THE PLACE OF BUSINESS IN AMERICA'S FUTURE/ *A Study in Social Values*

THE PLACE OF BUSINESS IN AMERICA'S FUTURE/*A Study in Social Values*

NEIL W. CHAMBERLAIN

BASIC BOOKS, INC., PUBLISHERS
New York

© 1973 by Basic Books, Inc.
Library of Congress Catalog Card Number: 72–89186
SBN 465–05778–0
Manufactured in the United States of America

73 74 75 76 77 10 9 8 7 6 5 4 3 2 1

CONTENTS

THE PLACE OF BUSINESS IN AMERICA'S FUTURE / *A Study in Social Values*

Introduction

The question of whether America's social values are changing has become as immediate and vital as whether America's physical environment is dangerously deteriorating. Employers testify that younger workers no longer subscribe to a work ethic. Effortless consumption, as a matter of right, is claimed by some as a new way of life, at the same time that others turn away from mass-made materialistic objects to pursue lives of contemplation, inspiration, or communal fraternity. Technological regimentation is damned by some, while others cling to technological salvation as the rock of the modern age. Racism and sexism are denounced by egalitarians, while these explanations for differential performance are viewed as the evasion of personal responsibilities by the more traditionally individualistic and self-reliant. Seemingly American society is being fragmented and devitalized by contention over the goals we seek. Does the nation still profess any common set of values such as seemed to guide its citizenry of an earlier day, or have these been outworn? Are there "self-evident" truths to which all men may repair, and if not, what are the consequences for America's future?

If these are issues whose very weightiness is depressing, they cannot for that reason be laid aside. But they can be and often are dismissed because they are argued so inconclusively and unpersuasively, by people with a sense of prophecy or mission, from premises deriving from purely personal experience or predilection. Of such argument we have had a surfeit. What I have tried to do in the present study is to start with the basic concept of social values itself, attempting to hone it to a degree of clarity that endows it with analytical utility, permitting—at the last—a more objective and fruitful attack on the questions which prompt the study: Are America's values changing? If so, why, in what direction, and what difference does it make?

If this seems an excessively ambitious undertaking, I make no apology for an effort set in motion by simple intellectual curiosity. What better excuse can I offer? But the satisfaction of such curiosity would remain incomplete if it did not elicit a response from others. And I am mindful that a study which traverses twelve chapters of conceptual development in order to make the application which is the objective presents a formidable obstacle to most readers. So much rough terrain to be covered before one reaches the promised destination! Will it prove to have been worth the effort?

To induce the reader to journey with me, I have sketched in this Introduction the architecture of my concept of social values, with the hope that this will help to clarify the relationship of its several parts, as these are successively developed. Obviously, however, the sketch is not intended as a substitute for the finished effort. I have not even followed the same sequence in putting the elements together. This preliminary statement is only a maquette to convey a suggestion of what is to come.

"Society" is of course an abstraction of a high order. It is not a monolith composed of numerous homogeneous parts, so that it constitutes a simple sum of its uniform ingredients. A society such as that of the United States—and others, to a greater or lesser extent—is made up of many parts. It has become common these days to think in terms of systems, composed of a number of subsystems, integrated and interrelating to maintain continuity and achieve purpose. In such a view we might conceive of business, labor organizations, educational institutions, churches, the military, and governments at all levels as constituting components of the larger social system. This is a functional view of society, and incomplete, since most societies are also divided along nonfunctional lines of ethnicity, race, religion, language, status. At times the nonfunctional and the functional overlap, as when race or religion identifies a group with certain occupational characteristics, or status results from role. But this is not necessarily the case. We need only note that the groups and divisions of which a society is composed are numerous, overlapping, and diversified.

Membership in a particular set of groups operates over time to endow an individual with a sense of personal identity—that concept whose *social* significance Erik Erikson has led us to appreciate. The individual's development of a sense of his identity thus derives not only from his innate psychic characteristics but also from the shaping and governing of that raw self by the values of those with whom he is most closely associated—his parents at first, then his peer groups, his ethnic or racial pool, his occupational or professional associations, and—not least—the political units (local and national) of which he is a member.

All these groups express certain sets of values which the individual, in identifying with them, comes to accept in varying degree. His identification with (and his own value-positing sense of personal identity deriving from) a particular group may be weak or strong, temporary or lasting, reinforcing of or conflicting with other identifications.

What are these "sets of values" which we associate with the numerous component groups of a society? By a process of gradual approximation, we identify them as consisting of three separable but related strands. The first is the *focal value,* a sense of what constitutes the good life, the *summum bonum.* On this aspect of their identity, groups have differed throughout recorded history. There is in fact a whole array of focal values, including a variety of preoccupations with materialistic accumulation and consumption; a variety of religious, intellectual, and esthetic fixations; a range of military orientations; a cluster of relational and familial satisfactions. *Some* trace of *all* these valued aspects of society enter into most people's lives, but for particular individuals and groups some *one* of these desiderata becomes dominant, transcending the others, and central (focal) to their way of life. We need not concern ourselves with how particular groups come to espouse certain focal values at a given time or place. We simply take the empirical evidence as establishing the fact.

The second strand of a group's value set is the *constitutional value.* This consists of the authority and coercive relationships which it accepts and prefers to other alternative authority relationships as conducing to its survival or advancement. We may conceive of this value as a spectrum, ranging, at one extreme, from a strong sense of coherence and order, relying heavily on hierarchic authority, to its polar opposite of a strong sense of personal autonomy (self-actualization, in the jargon of the day), just short of actual dissociation from the group.

The third strain, the *distributive value,* can likewise be regarded as a spectrum. Here we are concerned with the distribution within the group of all the good things which it produces—not only real income but social status and political preferment. Some groups, at one end of the spectrum, believe in privileged and unequal distribution, whether through the aristocratic sanction of bloodlines or the "democratic" sanction of personal merit competitively demonstrated against others. At the other end of the spectrum we find those who espouse full egalitarianism—not only of "opportunity" (which leaves room for highly disparate circumstances among members of the group), but of actual conditions.

These three strands—focal, constitutional, and distributive values— collectively compose the values of a group. They are vital in establishing its *particular* identity, in distinguishing it from other groups and giving it coherence and continuity. The three strands tend to be interrelated in subtle and complex ways. Rational materialism may be linked with a belief in constitutional individualism which requires distributive inequalities, or it may be tied to an egalitarian philosophy which can be achieved only by a strongly centralized authority. A focal military value virtually dictates hierarchical order and inequalities of rank and deference. Focal religious values may be coupled with Catholic centralism or Lutheran autonomy, and associated with sumptuary privileges of office or the purest form of communal living. Whatever the interrelationships of the three value strands, they weave together with a consistency and harmony that makes for group integrity—until or unless certain circumstances (yet to be introduced into our analysis) begin an unraveling process which saps the unifying strength of the group's value core.

Within a populous society beyond the stage of primitive development, a wide assortment of focal values and many shadings of constitutional and distributive values are exhibited by its constituent groups. For whatever historical reasons, its functional and nonfunctional components offer a smorgasbord of value combinations. But at most periods in its history some one group is likely to have established a strength and importance which surpasses that of other groups, emerging—sometimes gradually, occasionally precipitately—as a dominant influence in the society. It effects alliances with other strategic groups, wins supporters from among its beneficiaries, elicits the tolerance of still others (especially those to whom success itself is magnetic), and is observed noncommittally, if at all, in its upward climb by the often large numbers of unconcerned and uninvolved members of the population.

The group which thus becomes dominant succeeds over time in impressing on the society the set of values which characterizes it. It need not employ repressive force in achieving this end; it simply makes manifest, through its widening influence, the growing identity between its own and the nation's welfare. Its values tend to become recognized as the nation's values, both internally and externally. The values of other groups within the society are not extirpated but submerged. The assortment of value sets may be as prevalent as before the rise of the dominant group, but the hold of these particularistic values on their members is muted and compromised. Since each individual takes his identity in some degree from the multiple groups with which he is associated, and since the political unit plays so important a role in structuring all intergroup relations, for most individuals the values of the political unit (largely impressed by the dominant group) surmount in importance those of the other groups to which he belongs.

In shaping the national identity (sometimes the provincial or tribal identity) in this fashion, the dominant group is likely to modify its own values in some degree. As it associates itself with the national interests (by definition broader than its own), it develops a wider orientation which softens somewhat its previous particularistic concern with self-interest. Yet self-interest must be served: why else should any group strive to extend its influence? The rationalization for preferment of one's own group interest is easy to come by: insofar as the national welfare becomes more closely identified with the values of the dominant group, the latter must remain dominant in order to advance the national welfare. The justification, however circular, is sufficient. To take a contemporary example, policies to increase the Gross National Product do not benefit all members of the population equally; the dominant groups tend to benefit disproportionately. But all members of society have learned to regard any increase in the GNP as a *social* desideratum, and most of all, those responsible for the policies leading to it.

To describe a group as dominant does not imply that it can have its own way. It means only that it is strong enough to impress its values on the society to a greater extent than any other group is able to do. This does not relieve it of the necessity of effecting compromises at times with those whose support is important to its security. To achieve its position and then to maintain it may require that it make concessions to a former dominant group, now slowly passing from the scene, or to a contending group rising in influence. Within large contemporary societies this function of effecting compromises is generally performed by specialized intermediaries—the professional politicians. They act as brokers among those actively contending for influence, and in performing this function must accord heavier weight to those whom we have called the "dominants." Thus there is a built-in political tendency, over long stretches of time, for the preservation of the status quo, or at least only its slow modification by concessions. Because this process seldom involves direct negotiations between contending interests it is referred to as *implicit bargaining.*

But a society's values—its *summum bonum,* its sanctioned use of coercive authority, the distribution of its benefits which is viewed as equitable —can hardly be cherished and endowed with emotional content if it is recognized as *only* the success story of a particular interest group, somewhat watered down by the implicit bargains effected through the brokerage function of professional politicians. To achieve a more compelling, a more abstract, a more justifiable appeal, the values which a dominant group has bestowed on a society must be given a *philosophical validation.* The writings of intellectuals, both past and present, are drawn on to clothe a society's values in more durable, more affective, more disinterested language. Gradually there builds up a body of doctrine which becomes the sacred works of a society, lending itself to exegesis and interpretation with the passage of time.

Moreover, the influence of the dominant group and its values extends into the institutions of a society. Historically, the dominant group has come from one of three basic institutions—the military, the religious, or the economic. At times these three, or two of them, have shared in dominance, as allies, but in general no one of these can maintain a secure position without at least passive support from the other two. The government, as already noted, tends to act as a supporter of present interests and a mediator of change. In addition, the educative institutions—principally family and school—become instruments by means of which the social values, as philosophically validated, are passed from generation to generation.

Despite the flexibility which is provided by changes in the implicit bargain, by philosophical reinterpretation, and by institutional modification, a dominant group cannot be assured of indefinite continuity in its privileged position. There are a number of reasons why, with the passage of time, it may recede toward a mean advantage. It may be too shortsighted, too rigid in its determination to hold fast to its position, to make the concessions which are called for. It may experience an erosion in credibility with respect to the values it professes, since purity in adhering to them cannot be maintained in the face of the need for compromise that goes with the exercise of power. The values which it necessarily excludes in the process of affirming its own may become in time, like forbidden fruit, more attractive for being excluded, particularly if the stressed values lose some of their appeal due to familiarity or satiation.

None of these conditions guarantees any transition to a new set of social values, however. For that to occur, something else must be present—a challenger group. The process is envisaged as follows.

A society at any point in time is characterized by certain *objective conditions* by which it can be described. For sake of analytical convenience, we can group these into four categories: its knowledge authority (the source from which it derives what it believes to be truth, as from the church in an earlier day, from science today); its economic and technical circumstances; its population characteristics (composition, location, qualitative attributes, as well as numbers), and its political organization. Changes in these objective conditions occur over time, sometimes by process of social evolution and incremental modification, sometimes because of intrusive and unpredictable events. A new source of knowledge arises, economic and technological developments occur, a population grows or redisposes itself (as in urbanizing) or becomes more heterogeneous (as through immigration waves), the governmental apparatus is reorganized (perhaps centralized or decentralized).

These changes in objective conditions may create what some subordinate group within a society perceives as new opportunities for its own advancement. It experiments, risks breaks with tradition, becomes more energetic in taking advantage of the new circumstances. We call such a group a *thruster*. Its efforts may be sharply focused, in a revolutionary surge to make good, but they may also be gradually cumulative, almost self-revelatory, so that any newly achieved position comes as a surprise, requiring time to become accustomed to.

Of course, a thruster group may fail because it is ambivalent as to its own intentions or because it is shunted aside by another thruster group whom the changed objective conditions have benefited more or which is better positioned to benefit from those changed conditions. Moreover, there is no guarantee that a thruster, however purposeful, will unseat a dominant group. At times, some segment of the dominant group may itself break away and become an *inside* thruster group, taking leadership away from an older generation, adapting as necessary but without fundamentally upsetting the dominant values.

If a thruster group achieves some measure of success it is likely to draw to it its own allies and supporters, its own coterie of admirers—other groups of lesser or more timid thrusters who find larger benefit for themselves in shifting loyalty. The old dominants may seek to counter in one of three ways: through concessions which are intended to blunt the thrust, through co-optation which drains off the ablest leaders of the thrusting group and admits them to the still-prestigious circle of the privileged, or through repression using the institutional instruments which it may still sufficiently control.

But if objective conditions have significantly changed, in ways to which the old dominants find difficulty in accommodating, and if the thrust is vigorous and sustained, in time the thrusting group will emerge as a new set of dominants, impressing their own values on the society, creating a new national identity. For a time something of the old values and identity may lag on, creating a degree of confusion of identity before, ultimately, taking their place in the array of lesser or excluded values.

Only with a thruster group achieving dominance will a new set of social values emerge within a society. The notion of a change in social values by some form of self-induced mass conversion is specifically rejected. In the absence of a vigorous and successful thruster group, the passage of time and changes in objective conditions which act to undermine an existing dominant group will lead only to a diffuseness of social values. The numerous constituent groups of the society will assert their own particularistic values more vigorously, in an effort to make secure such advantages as they possess or to expand a bit the social territory which they occupy. Contentiousness will displace coherence, though something of the latter must remain if a society is to survive as a political unit. Some social values always obtain, since a society—however it is politically defined—is inconceivable without some trace of purpose and morality; however, the intensity with which they are felt, the clarity with which they are understood, the consistency with which they are observed, and the extent of their hold on components of the population can and do vary between societies and within the same society at different points in time.

It is in the light of this analysis, supplemented by an international dimension which I refrain from intruding into this summary statement, that I have sought to appraise the likelihood of value change in the United States. Three "most likely" possibilities seem to emerge.

1. A diminution in the present dominant position of large-scale business management, in the absence of a thruster group, may lead to a growing diffuseness of social values. This is another way of saying that an increasing assertion of the particularistic values of contentious groups may be expected.

2. From within business there may emerge a new leadership (an inside thruster group) embracing a more technocratic and systems-planning approach to the solution of social problems which changing objective conditions have forced on American society. This would involve some reinterpretation of values but no radical modification.

3. For reasons both internal and external (urban breakdown and foreign challenge), an enlarged role may be foreseen for the military establishment, which would then emerge as a genuine thruster group, seizing on the changed conditions confronting the nation as opportunities for the advancement of its own values and interests. An alliance with large-scale business management would be logical and strategic and could be expected. I do not envisage this as the now familiar bogey of a military-industrial complex fastening itself like an incubus on the nation, but as a thrust which would engender strong support from numerous groups, including some which now consider themselves "liberal."

Unpredictable events may remove one or all of these possibilities and bring brighter alternatives, but that is a matter for hope or faith. These seem to be the most likely expectations which can be drawn from the analysis.

So much for the skeleton of the argument. Perhaps it will serve some usefulness in aiding the reader to anticipate the relationships of the constituent parts as they are developed more fully in the extended analysis.

1 / Social Values—
Meaning What?

Periods of social unrest seem to generate an interest in social values. The existence of the former is often attributed to a breakdown in the latter. Some people talk of the need for restoring the "old" values, while others urge the necessity of new ones. Thus, the long-standing interest of philosophers and sociologists in the subject has, in the declining years of the twentieth century, been joined by a more popular concern with what is happening to the values of Western society, a concern induced by a sense of general deterioration of institutions and behavior patterns.

It is this situation which has prompted this book. The questions to which it is addressed are: What *are* social values? How do they get established and how do they change? What is their significance? While seeking general answers to these questions, the book attempts to make specific application to American society.

At the outset, one is faced with an agenda of questions indicative of the fuzziness and vagueness which have surrounded the subject. I shall do no more than touch on some of these now, since we shall examine them in greater detail shortly.

When we speak of social values, do we have in mind a simple catalog of a society's preferences, not necessarily related to each other, or is there some integrated core of values? If the latter, how do we distinguish what is part of the core and what is outside it?

Are a society's values related to its actions? Is it possible for behavior and values to be at odds, and if so, only episodically or over longer periods of time? Are values only beliefs or intellectual constructions, or are they also behavioral modes?

What is the relation between personal and social values? Are the latter simply the sum of the former, or are the former a product of the latter, molded in the process of maturation? Are social values simply some individuals' projection onto a larger social unit of those values which they have persuaded themselves ought to be pursued? Can persuasive individuals convert their fellow citizens to their own value perceptions, so that the individual becomes the molder of social values?

How are economic and social values related, if at all? One student has said that "economists draw the indispensable distinction (largely lost to sociologists) between, on the one hand, the *value* of things, and on the other, the *values* of individuals or societies." [1] But the values of a society determine the value of things. One is the mirror image of the other. (The market system does this through a process of pecuniary weighting, which thus fails to encompass those things which are unsalable. This may indeed be the overriding criticism of the market mechanism as a carrier of liberal values: it does not *and cannot* encompass all social phenomena and tends to exclude those it cannot encompass; it may be that the radical objection to the market system is not that it is too extensive but that it *cannot* be extensive enough. On the other hand, those who seek to extend pecuniary measurement to a larger range of social transactions, in order to salvage the market system, are violating the incommensurable nature of certain kinds of relations by attempting, with an almost Wildean cynicism, to set a price on everything. Hence, we have been treated to discourses on the pecuniary value of love, irreplaceable natural resources, human life itself.)

If we distinguish between a society's values and the "objective" conditions or context in which it finds itself, including such variables as the state of knowledge and the arts, economic organization, population magnitude and composition, its government and its relations with other peoples, we may ask whether that society's values give rise to these objective conditions or whether these objective conditions determine the society's values. Or perhaps there is some indeterminate interaction between the two. We may ask, for example, whether Max Weber was more nearly right that values have their independent and determining influence over the economic and social structure of a society, whether Karl Marx saw more clearly that it is the economic relations of a society that determine its values, or whether R. H. Tawney more persuasively argued their interaction. In terms of contemporary writers, is Charles Reich (or to a less certain extent John Kenneth Galbraith and Lewis Mumford) right in believing that psychological attitudes ("consciousness") can develop independently and successfully modify institutions and society, or is Andrew Hacker (or to a less certain extent Herbert Marcuse) on sounder ground in believing that monolithic institutions force individuals to conform to institutional needs and patterns of action (and that therefore American society is basically incapable of changing its outmoded values)?

What is the time dimension of social values? What stability can be attributed to them? Do the preferments which characterized the United States a century ago still persist, or have they changed, and if the latter, did the change occur precipitously or slowly? Do the values of earlier times linger on even as new values make their appearance? When a writer in 1957 described the college generation of that time as aspiring "for material gratification," fully accepting "the convention of the contemporary business society," expecting to "conform to the economic status quo," unwilling "to crusade for non-discrimination" but merely accepting it "as it comes," respecting the "traditional moral virtues," "dutifully responsive toward government" [2]—was he describing a temporary phenomenon which was to be radically altered in not much more than a decade, or is it the intervening set of "New Left" attitudes which will prove ephemeral? Are social values almost matters of the moment?

In contrast, are there some values which are timeless and universal, so that they can be ascribed to all humanity, in the great tradition of Immanuel Kant's categorical imperative, values which, whether men actually practice them, all thoughtful men believe should be practiced? But if there are such universals, where can we discover them? Even the principles we tend to honor most in the abstract, such as the "sanctity" of human life, are breached repeatedly for reasons which are viewed as more compelling. The notion of human sacrifice for a higher purpose is an exculpatory way of rationalizing murder, and can be elastically extended to cover wars for righteous cause.

Are the social values of a people mutually consistent or do they sometimes embrace opposing outlooks and dichotomous or at least mutually exclusive principles of behavior? One student maintains that "no system of values can encompass genuine contraries," and "oppositional propositions in any value system are spurious." [3] But others, at least from the time of Jeremy Bentham on, have accepted the contradiction inherent in, for example, the mutually desired values of equality and security.

How are social values related to national character, that problem which Henry Adams considered the most difficult and yet the most important facing the historian? Indeed, what is the connection between *social* values and the political phenomenon of *nation?* Does nationality generate common social values, or is it the other way around?

These are all questions which we shall want to explore at one time or another in the course of this study. There are others which will emerge as we proceed. The answers at which we shall arrive will likewise emerge only gradually. Still, in order to gain some tentative footing in this slippery territory, from which to begin to explore the terrain, let us benefit from the work of previous investigators and survey the content which they—one or another—have found in this concept.

An Approach to Social Values

There are at least four ways in which we can regard social values, and while each is distinctive they are mutually compatible.

VALUES AS THE SPIRIT OF AN AGE

The school of thought best represented by Vico, Herder, Hegel, and Oswald Spengler believes that there is some transcendental "spirit of an age," an outlook peculiar to a society of a given time and place which infuses all its institutions and activities, which gives a unique coloration to its pursuits and preferences. One can approach this conception by the dialectical path if he wishes: the spirit of the age is defined by what it tends to exclude. If the style of the times is secular and intellectual, it downplays the religious and the emotive. If it is materialistic, it de-emphasizes the esthetic. But some theme dominates and determines the temper of the times.

With some expositors this view takes on a mystical and even supernatural character. Hegel, for example, believed in a World Spirit, toward the realization of which mankind moved teleologically, each culture unconsciously making its contribution by a dialectical process, until the day of the ultimate Universal synthesis. The Spirit of a Nation is the idiosyncratic expression of this movement, concretely manifesting itself in every aspect of its consciousness and will—its religion, its polity, its ethics, its legislation, and even in its science, art, and technology. All of these are reflections of "the particular principle that characterizes a people," which incorporates a "capacity of potentiality striving to realize itself." Elsewhere Hegel speaks of a nation's "vital principle" and its "matured totality," the latter representing the fulfillment in each individual of the spirit of his age.[4]

The same basic theme, though without the same mystical tenor, is to be found in Mosca, who wrote of a current peculiar to an epoch; in Spengler, who believed that each of the great civilizations was characterized by its own *geist;* in Simmel, who thought that each uniquely definable age was driven by a sovereign idea; and in Mannheim, who argued that every fact and event in an historical period expressed or revealed a unity and interdependence of meaning.

Pitirim Sorokin has given as clear a statement of this conception as one could ask for.

Any great culture, instead of being a mere dumping place of a multitude of diverse cultural phenomena, existing side by side and unrelated to one another, represents a unity or individuality whose parts are permeated by the same fundamental principle and articulate the same basic value. The dominant part of the fine arts and science of such a unified culture, of its philosophy and religion, of its ethics and law, of its main forms of social, economic, and political organization, of most of its mores and manners, of its ways of life and mentality, all articulate, each in its own way, this basic principle and value. This value serves as its major premise and foundation. For this reason the important parts of such an integrated culture are also interdependent causally: if one important part changes, the rest of its important parts are bound to be similarly transformed.[5]

The philosopher-novelist Hermann Broch constructed his major work, *The Sleepwalkers,* around this basic theme. In his more compact and poetic expression: "Every historical unity depends on an effective or fictive centre of value; the style of an epoch would not be discernible unless a unifying principle of selection were assumed at its centre, or a 'spirit of the age' which serves as a standard for judging the value-positing and style-creating forces in operation." [6]

The psychoanalyst Erik Erikson has likewise found his own form of expressing a basically similar conception. He speaks of the "cultural consolidation" of a period, which creates satisfaction in social activity which is somehow seen as "right"—"a rightness proven by the bountiful response of 'nature,' whether in the form of the prey bagged, the food harvested, the goods produced, the money made, or the technological problems solved. In such consolidation and accommodation a million daily tasks and transactions fall into practical patterns and spontaneous ritualizations which can be shared by leaders and led, men and women, adults and children, the privileged and the underprivileged, the specially gifted and those willing to do the chores. The point is that only such consolidation offers the coordinates for the range of a period's identity formations and their necessary relation to a sense of inspired activity. . . ." [7]

There are clearly differences of emphasis and detail in these several conceptions of a value core or a style of an epoch or a spirit of the times or a cultural consolidation, but equally clearly they all constitute variations on a particular theme which helps to illuminate the concept of social values.

VALUES AS PURPOSE

Social values are also expressed in the broad purposes and objectives of a society. We are now concerned not with the style or spirit which is thought to dominate the whole of an epoch, but with the grand design which expresses this in its successive stages.

Let us suppose that a society, manifesting a dominant theme to which its institutions and efforts are largely directed, conceives of that theme as a succession of desirable future states of affairs. Looking into the future, it (in the person of its leaders and thinkers) perceives a time stream in which the style of that epoch unfolds through a series of events, which can be partly planned for and partly dreamed of. To the extent that these national aspirations are firmly held, the society's institutions become linked with them, purposively, and take on some of the values associated with the national purpose.

The spirit of an age is not uniquely determinative of such a national agenda. The religious or rationalistic style characterizing a period might be reflected in a variety of grand designs. But for particularistic and idiosyncratic reasons, which we shall examine later, it becomes identified with a more or less specific grand design, a national purpose, a social aspiration, which gives a larger meaning to the more transient and trivial day-to-day events of the nearer time dimension.

The nineteenth-century United States provides an illustration of this meaning of social value. As Russell Nye has so succinctly set forth in his study, *This Almost Chosen People*,[8] the dominant theme of American society was the creative power of the liberated individual, as expressed within a democratic political system. If "individualism" or "liberalism" was the spirit of the age—a philosophically expressed value which was officially reaffirmed as late as 1960 in the report, *Goals for Americans*,[9] the national purpose embodied more specific states of affairs. First, the United States was to provide a positive example to the rest of the world of the regenerative powers of democracy and the creative powers of individualism, by its own economic achievements. This involved the settlement of the West and the consolidation of the continental empire. Its cumulative success would, it was believed, prove irresistibly persuasive to the rest of the world. But to expedite the conversion of the backward, to ensure the earlier arrival of the day when the world would enjoy the blessings of the American epoch, and perhaps—one might add—to give a more active sense of purpose to a restless and ambitious people caught up in the spirit of their time, there gradually emerged the idea of the nation's "manifest destiny" to extend its political influence and authority throughout the Western Hemisphere and perhaps, indeed, beyond. Poets and preachers no less than politicians lent themselves to such a grand design. This sense of mission justified a succession of interventions around the world, even as national leaders continued to assert that these were "not rooted in any national material interest," unlike the foreign policies of most other countries in the past.[10]

As long as the spirit of the times remains vital, the national purpose can be extended and even redefined. If such national aspirations are felt with intensity and command the support of most of the population, they get worked into national policy and even a national agenda which concretely manifests its spirit in its time.

VALUES AS NORMS OF CONDUCT

Beyond these more grandiose aspects, social values have a specific significance for the individual in providing him with norms of conduct. A society cannot rely solely on laws and written codes but must depend also on unwritten rules and customs as guides to the appropriate behavior of individuals in a variety of situations—behavior which each individual can *expect* of others almost as a right. These responses become so ingrained and conventionalized that the individual is scarcely cognizant of them. He is made aware of them when confronted by departures from conduct which he has come to take for granted. One of America's leading industrialists, observing the deterioration of this quality in the activities involving him and sensing a gradual discarding of what were once automatic responses to unwritten codes of interpersonal and institutional relations, remarks on the "terrible danger" implicit in this rejection of social norms. "Unless the great majority of citizens are willing to govern themselves by generally accepted standards, the only alternatives are chaos or a police state which governs by force and by fear." [11]

Earlier observers of the American scene remarked on the extent to which shared norms—common codes of what was viewed as ethical conduct and the automatic responses which were expected in particular situations—created a degree of conformity of behavior, so that the individualism associated with this experimental nation was capable of being turned into a kind of tyranny, buttressed by a strong sense of the rightness of the democratic majority. Certainly Tocqueville and John Stuart Mill were keenly conscious of this potential. In reviewing this nineteenth-century background, the economic historian W. W. Rostow likewise commented that American individualism largely meant the substitution of "a structure of masters" different from those of the Old World. Among the New World masters were a tendency to conform to the will and manners of the majority and a written Constitution "elevated to a peculiar sanctity." [12] But despite any fear of excessive conformance to socially prescribed modes of behavior, there was no rejection of their need or desirability.

The ethical content in such social norms had already been nicely identified by that Scottish scholar Adam Smith, whom we now remember primarily as the father of modern economics, in his first great book, *The Theory of Moral Sentiments*. There he laid primary stress on sympathy, or fellow-feeling, as the cement which bound a society together. This sentiment did not derive from any separate moral faculty in the individual but rather as an instinctive product of the imagination, which pictured how other people felt in all the intricate patterns of social behavior in which any of us might find himself, and what reactions from others we ourselves would like to experience in comparable situations. We seek the sympathetic response of others, but this is elicited only to the extent that our actions and purposes seem "proper" and accord with others' notions of what should excite sympathy. The morality which derives from the sentiment of sympathy is thus a social product.[13]

This ingrained conformity with the norms of conduct imposed by society can sometimes lead us into actions which run counter to our own individualistic welfare. "Thus under ordinary circumstances the coward has a better chance of survival than the brave man, yet all societies try to establish in their members value-attitude systems which will promote brave behavior. Since courage is necessary for the successful defense of the group, such systems contribute to the survival of the society at the expense of its individual members." [14]

This sense of social values as the appropriate behavioral norms of a society has been given special conceptual significance by Sigmund Freud in the form of the superego, which has been described (I regret to say I cannot recall by whom) as "the internalized code of a society which has accumulated the experience of many egos and which communicates its standards by means of parental authority." Here we have the succinct expression of the gradual building up over time of modes of behavior which a society regards as "right" and which act as a governor on the individual's own instinctual drives and personal preferences.

Though this code is internalized by all those who have been socialized, this fact carries no implication that personal disposition and social norm always coincide. In any given situation, the individual's preference may be to act in ways other than social norms prescribe; forms of group and personal prejudice which run counter to generalized norms of equal treatment are obvious examples of personal disposition coming in conflict with social norms. In this conflict, whose outcome cannot be predicted in any specific circumstance, we receive a partial answer to our earlier question of whether the reality of social values is revealed by actual behavior. In any given situation, personal disposition—Freud's *id* and *ego*—may prove stronger than the relevant social norm—Freud's *superego,* but this does not mean that the latter is nonexistent or unimportant. Of course one can add that unless individual behavior does in fact conform to the social norm on enough occasions to create some probability of the expected response, we face the situation referred to by Henry Ford II—the social norm, the automatic response, has broken down in this particular, and Freud's super-ego no longer performs as a satisfactory governor. This may be true with respect to one subset of social relations without, however, invalidating the general reliability of a society's values conceived as norms of conduct.

VALUES AS SANCTIONS

Social values do not merely set the style of an epoch, identify national purpose, and ensure some consistency of individual conduct; they have the additional function of integrating and coordinating the society's activities. Values endow a society with certain cohesive qualities—this is the essential truth of the "consensus" theory of social values adopted by Talcott Parsons and his followers. A certain unity of world view and a certain agreement on what constitutes right conduct in generally encountered social situations are prerequisites to a society's even being a society. But this is not enough. A society's activities do not proceed solely according to tradition or animal instinct. Although there is a large element of routine present in any social group, there are also fresh decisions which must be made, some of minor importance but others relating to the society's very survival. These nonrepetitive decisions (today many would say unprogramed decisions) cannot be arrived at by some form of consensus-osmosis. They require the deliberation of individuals in positions of formal or informal authority and determinations which, once made, are accepted by others, even if necessary under coercion. This means more than simply the general acceptance of some form of political government, since it is not always—or only—government which makes such decisions. It involves an acceptance by individuals within a society of the appropriate roles which they may be called on to play and a consensus as to the forms of coercion which are appropriate in prevailing on them to play those roles. Coercion cannot be avoided in any society, but it is only an underlying consensus as to its proper use that makes coercion a reliable tool. This invokes a sense not only of the value of making the social system work but also of the general way in which it will be made to work—the role of institutions, and of people in institutions, and their relationships to each other, not simply in traditional modes prescribed by codes, but in new situations which had not been contemplated.

This sense of social values embodies a more dynamic element than the social norms provide. It creates the basis for individuals feeling themselves attached to and integrally responsible for an ongoing social system which has special significance for them. People can conform to all the ethical prescriptions their society demands of them without experiencing that sense of interaction and integration in a common endeavor. Some writers have spoken of social values in this sense as energizing norms, in contrast to the constraining norms discussed previously.[15]

Here, then, we have four versions of social values, each of which has an appealing claim to conceptual respectability and all of which are mutually compatible and even interrelated. There is no logical ground for excluding any from our investigation. I propose, therefore, to take as our point of departure this tentative definition: Social values consist of a spirit or theme which characterizes an historical period of a given society, expressed in the form of an agenda of national purpose (a grand design), also defining the norms of social conduct for all those sharing in the enterprise, and integrating the members of the society into the ongoing activity through acceptance of role responsibility and initiative and a consensus as to appropriate forms of coercion.

These constituent elements may not always be present in every society, or they may be present with varying degrees of intensity, both as between societies and within the same society, and at different times in a society's history. But if we are examining social values, we cannot very well fail to consider how these several aspects work together.

In summarizing this definitional phase of the study, we can benefit from the insight of philosopher C. I. Lewis. There are two basic problems, he wrote, which have traditionally been dealt with under the same rubric— the question of the *summum bonum,* which is a matter of values, and the question of justice, which is a matter of ethics. For those, like Kant, who seek to subordinate the good (that which is valued) to the right (that which is ethically justified), "correct" values depend on ethically justifiable action. But this creates a philosophical difficulty: although ethical virtue may be a highly prized good, it cannot be the highest good, since that requires some satisfaction of the human capacity for happiness. And that is not a moral matter. Thus one is driven to the conclusion that the "finally valuable is not determinable from the moral." "And for any naturalistic ethics, determination of the good must be prior to determination of what is right, since the justification of action depends on the desirability of the contemplated result. Consonantly, general questions about correctness in valuation comes first, and questions about right conduct come afterwards, so far as these two can be separated." [16]

Thus, in the realm of its values, a society is faced with two choices—an affective choice, involving states of desire, and an ethical choice, involving the morality of its relationships. And the former must precede the latter;

goods must be desired before theft becomes an issue. In the conceptual framework we are developing, the spirit of the times and the national purpose constitute the affective choices, the determination of what states of affairs a people considers desirable, while the social norms and the integrative responsibilities and initiatives, with their necessary coercive element, constitute the ethical choices, the determination of what states of affairs a people considers just. These affective and ethical choices, these conceptions of the socially desirable and the socially just, jointly constitute social values.

Internal Divisions within Society

To this point we have been talking as though society constituted some homogeneous unit, characterized by a single set of values. But of course this is not the case. Every society, even the most advanced, is subdivided along certain lines. The most prevalent but for our purposes the least interesting categorical divisions are those of age and sex. But beyond these elemental classifications, even the most egalitarian societies recognize class divisions. In some instances classes may be so removed from each other that they virtually live in different worlds, like Disraeli's "two nations" of nineteenth-century England.

Schumpeter, the eclectic scholar, gently chastised his fellow economists for their reluctance to recognize the reality of social classes, and suggested that, by comparison, Marx moved into a more favorable light for having seen their importance. "Social classes . . . are not the creatures of the classifying observer but live entities that exist as such. And their existence entails consequences that are entirely missed by a schema which looks upon society as if it were an amorphous assemblage of individuals or families." [17] Here Schumpeter was obviously scanting the utilitarian-schooled classical economists who, following Bentham, had indeed viewed society as nothing more than the aggregate of the individuals who composed it, and who could therefore express their *summum bonum* in the famous but meaningless phrase, the greatest good of the greatest number.

The diversity of a society extends beyond its broad social class divisions and is also based on such factors as professional specialization and institutional affiliation—functional divisions. Following Durkheim, we might say that the more developed a society the greater is the range of its specialized group interests and the larger is the number of its smaller constituent societies.

This multiplicity of groups with their specialized interests gives rise to group values, performing in the smaller society of the group the same functions as social values in the larger context, each group possessing (in some degree) its own spirit of the times, its own specialized purposes or design, its own norms of group behavior, its own integrating dynamic. These group values perform a double function: on the one hand, they serve to support and advance the special interests of the group; on the other hand, they act as a means of excluding other groups which might conceivably trespass on their social territory. Jurisdiction is preserved not simply by juridical formula or organizational agreement, as in the case of labor unions, but also by creating distinctive value systems which are peculiar to the role performed, emphasizing class attitudes or professional missions.[18]

The medical profession, one of the oldest of these specialized groups, provides an effective example of the preservation of a separate identity—indeed, virtual autonomy—not only through governmental licensing but perhaps as importantly by means of its own code of values. This professionalization of function, which has gone farthest in the developed societies, with its effect of specializing values, has been nicely caught by Hermann Broch, whom I previously had occasion to quote. Speaking of Western man generally, he writes: ". . . no matter how romantically and sentimentally he may yearn to return to the fold of [universal] faith, he is helplessly caught in the mechanism of the *autonomous* value-systems, and can do nothing but submit himself to the *particular* value that has become his profession, he can do nothing but become a function of that value—a specialist eaten up by the radical logic of the value into whose jaws he has fallen." [19]

The existence of a diversity of groups, each with its own value system, necessarily means that there will be some loss of unity within the larger society. The spirit and purpose, the norms and integrative functions of the particularistic groups cannot possibly be identical with the values of the society at large, since that would preclude their separate identification. It is only by distinguishing their mission, by particularizing their values that they establish a basis for inclusion and exclusion. Hence the existence of semiautonomous groups or classes is equivalent to some divergence from the overall pattern of social values.

But though group values diverge from social ones, they cannot diverge completely. Without some congruence the group would be totally alienated; the "society" would lose all cohesiveness, and we would be left with a definition of society as no more than the sum of its groups—hardly more satisfying logically than the utilitarian conception of society as the sum of its individuals. In order for groups to survive, they must maintain some network of relations with other groups; in order for social classes to persist in their hierarchical order, there must be other classes within the *same* society. To achieve this necessary integration, however weak or strong, requires some common set of values to which all men can repair, in the phrase of the American founding fathers. The presence of diverse groups and classes within a society does not dispose of social values; it both weakens their hold and strengthens their importance, at one and the same time.

There is one other aspect of the relationship between group and society which deserves at least quick note. In examining social values as a code of conduct or set of norms, we observed that at times they require a degree of conformity of the individual which may be oppressive. But group values, because more particularistic, are likely to be even more tyrannous. Society as the larger system, encompassing all of its constituent groups, offers the individual some opportunity to escape from the more confining group value system when it becomes unbearably constrictive.[20] If social values are partially undercut by the competition of group values, it is no less true that group values are weakened by the presence of the larger social value system.

Thus the values of group and society partially converge and diverge, but the degree of convergence must be greater than the degree of divergence or the society is in danger of disintegrating. Localism and regionalism sometimes display the same congruence and deviance from national social values, especially in societies in which feudal forms persist. In the rural and particularly the Indian communities of Latin America, a social equilibrium, with its own peculiar social, religious, and feudal values often obtains, but it remains consonant with the values of the larger social system despite a kind of primitive autonomy.[21] The villages of pre-Meiji Japan displayed community values which closely controlled the individual as in an extended family clan, but not in opposition to national values.[22] By contrast, in the United States, the value system of the pre-Civil War South stood in marked conflict with the social values which presumed to encompass that region. Divergence was stronger than congruence, and disintegration was prevented only by military force, not by the superior affective power of the values of the larger social system. Similarly, the fear that large-scale immigration, importing an assortment of divergent values, would weaken the "homogeneous" value system presumed to characterize the United States was a major concern of American social scientists from 1850 on.[23]

The strength of group values, their diversity and multiplicity have led some analysts to dismiss social values as unimportant if indeed nonexistent. "It is futile to speak of any homogeneous attitudes. . . . The heterogeneity of ideological trends in present-day America is its most outstanding feature. . . . The cultural structure in our dynamic civilization is complex and changing and accordingly offers an infinite selection to individuals of how they will be influenced by the culture." [24] "Theories that center on 'social approval' can be criticized because, in many societies, stratified and complex as they are, approval by some groups is paralleled by disapproval by others; and a single system of dominant social values is little more than a fiction." [25]

But such skepticism goes too far. If the culture of a "dynamic civilization" offers an infinite selection of possible modes of behavior, this does not mean that everyone will behave wholly idiosyncratically. As Kluckhohn and Murray observe, every man behaves in certain respects like all other men, in certain respects like some other men, and in still other respects like no other man.[26] The first category of behavior involves social values, the second category relates to group or particularistic values, the third to personal values. Clearly, there is no warranty for concluding that only the first category, social values, is real and important, but equally clearly there is no ground for maintaining that either of the remaining two categories occupy the field of values exclusively.

Obviously, particularistic (group) and individual values may clash with social values, and group values may conflict with other group values. We are accustomed to daily confrontations of such specialized codes and interests, but they commonly take place within a context of system values which allows for them, within certain not clearly defined limits. The degree of toleration of group conflict and of divergence from common norms is—as we shall later develop—itself a constituent part of a society's values. Thus the values of different classes, clearly distinguishable from each other, can coexist within a society—but if they do, free of any externally imposed force, it is only because they are linked together within some *common* system in which all find a way of life more satisfying than some other way, and role relationships embody rights and obligations which have accumulated an ethical coloration.

Even Marx, who built his doctrinal edifice on the foundation of class conflict, recognized the reality of common social values, explaining them as a superstructure erected by the dominant ownership class to undergird its position. That multiple values—specialized group values—exist in a complex society is readily apparent, and that at times these may erode the integrative social values of the larger system can be readily conceded. But this is only to say that social values are not equally pervasive and constant in all societies at all times. Whoever supposed such nonsense? But it is quite another thing to identify the dimensions of social values, and to recognize that these may be strong or weak, in part or in whole, in one country or another, at one time or another, and that these diverse characteristics are exactly what give the concept its importance. At times there may be a strong and discernible value system characterizing a people, setting them apart from others, giving them a clear historical unity and importance. At other times, for the same people or a different one, the social value set, or some aspects of it, may be weak or confused: some norms may persist from an earlier day; the last expression of a fading style may manifest itself from time to time, but there is no general or pervasive national purpose or dynamic. Hence, when we ask what the social values of a given people are, we may expect *some* answer, but the latter may fall within a very considerable range of strength, pervasiveness, and effectiveness.

The Political Unit

Social values are shared within some unit of population. We have spoken of the nation and its constituent functional groups as such units. For purposes of a more general designation, let us use the term "political unit." Some notion of a *political* entity within which values are shared is necessary, since one aspect of a social value system is the general acceptance of responsibility for the performance of particular social roles in a variety of circumstances, under sanctioned measures and forms of coercion —a distinctly political relationship which requires some social approval as to the justice it involves.

Indeed, the presence of common social values, however weakly or strongly held, is one influence making for the definition of a political unit. At the same time, a political unit, once identified, helps to shape and mold the social values themselves simply by *using* the powers with which commonly held values endow it—powers of giving explicit expression to inchoate purpose, of exercising the coercive authority which its population sanctions. The political unit thus has considerable significance for our study of values. More specifically, that significance lies in the part it plays in the identity formation of all its members.[27]

How an individual sees himself, the values he affirms derive in large part from his association with a place, a religion, a profession, a class, some sense of unity with all of which he acquires in the course of his growth. This comes partly and initially through his family but also through later peer associations and independent exploration. As we know, the number of such group associations may be considerable, and diverse among individuals of the same society. One of the most important of these associations—and the only one held in common by all members of the society—is his identification with the political unit of which he is a member. His integration with the political unit involves the absorption of the social values which that unit helps to define. The absorption of those values assists the individual in adjusting to his roles within his society, to the expectations held of him by others and by him of others, and to the degree of autonomy which is allowed him. It helps him to define himself in a way which is satisfying.

Tocqueville has captured this effect of communal values on a person's identity in the introduction to his *Democracy in America*. Taking as his overall theme the seven-centuries long movement toward increasing egalitarianism, he nevertheless recognized that the medieval period, at the start of that movement, was not necessarily one of misery arising out of the differentiated and unequal roles in which it cast its members.

As the noble never suspected that anyone would attempt to deprive him of the privileges which he believed to be legitimate, and as the serf looked on his own inferiority as a consequence of the immutable order of nature, it is easy to imagine that some mutual exchange of goodwill took place between two classes so differently endowed by fate. Inequality and wretchedness were then to be found in society, but the souls of neither rank of men were degraded.

Men are not corrupted by the exercise of power or debased by the habit of obedience, but by the exercise of a power which they believe to be illegitimate, and by obedience to a rule which they consider to be usurped and oppressive.[28]

Tocqueville is here referring to the integrative aspect of the value system, by reason of which the individual accepts the coercive authority which defines his roles and responsibilities; the reference to "the immutable order of nature" conveys as well a sense of the purposive or "grand design" aspect of the value system. At the time about which he wrote, the political unit was much smaller and less stable than the nation-state of today, but the function it performed in assisting the individual to establish his identity through the value system it expressed was the same.

But now we encounter a negative aspect of this process. In some cases this sense of a developing personal identity, supported by, but still uniquely distinguishable from, group identity precisely because it is personal, is thwarted or short-circuited or fails to develop adequately. In these instances the individual, and sometimes individuals in the aggregate, substitute a synthetic identity in the form of nationalism or ethnicism or racism or class, which provides the missing sense of oneness or wholeness. Erikson refers to this false identity as "pseudo-speciation," the intent to endow one's own kind with characteristics which are considered superior to those of other populations, which are indeed viewed as lesser species. This is something quite different from the assimilation of a value system defined within a political unit, which gives support to the individual in establishing his personal identity. Rather, this is the identification of the individual with an abstract political unit. Values in both the sense of purpose and ethics go out the window before the unreasoned affirmation, "My country, right or wrong."

Thus the process of pseudo-speciation leads to the substitution of pseudo-values for social values. Nationalism, for example, becomes something to be asserted as though somehow the political unit, however that elastic concept may be defined at the moment, contains some mystical good in and of itself, without respect to what it stands for, expressive of some superior quality which its members enjoy over lesser breeds. Nationalism is of course capable of arousing strong passions and does possess some integrative power, but it does not constitute a spirit of a particular period or spell out some grand design or purpose or provide norms of conduct or— even as an integrative force—does not by itself offer any basis for the forms and limits of coercive power which gives a society its dynamic. It represents the defeat, though sometimes only temporary, of the individual's search for personal identity and the substitution of a ready-made means of endowing himself, without effort, with special importance relative to certain others.

The political unit thus has genuine significance for the definition of social values, but it also creates the potential for intruding pseudo-values in the form of conceptions of "national conceit," as Vico expressed it, or presumed "absolute superiority over other groups," as Mosca put it.[29] It also gives rise to competition between nations for little purpose other than to show superiority. Joan Robinson has spoken of the "League tables" or team standings of national income growth. "When the poor old U.K., as often happens, appears rather low, we are filled with chagrin; or else we set about picking holes in the statistics to show that the placing is wrong; or we point to all sorts of unfair advantages that the wretched foreigners have, which make the comparisons misleading." [30]

On a more sordid level of international competition, published official documents have made clear that perhaps the overriding reason for prolonging the war in Vietnam was the unwillingness of U.S. officials to concede that they could not best an "inferior" enemy. And the Soviet Union has found euphemisms for covering its obvious feelings of national superiority over lesser socialist countries, even though all embrace a Marxist formulation which presumably eschews such nationalism.

The political unit enjoys a notably elastic character, as it expands and contracts in line with historical circumstance. Expansion and assimilation have the effect of giving greater diffuseness to social values, as they are made to accommodate a greater number of particularistic value formulations. The common perspective which emerges, the value system which is coincident with the larger political unit, is likely to lose some of its sharpness as it serves the expanded population. Its concepts become more abstract, and therefore support a wider range of possible applications and interpretations, making possible the enlarged political unit but at the price of clarity of its ideology.

The reverse is true with the dissolution of political units and the devolution of authority to local levels. Separatist movements are sometimes sparked by constituent parts of a larger political unit which seek to define a more satisfying value system for themselves, which see a different group or national identity as more supportive of their own personal identities, in Erikson's terminology. Assume, for example, with Eugene Genovese [31] that the American South was motivated to assert its independence by a perfectly rational determination that this was the last desperate means by which it could preserve a way of life—hierarchical, chivalric, organic— which it preferred to the more industrialized, competitive, materialistic life of the North, whose numerous reform movements, ranging from abolitionism through feminism and associationism to labor unionism, seemed to be creating disorder and threatening institutional disintegration. Is there any doubt that if it had made good its attempt the social value system which it would have evolved would have been significantly different from that supported by its cousins to the North, and more to its taste?

We have been noting the political unit as the locus of social values, but it also has economic, political, and social functions. If we shift our attention from the common *values* to the divergent *interests* of its members, we find ourselves confronting economic inequalities, political preferment, and social status distinctions—something which, in an earlier study, I called "the distribution of the social advantage." [32] Within the political unit some benefit more than others. The nation represents not only communal values but specialized interests. Indeed, the value system often sanctions such inequality of interests, as Tocqueville observed of the medieval age and as we could observe of our own contemporary societies. The same political unit which supports the common value system likewise supports the unequal distribution of the social advantage.

At times the inequity of the distribution of advantages is so great that it threatens maintenance of common values. Thus the Abbé Sieyès, who for a short time during the French Revolution became the spokesman for the Third Estate, used abuse of privilege as justification for violent change, interestingly enough anticipating the idea of pseudo-speciation in the process. As K. R. Minogue reports Sieyès' views: "Privileges are desired by men because of the 'intoxicating charm' of superiority, but they are incompatible with liberty and self-respect. The privileged constitute a 'nation within the nation' and their first thoughts are for the interest of that narrow caste, not for the nation itself. Indeed, the privileged come to think of themselves as a different species of beings from ordinary men." [33]

Inequalities of advantage exist in every society, even though not always to the degree that affronted Sieyès. Support of the political unit, and of the government which administers it, is of greater importance to some than to others, since it is equivalent to support of their own special advantage. Thus support of common values and support of differentiated interests become confused within the political unit, creating problems not only of identification but sometimes too of justification. The latter can and is occasionally met by appealing to pseudo-values, the sense of national superiority (in which all can share equally) as against other nationalities. If patriotism is the last refuge of the scoundrel, it is also at times a mainstay for the solid citizen.

Thus interests no less than values (and interests in the name of values) motivate the actions of political units. "In America, the truth of this has been made manifest by civil war. A majority has imposed their political and social systems on a minority; and, in order to maintain the sanctity of the constitution, a president destined to everlasting fame as a democratic hero had sent armies marching throughout his country to stamp out the doctrine of self-determination, bred among men as freeborn as himself." [34] Was this in the service of an ethic which would not countenance the possession of coercive power without using that power to further a way of life for which it stood, or was this the use of power to further special interests? Perhaps even those responsible for the decision could not answer. The ambiguity repeats itself at the end of the century. John Fiske, the Harvard historian, dreams of a time when the whole of mankind should constitute one huge federation along the American design, in which conflicts would be decided not by arms but "by the decision of one central tribunal, supported by the public opinion of the entire human race." And yet this version of the American grand design had as its counterpart the expansionist view exemplified by Senator Albert Beveridge, who believed that "American law, American order, American civilization, and the American flag" were "agencies of God," who had "marked the American people as his chosen nation to finally lead in this regeneration of the world. This is the divine mission of America and it holds for us all the profit, all the glory, all the happiness possible to man." [35] How draw the line between the missionary sense of value-rightness and the imperialistic sense of might-rightness, while they coexist? How distinguish, unerringly, in each instance, between the political unit which seeks to maintain itself against subversion and aggression, in support of its own autonomous values and distribution of interests, and the political unit which asserts itself against the autonomy of other units, in furtherance of its own sense of mission or pursuit of special advantage? Both within a single political unit and between political units, values and interests tend to become fused and confused. We shall have occasion to revert to this later.

The "Little Nationalities" and Minority Races

Thus nationalism becomes a multifaceted phenomenon: the support of social values which (more or less) integrate a people, the protector of special interests which are (more or less) consonant with those common social values, and the basis of a pseudo-value which asserts a genetic or inspired superiority over other nationalities. But we have not yet complicated the picture enough.

Within most contemporary nations there are pockets of population of alien ethnic origin. Few nations in the world do not encompass constituencies which have migrated from other areas and constitute "little nationalities" within the larger nation. These, like the functional groups which we took note of earlier, have their own particularistic value systems, in part an historical residue from the country of their origin and in part the product of their history in making their way in a strange, sometimes frightening, and at times even hostile, new country. These value systems, again as in the case of the functional groups previously examined, are partially divergent from the value system of the host country, but necessarily also partially congruent. The values of the foreign-born assert their own particularity but at the same time avoid bringing them into direct conflict with the majority population among whom they live. Their children grow up establishing their personal identity with a degree of ambivalence not characteristic of the indigenous stock, since they imbibe the social values of their ethnic-oriented parents and at the same time are exposed to the values of the larger society in other environments outside the home.

In those societies in which the alien ethnic group is made to feel uncomfortable or inferior, the bonds among its members are likely to be maintained and cultivated since the survival of the group constitutes a source of security. The particularistic values are likely to be nourished as a means of ensuring the group's integrity. Reversing the case where a group's imposed conformity becomes tyrannous to some individuals, who escape its control by moving out into the larger society, here the very strength of the ethnic group may provide "an inner emancipation from a more dominant group identity, such as that of the 'compact majority.' " [36]

In an unpublished manuscript Edith Carlson has surmised that the finicky obsession with orthodox practice on the part of the Jewish rabbis, against which Jesus rebelled, stemmed from their conscious intent of protecting the integrity of Jewish society, through heightened conformity with its own particularistic customs, against the erosion that would surely follow from the absorption by the young of the values of their Roman rulers.

This last example illustrates how the process of pseudo-speciation makes its presence felt within ethnic minorities—the little nationalities—of a society. The Jews preserved their cultural identity through the mythology that they were "chosen" people, even in the face of discrimination and abuse practiced against them by a dominant majority, in the same manner that Senator Beveridge trumpeted to the world that the American nation was God's chosen instrument. For an ethnic group subordinated to a dominant majority, the assertion of superiority over other ethnic minorities becomes an important crutch for the cultivation of a sense of personal pride. The individual member gains support for his personal identity through his association with a group which is "better" than others. Gang fights may erupt between youths of different ethnic backgrounds in support of such claims of superiority, just as wars among nations at times are occasioned by similar preening of national identities. We must distinguish such pseudo-values from the social values with which this study is concerned.

Just as social value systems become confused with special interests within the nation, so is this also the case within the little nationalities, the ethnic minorities. Some members of the clan benefit more than others. For some, the larger advantages which they reap from preferred positions *within* the ethnic group may compensate for the badge of inferiority they are made to wear within the larger society. Indeed, the cultivation of ethnic bonds and the protection of their integrity against assimilating tendencies may be fostered by those for whom the group provides special advantages which might not be duplicated outside that group.

Most of these comments concerning ethnic groups have equal applicability to racial minorities. These too tend to be segregated, at least when they appear in large enough numbers to make the dominant majority race conscious. With segregation they maintain their own value systems, within a shadowy context of the larger system's values. If the degree of prejudice displayed against them or of isolation thrust on them is great enough, the congruence of their particularistic values with the values of the larger society is proportionately lessened. The notion of a separate society with its separate values takes hold, and only when the minority member goes "abroad," entering on the "foreign" territory of the racial majority, is he likely to simulate adherence to the latter's codes of conduct. This may even involve a simulated adherence to the latter's pseudo-values, in the form of playing the stereotyped role for which the dominant race has cast him. Thus in the United States, until the civil rights revolution of the 1960's, the "good" Negro was one who, knowing "his place," conformed to the obsequious, slow-moving, good-natured, not very intelligent, "Step-'n'-fetchit" character which many whites expected of him, even though back in the midst of his own people a quite different character would emerge.

As has been observed, the Negro in the United States actually exemplifies caste more than race. "For caste membership and caste-bound social status are decided exclusively by descent; caste membership is determined for life before a child is born, and the barrier dividing the two classes cannot in principle be crossed. Between white and coloured there is no intermediate status." [37] This assertion of racial superiority has the same roots of pseudo-speciation as the assertion of national superiority, though they appear to run deeper. They likewise show the same purpose of removing by arbitrary specification an element of the population from competition with the majority. In effect, jurisdictional lines are drawn around economic, political, and social roles which are allocable to both groups, with the "inferior" race winding up with the inferior share.

Where prejudice is virulent it is small wonder that the rejected race in turn rejects the values of the master one, and that the latter's values in turn are corrupted by such a profoundly held pseudo-value. Indeed, the dominant race may succeed in effectively excluding the minority from participation in the active life of the community, so that the excluded in effect cease to exist as human beings. Confronted by that denial of their existence on all sides, it is small wonder, as Erikson has pointed out, that the more sensitive American blacks have engaged in an "almost ritualized affirmation of 'inaudibility,' 'invisibility,' 'namelessness,' 'facelessness' . . ." [38]

Even in the case of race, however, as in the case of ethnic minorities, there are those who, out of such opportunities as are allowed the group, obtain a preferential share. The distribution of social disadvantage, like social advantage, is unequal. Some make out very well indeed, as leaders within their own communities or as representatives of their communities to the larger society. For these the elimination of prejudice and the assimilation of their race would not always come as a blessing, since it might sweep away the foundation for their advantageous position. Values and interests again become confused.

Nor do all members of a racial minority identify unambiguously with their race. Those who have become more integrated with the dominant class may resist the intrusion of others of their color, partly in fear that the increase in their numbers might excite a dormant prejudice and spoil their present advantage, partly in fear that the clash of particularistic values (which they are in the process of shedding) and of common dominant social values (which they are in the process of acquiring) will create a tension and ambivalence they are unwilling to face.

Thus race, like ethnicity and nationalism, gives rise to genuine particularized social values, which are of prime importance in helping the individual establish his personal identity. However, along with these goes the pseudo-value which attributes some special significance to the group itself, relative to other groups, and a confused identification between common social values and differentiated social advantages. We shall have occasion to make use of all these ingredients as we pursue the tangled thread leading us to the origins, significance, and means of change of social values.

We have not yet finished with the definition and elaboration of social values, but before we return to that task it will be helpful if we first achieve some understanding of the process by which they become established.

Notes

1. Kurt Baier, in *Values and the Future,* ed. K. Baier and Nicholas Rescher (New York: The Free Press, 1969), p. 36.

2. Philip E. Jacob, "Changing Values in College," in *The American Style,* ed. Elting E. Morison (New York: Harper & Row, 1958), pp. 163–165.

3. Michael McGiffert, in *The Character of Americans,* ed. McGiffert (Homewood, Ill.: Dorsey Press, 1965), p. 225.

4. This is from the Introduction to Hegel's *The Philosophy of History,* trans. J. Sebree, selections from which are to be found in *Theories of History,* ed. Patrick Gardiner (New York: The Free Press, 1963), pp. 60–73.

5. Pitirim Sorokin, *The Crisis of Our Age* (New York: E. P. Dutton & Co., 1945), p. 17. Sorokin's position with respect to such transcendental values is very similar to Spengler's, but he quite explicitly distinguishes himself from Spengler in disavowing the notion of a life cycle of a civilization. A society can continue indefinitely, but only if its overriding value principle changes as circumstances make appropriate.

6. From *The Sleepwalkers,* by Hermann Broch, trans. Willa and Edwin

Muir (New York: Pantheon Books, a division of Random House, Inc., 1947), p. 562. Quoted with permission.

7. Erik H. Erikson, *Identity: Youth and Crisis* (New York: W. W. Norton & Co., 1968), p. 32. Quoted with permission.

8. Michigan State University Press, East Lansing, Michigan, 1967, Chapter 4, especially pp. 168–169, 195–196.

9. *Goals for Americans,* Report of the President's Commission on National Goals (Englewood Cliffs, N.J.: Prentice-Hall, Spectrum Book, 1960), p. 1: "The paramount goal of the United States was set long ago. It is to guard the rights of the individual, to ensure his development, and to enlarge his opportunity."

10. C. L. Sulzberger, citing Charles E. Bohlen with approval, *New York Times,* 26 November 1969.

11. Henry Ford II, *The Human Environment and Business* (New York: Weybright & Talley, 1970), p. 17.

12. W. W. Rostow, "The National Style," in *The American Style,* ed. Morison, p. 251.

13. "The desire of approbation and esteem of those we live with, which is of such importance to our happiness, cannot be fully and entirely contented but by rendering ourselves the just and proper objects of those sentiments, and by adjusting our own character and conduct according to those measures and rules by which esteem and approbation are naturally bestowed." Adam Smith, *The Theory of Moral Sentiments* (2nd ed.; 1761), p. 191.

14. Ralph Linton, *The Cultural Background of Personality* (New York: Appleton-Century-Crofts, 1945), p. 114. Adam Smith made the same point in his *Moral Sentiments,* p. 286: "The soldier who throws away his life in order to defend that of his officer, would perhaps be but little affected by the death of that officer, if it should happen without any fault of his own; and a very small disaster which had befallen himself might excite a much more lively sorrow. But when he endeavors to act so as to deserve applause, and to make the impartial spectator enter into the principles of his conduct, he feels, that to everybody but himself, his own life is a trifle compared with that of his officer, and that when he sacrifices the one to the other, he acts quite properly and agreeably to what would be the natural apprehensions of impartial bystanders."

15. For example, Alvin Gouldner, *The Coming Crisis of Western Sociology* (New York: Basic Books, 1970), p. 191.

16. C. I. Lewis, *An Analysis of Knowledge and Valuation* (La Salle, Ill.: The Open Court Publishing Co., 1946), pp. vii–viii.

17. Joseph A. Schumpeter, *Ten Great Economists* (New York: Oxford University Press, 1966), pp. 15–16.

18. Robert F. Murphy, citing Georg Simmel, emphasizes that "the very inclusiveness central to the definition of the group bespeaks its exclusiveness." He goes on to point out that "groups, by coming into conflict with each other, also define and preserve their boundaries, obtain a modicum of internal solidarity, and sometimes combine and transform each other." *The Dialectics of Social Life* (New York: Basic Books, 1971), p. 137.

Herman Turk has provided a nice case study of this phenomenon with respect to student physicians and student nurses, each of which groups, though presumably oriented toward the same functional objective of patient care, emphasized its special role in part by its own distinctive value set, which both supported its own specialized activities and excluded the other group from sharing in them. "Social Cohesion through Variant Values: Evidence from Medical Role Relations," *American Sociological Review* 28 (February 1963): 28–37.

19. Broch, *The Sleepwalkers,* p. 448. Italics supplied.

20. Talcott Parsons and Winston White refer to this aspect, citing David Riesman, in Seymour Martin Lipset and Leo Lowenthal, *Culture and Social Character* (New York: The Free Press, 1961), p. 97.

21. Rodolfo Stavenhagen describes this situation in "Marginality, Participation and Agrarian Structure in Latin America," *International Insitute for Labour Studies Bulletin* 7 (June 1970): 76.

22. Barrington Moore, Jr., *Social Origins of Dictatorship and Democracy* (Boston: Beacon Press, 1966), pp. 258–265.

23. R. Jackson Wilson has provided several nice examples of this fear in *In Quest of Community* (New York: Oxford University Press, 1968): The sociologist E. A. Ross believed that "the new America was being overrun by immigrants from southern and eastern Europe, Catholic in religion, living in industrial slums, threatening to eat away the old fund of common ancestry, common faith, and common experience . . ." (p. 109), and Josiah Royce deplored the fact that "the rush of immigration made it more and more difficult to maintain the core of moral homogeneity" (p. 164). The number of other social scientists who might be cited on this same score is legion.

24. Franz Alexander, "Educative Influence of Personality Factors in the Environment," in *Personality in Nature, Society, and Culture,* ed. Clyde Kluckhohn and Henry A. Murray (New York: Alfred A. Knopf, 1949), pp. 334–335. It is perhaps in point to note that Alexander, as a psychoanalyst, might be expected to emphasize individualistic values.

25. Alexander Gerschenkron, *Continuity in History and Other Essays* (Cambridge, Mass.: Harvard University Press, 1968), p. 135.

26. Kluckhohn and Murray, *Personality in Nature, Society, and Culture,* pp. 35–38.

27. Much of what follows in this section is taken from Erik H. Erikson's pioneering and thought-provoking book, *Identity: Youth and Crisis,* though I have had to condense his thesis drastically.

28. From Alexis de Tocqueville, *Democracy in America,* ed. Phillips Bradley. Vol. 1 (New York: Alfred A. Knopf, 1945), p. 9. A Reeve/Bowen/Bradley Translation. © 1945 by Alfred A. Knopf, Inc. Quoted with permission.

29. From *The Ruling Class* by Gaetano Mosca. Trans. Arthur Livingston. Page 72, also citing Vico. Copyright 1939 and used with permission of McGraw-Hill Book Company.

30. Joan Robinson, *Economic Philosophy* (Chicago: Aldine Publishing Co., 1962), p. 126.

31. Eugene Genovese, *The Political Economy of Slavery* (New York: Random House Pantheon, 1965).

32. Neil W. Chamberlain, *Beyond Malthus: Population and Power* (New York: Basic Books, 1970), Chapter 2.

33. K. R. Minogue, *Nationalism* (New York: Basic Books, 1967), p. 47.

34. A. P. Thornton, *The Habit of Authority* (London: George Allen & Unwin, 1965), p. 239.

35. Both the Fiske and Beveridge quotations are from Russel B. Nye, *This Almost Chosen People* (East Lansing, Mich.: Michigan State University Press, 1967), pp. 199–200.

36. Erikson, *Identity: Youth and Crisis*, p. 22.

37. Stanislaw Ossowski, *Class Structure in the Social Consciousness* (New York: The Free Press, 1963), p. 108. © Stanislaw Ossowski, 1963. Quoted with permission of the Macmillan Company and Routledge & Kegan Paul, Ltd. The same point is made by Gordon W. Allport in *The Nature of Prejudice* (New York: Doubleday Anchor Books, 1958), p. 304.

38. Erikson, *Identity: Youth and Crisis*, p. 25.

2 / The Objective Conditions

What gives rise to social values? From one point of view, values may be regarded as determining the character of a society. This makes them the primary causal (independent) variable, and the question of what determines the values is in effect waived. Alternatively, to identify something else as determining such values (the technical conditions of production, for example) would elevate that something to primary causal (independent) status and demote values to a dependent role, determined rather than determining. Rejecting both of these extremes, I assume that the objective conditions characterizing a society, and changes taking place in those conditions, give greater support to one or more conceptions of what kind of life is to be preferred, what purposeful design shall be pursued, what behavioral norms are followed, what coercive and integrative authority is accepted—all these in contrast to opposing conceptions which are downplayed or even eliminated. Most of this study is concerned with the working out of this general proposition.

There are four main classes of objective conditions which provide the constraints and opportunities within which purposive action takes place: the knowledge authority; economic and technical organization; population; and political organization, including relations with other political units. Some elaboration of the content of these four categories is essential to clarify the later analysis.

The Knowledge Authority

At any stage in a society's history there is some expert source of explanation as to how and why things happen as they do, some class of people who are credited with the capability of prediction. We call this the knowledge authority. In primitive societies such people are believed to be possessors of magic; at a later stage they are the priests of a society's religion; in our own day they are the scientists.

The kind of knowledge to which these authorities give rise creates one set of objective conditions which influence the social values which are adopted. It is not necessarily the knowledge authority itself which defines the values, though that is sometimes the case. It is simply that it helps to create a system of knowledge which is more congenial to one set of values than to another. The gradual rise in importance of utilitarian values in the West, for example, depended in part on the gradual displacement of religious authority by scientific authority as the principal source of knowledge.

John Stuart Mill has given eloquent testimony as to the importance of this influence.

Every considerable change historically known to us in the condition of any portion of mankind, when not brought about by external force, has been preceded by a change of proportional extent, in the state of their knowledge, or in their prevalent beliefs. As between any given state of speculation, and the correlative state of every thing else, it was almost always the former which first showed itself; though the effects, no doubt, reacted potently upon the cause. Every considerable advance in material civilization has been preceded by an advance in knowledge; and when any great social change has come to pass, either in the way of gradual development or of sudden conflict, it has had for its precursor a great change in the opinions and modes of thinking of society. Polytheism, Judaism, Christianity, Protestantism, the critical philosophy of modern Europe, and its positive science—each of these has been a primary agent in making society what it was at each successive period, while society was but secondarily instrumental in making *them,* each of them (so far as causes can be assigned for its existence) being mainly an emanation not from the practical life of the period, but from the previous state of belief and thought.[1]

The two types of knowledge authority which have been of dominant importance in the course of human history have been the supernatural, which for our purposes we can simply let stand for the religious, and the scientific. Max Weber probably remains the most insightful and subtle student of the role and manner of functioning of the religious authority. To do even minimal justice to the range and perceptiveness of his analysis would take us far beyond the needs of this study. For our purposes it is perhaps enough to note two distinctions which he makes. The first is between the prophet, the charismatic individual whose authority rests on some presumed personal and direct relationship with the divine power, and the priests, the institutionalized representatives of the ongoing church, who systematize and nourish the religious expression and give it its continuing authority. The second distinction of relevance for us is between the preaching types of religious authority, such as have largely characterized Buddhism and Protestantism, and the pastoral type, which is concerned with "the religious cultivation of the individual," represented preeminently by the Catholic Church.

Preaching and pastoral care differ widely in the strength of their practical influence on the conduct of life. Preaching unfolds its power most strongly in periods of prophetic excitation. In the treadmill of daily living it declines sharply to an almost complete lack of influence upon the conduct of life, for the very reason that the charisma of speech is an individual matter. Pastoral care in all its forms is the priests' real instrument of power, particularly over the workaday world . . . . In fact, the power of ethical religion over the masses parallels the development of pastoral care. Wherever the power of an ethical religion is intact, the pastor will be consulted in all the situations of life by both private individuals and the functionaries of groups. . . .[2]

To the extent that religion reveals the divine order, which can only be viewed as the *good* order within a monotheistic system of beliefs, and to the extent its revelatory authority is in fact accepted as *the* knowledge authority, its value-positing and style-creating capabilities are enormous. Weber's own conclusions on this score are well known, particularly with respect to the influence of the Catholic and Protestant versions of Christianity on the rise of rational economic (capitalistic) activity. He credits medieval Catholicism with completely preventing the rise of such a systematic worldly activity *within* the religious obligations it imposed through its pastoral care. (". . . people with rigorous ethical standards simply could not take up a business career. . . . A business career was only possible for those who were lax in their ethical thinking." [3]) It remained for Protestantism to encompass systematic, rational economic activity within its ethic. Among contemporary sociologists, probably Parsons has most emphasized the dominant impact of Christianity on Western culture, in a kind of two-stage movement, with the medieval church serving as the unique conduit for the transmission of classical culture to the modern world, and with the Protestant development giving form to our contemporary economic and political institutions.[4]

From a different perspective Mosca has argued that it was the *loss* of authority by the church in the West which opened the door to the concept of popular sovereignty. By cutting away one important support for the royal prerogative, the *divine* right of kings, it created a political vacuum which, as he sees it, was difficult to fill short of some version of a popular mandate, even though it might entail, at least initially, some limitation (of property, of income, of education) on those exercising it.[5]

This ebbing of the authority role of Western organized religion coincided, and was in part due to, the rise of the rational, scientific mode of thought: a new knowledge authority unseated the old. The process was not swift and violent—it extended over four or five centuries—but it was persistent and relentless. Nef attributes to the rise of mathematical reasoning from 1500 on this new way of looking at the world. Mathematics became the handmaid of science and industry both, though Nef stresses the independence of those two streams of activity. It was principally out of Catholic France that mathematics, arising as a means of pure reason, speculative and nonmaterial, gave impetus to the development of science for its own sake. It was principally out of utilitarian Protestant England that mathematics laid the basis for industrial applications. The two streams eventually merged in the modern world of science and technology.[6]

The impact of science on ways of conceiving society was early recognized, by the new breed of thinkers and the old theology both, but it entered into formal social-systems analysis only after 1800. In England Jeremy Bentham aspired to become the Newton of social science, and although his writing continues to evidence religious sympathies and beliefs it is predominantly secular in its significance, since he defined morality only as the rational anticipation of all the consequences flowing from one's actions. In France Auguste Comte, commonly regarded as the father of sociology, developed the doctrine of "positivism," explicitly based on scientifically certified knowledge. Positivism "preached 'an end to ideology' under the formulation of 'an end to metaphysics.' "

In other words, Positivism assumed that science could overcome ideological variety and diversity of beliefs. Comte had, in this vein, polemicized against the Protestant conception of unlimited liberty of conscience, holding that this led men each to their own differing conclusions and thus to ideological confusion. This disunifying liberty of conscience was, in Comte's view, to be supplanted by a faith in the authority of science . . .[7]

It was the demonstrable "validity" of scientific knowledge, in the form of technological advances, that constituted the secular counterpart of miracles in religion, leading men generally to believe not only in what they could see but in the authority of the knowledge that could lead to such accomplishments. As Leslie Stephen put the matter, "the prospect of bringing the ordinary creeds of mankind into harmony with scientific conclusions depends, in no small degree, upon the general respect for men of science; and that respect, again, depends materially upon the fact that men of science can point to such tangible results as railroads and telegraphs." [8]

Despite the seemingly irresistible centuries-long march of science, we do well to remind ourselves of the recency of its acceptance as knowledge authority in the West. R. Jackson Wilson has documented through the biographies of notable nineteenth-century social philosophers in the United States the painful intellectual dislocations that came with the new way of thinking about society. "On the whole, the new empirical psychology was a critique of Revelation, and anthropology a critique of Providence." The ambivalence cut deep into the intellectual community. John Dewey noted the "primary inconsistency" between science and morality. The new disciplines "seemed to require that the intellectual relinquish or at least mask the moral stance," but they also "held out the possibility that intellectuals could deal with subjects more obviously relevant to society than the inherited body of theology and moral philosophy." [9]

By mid-twentieth century, however, it did appear that science and its cohort technology had made good their claim to constitute the preeminent knowledge authority, swamping all but minuscule opposition, accommodating all social interests, rewarding everyone with their bounty. Scholars like Jacques Ellul and Herbert Marcuse have stressed the way in which the scientific and technological modes of thought have dominated the way in which we perceive ourselves and society.[10] As the reverse of this coin, other scholars have testified to the "death of God." Erich Fromm has said: "In fact, whether a man in our culture believes in God or does not makes hardly any difference either from a psychological or from a truly-religious standpoint. In both instances he does not care—either about God or about the answer to the problem of his existence." [11] And Herbert Kohl comments:

. . . contemporary philosophers, with few exceptions, have faced the fact that religion is no longer an active part of the everyday life of men in the Western world. Philosophy insofar as it considers the actual lives men lead these days must consider life as lived without divine guidance or grace. Life has become too complex for simple answers; hence philosophy insofar as it is modern does not consider religion as an issue.[12]

What may be true of the West is not, of course, necessarily true of other parts of the world. Arthur Koestler has made the point that while India is going through a kind of industrial revolution of its own, this consists largely of borrowed forms, unsupported by a prior scientific revolution which transformed people's ways of thinking. "In half a million villages, where eighty per cent of the population lives, every important activity and decision is still regulated by consulting the stars." [13] For the largest part of this society the knowledge authority is still the interpreters of the supernatural.

But there is reason even to question the supremacy of science in the West, if one means by that a final stage of the progression in ways of thinking—from the supernatural to the metaphysical and then to the ultimate stage of the scientific, following Comte's classifications. "Ultimates" have a way either of not materializing or of coming undone, and this may be true of science as the final knowledge authority no less than of Hegel's realization of the World Spirit, which he half believed had arrived with the Prussian state, or Marx's classless society, which he thought would be ushered in by the extirpation of the bourgeoisie. For one thing, the scientific ethic itself, opening up everything to investigation and criticism, has permeated the secular universities of the West. For them there is no "proscribed list." But this very openness of investigation has exposed science's own authority and the values it supports to questioning, even to the questioning by some (like Marcuse) of the value of open inquiry itself.

Marcuse has proffered his own alternative to scientific, conceptual thinking and operational analysis. In an ingenious and impressive piece of reasoning, he has pointed out the significance of the movement from Plato's ideal Forms to Aristotle's conceptual logic. Plato's Forms (ideas or ideals) were the only "truth," since any "real" (immediate) phenomenon was "contingent" in that it did not fulfill or realize the full "potential" of the Form. Since the Form is the only *true* reality, then what *is* (the contingent experience) really is *not* (is not, that is to say, the whole reality of the Form itself). This Platonic view of the world as comprehending two antagonistic versions of reality, the contingent and the potential, constitutes what Marcuse calls two-dimensional, or dialectical, thinking.

With Aristotle came formal logic. Since the philosopher found himself blocked in dealing with contingent experience, as particularistic expressions of an ideal Universal Form, he pursued the alternative of *abstraction,* as applied to a class of contingent experiences, deriving a "concept" which could be employed analytically. A class of objects had homogeneity with respect to the aspects abstracted from them and embodied in the concept; anything which differed in respect to this abstract concept was excluded from the class. Here was laid the basis for scientific reasoning. Such formal logic does not deny truth or reality to what it observes, nor does it judge it, as was the case with Platonic idealism. It deals with "abstracted" experience from which it derives testable propositions. Marcuse considers this one-dimensional thinking, since it proceeds only by excluding aspects of reality.

Marcuse would return to the Platonic mode, reviving the old conflict between contingent expression and potential, now, however, not in the realm of knowledge (ontology and epistemology) as such, but in the area of social policy and action. This dialectical mode of reasoning would not abstract from social reality, but would deal with it in its concrete particularities, in the wholeness of its historical expression. With this approach, *no* expression of social behavior can be accepted as "truth," since it represents only a partial fulfillment of the values (social policy) which called it into being. Over time what it does *not* do (the unrealized aspect of its value purpose) becomes more important than what it does, and creates the basis for critical attack. The dialectical mode thus continually moves away from present reality, demanding a break with it as failing to achieve its potential. Marcuse recognizes quite explicitly that this is a nonoperational, nonscientific mode of thinking, but this is precisely what he has set out to provide. He likewise recognizes that such a mode of thought is unlikely to win acceptance in an age of science and operationalism, which is the basis for his underlying pessimism, though he does allow himself the luxury of occasional apocalyptic moments.[14]

A recent suggestion by Thomas R. Blackburn, a chemist, blends the idea of intuitive (in his terminology "sensuous") training with Marcuse's view that scientific conceptual reasoning by itself fails to capture the whole of reality. ". . . by relying lopsidedly on abstract quantification as a method of knowing, scientists have been looking at the world with one eye closed. There is other knowledge besides quantitative knowledge, and there are other ways of knowing besides reading the position of a pointer on a scale." Blackburn would complement such quantitative abstraction with "direct, intuitive, sensuous" knowledge of phenomena, a method of observation for which an individual would require training. "What is urgently needed is a science that can comprehend complex systems without, or with a minimum of, abstractions. To 'see' a complex system as an organic whole requires an act of trained intuition, just as seeing order in a welter of numerical data does." [15] Blackburn obviously does not intend to advocate a displacement of science as a mode of thinking, but equally clearly he is recommending a major change in the scientific mode.

A loss of status by science in recent years has indeed been apparent, not only among the youth culture in the sixties but also in scholarly quarters. Alan Watts, a student of comparative philosophies and religions, has argued that "we have confused knowledge with what can be expressed in words or numbers as against what can be felt and sensed. Thus Western religions have stressed the overwhelming importance of dogma and belief, that is, of correct ideas even beyond the importance of correct behavior." [16] Watts foresees a trend toward Eastern "states of consciousness" which apprehend "reality" in a nonconceptual way, as experiences which cannot be reduced to words but are no less valid for that fact. Although he does not dispute the validity of scientific—conceptual—reality, those of his persuasion no longer recognize science as the sole or even supreme knowledge authority. If I interpret him correctly, they would not, however, regard nonconceptual experience as a supernatural expression. (Indeed, Watts speaks of it as more "materialistic and empirical than even Western science.")

Beyond such a divided but materialistic knowledge authority, L. P. Elwell-Sutton has argued that scholars should not ignore "the possibility of extra-human intervention in human affairs. Indeed, to do so is to emulate the example of the medieval inquisitors who refused to consider Galileo's theory that the earth was round." [17] When taken to task by scientist Jacob Bronowski for advocacy of "a return to historical obscurantism," Elwell-Sutton rejoined that what really troubled Bronowski was "the suggestion that scientific rationalism may not be the whole truth." Reversing the historical trend of 500 years, he charged that Bronowski was in fact bound by "scientific dogma." [18]

The apparent but still rather limited challenge to scientific supremacy constitutes no intimation of the rise of a new or substitute knowledge authority, but it does suggest that such an outcome is not to be ruled out.

There is no point in further speculation concerning ways in which our present knowledge authority may be altered in the future. It is enough to suggest that such a change is entirely possible. Whatever knowledge authority rules within a given society at a given time, it presents, as an objective condition, a particular way of viewing reality and realizing knowledge, and any change in that authority opens up new possibilities for perception and valuation.

Economic and Technical Organization

A second major class of objective conditions is given by the characteristics of the economic organization of a society. Here the overriding consideration is its stage of economic advancement. Following Colin Clark we may refer to primary (raw materials and food), secondary (manufacturing), and tertiary (service) economic organization, and the proportion of each type of activity present. In more current terminology, we might prefer to label these stages of development as preindustrial, industrial, and postindustrial.

The movement from a predominantly agricultural to a predominantly industrial economy carries with it the profoundest consequences. The growth of technology, powered by the development of science, creates new institutions which disrupt the natural rhythms of an agricultural existence and require a reorientation of family life, of attitudes toward work, and of one's own place in the working community. In Durkheim's phraseology, the individual leaves a world of social solidarity based on likeness (commensals, any of whom could substitute for each other) and moves into a world of organic solidarity (symbionts, specialists, complementing each other). Occupational differentiation becomes increasingly important. Cities come into existence to facilitate the division of labor. Specialization becomes the means of ensuring economic security by performing more effectively some service which others do not and cannot perform so well.[19]

Industrialization and urbanization create new classes. The concentration of wageworkers in geographical centers gives rise to their organization to protect their interests against the masters. The growth of industrial and governmental bureaucracies to supervise the new institutions and to regulate the activities of concentrations of people produces a middle class.

The impact of technology on the intellectual life of a society is complex and uncertain. A number of earlier observers, ranging from Tocqueville in France to William Morris in England believed that industrialization, with growing division of labor, would lead to a "dulling" of the intellectual life of workers, even in the process of increasing their material well-being. Reversing Marx, Tocqueville saw a growing divide between a prosperous but conformist laboring class at large and a kind of new industrial aristocracy which would arise even within democratic societies.[20] While some contemporary observers believe that Tocqueville has been proved right, others, from the turn of the century on, have concluded that industrialization, by reducing the hours of work and creating more leisure, has made possible a fuller cultivation of the mind. Even if one adopts the latter view, insofar as industrialization has been associated with urbanization, with its more varied cultural fare, the respective contributions of these two influences cannot be measured.

Industrialism, whether or not it has stimulated intellectual vitality, has created a need for basic education. Societies which have advanced beyond the agricultural stage invariably are better-educated societies. In part this may be due to the simple fact that they are likely to be more prosperous and can afford the luxury of teaching children to read and write, but it also has its rationale in the greater demands which technical operations place on individuals who must be able to decipher posted notices and elementary instructions, fill out forms, communicate information to others, and exercise a degree of self-discipline which is most likely to be learned in school. The more complicated the technology, the greater the need for more highly educated technicians.

Industrial advancement depends on an agricultural surplus or on export of manufactures in exchange for imported food and raw materials. In either case, as a society moves away from a condition of subsistence to one of greater prosperity, it achieves a discretionary surplus—some production beyond what is needed for subsistence, at whatever level subsistence may be culturally defined. The discretionary surplus may accrue either to individuals or to the government, or to both in some measure. It may be plowed back into capital equipment, used for private enjoyment, or expended on public improvements. But with growing affluence and increased discretion in how much can or must be spent, the possibility of a Keynesian imbalance between production and consumption comes into the picture, necessitating government regulation and planning.

With the expansion of population and the advancement of technology, the producing establishments expand appropriately. Large-scale institutions are necessary to large-scale economies. Organizational change is a constant requirement to accommodate growth. This requirement of changing scale, specialization, and organization is equally applicable to socialist as well as private-capitalist countries. The ministry with its industral subdivisions, in the former, has a rough counterpart in the supercorporation in the latter—in the United States, for example, the conglomerate firm, in Japan "the group" (an outgrowth of the prewar *zaibatsu,* now no longer a single entity but still operating interdependently). Under one organizational umbrella are gathered a number of industrial and commercial activities, some functionally related and some unrelated. To a greater or lesser extent, they draw on a common pool of capital, placing it where it promises to be used most effectively.

With respect both to the internal operations of the enterprise and the integrated operations of the economy there are varying degrees of discretion and authority on the part of subordinate and superior. The standards and methods of efficiency differ. In all cases, however, as Weber, Simmel, and Schumpeter anticipated, bureaucratization of the organization is inescapable; organizational integration requires levels of authority, defined spheres of discretion, standard operating procedures, highly detailed methods of accounting, increasingly sophisticated planning and budgeting systems. And as Arnold Toynbee and John Kenneth Galbraith predicted, the large corporation, even in a private-enterprise society, becomes increasingly an agent of the government, an arm of the civil service bureaucracy, an extension of the government's administrative organization.

The improvement in working conditions and compensation of industrial workers, the shift from industrial production to services for an increasing proportion of the labor force, the continuing expansion of industrial and governmental bureaucracies, and the rise of new professions transform the population of the advanced economies into a predominantly middle-class society, though that term loses much of its meaning in the process. If it is intended to convey the idea that advanced economies are largely one-class societies, it is obviously (and semantically) misleading, since classes continue to exist, even if the economic and social distances separating them are reduced. If it is intended to suggest a sameness of interests characterizing a "mass" urbanized culture, it exhibits partial validity, since the mass constitutes the main market for the culture producers, who can be expected to gear their culture products to popular tastes. But it carries partial falsity, as well, since there are, as we noted earlier, a large number of special-interest groups, with their own particularistic values, which are partially divergent from, and even in conflict with, those values which are held in common. To speak of a whole population as "middle class" is to use an historical concept in an ahistorical way. Perhaps the vague implication in the continued use of the term that a large proportion of the population has achieved a stake in the continuity of the system and its underlying values is its most important conceptual content.

This last consideration intrudes the question of ownership of the means of production. In the case of agricultural societies, ownership of the land takes on overriding importance. In many instances, even in the contemporary world, this gives rise to a feudal structure, with great landholders, proprietors of latifundia, sharing most of the country's landed wealth among themselves, with a largely landless peasantry subject to their dictate and direction. As a country moves toward industrialization, there is a tendency for these large landholdings to be divided among lesser proprietors, a stage which is then often followed by recombination in the form of agricultural cooperatives or enterprises, either under socialist (state) or corporate (private) control.

The influence of ownership which has received greatest attention in the Western world, however, is not with respect to landholding but industrial enterprise, a fact for which Karl Marx is largely but not wholly responsible. Although a number of contemporary writers have dismissed as unimportant the matter of ownership of the large, modern corporation, on the ground that control is more important, and has been separated from dispersed ownership, this goes too far. As long as ownership rights, even though not actively exercised, provide at least the legal basis for the control by others, they remain important.

Their significance lies in two aspects. Ownership of means of production conveys discretion, however hedged, to determine the direction of economic activity. The resources of a society are used for those purposes conducing to the advantage of the owners of the resources. In a private-enterprise economy, that means activity directed into profit-making channels. Advertising promotes such activity, creating and stimulating wants which might not have otherwise been felt. In doing so it contributes to the growth of the economy, constituting something of an engine powering economic development, linked as that is to technological innovation and scientific advancement. The relation here to consumption as a value, and to technological order as an instrument for promoting consumption, is readily apparent. In socialist economies, although profit cannot be ignored since it remains a measure of efficiency, it need not direct the flow of economic activity. Housing, for example, might conceivably be given higher priority than automobile construction, as a matter of social choice, even though in carrying out that mission the housing authority could be expected to operate as profitably (efficiently) as possible. Nor need profit in socialist economies provide the same motivating force for economic expansion. Such motivation would presumably have to derive from hierarchical authority or social idealism.

The second significance of ownership lies in the special claims it provides in the distribution of the rewards of economic activity. Over and beyond any earnings flowing from personal contribution to the production process, owners of enterprises reap an additional return from the "rent" which they are able to charge for the use of their property. In socialist economies rewards of ownership accrue to the state.[21]

Even in so summary and partial a survey of the possible economic conditions of a society, it is evident that particular conditions promote certain values more than others. An agricultural society is more likely to be status structured and less egalitarian as to the distribution of material advantages than an industrial type. Small industry and active ownership is more likely to emphasize individualism and pecuniary accumulation than large-scale corporate activity. Changes in these economic characteristics of a society provide occasion for the redirection of its values.

More recently, a school of environmentalists has been stressing the potential consequences of the worldwide effort to increase output and raise the level of consumption—an effort which has turned into a race between nations contending for international influence (when will the U.S.S.R. overtake the U.S. in total production; when will Japan overtake the U.S.S.R.?), and which has also set goals for the developing nations which are striving to break out of their circle of poverty. Some scientists, notably Barry Commoner, have argued that continued rates of growth simply cannot be sustained at anything like current levels, if indeed at all.[22] This for the reason that increased output in recent years has stemmed largely from the use of chemical products which do not fit into the "circle of life," which do not get fed back into a self-sustaining natural system. Imbalances occur which threaten the continuity of the ecosystem. Thus scientific technology, on which we have relied so largely for economic growth, will within the foreseeable future be restricted as an engine of expansion. What then, Commoner asks, will be the effect on economic institutions which have been based on growth-motivation? How resolve questions of economic equity when one can no longer count on rapid economic expansion as the means of extricating the disadvantaged from their mean condition? Without necessarily accepting the whole of his carefully reasoned argument, we have here another instance of (potentially) an objective economic and technological condition which would certainly affect people's attitudes of what constitutes the good life and what can be considered equitable relations with each other.

Population

The third set of objective characteristics importantly influencing the values asserted within a society entails its population.[23] Among these is simply the effect of numbers of people—population growth and occasionally population decline. The Malthusian thesis posits that since population tends to grow at a faster rate than food, malnutrition and famines will take their periodic toll to reestablish some balance between the two. Sexual continence and technological advantages in the raising of food may slow the evil day, but since the amount of natural resources is immutably fixed while the procreative urge has no limit, sooner or later the Malthusian trap has to be sprung.

While a number of scholars and politicians have sought to rebut Malthus by pointing to the gains which have been made in contraception, the spread of the concept of family planning, and the enormous improvements which have been forthcoming in food production—by industry no less than agriculture, by chemical means no less than biological, the pessimists are still largely (and I think correctly) anticipating catastrophic Malthusian effects in parts of the underdeveloped world, where even a successful reduction in the rate of reproduction now, without further delay, would still leave in prospect an enormous increase in the output of the human pipeline simply because it is already filled with so many people of reproducing age. The spigot cannot be turned off, even if the rate of output is slowed, and the volume still to be put through the pipeline will go on increasing for decades. It has been pointed out that even such a natural disaster as the tidal wave which destroyed an estimated half-million lives in East Pakistan in 1970 was simply a gruesome Malthusian consequence of the fact that pressures of numbers had driven people to settle in the low-lying areas at the mouth of the Ganges, for lack of any other place to live.

One of the major objective conditions confronting a society, then, is the extent to which it is capable of providing adequately for the size of its population. This has been the chief concern of the population experts. But other considerations are also present.

In addition to simple numbers of people, the composition of a population is important, particularly with respect to its ethnic and racial groups.

There is no need to dwell on this aspect, since we have already touched on it with respect to the concept of pseudo-speciation. Minority groups tend to be subject to discrimination, unless they are minority masters, so that in the distribution of the social advantage they get the short end of the stick. Sam Bass Warner offers an example of this process with respect to housing in the city of Philadelphia over the period 1860–1930 which could be duplicated many times over with respect to other goods, other places, and other times. As the population of Philadelphia expanded, the wealthier moved to the more open outer spaces and suburbs. "All the disfavored racial and ethnic groups—the Negroes, Italians, Russian and Polish Jews—were crowded into those areas of old housing and low-paying industries." [24] Every society distributes its resources unequally among its members. For a variety of reasons which need not now concern us, some receive more advantages than others. With population growth, the effect is not an equal tightening of the belts of all the members of a society. The wealthier and politically privileged are better able to protect themselves from shortage of food, living space, educational and recreational facilities, and other amenities. It is those who are already disadvantaged who become even more disadvantaged by the pressure of numbers; those who are already given the inferior jobs, those who are discriminated against in housing and education, find the pressures increasing in the limited social space to which they are confined.

The consequence may not be simply discomfort for the underprivileged but political instability. An increase in political sensibility by a growing subpopulation which already is dissatisfied with its share in society, or which suffers because its restricted share must be parceled out among a larger number of its own people, is likely to lead to a diminished sense of congruence with the values of the larger society, and a preferment of its own particularistic values. Determined actions by the grossly exploited can build the base for a demagogic leader to challenge the status quo. The defense of private property, particularly in the form of exclusive use of sizable parcels of land or natural resources such as beaches, becomes increasingly difficult.

Inequality in wealth and income, always a potential threat to political stability, increases with population expansion unless redistributional policies are adopted. Land is fixed, and some forms of capital (major plant and equipment installations) are *relatively* fixed in amount. The value of these usually rises as they become relatively scarcer, and this, in private hands, leads to greater concentration of wealth. The nonpropertied suffer a relative and sometimes absolute deterioration of economic position unless political actions are taken to offset this effect. With continued growth in numbers and density of people, it becomes increasingly difficult to defend the rights of private property against the demands of public interests. Property may be left in private hands, but it is subject to more intensive public regulation. Incomes may remain greatly unequal, but taxation to raise the revenues for social welfare programs ultimately must weigh more heavily and effectively on the wealthy if social cohesion is to be maintained, if social values are to be held in common.

The form of government is also affected by the size of a population. As a people increases in numbers the government must expand its activities in order to regulate the pressures of people on people—to limit discretion in such matters as the use of streets, the disposal of refuse, the care of sickness, the diffusion of smoke and noise, the movement of traffic, and in a variety of other matters. In a society which is also industrializing and expanding, and therefore becoming more specialized as to its institutional forms, it is more necessary to centralize the role of coordination and integration. The society which numbers its population in the hundreds of millions must of necessity resort to more authoritative forms of central control in matters of greatest importance, and devolve on smaller political units—still substantial in scale—the provision of such services and the regulation of such activities as can best be left to more localized discretion.

More generally, population growth has its impact on a society's organizational structure, both private and public. In effect, as a society grows this imposes a necessity on its organizational skeleton to modify its form. Form becomes more formal; specialization of functions leads to departmentalization and divisionalization. Control is likewise affected. The local units—whether of government, of enterprise, of workers' unions—become more and more subordinated to a central authority, usually national in its scope. The larger and now more dispersed membership or constituency tends to organize and factionalize and press for participation in the making of decisions which affect it. Leadership in such groups tends to gravitate toward a few activists, who in time play a formal representative role within the existing organization or within a new organization; the variations are numerous, ranging from national labor unions engaged in collective bargaining with national corporations to conferences of mayors and governors conferring with national executive and legislative authorities, from associations of local dealers or suppliers agreeing on codes of equitable relationships with national manufacturers to local political parties sending delegates to national political conventions.

More formal methods of control are required. The economy becomes knit into a complex system of planning, with the government as the overall manager, using its own and private organizations as well for the accomplishment of social objectives, within a framework of specifications necessarily leaving some degree of discretion to the lesser administrative units —obviously more in a private-enterprise than a socialist economy. Within the enterprise the planning process continues, as top management sets guidelines within which its own subsidiaries or divisions act to accomplish corporate objectives, and so on down to the smallest shop unit. The larger the society and the organization the more intricate is the network of control relationships, but also the greater is the amount of discretion which must be accorded to the lesser administrative units, whether private or public, in carrying out objectives which are more and more broadly defined.

Even a people's technology is significantly affected by the size of its population. The amount and direction of inventive activity tend to be responsive to the economic needs a society manifests. An expanding population increases the market and profitability of certain industries, thereby stimulating inventive activity in solving their technical problems. It also increases the number of enterprise units, and hence the number of opportunities for technical experimentation. This does not mean that the larger the population the more inventive and technologically advanced it becomes relative to other smaller countries, as, say, India would then be relative to Sweden. It means only that within a given culture, and for a given stage of economic development, a larger population will change the structure of economic demands, creating new problems calling for innovative solutions and offering greater rewards—of prestige and service as well as of money —to those meeting such needs.[25] As one example of this process at work, a "mass" middle-class society creates a demand for mass consumption, which can only be met through industrial mass-production techniques. In this sense Henry Ford was created by his times.

Urbanization too is a demographic phenomenon, with significant consequences. For one thing, it creates its own class—that middle class of which we have been speaking, and in any industrialized society it tends to draw to it the social, political, and economic leadership. But the anonymity which the city provides and the sheer magnetism of its numbers also draw to it deviant and marginal persons, as well as new classes, dissident masses, expatriates, and migrants. It is the cities, not the countryside, which typically spawn radical programs and liberal causes. Tocqueville, viewing the United States in the 1830s, found its cities populated by a "rabble even more formidable than the populace of European towns." [26]

Urbanization is not only marked by the rise of a new class but also by a new way of life. If, from medieval times on, the town has emphasized its economic functions, it has also become the culture-creating center of society and a potent influence for the secularization of social behavior. Urban culture lays stress on civil manners; innovation (particularly as represented by style); the institutionalization of many aspects of social life through societies, clubs, associations for specialized purposes; and the commercialization of many relationships and activities (urban culture is notoriously a money culture). Not of least importance, cities encourage the spread of literacy; within any society the educated are to be found disproportionately in its population centers. In the more advanced societies, with widespread popular education, this gives rise to what has been called "mass culture," the domination of taste by the many.

Thus in manifold ways a society's population—its numbers, rate of growth, composition, location—create a set of objective conditions, which in their particularities are likely to support certain social values in contrast to others.

Political Organization

The final category of objective social conditions influencing which values get stressed within a given society is its political organization.

The source of the powers of government and the degree of centralization of those powers constitutes one vital characteristic. Though we frequently refer to governments as "sovereign," we likewise recognize that some exercise a more limited authority than do others, whether from custom, constitution, or capability. Governments imposed on a people tend to display an almost absolute power. A military leader slips into—more correctly, creates for himself—a seat of authority, from which he enjoys feudal privileges over those whom his might protects. Down through the Congress of Vienna in 1815 the heads of most European governments were monarchs with virtually absolute power inherited through family succession. The king of England shared power with Parliament following the Glorious Revolution of 1688, and an occasional small territory observed republican principles—Switzerland, and at various times such centers as Florence and Genoa, but the monarch's inherited right of rule was *generally* the rule. As Bertrand Russell has expressed it:

Roughly speaking, territory was treated as we still treat landed estate: we do not think that the tenants of a landowner can acquire a right to own the land on which they live by merely deciding that they would like to do so. This would seem absurd to most men of the present day; and the principle of self-determination as regards government would have seemed equally absurd to the negotiators at Vienna.[27]

Nevertheless, as Castlereagh anticipated at the time, "It is impossible not to perceive a great moral change coming on in Europe, and that the principles of freedom are in full operation. The danger is, that the transition may be too sudden to ripen into anything likely to make the world better or happier." And a thoughtful French aristocrat, politician, and philosopher, Alexis de Tocqueville, likewise perceiving the "great moral change" which was in Europe's offing, traveled throughout the youthfully exuberant United States so that he might prepare for his fellow countrymen a document alerting them to the best and the worst of the possibilities inherent in democracy as practiced there.

But over the years democracy has come to mean such a variety of forms that the word has lost its conceptual value. As originally conceived, it referred to direct self-government by a citizenry of free men. In the sense given its clearest expression by Rousseau, it was the governmental form of a community sufficiently small that all could be directly involved in its decisions; representative of the general will, it was the sovereign voice of the people, binding on all. Thus every individual was both sovereign and subject, at one and the same time participating in making the laws of his state and in being bound by them, on terms of equality with all other citizens. But this concept of pure democracy lost any applicability with the growth of the modern state: millions of individuals cannot effectively participate in devising the general will.

Democracy subsequently came to be understood as a representative form of government. Representation could take numerous shapes. A government might be viewed as representative of a people if elected by a majority. It might even be considered representative if, however chosen, it acted in the common interest. But since majorities could be tyrannous over minorities, and the common interest was difficult to define in a population of heterogeneous interests, there emerged the concept of democracy as consisting, *along* with popular representation in some sense, of a sphere of immunity from governmental authority. Thus in the Lockean formulation democratic governments (in contrast to authoritarian forms) were barred from violating the property rights of those whom they represented. The Bill of Rights of the American Constitution is perhaps the clearest expression of this conception of democracy as embodying both public representation and private immunity. This is the conception which Tocqueville so eloquently elaborated as characterizing the United States of the early nineteenth century.

With the passage of time, increase in the size of populations, and the extension of education and suffrage, notions of democratic representation have continued to undergo modification. It would be almost correct to say that most governments today view themselves as representative and limited in some respects, even those which are clearly authoritarian in form. This follows from equating democracy with some variant of populism. Since it is the rare government which can maintain its office *solely* on the basis of force, even though it may liberally resort to its use, it is more or less compelled to strive for at least a modest degree of popular acceptance.

In meeting this requirement governments can move in either of two directions. They may conform themselves to the interests of the principal power centers of a society while somehow satisfying the general (and often heterogeneous) population, or they may play for a mass following by a combination of demagogic and public relations efforts while placating the major interest groups on whom they must rely for the functioning of an increasingly complex society.

According to the first approach, governments are the locus of interest-group control, the arena for a contest of powers out of which emerges the actions which satisfy the most powerful groups. There are several variations on this theme, ranging from the pluralist school of thought which believes that interests are so numerous and so fragmented that public policy represents a kind of consensus, through the position popularized by C. Wright Mills which views public policy as the product of a much smaller number of power elites, to, at the other extreme, the Marxian position that government is explicitly and necessarily the representative of the dominant class (in his time the capitalist, or "bourgeois," class).

If governments move in the other direction, they follow the path described (but despised) by Ortega y Gasset.[28] They are responsive to the demands of the voting masses, pandering to their ill-conceived wants and fancies. Bereft of and unconcerned with the guidance of an intellectual elite which could create a sense of style and standards, such a government tends to emphasize bread and circuses (or wars or welfare), satisfying common tastes. Public opinion polls become barometers of popularity, and hence public opinion becomes something to be manipulated. Politicians and parties are products to be sold. If interest groups become restive, threatening withdrawal of support, the populist program can be explained as a necessary palliative, lacking which, more radical programs might be demanded.

Clearly these two types of governmental philosophy are simply opposite ends of a spectrum, along which any government can position itself. What is at issue is how a government seeks to ensure its acceptance and continuity. The deeper the divisions within a society, the more difficult does it become to satisfy the component interests. The powerful and therefore the advantaged groups seek to preserve the status quo, and are therefore on the side of repression of dissidence. The disadvantaged groups seek change, and may be numerous and desperate enough to threaten disruption of civil order unless they obtain it. Under such circumstances a government must choose between steadfastness and repression, on the one hand, or permissiveness and change, on the other, or some blend of the two. In any event, different values are involved.

One important objective characteristic of political organization is the degree of its centralization, since this affects the opportunities for diversity of views and divergence of policies. It reflects whether the social system is tightly or loosely organized. Generally speaking, the more specific are social objectives, the greater is the need for central control. If social goals require spelling out a particular investment pattern (so much of the nation's income to go into transportation or housing or educational facilities), then the government must exercise authority specific enough to command this performance. The authority may be only in the fields of fiscal policy, but under some circumstances it involves actual direction of men and capital—most obviously in times of crisis.

The more general the national objectives, the less central control is required and the more private or local discretion can be released. A vague and modest full-employment goal may be satisfied with limited powers over taxation and credit supply. Nevertheless, whenever there is *any* effort, however limited, at coordinating units, public or private, to achieve social goals, some measure of control is inescapable. Loose coupling of the organizational parts of a society, lack of standards for their performance, haphazard or perfunctory review by higher authority—all imply a weakness of social objectives but never their absence.

Even if one were to advance the laissez-faire argument that the objective of government is to create an atmosphere of general permissiveness, extending maximum autonomy and encouraging maximum initiative on the part of private enterprises, some review and control would be necessary to achieve *that* objective—to ensure that private grasping for monopoly positions and conspiracies aimed at short-cutting interpersonal competition did not subvert the general objective. Thus even in the most individualistic of economic systems, some centralized purpose and control cannot be avoided.

Centralization of authority takes place on two fronts—not only in the division of power between national and local bodies but also in the division of power between executive and legislature. If promptness and decisiveness of action are considered important, if technical expertise must be relied on, if the administrative agencies of government increase in number and scope, the balance shifts to the executive branch. Large debating bodies are ineffective under such circumstances.

With respect to the balance between national and local authority, the trend has been toward consolidation of power in the central government, a trend perceived more than a hundred years ago by Tocqueville. In a democracy, he argued, the stress on equality under the law encourages the idea of a single government over the whole of the country, affecting all equally. The rise of a middle class, which democracy promotes by giving rein to private actions, means that large numbers of the ablest citizens will be preoccupied with their own affairs and disinclined to take part in public business; they prefer to leave that to an elected government. With a propertied and numerous middle class also comes the desire for a strong central government to preserve law and order. Thus everything predisposes a democracy toward the support of a centralized administration.

But Tocqueville need not have confined his conclusion to the American democracy. Even in socialist societies the trend has been in this direction. The salient reasons are the increase in size of population and the number and complexity of economic enterprises requiring central coordination. Nevertheless, with centralization in certain important particulars there necessarily goes decentralization in other respects to the more local governmental units, to avoid choking the national management with excessive detail. But even at the local units the same forces of size and complexity impose the same requirement, of centralizing—but now in the local government—many of the coordinating powers, delegating to lesser decentralized units (enterprises, neighborhood associations, voluntary groups) such discretion as is consonant with efficient performance, without jeopardizing objectives.

We have now canvassed, enough for our purposes, the four major categories of objective conditions which describe a society at a point in time: the knowledge authority on which it relies, its economic and technical organization, its population characteristics, and its political organization. Obviously we cannot say that these encompass the whole of the circumstances describing a people, but they emphasize those which are of strategic importance. Significant changes in these characteristics are likely to shift support from certain social values to other values. The period and movement which we call the Reformation, for example, witnessed in northern European societies a change in the conception of the knowledge authority, coinciding with major changes in economic and technical organization, and accompanied in the political field by an assertion of a secular and national authority against the imperial and supranational authority of the church. The consequence was to unleash a cumulative movement supporting a significant shift in the values of the societies where these events occurred, values which did not spring forth newborn and dewy-fresh, but which had been present all along, requiring only the nourishment of specific changes in the objective conditions in order to flourish and spread.

Notes

1. John Stuart Mill, *A System of Logic*, 8th ed. (London: Longmans, Green & Co., 1872, reprinted 1961), p. 605.

2. Max Weber, *Economy and Society*, Vol. 2 (New York: Bedminster Press, 1968), pp. 464–465.

3. *Ibid.*, p. 587.

4. Talcott Parsons, *Sociological Theory and Modern Society* (New York: The Free Press, 1967), especially pp. 393–409.

5. Mosca, *The Ruling Class*, p. 359.

6. John U. Nef, *The Conquest of the Material World* (Chicago: University of Chicago Press, 1964), particularly pp. 308–322. © 1964 by The University of Chicago. Quoted with permission and permission of John U. Nef. Essentially the same point is made by John Merz, *A History of European Thought in the Nineteenth Century*, Vol. 1 (New York: Dover Publications, 1965), pp. 92–103.

7. Gouldner, *The Coming Crisis of Western Sociology*, p. 114. The outlooks of Bentham and Comte with respect to the application of science to society were radically opposed. Bentham believed in an individualistically oriented society, while Comtian sociology tended to put the stress on social institutions.

8. Leslie Stephen, *History of English Thought in the Eighteenth Century*, Vol. 1 (New York: G. P. Putnam's Sons, 1927), p. 11. Quoted with permission.

9. Wilson, *In Quest of Community*, pp. 39–40. Also underscoring the continuing hold of the old faith, Robin Williams reminds us in his essay, "Values and Beliefs in American Society" (in McGiffert, *The Character of Americans*, p. 205) that the Scopes trial over the teaching of the doctrine of evolution took place only a few years ago.

10. Jacques Ellul, *The Technological Society* (New York: Alfred A. Knopf, 1964) and Herbert Marcuse, *One-Dimensional Man* (Boston: Beacon Press, 1964).

11. Erich Fromm, *Man for Himself* (New York: Holt, Rinehart & Winston, 1947), p. 67.

12. Herbert Kohl, *The Age of Complexity* (New York: Mentor Books, 1965), p. 271.

13. Arthur Koestler, *The Lotus and the Robot* (New York: Harper Colophon Books, 1966), p. 113.

14. Marcuse, *One-Dimensional Man*, especially Chapter 5. I find Marcuse's philosophical reasoning subtle, complex, and compelling, but his prescriptive analysis—when he permits himself the hope of change—is turgid and obscure.

15. Thomas R. Blackburn, "Sensuous-Intellectual Complementarity in Science," *Science* 172 (June 4, 1971): 1003–1007. It is apposite to note that the present widespread "sexist" or "new feminist" movement, aimed at establishing equality between the sexes or diminishing the differences between them, is often said to hold a "liberating" potential for the human race. One aspect of this would be the encouragement to blending in one person the so-called "intuitive" quality of the female and "rational" quality of the male. The reality of these stereotypes is denied, thus freeing each of the sexes to cultivate a quality which is not now considered "appropriate" to it, holding the promise of that blend which Blackburn advocates.

16. Alan Watts, "The Future of Religion," in *Toward Century 21*, ed. C. S. Wallia (New York: Basic Books, 1970), p. 301.

17. L. P. Elwell-Sutton, "Mohammed Muckraked," *New York Review of Books*, 27 January 1972, pp. 24–25. Elwell-Sutton is Head of the Persian Department of the University of Edinburgh.

18. This interesting exchange of letters appeared in the *New York Review of Books*, 9 March 1972, pp. 36–37.

19. This is one reason why contemporary urbanization in so many underdeveloped countries, as in Asia and Latin America, cannot be equated with urbanization as it has taken place historically in the West. The former is more the replication of village life in city streets, with numerous individuals holding on to a bare subsistence through menial services of little economic value, while the latter occurred in response to an industrial development which reflected increasing occupational specialization.

20. Tocqueville, *Democracy in America*, Vol. 2, pp. 164–165. On Morris and other like-minded English literary men, Raymond Williams has written illuminatingly in *Culture and Society, 1780–1950* (New York: Columbia University Press, 1958).

21. Yugoslavia has, however, embarked on the highly interesting experiment of using profit as a motive for efficiency and expansion, and as an instrument for distributing income, in socially owned enterprises. It has accomplished this by entrusting the operation of communally owned establishments to the workers of such an establishment who derive a profit from its efficient operation—not a bonus given to them by a higher authority, but a "dividend" which they declare for themselves. They are otherwise responsible only for taxes (as would be true of a private enterprise) and for maintaining the facilities in good condition, including reasonable but unspecified innovation and investment—this in fulfillment of their obligations to society which has entrusted them with these resources.

22. Barry Commoner, *The Closing Circle* (New York: Alfred A. Knopf, 1971).

23. Most of the material in this section, unless otherwise noted, comes from my previous study, *Beyond Malthus: Population and Power*.

24. Sam Bass Warner, *The Private City* (Philadelphia: University of Pennsylvania Press, 1968), p. 173.

25. This thesis has been adapted from Jacob Schmookler's *Invention and Economic Growth* (Cambridge, Mass.: Harvard University Press, 1966).

26. Tocqueville, *Democracy in America*, Vol. 1, p. 299.

27. Bertrand Russell, *Legitimacy versus Industrialism, 1814–1848* (London: George Allen & Unwin, 1965), p. 24. The Castlereagh quotation which follows comes from the same source, p. 25.

28. José Ortega y Gasset, *The Revolt of the Masses* (New York: Mentor Books, 1951).

3 / Thrusters and Dominants

In trying to ascertain how values get established and maintained, we obviously have to break in on a society at some point in time. At that point certain objective conditions prevail, embodying some of the characteristics we have been concerned with in the preceding chapter. There also exists, with whatever degree of preciseness or diffuseness, of strength or weakness, some set of values.

We assume that with the further passage of time, certain changes take place in the objective conditions. Depending on the nature and magnitude of these changes, they may provide the ingredients of new opportunities to some group or class of individuals within the society. What to others may be simply a source of interest or concern or even a threat to be countered appears to it as the occasion for new or renewed activity. If we conceive of the objective conditions, the social-political-economic context of the times, as constituting the "assets" which society uses to whatever advantage it conceives possible, then a change in the composition of those assets invites a possible speculation for new advantage.

And not necessarily only some *one* new possible line of activity is suggested. Conceivably the change in circumstances may suggest several possible applications, inviting the attention of several different groups or classes within the population; there may be some competition among them for favored position. Conceivably their projects may permit collaboration. But whatever new or alternative lines of action may be adopted depends on the qualities of the individuals and groups confronting them. Those who respond by seizing them for their own advantage, whether promptly and perceptively or more slowly and with only a gradually dawning sense of their significance, we call *thrusters*.

Now obviously a society, even in the face of rather great changes in its conditions, may not give rise to any thrusting group. It may simply shift the nature of its activities as little as is necessary and continue in its traditional ways to the extent possible. Some analysts, with perhaps an unconscious concentration on Western societies, have held, in contrast, that *every* generation sifts to the top particular types whose talents are those needed at that time, and these help to shape the course of a society's history.[1] My argument is not that there is some speculative social *need* which somehow gets served, but simply that the changing objective conditions of a society offer challenges which some resist and opportunities which some attempt to seize. The latter type are thrusters.

From Thrusters to Dominants

Thrusters are likely, as a group, to be less wholly integrated into the ongoing activities, less satisfied with their position in it, and less firmly persuaded of the values of their society. They entertain more skepticism about a "natural order" quality to existing arrangements and relationships. As Robert Murphy has pointed out, the controls over individuals established by the Freudian superego are only partially effective; to varying degrees individuals remain alien to their society. The social norms "can be manipulated to personal advantage, and they can serve to mask activity as well as to determine it. This is to say that the same ambivalence that pervades all human attachments pervades man's attachment to his fellows and to culture, as an abstracted set of norms." [2] The thrusters exhibit this ambivalence toward the values and codes of their society to a greater degree than others. They have a stronger sense of personal or group objective and some sense that, given the appropriate conditions, they can modify or control the future to their advantage. They act on the principle of purposeful and opportunistic thrusts into the future rather than continuity of present circumstance. In aspiring to make their impression on the future, they sometimes intend—whether they realize the audacity of their intent or not—to bend the existing social system more to their will, to mold it, if possible, more to their design, to play a larger part in shaping its style, developing its mosaic of purposes, modifying its norms and modes of coordinating its activities.

Of course not all thrusters are motivated, even subconsciously, by such an intent. Some are only looking for greater recognition within the existing society, a greater degree of acceptance. For them the opportunity on which they seize may have no larger consequence than to give them more of a share in the distribution of the social advantage, without shaking the system whose benefits they seek to enjoy.

Thrusters are thus likely to be people with particular personality characteristics, but whether their particular capabilities ever have an opportunity to manifest themselves depends on the changes occurring in their environment, on which they can build. A society may have numerous individuals and clusters of the thruster type, who live out their lives without having the chance to display their characteristics, for all ostensible purposes conforming more or less—more likely a little less—to the social values of the time, simply because the lightning of opportunity never strikes. But for some, the lightning performs—perhaps only a few weak flashes which merely flutter their hearts and fortunes, but at times perhaps with great storming flares by means of which they are able to light not only their own progress but to affect the currents of history.[3]

Not that we need assume that thrusters are always poised and at the ready. It may take a while before they recognize that opportunity has struck, and their first attempts at profiting from the change in circumstance may be faltering and feeble. The nature of the changed conditions must be understood before they can be put to advantage. Particular knowledge may have to be acquired, perhaps by their sons rather than themselves; for Saint-Simon the first great industrialists achieved their position not simply on the strength of accumulated property interests, as Marx would later have it, but because they knew what to do with it—they had discovered the value of the new knowledge authority.[4] There also may be numbers who perceive the same opening chance, but they may be without any sense of unity or common cause, so that in effect they must pass through a period of identity formation as a new class or group, before they can become effective.[5]

One is embarrassed at the problem of selecting examples of thruster groups from among the numbers that history supplies. The early Christian church in the West seized on the disorder precipitated by the barbaric invasions, at a time when a "wave of mysticism was sweeping the empire." The edict of Constantine making Christianity the official faith was a major assist, to be sure, but the underlying conditions were propitious to its spread. The confluence of civil disintegration and rampant superstition were made to order for a church preaching rewards in an afterlife for those faithful to its tenets. "It is noteworthy that toward the end of the fourth century and in the first half of the fifth, while the western empire is crumbling, the Church glitters with a constellation of superior men . . ." [6]

For all its growing strength in this period following the dissolution of the Roman Empire, the Christian church at first exercised at best a loose hold over the disorganized continent, subjected as the latter was to recurring depredations, and broken up as it was into pockets of local and almost primitive culture. It was only after the tenth century when a period of relative peace permitted a consolidation of its influence, that the dominant role of the church fully emerged. "During the epoch when the greatest gothic cathedrals were conceived and built, from the mid-twelfth to the early fourteenth century, the religious and the secular clergy combined formed apparently one of the most important elements numerically in European society. The peasants alone outnumbered them. In such a society, without newspapers or organized entertainment for profit, the religious exercised an enormous influence on daily living. Their example was impressed on the secular priests and it often determined the way they dealt with their lay charges." [7] The thruster had become the dominant.

Warriors and a military caste become a thruster group under certain circumstances. Mosca has noted that when a primitive society is moving from the hunting stage, when all men are hunters and warriors, into a more settled agricultural life, the warriors tend to become separated as a special protective class, little by little acquiring "such ascendancy over the other as to be able to oppress it with impunity." [8] John Millar in his early and classic work, *The Origin of the Distinction of Ranks,*[9] has described how, in western Europe, aristocracy grew out of the military dependency of some on others: in a period of insecurity, lesser individuals allied themselves with the stronger and more war-worthy, subjecting themselves to various liabilities in return for protection. Feudalism and the system of feudal privileges emerged out of the unsettled and invasion-prone condition of Europe down through the tenth century, which, while creating a life of hardship for the many, provided extraordinary opportunities for those few capable of seeing and seizing them. In this period the secular nobility and the church authority were teamed in an alliance which at first was mutually advantageous but which over time became increasingly contentious.

As the feudal state was transformed in time into a bureaucratic one, through a succession of changes in conditions which cannot detain us now, opportunities were created for a new class of thrusters, whom we would now call the civil service. This process, which has been occurring in Europe and later its North American offspring from approximately the eleventh century on, has in more contemporary periods become a notable characteristic of the developing economies, particularly those dominated, until recently, as in Latin America, by a landed oligarchy exercising feudal privileges. In these countries the new urban, white-collar middle class has not yet coalesced, however, in part because of an ambivalence as to whether they wish to play a larger role in a changed society or simply share a larger portion of the advantages of the existing order. As Erikson would say, they have not yet determined their identity.

Similarly the objective conditions giving rise to industry provided opportunities for people who would otherwise have been dependent on a landed aristocracy to establish new positions of influence for themselves. The bourgeoisie began as thrusters and ended as dominants. At a later stage, a new breed of "captains of industry," thrusters if there ever were such, took advantage of continuing changes in the objective conditions of

Western society to swamp the small, local, family proprietorships of the period of classic capitalism, carrying off what has sometimes been termed "the organizational revolution."

Since we are now concerned with changes occurring internally within a society, we do not—for the moment—include those imperialists and conquistadores who are thrusters on a larger world stage. But even with that exception, we can add as another significant example the thruster group *within* a colonial society, composed of those indigenous elements of the population who work with the metropolitan power and who become administrators in their name. Taking over the reins of power from the old traditional dominant class, the new, younger, often Western-educated elite thrusts its way up within its own society, and in modern times has then often turned against its colonial masters to work with and even to lead the nationalist causes.[10]

A final example comes from the Communist countries, notably Russia. There the thruster group which precipitated the basic revolution has gone on to make use of that revolution in its own interests, establishing itself as —in the term made familiar by Milovan Djilas—a "new class" of dominants, the "product of specific opportunities." "The new class obtains its power, privileges, ideology, and its customs from one specific form of ownership—collective ownership—which the class administers and distributes in the name of the nation and society." [11] We could add other and important examples of thruster emergence—the fascists in Italy, the Nazis in Germany—but these are surely enough to give concreteness to the concept.[12]

As we have previously noted, a thruster group may simply be accommodated by the existing dominant group or groups, either by being allowed certain privileges formerly denied or through some slight modification in the norms of social behavior patterns. But if the thrusters are not content with being bought off in such a fashion, and if they have indeed seized hold of an opportunity which becomes more and more realized, they will in time themselves become the dominants, accommodating rather than being accommodated. But they can achieve this status only to the extent —it is virtually a truism—that they are recognized as such by the society. Kitchen cabinets and gray eminences may rule administrations but they are unlikely to influence the way of life of a people. ". . . A new emerging group can, of course, only be considered an elite when it manages to prove its superiority by setting new standards which are accepted by the others." [13]

This carries no connotation that the new standards or values need be digested by everyone in the society, but only that they be accepted by all those who are functionally important to the ongoing life of the people and particularly by those who are important to the emerging design. By slipping into the seat of primary influence, the thrusters-become-dominants inherit responsibility for the successful functioning of the system. No group, however, can be so dominant as to subordinate all others to its will. Power is never so absolute, and especially the power of a group which has to learn a new role. There is no escape from the necessity of coming to terms with other sources of authority within the system, of accommodating others whose goodwill or at least tolerance is essential, of silencing criticism where it cannot be converted into faith.

There is another aspect to this process of accommodation which goes back to our earlier examination of the multiplicity of groups operating within a society, each forming its own value system which is partially congruent with but also partially divergent from the common value system of the larger society. Each individual, it will be recalled, in part acquires his identity through affiliation with one or more of such groups, absorbing its outlook and behavior patterns as part of his own. Since a total population is thus divided into numerous group identities, as well as possessing some identity in common, a new dominant cannot simply impose its own particularistic values on others as something that henceforth will be held in common. It cannot crassly ignore the special values and interests which pockmark the social landscape, but must recognize and respect them to the extent possible if it is to win acceptance for itself. In doing so it must conceal and dissimulate, concede and modify, practice patience and diplomacy, employ rewards and punishments. It is successful to the extent that, over time, its own values and interests become seen by others as identical with those of the nation.

In the pursuit of this object, the thrusters-become-dominants cannot help but change themselves. Their very struggle and success must lead to greater coalescence within their group, more of a sense of their own special identity, and along with this some tightening of their particularistic values as a source of strength. But as they move from being a special-interest group into a position where they are identified with the interests of the nation, and as they learn the process of accommodating others for their own interests, their own identity conception and value system cannot help but acquire a larger perspective, more befitting a leadership class. Even the big-business class in the United States, often pilloried for its pursuit of private advantage, quite genuinely if sometimes misguidedly attempts to act for the "balanced best interests of all." The phrase is not solely a public relations invention.

Thruster Supports

There are a number of possible supports assisting a thruster group in winning acceptance. For one thing, it may seek or be presented with allies. Barrington Moore has described in some detail how members of the English landed aristocracy, commercializing their estates in response to the profitability of the wool trade, in effect constituted themselves into a class of agrarian entrepreneurs. Thus—quite in contrast to France—an important element of the old aristocratic elite found itself on the same side as the rising industrial bourgeoisie in seeking the acceptance of liberal, laissez-faire principles.[14] Similarly, German National Socialists found both willing and reluctant allies among members of the industrial and military. In Latin America the Catholic Church has constituted one such support group to a succession of thrusters and dominants, advancing its own interests in the process. During the colonial period, it "served as an agent of colonial expansion, as an administrative and economic organization, and as a key institution of social control" under the feudal nobility. In the period following political independence, it aligned itself with the conservative, landholding oligarchs.[15] In more recent years some segments of the church have given support to radical popular causes. In some countries the military has served as ally to thrusting nationalist and modernizing groups. At times members of the once powerful but now declining interests can be co-opted by the thrusters to smooth the transition.

The attraction of a following constitutes another phenomenon whose importance increases. As a thruster group rises and consolidates its position within a society, its own values will be asserted more vigorously and openly. The special purpose which characterizes it, from among the array of purposes represented within the society, becomes expressed with more confidence. Differing in degree, however subtle or flagrant, from the preceding or coexisting values which have till that time characterized the society, the new purpose may at first create some ambiguity or diffuseness of values. If the thruster group accumulates more influence within the society, permeating more of the society's total activity, it is more likely that others will be induced to adjust to its mode of behavior, and the more likely are its values to win acceptance. As its very success helps to consolidate the changes in objective conditions which are taking place and which support its thrust, or as its activity gives direction to those changes, more and more "little thrusters" or timid opportunists will see their own futures benefited by tolerance of the new values or explicit acceptance of them. Its growing position in effect creates new opportunities for *other* thruster groups to take advantage of, or for the thruster element in *every* group to seize on in an effort to improve its position. Thus the emerging dominant values may, in time, tend to redirect the current values, activities, and interests of a society's functional groups, through the instrument of aspiring leaders *within* those groups. Behind those who initially seized the main chance swarm numbers of less perceptive or more timid individuals and groups who are ready to take advantage of the new direction, now that it has been charted. Thus a value which was already present in the society, as one among others, wins a larger and larger following, and in time displaces contending views.

Some individuals and groups may even establish new identities in the process; these are not necessarily shallow and ambitious characters who are willing to sell short their previous selves for quick success; they may be realizing a self that was always there but had had no opportunity for assertion. Nor need these be pale carbon copies of the thrusters who have broken the trail for them; they may be congruent in important respects while divergent in others. Thus K. H. Silvert speaks of the Latin-American traditionalists who "have modified both action and ideology to accommodate themselves positively to a certain kind of industrialization"—not the kind which we associate with private competitive or even socialist industrialization, however, but their own syndicalist or corporativist type, "essentially but a complication of the hierarchical order of medieval society." [16]

But everyone in a society is not likely to turn ally or follower of the rising dominant. Some are skeptical or suspicious, whether because of threat to present advantage or simply out of cynicism or dislike of any disruption to familiar patterns of existence. Max Weber has generalized, with respect to the influence of religious groups, that "the more a priesthood aimed to regulate the behavior pattern of the laity in accordance with the will of the god, and especially to aggrandize its status and income by so doing, the more it had to compromise with the traditional views of the laity in formulating patterns of doctrine and behavior." [17]

A former elite may be allowed to retain many of its social, political, and economic advantages because it is recognized as functionally useful to the new dominants. Thus in England, in the period between 1832 and 1868 when the industrial managerial-owner class was making a rapid climb to influence, "the power of the old-established ruling-class remained largely unimpaired. Within that class the balance of power had shifted somewhat in favour of newer wealth and away from mere landed property and this process had not gone on without some tension and conflict." [18]

But the rising industrialists displayed no great impatience at this seeming lag. Change was taking place, albeit slowly, in a way which preserved the confidence of the population at large as to the stability and continuity of a familiar way of life. As one officer of Parliament during this period philosophically observed:

Notwithstanding the more democratic tendencies of later times, rank and station still retained the respect and confidence of the people. When the aristocracy enjoyed too exclusive an influence in the government, they aroused hostility and jealousy; but when duly sharing power with other classes and admitting the just claims of talent, they prevailed over every rival and adverse interest and—whatever party was in power—were still rulers of the state.[19]

In this latter case one might well ask, who was accommodating whom? The old dominants accepted the best of the thrusters, the increasingly successful thrusters were unwilling to turn out a privileged but respected leadership group which was slowly giving way to them. Such a situation of mutual accommodation may remain confused for some time before it becomes clear whether there has in fact been a shift in the style and direction of the society.

In this connection it is worth reminding ourselves that social *systems* are composed of functionally related component groups, but there are nonsystem—which is to say nonfunctional—groups as well within a society. Among these are ethnic and racial groups. A rising thruster group may very well accommodate such nonfunctional groups to win acceptance, but it may also discriminate against them if it believes it can thereby win a following from others. In either case the values (here, pseudo-values) which are accommodated may have little effect on the real design of the thrusters.

Along with the accommodated we may include the beneficiaries of the new dispensation. These may be members of categories of occupations whose functions assume greater importance and who therefore share more fully in the rewards. Or they may simply be a "public" with whom the thrusters feel ethnic kinship or religious sympathy, or a class of persons —the industrious, the thrifty, the self-reliant—who fortuitously share certain of the values now being stressed. The exploitation of Argentina's natural resources was effectively begun in the 1880s, under a native landholding elite known internally as "the oligarchy," supported chiefly by British capital. These "paternalistic but capable modernizers" saw their country's future lying in the exportation of primary produce (wheat, wool, and meat). They themselves spent most of their time in the urban centers. The success of their design for the country fattened their own earnings, but this wealth "filtered down to the quarter of the nation's population already urbanized by the turn of the century." [20] The values and interests which they espoused served the country for almost half a century, benefiting many besides themselves, before being submerged by change. In the United States, Andrew Carnegie, one of the nineteenth-century industrial magnates, may not have been viewed benevolently by his employees at the Carnegie Steel Works, but he was widely praised by the American public generally for his gift of free public libraries to communities throughout the country.

Still another category, taking its place alongside the allies and followers, the accommodated and the beneficiaries, are those whom we may simply call the adaptable. For a large segment of the middle-class population of industrialized nations, success itself is entitled to respect. Those who are able to ride the currents of their time to position and fortune have demonstrated the capability of exercising authority. Since in every society some authority must exist, why not they? Thus those who have made good constitute a "natural" locus for society's main decisions. Such an attitude [21] does not require that the successful be a unitary group; it is perfectly capable of responding to both an older elite which has retained its privileges (and therefore is still successful) and to the thrusters who are metamorphosing into dominants. It thus contributes to some ambiguity as to the value center of the society, but at a minimum it is tolerant to the new authority.

On the lower fringes of the middle-class population of industrialized societies, and among its lower-class and more disadvantaged groups, there are large segments which are only loosely integrated with the rest of society. They may have a functional relationship which keeps them afloat, or a dependent relationship, but if they are tied to the rest of society in any emotional way at all it is likely to be only through such symbols as national sporting events or holidays or the throne or religious events. Like the plebes in George Orwell's society of *1984,* they are outside the society that counts, a position which gives them greater freedom from certain cultural inhibitions but greater restraints with respect to cultural participation. Genevieve Knupfer has presented evidence with respect to the United States that "the economic and educational limitations accompanying low status produce a lack of interest in and a lack of self-confidence in dealing with certain important areas of our culture; as a result, there is a reduced participation—a *withdrawal from* participation in these areas.[22]

For people in such low-status or depressed circumstances, the rise of a new dominant class may be a matter of little significance. They may even be ignorant that any shift of social values is in process. The norms affecting their own lives remain largely unchanged. Looking inward on their own parochial interests and particularistic values, they are scarcely aware that the objective conditions of the larger society have changed in ways that could affect them, or if aware of such changes they can scarcely conceive of any response of approval or disapproval which they could register which would mean anything to anyone. They are the unconcerned.

In less developed, more traditional, more agrarian-based societies this situation is multiplied many times over. Consider Celso Furtado's description of the Brazilian scene in 1930:

Some four-fifths of the population was rural, and economically and socially organized around these estates, which were sometimes extremely large, supporting thousands of persons. About four-fifths of the population was also illiterate, and then as now such people were constitutionally without political rights. Those who effectively participated in the electoral process comprised scarcely more than 1 per cent of the total population of the country. For the great mass of the people, the state existed only in its most obvious symbolic forms, such as the person of the President, who to them had merely taken the place of the Emperor.[23]

Add to this picture "the general climate of fear and insecurity in which the peasants spend most of their lives," [24] and one completes the portrait of the unconcerned. As Barrington Moore comments:

Large masses of people, and especially peasants, simply accept the social system under which they live without concern about any balance of benefits and pains, certainly without the least thought of whether a better one might be possible, unless and until something happens to threaten and destroy their daily routine.[25]

It is with respect to this mass of the unconcerned that Marx's view of religion as the opiate of the people makes sense. The seat of civil society lies farther away and is almost less real than the heavenly society which is physically present in the local church. Or if not dedication to religion, then it is often the pseudo-value of superiority over some other segment of the disadvantaged, either a component of the local society or another people geographically contiguous, who must be kept in their inferior position at all costs. This becomes the core value giving meaning to one's life, around which passions can be aroused and bloody battles inconclusively fought.

It is the presence of the adaptable segment of society, and even more of the unconcerned, that raises a genuine question as to the validity of a concept of social values which embraces the whole of a society and is viewed as essential to its effective integration—the Parsonsian perspective. It is easy to convince ourselves that as long as the social system functions reasonably well, then it amounts to a consensus on values, on purpose, which induces the desired responses and elicits the necessary participation of all in their complex and interdependent activities. But there is little empirical basis for this belief. It seems highly likely that it is only the relatively small proportion forming the architects and principal beneficiaries of the social values who really affirm them or even think about them at all. Many members of a society—the less developed the higher the proportion—may simply ignore them or give lip service to them or cling to their own particularistic beliefs. Their functional contribution is induced more by reward, fear, routine, and apathy than by empathy. To assign a common set of values to all the actors in a social system would appear to be a grave error.

And yet this is not to deny the validity and significance of the concept of social values in a more limited sense. As I have already urged, there is significance in the *extent* to which some values *are* held in common: this differs among societies, and within the same society over time. There is significance in the fact that the principal actors on the social stage in some countries feel a need to affirm certain values as relevant and desirable for the whole of a society, almost like a runty and slightly watered-down version of a Kantian categorical imperative.

And not least, there is significance in the fact that in our time the direction of change seems to be moving (to the regret of some, and the hope of others) toward the greater weight which must be accorded the "masses" in the population. The mute are acquiring a voice. As Mosca noted: "Whatever the type of political organization, pressures arising from the discontent of the masses who are governed, from the passions by which they are swayed, exert a certain amount of influence on the politics of the ruling, the political, class." [26] And from Djilas: "The Communist regime, in common with others, must take into account the mood and movement of the masses. Because of the exclusiveness of the Communist Party and the absence of free public opinion in its ranks, the regime cannot discern the real status of the masses. However, their dissatisfaction does penetrate the consciousness of the top leaders." [27]

Passions arising from discontent and dissatisfaction of the masses with their condition may seem a long way from an involvement with social values. But it is not as far away as it seems, as we shall soon have occasion to discover.

Opposition and Placation

A discussion that deals with allies, followers, accommodated interests, beneficiaries, the adaptable, the unconcerned, and the coerced conveys a picture of a thruster group which carries the day to become a society's new dominant. But we should avoid any connotation that thrusters are always successful, even if only temporarily. Indeed, that would be impossible, since at some moments in a country's history there are a number of thruster groups vying for position, sufficiently incompatible in their interests to make a pluralistic accommodation impossible.[28] For every group which has successfully seized the opportunities presented by change, there are numbers whose thrust has been blunted or turned aside. If they are to succeed, thrusters either must first work within the existing power structure of government and police, perhaps dissimulating or deprecating their activities until they have acquired enough influence to force the government to accept their presence and perhaps even facilitate their purposes, or—as the more desperate alternative—they must convert themselves into a revolutionary movement to conform the society to their objectives. The responsibility which such a new authority shoulders to make the system work, to keep all functional interests performing their function even as the style and design of the times begins to change around them, connotes the possibility of failure. This is likely to occur when, along with the supporters, strong opposition groups form.

The opposition may come from the former dominants who not only fear the loss of their privileges but who may have a strong dislike for the new style. Most of the landed aristocrats of nineteenth-century England had a dark distaste for the new "moneymen" whose influence was spreading. As we have noted, there was in fact a gradual accommodation of the new interests by the old, leaving the outcome ambiguous; yet the aristocratic accommodation was not due to any loss of belief in the rightness of their own position and their own identification with society's best welfare.

It is doubtful whether the aristocracy would have been so successful [in retaining its political and parliamentary position over the period when the new industrialists were rising fast] if, on the whole, it had not been convinced of the justification of its own exercise of power and, in addition, had managed to persuade a large section of the population of the righteousness of its claim. . . . Individual noblemen might seek the destruction of the old order and propagate measures to bring about the rule of the middle class, but the majority of the landed proprietors clearly believed that in holding positions of political power they and the group closely allied to them, were acting in the best interest of the nation.[29]

Opposition may also come from other thrusting groups likewise seeking to capitalize on whatever opportunities they descry in the changes which have occurred in the objective conditions, particularly in time of disorder. A country may be thrown into a prolonged period of political instability as the sparring proceeds between groups with fundamentally opposed outlooks.

But I should like to avoid any impression that the social values championed by the thrusters-become-dominants and ultimately impressed on society have nothing behind them but a successful coalition of separate interest groups, in the same manner that a political convention puts together a temporary and often contentious coalition of factions to nominate a candidate. The private interests are there, but along with them goes a sense of *national* values and interests with which they are identified and which endows what otherwise would only be selfish with some larger meaning, a public spirit.

Thornton, in trying to explain why a British electorate enlarged to include workingmen and the middle class continued to give much of its support to parliamentary representatives from the aristocracy, puts his emphasis on this sense of common national identity based on common values.

For English society, despite the dislocations that the processes of industrialism had caused, was still close-knit. There was such a thing, although never so publicized as its fellow in the United States, as a national outlook, a generally accepted method of dealing with life, even if it was most often defined in terms whose negative aspects had an easily-exploited comicality: "not playing the game," "not cricket," "not done," all of them implying the existence of some aristocratic code of action and doing. . . .

General acceptance of this social structure, based on the conviction that everyone either had or could get a function of value within it, made life in England in fact easier than was often supposed by foreigners, who were able to see the distinctions between the classes more clearly than the unity of the society these classes composed. Unity allowed a genuine sense both of leadership and of public spirit to develop. . . .[30]

Nor do I wish to overplay the way in which the particularistic values of a thruster group may become the common social values of a society. We shall have occasion to examine this matter more thoroughly later. For the moment, it is perhaps sufficient to suggest that the rising dominant group, in an effort to placate the preceding dominant class, may be willing to muddy or distort its own position to avoid too direct a confrontation of values. Old values lag on and are not easily dislodged from the minds of many older people. Some aspects of the former value system may not be particularly important to the new dominants, so that they are content to leave them in place. The old dominants may be allowed to retain status and custom, the new dominants deferring in these respects or perhaps even relishing a bit the color of behavioral patterns which have no impact on the main drift. Thus the English bourgeois for many generations, even while asserting more and more vigorously a new social vision, did little to dislodge the landed aristocracy from its positions of political and social privilege, as long as it did not excessively block the path of change. The pomp of royalty gave them a tie to a glorious past which they could, in part, use to commercial advantage but also enjoy for its own sake without sacrificing anything of what they were after. In part it was also a matter of accustoming themselves to the very changes they were in the process of introducing.

In some instances a new dominant may resort to coercion or repression to make its values accepted. It may undertake reeducation through schools and censorship. It may invoke the pseudo-values of race or nationalism as a means of bolstering its position. But such crude forms are scarcely necessary when a thrusting group has in fact made good in its endeavor to reorient its society in the light of changed objective conditions which support its position. As in time it mans or controls the decision positions of the major institutions, its creed seeps into the fabric of the society. As Carl Kaysen has pointed out with respect to the influence of the large corporations in the United States, just by virtue of their positions the men who control them cannot escape making social and political as well as economic decisions. This is what makes us a "business society." [31] These decisions collectively compose a style, a way of life, the national objectives, norms of conduct, and modes of integration—in short, they come to spell out, in practice, a set of social values.

All members of the thrusting group do not have an equal impact in effecting this result. Every member, just by virtue of being one of the thrusters and behaving as one, adds to the cumulative effect, but some individuals are clearly more dominant than others. Perhaps they are personally more impressive or more daring or of larger vision; perhaps they occupy positions of larger importance. All of a society's diverse groups develop their own leaderships, formal or informal, as we previously noted, and this is no less true of the thrusters who achieve dominance. Some become recognized spokesmen, head whatever associations are formed, establish more effective working connections with members of the former dominants or members of government or high-status groups or supporting groups. They are the most influential in formulating policy positions. The character of this leadership changes over time, depending on the relationships of the group to the rest of society in the course of its rise to dominance and its subsequent enjoyment of that position.

In presenting the foregoing picture of how some groups within a society coalesce in the face of changed conditions which they perceive as opportunities, thrusting their way upward—sometimes failing, sometimes succeeding, and when succeeding sometimes compromising and sometimes dominating—I have purposely tried to avoid the confusing terminology of elites, strategic elites, power elites, ruling classes, and upper classes. It is not that I reject such terms, but that they have usually been employed to make points quite different from those which concern me. I am only interested in how, out of the flux of manifold social interests and activities, there does emerge something which can meaningfully be labeled social values, even though they are at times diffuse and weak. Their very weakness and diffuseness, when such is the case, is a matter of significance, just as, on other occasions, their specificity and strength are important.

Perhaps I can most effectively summarize the conceptual intent of this and the preceding chapter by quoting a methodological aside from the classic study on the Polish peasant by Thomas and Znaniecki. In comparing the difference between the physical and social sciences, they commented that "while the effect of a physical phenomenon depends exclusively on the objective nature of this latter's empirical content, the effect of a social phenomenon depends in addition on the subjective standpoint taken by the individual or the group towards this phenomenon and can be calculated only if we know, not only the objective content of the assumed cause, but also the meaning which it has at the given moment for the given conscious beings." [32] Even though the objective conditions which we examined in the foregoing chapter include social phenomena (economic and political institutions, for example), and to that extent differ from the objective conditions to which Thomas and Znaniecki refer, the analogy holds. We can similarly argue that it is not just these empirical realities which determine the values of a society, but rather how those objective conditions and changes in them are viewed by particular individuals and groups, their subjective attitudes toward the changing conditions. Thus it is the interaction between the objective conditions and the subjective attitudes of thruster groups which set in motion a sequence of events which may in time lead to a reorientation of the society's value structure.

Values and Interests

A thruster group does not live by values alone. These are accompanied by social, political, and economic interests which, like other groups, it tries to acquire for itself. Indeed, these can be seen as furthering its values; without the security which these provide, the values which it seeks to impress upon its society are always in danger. Unless the thrusters aspire to certain advantages of position, how can they become dominants? Thus they tend to see the reinforcement of group advantage as necessary both to the preservation of the way of life they deem "good" and to their own specific enjoyment of the good life. As we earlier noted, values and interests tend to become fused.

As the thrusters spread their influence throughout a society and become its dominants, they tend to acquire a disproportionate share of the social advantage. There is a tendency for them to establish the standards by which most individuals are screened out from privileges and others are screened in. Even in a presumptively open and freely competitive society the terms on which competition takes place are structured not only to further the perpetuation of values but also the structure of interests which reinforces them. Not that all members of the dominants enjoy a larger share of social advantages than do nonmembers. The privileged groups of former years may retain many of their privileges; some members of the new dominant class may not make out very well. But generally speaking, if a thruster group achieves dominance and spreads its influence, as a class it tends to receive a disproportionate share of the social advantage. And the leaders of that class tend to be the principal beneficiaries.

Again, history provides a profusion of examples. As Nef has documented, for centuries

. . . the church exercised everywhere in Europe considerable, and in some regions, preponderant, influences on the ways in which the soil and the resources of the subsoil were exploited. Through their possession of land, their income from all kinds of property, and through the immense contributions which they obtained in various ways from laymen (at a time when what we now call charitable contributions almost took the single form of contributions to the church), churchmen determined to a large extent what building should be done. They provided the principal orders for many durable goods, especially works of art in stone, glass, wood, cloth, iron, and other materials. Persons who had, by their vows, renounced the life of the world to devote themselves to the service of Christ, persons whose primary obligations were spiritual, whose proper allegiance was not to Caesar but to God, made the decisions which settled the purposes of a large proportion of all economic efforts.[33]

Not the least of the beneficiaries of these activities was the pope himself. The increasing costs of papal self-indulgence were met in part by the increased sale of papal indulgences to the poor, a practice which in part was responsible for the mighty ire of Luther. The splendor of the papal way of life could only be supported by increased attention to worldly matters. A vast alum works was developed on the papal estates at Tolfa. "They produced so much alum that the papacy set about, with a measure of success, to monopolize the supply for all Europe. The pope threatened to excommunicate not only the traders who sold alum from the Levant but also the civil and religious authorities who tolerated such a trade." [34]

The historian Charles Beard has argued that a thruster group composed of dealers in public securities, shipping services, manufacturing, and banking, in contrast to those whose interests lay in land, was responsible not only for the values which are embedded in the American Constitution but also for the protection which that instrument provided to their own special interests. Both the leaders in the Philadelphia convention and the leaders in the state ratifying conventions were members of the same economic interests. "The Constitution was essentially an economic document based upon the concept that the fundamental private rights of property are anterior to government and morally beyond the reach of popular majorities." [35] While Beard received harsh treatment at the hands of a patriotic public and a tradition-bound profession, it is hard to take issue, except in detail, with his conclusion. It was chiefly the implication which others drew (and admittedly Beard did little to offset) that somehow a malevolent design had been imposed on a people by its most venerated founding fathers for selfish reasons that understandably sparked fire and aroused ire. But that a group of talented and dedicated men believed that the value structure which they sought to foster, and which they identified with the interests of the new nation, could best be preserved by their establishing institutions under which they could maintain a dominant position, and thus more effectively assure the survival of those values, only made good sense.

In the way of life developed in the cotton-based plantation system of the South, whose values rested squarely on notions of hierarchy and chivalry and the pseudo-value of racial superiority, the advantages of social status, political position, and economic well-being were concentrated in a small, dominant group; the remainder of the white population had to be satisfied with lesser material rewards, but could be soothed by the superior status which the system conferred on them relative to the substantial black population as a whole.

We have already encountered the accusation by Djilas that the new dominant class in the Communist states is less concerned with values than with its own privileges. Its members hold "an administrative monopoly," [36] presumably to further the proletarian cause, but in reality to advance their own interests. Years before Djilas wrote out of his own experience, Mosca had looked upon Communist Russia and made the same observation. "The rulers of a collectivist state pile economic power on political power and so, controlling the lots of all individuals and all families, have a thousand ways of distributing rewards and punishments. It would be strange indeed if they did not take advantage of such a strategic position to give their children a start in life." [37]

At times, however, the identification of dominant interests with social values may suborn the very values which the thruster group had presumed to secure for society. Within the church, the spiritual state of a person becomes a matter for commercial transaction. Within the infant American democracy, slavery is a protected institution.[38] In the socialist states founded on the principle of classlessness, "the elite that acts in the name of the nation develops common economic privileges and interests which eventually come into conflict with the great mass of people." [39] It is easy to judge others, but as Albert Camus has suggested in *The Fall,* are not most of us thereby also judging ourselves? By our willingness to live a style of life which, every day, in contrast to the lives of peoples around us in the world, affronts the values that we profess, are we not giving mute evidence of the identity we build between values and interests?

Notes

1. E. Digby Baltzell has identified a number of those of this persuasion in " 'Who's Who in America' and 'The Social Register': Elite and Upper Class Indexes in Metropolitan America," in *Class, Status, and Power,* 2nd ed., ed. R. Bendix and S. M. Lipset (New York: The Free Press, 1966), p. 174.

2. Murphy, *The Dialectics of Social Life,* p. 129.

3. Morris Ginsberg has expressed a very similar idea in his discussion of national character, in *Reason and Unreason in Society* (Cambridge, Mass.: Harvard University Press, 1948), p. 151. "The selection [of certain people over others] exercised by social forces need not operate by way of biological elimination or substitution. It operates rather by encouraging or inhibiting the expression of certain qualities and by determining their direction or mode of manifestation . . . . In the main the hereditary qualities of a people may well remain constant while changing circumstances bring different sides of the underlying character into play or give dominance to different elements of the population at different times."

4. Gouldner points up the contrast between these two in his *The Coming Crisis of Western Sociology,* p. 112.

5. Erikson has noted, in passing, the possible application of the "identity crisis" phenomenon to a rising elite in his *Identity: Youth and Crisis,* p. 16. S. M. Lipset argues (in Lipset and Lowenthal, *Culture and Social Character,* p. 158) that the American value system was dominant from the start, which would imply that no thruster group was needed, but a general consensus emerged out of dissatisfaction with the old social values left behind in Europe. However, if one considers the United States as a continuity of Europe, however separated geographically, then it is obvious that its settlers were chiefly

nonconformists and thrusters relative to the society from which they came. In effect, the thrusters of the old society transplanted themselves as the dominants of a new society, in the process making their own particularistic value system the common values of the new nation. Moreover, the process was not instantaneous. It took time, argument, provocation, and travail before divergences in views and interests could be sufficiently resolved to create a more or less common identity.

6. Mosca, *The Ruling Class,* pp. 369–370. He notes by name St. Ambrose, St. Jerome, St. Augustine, St. Paulinus of Nola, Paulus Orosius, and Salvian of Marseilles, and that "with the exception of Theodosius, and the unfortunate Marjorian, one of the last emperors in the West, there is hardly a native Roman of any character or brains who devotes himself to the service of the state," in contrast to the church.

7. Nef, *The Conquest of the Material World,* p. 226.

8. Mosca, *The Ruling Class,* p. 54.

9. Published by J. J. Tourneisen, Basel, 1793, especially pp. 170–227.

10. Thom Kerstiens has described this process in *The New Elite in Asia and Africa* (New York: Frederick A. Praeger, 1966), especially pp. 20–21. A somewhat similar phenomenon has been identified by John Waterbury in Morocco in *The Commander of the Faithful* (New York: Columbia University Press, 1970), p. 85. The British created such local elites as a matter of policy.

11. Milovan Djilas, *The New Class* (New York: Frederick A. Praeger, 1957), pp. 40, 45.

12. In recent years a number of scholars have proclaimed a future in which the new knowledge authorities, the scientists and technologists, would constitute the thrusting group. To Galbraith the future lies with the technostructure of the large corporation; to Daniel Bell, with the knowledge experts who are architecting a postindustrial society; to Zbigniew Brzezinski, with a "technotronic" elite. Harvey Brooks sees, not without misgiving, science as the new established church. That technoscientists are a thruster group of the present may indeed be the case, but that they constitute the thrusters who will rise to dominant positions is much more subject to dispute. They and their knowledge can be made *use* of by others, to whom they become simply tools or allies.

13. Kerstiens, *The New Elite in Asia and Africa,* p. 13.

14. Moore, *Social Origins of Dictatorship and Democracy,* pp. 6–9, 20–35.

15. Ivan Vallier, "Religious Elites: Differentiations and Developments in Roman Catholicism," in *Elites in Latin America,* ed. S. M. Lipset and Aldo Solari (New York: Oxford University Press, 1967), pp. 193–194. Quoted with permission.

16. K. H. Silvert, "National Values, Development, and Leaders and Followers," *International Social Science Journal* 15 (1963): 562.

17. Weber, *Economy and Society,* Vol. 2, p. 466.

18. W. L. Guttsman, *The British Political Elite* (New York: Basic Books, 1963), p. 39.

19. Thomas Erskine May, cited in Guttsman, *ibid.,* p. 39.

20. Eldon Kenworthy, "Argentina: The Politics of Late Industrialization," *Foreign Affairs* 45 (April 1967): 469.

21. This attitude has been nicely explored by Thornton in *The Habit of Authority*, especially pp. 230–241, 281–282, 335–336.

22. Genevieve Knupfer, "Status and Power Relations in American Society," in Bendix and Lipset, *Class, Status and Power*, p. 256. She also cites C. C. North to the effect that low status produces a kind of mental isolation which operates to "limit the sources of information, to retard the development of efficiency in judgment and reasoning abilities, and to confine the attention to the more trivial interests of life."

23. Celso Furtado, "Political Obstacles to Economic Growth in Brazil," *Obstacles to Change in Latin America*, in ed. Claudio Veliz (London: Royal Institute of International Affairs, Oxford University Press, 1965), p. 151. Quoted with permission.

24. Stavenhagen, "Marginality, Participation and Agrarian Structure in Latin America," p. 77.

25. Moore, *Social Origins of Dictatorship and Democracy*, p. 204. Quoted with permission.

26. Mosca, *The Ruling Class*, p. 51.

27. Djilas, *The New Class*, p. 64.

28. The situation in Spain today is a good case in point, where alongside church traditionalists and Franco supporters who would pursue a continuity of the present power structure and its associated values, there contends a modern, technocratic, autocratic but paternalistic movement largely centered around the church-born *Opus Dei*, which aspires to "rejoin" Europe, and a third, university-based, more loosely organized movement whose major objective is the establishment of a liberal, individualistic, secular society. It will be years before the outcome of this struggle can be known, but all these elements clearly cannot be reconciled.

29. Guttsman, *The British Political Elite*, p. 61.

30. Thornton, *The Habit of Authority*, pp. 281–282.

31. Carl Kaysen, "The Corporation: How Much Power? What Scope?" in *The Corporation in Modern Society*, ed. E. S. Mason (Cambridge, Mass.: Harvard University Press, 1959).

32. W. I. Thomas and F. Znaniecki, *The Polish Peasant in Europe and America* (New York: Alfred A. Knopf, 1927), p. 38.

33. Nef, *The Conquest of the Material World*, p. 227.

34. *Ibid.*, p. 74.

35. Charles A. Beard, *An Economic Interpretation of the Constitution of the United States* (New York: The Macmillan Co., 1948), p. 324.

36. Djilas, *The New Class*, p. 39.

37. Mosca, *The Ruling Class*, p. 418.

38. John Millar, in *The Origin of the Distinction of Ranks*, published only shortly after the American Constitution was framed, remarked ironically (pp. 282–283): "It affords a curious spectacle to observe that the same people who talk in a high strain of political liberty, and who consider the privilege of imposing their own taxes as one of the unalienable rights of mankind, should make no scruple of reducing a great proportion of their fellow-creatures into circumstances by which they are not only deprived of property, but almost of

every species of right. Fortune perhaps never produced a situation more calculated to ridicule a liberal hypothesis, or to show how little the conduct of men is at the bottom directed by any philosophical principles."

39. Michael Harrington, *Toward a Democratic Left* (Baltimore: Penguin Books, 1969), p. 212.

4 / Focal Values

Let us return now to the content of social values, which we opened for exploration in the first chapter.

Following C. I. Lewis, we accepted the broad division of such values into the two principal categories of purposive and ethical, those which stand for the *summum bonum* (and the design by which it is to be attained) and those which relate to the justice and morality of relations among men—in short, what is good and what is right. Here we shall be concerned only with the former, values which represent the "good life."

Every society harbors in it an array of such values, since there is no single conclusive way of defining what constitutes the good life. Its members, maturing along their individual paths, develop their own personal identities, shaped by a number of forces and permitting the emergence of unique personalities, encompassing particular values which may not be shared by any other. Or groups of individuals, perhaps organized around functional or ethnic backgrounds, may develop their own particularistic values which diverge in some measure from those of other groups and from the common social values, so that conceivably as many differentiable values are expressed in a single society as there are differentiable groups.

What are some of the major value orientations which may thus find some following? We can readily identify some which have been of historic importance. These would include the religious or spiritual concentration, the acquisitive or accumulative or materialistic outlook, the military life, the sensual and esthetic, and the intellectual preoccupation. But these constitute only broad classifications, given as examples, and are not intended as the basis for a typology. The importance of the distinction can quickly be shown.

As Weber and Tawney have both pointed out, acquisitiveness has always been present in every society, but it has manifested itself in markedly different ways. In some instances it has taken the form of sharp trading and mercantilistic dealing, in other instances the rapacious depredations of pirates and raiders. The Confucian Chinese showed as marked a predilection for the accumulation of works of art and fine household possessions as any Renaissance noble or papal authority. And these in turn differed fundamentally from the rationalized, institutionalized, maximizing, creative activities of the modern businessman. Yet all manifest an acquisitive and materialistic drive, which in all cases could even be obsessive, representing a way of life.

Similarly, the military life has always had an appeal for certain types of men, but the nature of that life as pursued has its numerous variations. For some it is the mobilization of might in the pursuit of conquest, the kind of satisfaction derived by an Alexander or a Bonaparte. For others there is enjoyment in the actual contest of arms, like the highest form of sporting contest (who can forget Teddy Roosevelt and his "Rough Riders?"), or the thrill of the ultimate gamble, or the spirit of high adventure. Mercenaries combined with it the appeal of plunder; especially in Renaissance times wandering bands of warriors would fight either for themselves, for loot, or on behalf of some city or noble, in the latter case perhaps winding up residing for a spell in the locale and demanding special advantages for themselves.

Even William James, in a more contemplative vein, found certain allurements in the militaristic ethic, like H. G. Wells, whom he here quotes approvingly.

In many ways, military organization is the most peaceful of activities. When the contemporary man steps from the street of clamorous insincere advertisement, push, adulteration, underselling and intermittent employment into the barrack-yard, he steps on to a higher social plane, into an atmosphere of service and cooperation and of infinitely more honorable emulations. Here at least men are not flung out of employment to degenerate because there is no immediate work for them to do. They are fed and drilled and trained for better services. Here at least a man is supposed to win promotion by self-forgetfulness and not by self-seeking. And beside the feeble and irregular endowment of research by commercialism, its little short-sighted snatches at profit by innovation and scientific economy, see how remarkable is the steady and rapid development of method and appliances in naval and military affairs.[1]

Religious affirmation has had perhaps the most persistent appeal throughout history. According to Toynbee, "It would indeed be a truism that religion is the true end of Man if one were saying this to any representative of the human species except the modern Western one." [2] The religion of which Toynbee speaks involves the faculty for "spiritual contemplation" and constitutes "the one boundless field for freedom and for creativity that is open for the unlimited aspirations of human nature." [3] But religion as Toynbee conceives it is quite different from the crusading religions of medieval Christianity and Islam, which invited not contemplation but compliance, or the messianic mission of the Mosaic code, whose "primary concern," as Weber has pithily put it, "was with foreign politics, chiefly because it constituted the theater of their god's activity." [4]

The difference in value-orientation of religions in different places at the same time, or at different times in the same place, has developed a voluminous literature. Perhaps nuance rather than sharp distinction will help to emphasize the point. Without accepting the Weberian thesis of the Protestant ethic, John Nef in his superlative study, *The Conquest of the Material World,* has delineated at some length the difference in "world view" (the style or spirit of the times, as we have referred to it) characterizing the Catholic countries of the continent and the Protestant countries of the north of Europe. In his treatment it is not religion in the sense of a creed by itself, shorn of any context, but a total way of life engendered by a particular religious orientation which gives distinctive color to a society.

In the traditionally Catholic countries, religion was coupled with a strong sense of community, esthetic sensitivity, and regard for the quality of one's activities and products. Though these are obviously large generalizations, they help to fix the flavor of the times, extending down through at least the seventeenth century. Nef argues that one can place the state of industrial organization in its proper historical perspective only if he grasps "the spirit in which the work was done." At the time of the Reformation wage labor was common enough, but it was not wage labor in the modern sense. Wages were almost always earned by work in one's own home or nearby. Many workers had their own plots of land. They or other members of the family engaged in "by-occupations," and some who worked for wages were at the same time master craftsmen, with apprentices and even journeymen working for them. All this puts quite a different complexion on what working for hire really meant at that time.

The objective of much industrial work was to raise monuments, to weave tapestries, and fashion decorations of every kind for the sake of their beauty and for the sake of sumptuous effects that would enhance the luxury and splendor of churches, public buildings, and of private houses of the very rich. The objective was not primarily, as in recent times, the manufacture of cheap goods in large quantities for profit. People shared in the products of industry mainly through their participation in the life of the church, the life of the sovereign, the life of a powerful landlord, or the life of a municipality. A large proportion of the persons engaged in industrial labor had a direct part in the actual fashioning of some object, designed generally to fit into churches, castles, palaces, or municipal halls and monuments with which they were familiar. Today a large proportion of so-called industrial work—such as advertising and sales promotion—has no direct relation to the production of a concrete object. Nor has the workman engaged in some particular task in a factory any part in conceiving the object as a whole to which his tiny increment of labor contributes. In the early sixteenth century a great many manual workmen were free to conceive of an entire piece of workmanship, such as a statue or an ornamental balustrade, and to solve by the thoughtful improvisation, which is a part of art, the aesthetic problems connected with its making. Quality still took precedence over quantity.[5]

Even in strictly commercial operations esthetic considerations were not slighted. West of the Rhine in Franche-Comté a saltworks whose magnificence was attested by the name given it, the *grande saunerie,* which in fact formed a self-contained village, boasted fountains playing in the squares, a "handsome edifice with a fine court and chapel" which doubled as a house of worship and a meeting place for the board of directors, towers, arcades, and Doric columns. Nef comments that, in terms of production, such embellishments were sheer waste. "Like the artistic craftsman in the Italian towns, the prince who sponsored them had his mind fixed on art rather than on profits." [6]

Even as the French state gained ascendancy at the expense of the church, the church continued to play its influential role in furthering these esthetic elements. In the seventeenth century, "by retaining its wealth, and by renewing and developing in novel forms its relation to beauty and to charity, the post-reformation Roman church, especially under French leadership, encouraged an economic evolution in which beauty, elegance, moderation, and gentleness provided the principal goals." [7]

As England, which before the Reformation had generally lagged behind France industrially, began at this time to outstrip her rival in the manufacture of most goods, France increased its advantage only in the output of lace, silks, tapestries, and works of art in glass, metal, clay, and stone. "Artistic craftsmanship consolidated a position in France which it had inherited from the age of gothic cathedrals and the age of the Renaissance at a time when Englishmen were coming to be interested primarily in technical progress designed to lower costs of production and increase output." "Under French leadership [which owed much to Italian models of the previous centuries] the traditional values of beauty, splendor, and elegance were renewed and given fresh life, at a time when French ways of craftsmanship, like French manners, were influencing the economic development of Continental Europe more than the new industrial outlook exemplified by the English. In the industrial life of most of Europe, considerations of quality retained their ascendancy." [8]

But the story in the north of Europe—in England, Holland, and the Scandinavian countries—was quite different. Here the Reformation had its impact not simply in revision of religious doctrine but in sweeping aside one way of life and substituting another. The church itself, as a landholding and wealth-creating influence, was stripped of its possessions, most thoroughly in England; the types of artistic creation for which it had stood were replaced by utilitarian production, and its hierarchically ordered institutional activities gave way to individual undertakings and governmentally organized enterprises. Nef's account is incisive.

The truly revolutionary character of the English industrial expansion which broke forth in the middle of the seventeenth century lay "in the shift in the objectives for which considerable industrial capital and numerous workpeople were employed." This shift was "away from production primarily for the sake of beauty, of delight in contemplation, toward production primarily for the sake of usefulness in the purely economic sense of substantial comforts in greater quantities." More utility, larger quantities, cheaper production, higher profits—these became the economic context in which the new religious outlook found its expression. "The stimulus of profits, calculated more and more exclusively in quantitative money terms, was heightened by the novel independence from government interference successfully claimed by private adventurers in a considerable way of business." "While individualism and utility had always been present to some extent wherever there had been economic progress in the past, no people before had centered their energies upon them to the same extent as those of England had begun to do by the early seventeenth century." "As time went on, the spirit of individual freedom in the pursuit of economic advantage was cultivated in northern Europe largely without those values of beauty and splendor in workmanship which were an integral part of the Renaissance spirit no less than individualism. Utility replaced quality as the mainspring of industrial progress." [9]

"Actually," Nef argues, "the ways of living and thinking, of feeling and worshiping, that once prevailed in Western Europe, as in other parts of the world, stood mainly in the way of the coming of industrialism. That depended upon a transformation of these ways of living and thinking, feeling and worshiping—upon revolutionary changes in the basic purposes for which the adventure of life on earth is undertaken." [10] How better can one express the concept of social values in the sense of a spirit of the times and a grand design?

The contrast between the two "world views" is sharply etched by Nef.

The period of late Romanesque and early Gothic architecture, from about 1050 to 1325, was marked by an extraordinary development of ecclesiastical building and of many forms of arts and craftsmanship under church guidance. It was as if the Europeans set about in those centuries to build for every village and town—with their monasteries, churches, and cathedrals—a splendid and permanent ascent from the city of man toward the City of God. Piercing the skies, these religious buildings, with their colored glass windows, their statues in stone, their great pillars and spires, were made of the raw materials provided by the immediately surrounding soil and subsoil.

But when, in the North, people begin to draw their identity from the new and more austere forms of religion, rather than the older and more sensual, a vast change intrudes.

Orders for glass, stone, iron, copper, bronze, wood, and other materials to be fashioned into works of art diminished wherever the Reformation triumphed; they almost vanished where extreme Calvinist austerity prevailed. In their enthusiasm for the return to rigorous Christian virtues as described in the Bible, for the elimination of much priestly intervention between man and God, the reformers were favoring the abolition of most tangible expressions of a heavenly city built on earth reaching to heaven. So they were abolishing what had once served their ancestors, especially during the eleventh, twelfth, and thirteenth centuries, as a mainspring for different kinds of economic development. In so far as the Protestants were successful during the sixteenth century in supplanting the papists, their success created a kind of economic vacuum.[11]

That vacuum was filled by the new quantity-produced articles of utility. And this transpired because the effect of the Reformation was to place control of large chunks of natural resources, formerly the property of the church, in the hands of "country gentlemen and merchants," as grants or leases from the crown. "The elements of the population which replaced the clergy in controlling supply and demand were represented by individuals who had different ideas from those of medieval churchmen concerning the uses to which the resources of the kingdom should be put."[12] Instead of artistic objects deriving from religious inspiration, it was the manufacture of cheap commodities, in large quantities, for their own profit upon which they concentrated.

We have dwelt at some length on these historic examples of religious values partly because of their importance but also because they illustrate so superbly the fact that it is not some pure element labeled "religion" which is found in a society, but a particular expression of the religious value, set within a congenial and reinforcing context. Further, it is not necessarily a single such religious orientation which is present within a population. Most countries of Europe in the post-Reformation period had their pockets of Protestants or Catholics living uneasily in the midst of a population which dominantly expressed the other competitive form of Christian theology. The array of life-values which are found in a single society, asserted tentatively or boldly by constituent parts of its population, may well encompass conflicting expressions.

Other life-styles besides the acquisitive, the militaristic, and the religious might be enumerated: there are those who profess a secular version of the religious emotion—naturalistic, sensuous, hedonic. For some the ascetic life represents the highest good; for others it is the cultivation of the intellect in the pursuit of scientific knowledge.

It is safe to assume that all these forms of value, and others too, are to be found in some degree in all societies, perhaps asserted by only a handful of individuals, perhaps the group value of some sect, profession, or ethnic minority. Certain cultures are clearly more hospitable to some values than to others. The East, for example, has been more marked by the presence of contemplative, spiritual, intuitive orientations, while the West has been more often characterized as materialistic and rational. It would be a mistake to assume that these are mutually exclusive values so that the presence of one makes impossible some expression of the other within the culture. It would be equally in error, however, to assume that all cultures exhibit neutrality or tolerance toward whatever values constituent portions of its population may espouse. Some values may be objects of opprobrium, of hatred, of fear. As we have noted, Catholicism was present in early Protestant England, but its followers were subject to frequent persecution. Protestant sects, such as the Huguenots, were to be found on the Catholic continent, but at times they paid for their beliefs with their lives.

But granted that every society shelters an array of conceptions of the good life, generally within any given society some value wins more widespread acceptance. It is assimilated by more individuals in the course of their maturation than any other competing life-value and so becomes built in to the personal identities of a larger portion of the population. In the preceding chapter we explored the process by which this takes place, how some group, become dominant through a timely thrust under appropriate objective conditions, is able to impress its values on a population. From among the array of values present within the society, it gradually makes modal its own view of what gives meaning to life. This conception of life's central purpose which comes to permeate a society, the commonly accepted criteria by which any person's achievements can be judged successful or not, we shall hereafter call the *focal value*.

This does *not* mean—the point needs stressing—that such a focal value precludes all other values, that once some value has become the dominant expression of a society it erases all others in the array. "Economic history, within the European framework, provides many cases where magnificent entrepreneurial activities were conducted in the face of a dominant value system that was violently opposed to such activities and continued to regard the working of the land that brought forth the blessing of its fruit as the only economic activity pleasing in the eyes of the Lord." [13] Nor is the focal value likely to be displayed with elemental purity. As we noted with respect to Northern Protestantism and continental Catholicism, the value core is an expression of a life-style rather than a doctrine, and can assimilate into one compatible whole components which at first impression seem unrelated. It may even contain apparent oppositions which its practitioners are unwilling to relinquish but which they strive to reduce to some consistency.

Perry Miller, in exploring the recesses of the New England mind, describes the "communal covenant" which the early settlers struck with God, whereby their physical and material welfare was viewed as divinely guaranteed by their moral conduct. "Success and morality here were linked together as nowhere else in the world by a specific promise of the same God who elsewhere regulated success or failure without the slightest regard to civic virtue." [14] Surely, comments Miller, such a conception seems considerably removed from the burning conviction expressed in Puritan doctrine of man's irreparable sin and God's stainless purity. Such a compact between God and the community smacks of a "downright commercial bargain." God is reduced "to the role of an economic schoolmaster, rewarding His good pupils for their model deportment and punishing His bad ones for neglect of their lessons." But, Miller adds, the same individuals who "most clearly voiced the commercialism of the national covenant" at other times reverted to the Puritan piety of God's omnipotence and man's unatonable evil. "There were," he notes, "latent oppositions among ideas entertained simultaneously." We would find no difficulty in exposing such inner contradictions in the value systems of most societies, but even in their presence it is possible to delineate the significant characteristics— the "value-positing and style-creating" characteristics, as Broch puts it— of the period.

This concept of the focal value of a society accords nicely with the concept of a national identity. The latter is not to be captured in a term such as "materialistic" or "spiritual," but requires a definition out of the expressed beliefs and behavior patterns of a particular time. The focal value constitutes part of the national identity, even though, as we previously saw, it diverges in greater or less degree from the value expression of constituent groups and individuals.

Of course it is possible that at certain historical junctures a society may lose its focus. From among a number of conflicting assertions none seems to command a modal following. Time must pass before some value asserts its integrating effect. It is also possible for short swings of value emphasis to occur, as the nineteenth century gave rise to periodic bursts of religious enthusiasm in an age largely colored by rational materialism, and as the twentieth century has displayed recurring youth reactions against the materialism of the age. But these do not suggest that focal values are subject to faddish cycles. One would hardly expect to find perfect stability or continuing uniformity in the way the focal value finds expression out of the array of values in which it is set.

Notes

1. The quotation appears in William James, "The Moral Equivalent of War" (1910), contained in *Living Ideas in America,* ed. Henry S. Commager (New York: Harper & Row, 1964), pp. 646–647.

2. Arnold Toynbee, *Change and Habit* (New York: Oxford University Press, 1966), p. 226.

3. *Ibid.*

4. Weber, *Economy and Society,* Vol. 2, p. 443.

5. Nef, *The Conquest of the Material World,* pp. 113–114.

6. *Ibid.,* p. 108.

7. *Ibid.,* p. 236.

8. *Ibid.,* pp. 210 and 277.

9. *Ibid.,* pp. 211, 212, 117.

10. *Ibid.,* pp. 211–212.

11. *Ibid.,* pp. 228, 230.

12. *Ibid.,* p. 231.

13. Gerschenkron, *Continuity in History and Other Essays,* p. 134.

14. Perry Miller, *The New England Mind* (New York: The Macmillan Co., 1939), p. 484. The following quotation comes from p. 485.

5 / Constitutional Values

The *objective* conditions include the actual manner of organization of the government and its coordinating authority within the society. They likewise include the actual economic organization and its attendant distribution of rewards. But both of these elements—the use of coercion and the division of advantages—likewise involve matters of ethics and justice. Is the government's use of its powers justifiable? Is the allocation of the system's productivity just? These are issues over which men have pondered at length, seeking standards to guide them. They are an integral part of the system of social values, as we tentatively defined it.

Thus we confront the ethical question behind the use of coercive force in society. Who should exercise it, in what forms, over whom, and to what ends? Even between societies which may be in close agreement on their focal values, there may be significant differences in the answers to these questions. It might reasonably be posited, for example, without arguing the matter closely, that both the U.S. and the U.S.S.R. pursue the same focal value of materialism, but it would be difficult to argue that they have similar views with respect to the proper uses of coercion over the way the society should be ordered to best achieve its ends. We shall call this aspect of the value system the *constitutional value*. The U.S. and the U.S.S.R. also clearly differ over how the benefits of their social system should be distributed. This too is a value question, which we shall subsequently pursue under the term *distributive value*. Thus focal values, constitutional values, and distributive values collectively compose the value system of a society. These three interlocked expressions of a society's morality will, in our further exploration, replace the four categories we first tentatively identified and the two categories of C. I. Lewis which subsumed those.

The Ambiguity of Self-Government

Central to the constitutional question is the issue of hierarchy. If we follow the line of thought initiated by Mosca in *The Ruling Class* and more recently generalized by Dahrendorf in *Class and Class Conflict,* some superior-subordinate relationship is inescapable in a society. In any form of social organization there must lodge some authority, as a matter of administrative necessity, and authority places hierarchical distance between those who exercise it and those over whom it is exercised.

Even if we go back to Rousseau and his dream of self-government, contained in units sufficiently small that every member was directly involved in the sovereign decisions of government, and the administrative function constituted the simple application of the general will to the particular case, the individual in his role as subject of the society was clearly subordinate to the sovereign will of which he himself was part—*wholly* subordinate, as Rousseau emphasizes, withholding nothing from the coercive authority which he, in his sovereign capacity, shared. The individual was subject to the collectivity.

Marxism shares this same paradox of subordinating the individual in the very process of raising him—in his aggregative manifestation—to the role of superior. The very notion of classlessness pushes Marx to the primacy of the individual, since in a classless society no man is any other man's tool. Men realize themselves through their individual work. "To Marx, the free man was the man who each day realized the potentialities of his being through works which gave his inner capacities the form of concrete embodiments." [1] But this gets a bit murky, for the industrialized society on which Marx relied for the achievement of abundance (the heritage and contribution of the capitalist stage) presupposes men integrated into production processes which "use" them as parts of the process, subjecting them quite explicitly, as in Rousseau's society, to collective control.

Marcuse recognizes this fact and at the same time rejects the Marxian escape hatch of the "realm of freedom" available to the worker, in his own time, outside the "realm of necessity" imposed on him by collective control over the instruments of production. For the free time available to the worker will be spent not in genuinely creative activities—something which is possible only for a small minority "even in the best of societies"—but in hobbies, sports, do-it-yourself time-filling activities which are themselves provided and stimulated by the authorities, private or collective, as a means of ensuring the consumption that is necessary to keep the system going. The only way out of this dilemma, if hierarchical control over the individual is to be avoided, is through direct worker control over their own productive operations. But the possibility of individual autonomy has been eliminated even from this utopian solution by the coercive demands of technology itself. A change in the "controlling powers" would of course be necessary to give autonomy to individuals in their workplace; it would also have to involve not simply the discarding of one set of authorities for another, but the substitution of the authority of the individuals themselves for any other authority—the "emergence of new needs and aspirations in the individuals, with needs and aspirations essentially different from, and even contradictory to, those sustained, satisfied, and reproduced by the established social process." One can reasonably assume that here Marcuse refers not simply to the established social process in private capitalistic societies but in socialist ones no less, and that he is arguing for a radical transformation of human wants away from emphasis on material goods toward other "goods." The old nonconforming Marxist is here at his radical best in asserting, dialectically, that the socialist emphasis on material production *excludes* (no less than it does in private, individualistic societies) a meaningful emphasis on nonmaterial outputs of which the individual is capable. He is back with his Platonic Ideas and Forms, whose potential cannot be realized by taking the part as the whole—hence his basic pessimism as to the likelihood that individuals can ever escape the coercion of some hierarchical authority, however that may be embodied, and achieve genuine freedom from others.[2]

But one need not go to the philosophical abstractions of Rousseau and Marx to find examples of how the very exercise of participatory decision-making—presumably the means of escaping hierarchical coercion—has coercion built into it. It is a very live and contemporary issue. Social psychologists have for years urged the desirability of involving people in making the decisions which affect their lives. We tend more readily to accept behavioral prescriptions which we have helped to write. But if such participation in planning represents a form of self-control, it can also be the basis for the imposition of controls over one's freedom of action. The decisions which emanate from a worker's council or a collective bargain have a compulsive power on the individual even though he has helped to frame them, and even if they should not carry the force of law behind them. When a group has decided, it is more difficult for the loner to exercise the discretion which may be his to exercise legally.

In the case of national plans, such as the "indicative plan" of France, when the whole effort results in an economic mosaic, individual units are placed in the position of spoiling the pattern if they do not accept the role which has been cast for them. Their participation in the definition of that role does not lessen the compulsion which arises from the logic of the overall design. Indeed, an argument could be made that the danger of freedom in the West may be less from authoritarian governments than from voluntary conformance to the discipline of economic and political logic in the formulation of which enough people have participated to give it a stamp of popular will. In this respect there is a parallel to the danger that arises within the business corporation with respect to its comprehensive budget-planning, in the determination of which all responsible managers

are presumed to have participated. The results usually—and necessarily
—have the effect of constricting behavior as much as releasing initiative.

Robert Murphy has suggested that democracy itself may be seen as
"simply another aspect of social control."

It derives part of its effect in mass societies because it gives the illusion of participation in the process of governing and thereby derives committedness from
the population. Socialism may become a higher form of the same process, for it
gives the illusion that the citizen joins in the ownership of the means of production as well as in the decision of the central policy. Through the involvement and co-optation of the citizenry in a process that they are controlled by
far more than they control, the citizen is given less a sense of power over than
of responsibility for the actions of government. Ambivalent though his attitude
may be toward the state, the citizen tends to justify its acts ideologically. In
this curious sense, the doctrine of collective responsibility may also result in a
fiction of corporate innocence.[3]

Coercion by Elite Authority

But let us move away from the more intractable and general problem of
the inescapability of coercive authority to the more specific question of its
placement in the hands of certain people: Who exercises the coercive
power and what is the justification for their doing so?

One point of view which has had a powerful appeal over the years has
been that political authority should be exercised by an elite class—elite by
reason of birth, of educational or intellectual attainments, of military accomplishment, or by some other standard. From Plato's philosopher-states-
men to Saint-Simon's scientist decision-makers, from Burke's "natural aristocracy" to Latin American oligarchs the idea of eliteness as the basis for
leadership has carried strong appeal. Even in the realm of private organizations the same notion has persisted. Carnegie's "gospel of wealth"
started from a recognition that God endowed some individuals with greater
talents than others; destined to leadership and financial success in the
world of business, they were also obligated to recognize their responsibilities to those less gifted and subject to their orders. George F. Baer, president of the Philadelphia and Reading Railroad, in one of history's most
memorable statements, asserted that "God in his infinite wisdom" had
placed the management of large corporations with those best capable of
carrying on that task. The "management prerogative" has been asserted
throughout history; within the present century scientific authority has come
to bolster its decisions.

In the larger affairs of a society Burke was one of the less dogmatic and more pragmatic supporters of the advantage of elite authority. He had few illusions that the English aristocracy of his day was composed entirely of able men, but as a class he thought them capable of providing the most competent leadership, in part due to the generations of tradition which had gone into their making, but more importantly because their own lives and interests were bound up in the welfare of the nation to an extent which would guarantee cautious change and avoid radical upheavals. There was a distinct touch of paternalism here. Like fathers whose interests are separate from yet bound up in their sons, the aristocracy had their own vested interests which yet were bound up in the general welfare of English society. John Adams, in the United States, held a similar view.

Raymond Williams has provided a fascinating account of the elitist views of some of England's best literary representatives in what he refers to as "the long nineteenth-century attempt to reidentify class with function. This took the form, either of an attempt to revive obsolete classes (as in Coleridge's idea of the clerisy), or of an appeal to existing classes to resume their functions (Carlyle, Ruskin), or of an attempt to form a new class, the civilizing minority (Arnold)." He caps this summarization with reference to Karl Mannheim's proposal to substitute for such old classes, whether based on birth or property, the new (professional) elites whose position is based on achievement, and concludes:

In practice, one can see our own society as a mixture of the old ideas of class and the new ideas of an elite: a mixed economy, if one may put it that way. The movement towards acceptance of the ideas of elites has, of course, been powerfully assisted by the doctrines of opportunity in education and of the competitive evaluation of merit. The degree of necessary specialization, and the imperative requirement for quality in it, have also exerted a strong and practical pressure.[4]

Concepts of an elite possessing special capabilities for exercising hierarchical authority, whether on an hereditary or term basis, have as their necessary complement the concept of an average or inferior majority, whether in terms of a "mass" or of a pluralistic society of many smaller masses. Ortega y Gasset has given a strong expression to this point of view, out of bleak humanistic despair rather than from authoritarian persuasion (he opposed communism and fascism alike).

The majority of men have no opinions, and these have to be pumped into them from outside, like lubricants into machinery. Hence it is necessary that some mind or other should hold and exercise authority, so that people without opinions—the majority—can start having opinions. For without these, the common life of humanity would be chaos, a historic void, lacking in any organic structure. Consequently, without a spiritual power, *without someone to command,* and in proportion as this is lacking, chaos reigns over mankind.[5]

Coercion by Representative Authority

Opposing this belief in the desirability of a mass majority recognizing the special claims of certain classes or elites to the positions of authority, which carry with them the coercive power necessary to the integrated operations of a society, is the idea of the popular election of a society's representatives. In such contests of popularity nonelite types may win favor, partly due to the populist thesis that every man is as good as any other and partly according to the equally populist tenet that the position makes the man. The rail-splitter and the haberdasher can occupy the seat of highest authority and grow to its measurements and demands. As Ortega y Gasset sees it, three major changes which took place in the objective conditions of Europe in the nineteenth and early twentieth centuries— a rapid increase in population, the triumphs of science and its industrial application (which he calls "technicism"), and the extension of democratic political institutions—have led to a sense of plenitude and self-satisfaction on the part of the masses, with singular results: in his acid words, "The ordinary man, hitherto guided by others, has resolved to govern the world himself." [6]

How effective this "resolve" may in fact be has been subjected to doubt on at least two scores. One is the old Rousseauian thesis that as the size of a population grows, the effectiveness of the vote of any one person becomes progressively diminished. As B. F. Skinner puts the matter, through the protagonist of his utopian novel, "The chance that one man's vote will decide the issue in a national election is less than the chance that he will be killed on his way to the polls." [7] The other is that with the growth in the size and complexity of institutions and society, the opportunity for individuals in their own communities or work centers to affect the decisions affecting them, taking place at distant locations, becomes more remote. How can one even know about—let alone have anything to say about— some decision affecting his job and status and community life which some computer may this moment be rattling off in the company or city where he works or in some other locale?

There is a further problem with the concept of popular representation. It is seldom if ever applied to the whole of a population, so that some groups are always excluded from representation. In the 1970s, the United States moved to enfranchise the group aged eighteen to twenty, previously deprived of the vote. One may reasonably grant that youngsters of limited experience and maturity should not be expected to participate in matters of "grave" national importance—but why a specific age limit, other than as some factor of tradition? In Switzerland women have only recently been given the right of participation in national elections. For many years blacks were denied the right to vote in the United States. Education and literacy have sometimes been made the basis for extending the franchise, as has possession of some minimum amount of property.

But beyond all such overt forms of discrimination against particular groups of the population lies the graver difficulty with the democratic mystique—that whatever the majority rules must be accepted. The enfranchisement of a minority group would, on this premise, be relatively meaningless, since it would always remain a minority. Conceivably in particular situations the latter might be able to bargain with some party representative of the dominant majority for concessions in exchange for its vote, but its interests could actually be less well provided for than in a government where the coercive authority lay with an elite rather than a popular majority.

If popular representation operates not only through the expressed preference of individuals but also through the influential pressures of interest groups claiming to control blocs of votes (resulting in the pluralistic political society, as it is so often referred to), this does not mean that all groups swing equal weight, or even weight in proportion to the size of their constituencies. Some constituencies are more influential than others, perhaps because they are wealthier, perhaps because they have access to the communications media, perhaps because their community positions give them more opportunity to influence others. Equal representation somehow can never be made to come out as such, since there are inevitably too many subtle factors affecting the weight accorded one man's views against another's. To some extent the differential weights of various groups are a product of tradition, partly contrived by the group itself competitively against other groups, and partly an artifact of the dominants, as they effect alliances favorable to their activities, values, and interests, and lend support to those whose support is important to them.

Popular representation and the need of the elected to put together a popular majority has the further effect of creating a perpetual potential for a demagogue. The masses, because they must be pandered to, can presumably get what they want. The demagogue, faced with a disoriented or fragmented or heterogeneous population, can seek out the lowest common denominator of want and offer it in flamboyant style. Josiah Royce believed that large cities were particularly capable of growing such a mob culture. The individual, washed up from some smaller community, found himself anchorless in the huge urban sea. He developed (anticipating Erikson) pseudo-loyalties to institutions like corporations, labor unions, political parties, religious sects, in which he submerged any identity of his own. Bereft of any genuine individuality, swept along and regimented in factions and causes, he developed a "mob spirit" on which the demagogue could build.[8] Though in different terms, Plato and Aristotle had long previously anticipated this fear. We shall have occasion to examine the phenomenon more fully later.

Although our concern has been chiefly with the governmental exercise of coercive power, other institutions—the corporate enterprise, the labor union, the educational establishments, the churches—have their comparable powers. It would extend our discussion too far to attempt to cover this ground, but suffice it to say that in certain areas this potential for coercion can carry grave consequences to the individual. The person who is dismissed from his job by a corporation because of doubtful security (and whose reputation is thereby blackened throughout the community) or who loses his membership in a labor union for factional activity or who is denied his degree or removed from a teaching position because of the voicing of certain opinions—all these types of coercion can be sprung on an individual often without warning. Increasingly in Western states legislation has sought to protect him from the excesses of such organizational zeal or the misuse of private power, but it is impossible to control all forms of private discipline, and the greater the government's intervention in private affairs the less the opportunity for local autonomy—another issue we shall be coming back to.

With respect to the exercise of coercive power both by governments and private organizations, the weight of opinion has been moving steadily toward providing forums in which individuals can make public protest. If the exercise of coercive power is a matter of social value, it is of interest to society that abuses of its ethical standards be revealed and enjoined. Courts of law are obviously designed to perform this function, testing whether the exercise of executive discretion has been in accord with the constitutional intent of the people.

In one-party systems the fact that courts of law are themselves subordinate to a unitary command casts suspicion on their independence.[9] Legal scholars have pointed out that in private organizations exercising significant coercive powers there is often the same unitary authority, and that effective protest is often infeasible. Some form of "due process of law" has been called for.[10] This is all the more pertinent to the extent one accepts Galbraith's view that the large corporation is becoming in effect an arm of government.

Individualism and Society

In discussing the role of hierarchical authority in society we come face to face with the remarkable concept of individualism, an idea so Western that most Eastern cultures still have no real equivalent for it, and so recent in origin that Tocqueville was obliged to define it for his readers of 1840. His construction accorded more nearly with the concept of liberty as it was coming to be conceived in England.[11] The term is here used in the related but more specialized sense associated with the philosophical thought of the Benthamite utilitarian school, which played so vital a part in English and American societies; its counterpart on the continent never carried the same weight, though the French donated the term which has generally been applied to its economic aspects, laissez faire.

In its most philosophical sense, individualism probably traces back to the Protestant Reformation, which insisted on the right of the individual to treat with God directly, without benefit of any religious intermediary such as the Catholic Church had insisted on. "Every man his own priest" was a battle cry for free inquiry, however much it may have been subverted by conformist Protestant sects in later years. The so-called Age of Enlightenment had given an intellectual connotation to the same exhilarating notion of the individual as the inquiring but responsible, the freethinking but moral, *unit of society*. The Enlightenment, by encouraging the individual to develop his own critical powers, did not aim to separate him *from* society. He was, if anything, better able to make his contribution.

This philosophical individualism inevitably had its counterpart in the economic sphere, where free competition, unfettered by any imposed authority, was viewed as conducing to the best interests of individuals and society both. Adam Smith's powerful polemic on this score had its impact on the continent as well as at home. But Smith had no intention—on this we can be sure—that his economic philosophy of self-interest, as best serving society, should be extended to all aspects of social activity. Nor did he feel that the policy of laissez faire, inviting the government to stay out of economic matters as much as possible, should be extended into a philosophy that that government is best which governs least, or that government as such must be regarded as something unfortunately necessary but basically evil and undesirable, that society itself was a nonreality, consisting of nothing more than the sum of the individuals who composed it, that, in a word, the individual was the only reality and society a construct of the imagination. If there is any individual who can be said to be responsible for such a perverted notion of individualism it was probably Jeremy Bentham.

For Bentham, personal morality consisted in the individual's rational striving to maximize his own balance of pleasure over pain, and this was dependent on his making a correct appraisal of the consequences to himself of his actions. Motivation—why he engaged in any act—was a neutral matter and unrelated to personal morality; only the consequences counted. The individual's choices were to be constrained by various sanctions whose purpose was to protect each person from exploitation by others in their pursuit of self-interest, to secure to everyone the maximum utility consonant with the maximizing activities of others. Indeed, Bentham defined the public good as simply the sum of individual interests. "The community is a fictitious body, composed of the individual persons who are considered as constituting as it were its members. The interest of the community then is, what?—the sum of the interests of the several members who compose it." [12] The greatest happiness of the community can thus be gained by allowing each person to seek his own pleasure, providing he does not cause an amount of pain to someone else greater than the pleasure which he thereby derives for himself—a purely quantitative conception. If one's pleasure, gained at another's pain, was quantitatively greater (and Bentham hoped to be able to develop a "felicific calculus" by which these sensations could be weighed), he was morally entitled to inflict the pain.

Obviously government and law were necessary in such a system (after all, Bentham was primarily what we would today call a political scientist or more narrowly a penologist), to ensure that appropriate sanctions were enacted to prevent an individual from exploiting others with greater loss to them than gain to himself. Bentham was thus one of the first of the cost-benefit analysts, and perhaps the very first systematic one. But in Bentham's utilitarian book, there was an a priori disadvantage to any law: law is a form of coercion, and coercion inflicts pain, which is a loss to society. The initial presumption against a law could only be rebutted by demonstrating that the law would produce more pleasure than the coercive pain it necessarily inflicted.

Government as an affirmative force, government as a promoter of social interests, Bentham could not conceive of. He extended Smith's laissez-faire reasoning in the economic sphere to social relationships generally. "The care of providing for his enjoyments ought to be left almost entirely to each individual; the principal function of government being to protect him from sufferings." Since the individual knows best where his interests lie, then just as in the economic sphere "it follows that the interference of government is altogether erroneous—that it operates rather as an obstacle than as a means of advancement. It is hurtful in another manner. By imposing restraints upon the actions of individuals, it produces a feeling of uneasiness: so much liberty lost—so much happiness destroyed." [13]

Karl Polanyi has argued persuasively against the notion that individualism, in this sense of "each tub standing on its own bottom," was far from being the "natural law" philosophy that its advocates sought to portray it as being; that instead of pushing the government out of the picture it required the active intervention of government to enforce an "unnatural" interpersonal competition that denied the reality of social institutions. [14] But the individualists became obsessed with the notion that power—coercive power—was the root of all evil. From the deep philosophical validity of Lord Acton's famous aphorism that power—all power—corrupts, which embodies the inescapable tragedy of all social systems since none can do without power, they moved to the absolutist position best expressed by Henry Simons when he said that "Power has no use save abuse." [15] "Perfect competition," that construct on which every beginning economics student has been brought up for generations, was defined as a condition in which no seller and no buyer had any power over any other, since each had innumerable equally acceptable alternatives to which he might turn. Market power demonstrated the absence of perfect competition and was to be avoided. The fact that the market itself coerces, and that no social system has yet discovered how to avoid the use of power to achieve its objectives, that the degree of governmental intervention which would be required to maintain "perfect competition" would itself require a monolithic government—somehow all these considerations were waived.

And yet there was in this flight from coercive authority something of beauty as well as something tawdry. As to the first, Frank Knight, the philosopher-economist, comes closest to the heart of the matter, tying together Bentham's rather crude self-serving system with the earlier conception of individualism out of the period of the Enlightenment.

"The saving grace of liberalism lay in the assumed moral and constitutional commitment to minimizing the functions of government and the sphere of its activity, i.e., to 'freedom' as the fundamental ideal, and the use of coercion negatively for the most part, to prevent coercion by individuals and private groups." (Here Bentham speaks.) "This means using it to enforce the ideal of *mutual free consent* as the basis of social relations, plus only such regulatory measures and 'public works' as are not seriously questioned." (Here is the voice of the Enlightenment, which recognizes the reality of society but seeks to put it on the Rousseauian plane of a general will expressed by consenting individuals.)

The beauty of this concept of government by "mutual free consent" is reserved, however, only to that small and uncomplicated a society such as Rousseau envisaged, a "state" of perhaps no more than five thousand souls. When societies expand and industrialization intrudes and private organizations become many times the size that Rousseau envisaged for the whole of his society, the vision of such a restrained use of the coercive power is no longer sustainable. And yet—Knight adds the most piercing irony—"apart from this *ideal,* as an accepted constitutional principle, the notion of majority rule would probably never have been seriously defended by competent thinkers as essentially better than other forms of tyranny." [16] We call to mind the reservations so strongly expressed by Tocqueville and John Stuart Mill as to the possibility of the "tyranny of the majority" in societies where all men exercised the vote.

The tawdry aspect of the flight from coercion lay precisely in the fact that, as industrialism pushed rapidly ahead and populations expanded and organizations grew, in the process necessarily acquiring that very coercive power which it had been the intention to exclude, the beneficiaries of these rapidly changing objective conditions, the new thruster group within the industrialist class, continued to speak of the rights of individualism as antithetical to the exercise of government controls. Laissez faire, the absence of coercion, remained for them the ideal, even though the circumstances which had provided it with its only conceivable philosophical justification had long since passed.

The heavy emphasis on individualism which pervaded the early United States, the competitive self-advancement which motivated each person, gave European observers concern that none would bother themselves with the public welfare. To English thinkers brought up in traditions which emphasized the responsibilities of enlightened individuals for the welfare of the society, Bentham notwithstanding, the price for material personal gain seemed high in terms of civic welfare.

If the impossibility of the individualist utopia revealed itself, among other ways, in the rise of the large corporation and the increasing application of advanced technology and scientific management to its operations, the quest for the grail had been pursued too assiduously to be abandoned. If necessary, the grail could be redefined. John William Ward has written perceptively of the changing content given to individualism in the twentieth century. It now came to mean that the individual would seek to find that place within his institution where he could best contribute to its objectives.[17] But this is hardly accomplished by a process of "free mutual consent," and the question of the proper exercise of coercion in bringing the individual to an awareness of where he fits best is left without answer.

Concomitant with the rise of the large corporation was the growth of the size of cities. "Individuals" were turned into coagulated masses of humanity, except for the few who were wealthy enough to buy a little zone of space around them. People pressed close on other people in living space, working space, playing space, and thinking space. R. Jackson Wilson points up the effects on people's attitudes. "In 1860 almost every American intellectual outside the South would have agreed that societies of men were aggregates of individuals, that the individuals were prior, in every sense but chronological, to their societies. By 1920 the order of priority, and everything it implied, was reversed. The individual, most intellectuals would have said, was the creature of his society." [18]

Finally, the ethical basis for Benthamite individualism wore thin. As long as one placed stress on the individual as prior, and society as an intellectual's artifact, no ethical support was needed other than the belief that by leaving each to his own devices the greatest happiness of all would be promoted. But with the recognition of the reality of society went a growing appreciation of the inequalities in the personal and inherited capabilities of the individual, both in terms of natural and property endowments. What ethical validation was there for a distribution of benefits proportional to such unequal endowments? The argument had been that the efforts induced by the prospect of reward benefited all of society—Adam Smith's invisible hand—but it was not altogether clear why pecuniary reward was necessary to elicit the effort. If individuals would undertake only those activities which promised personal benefit, then the European intellectual's concern that American competitive individualism would undermine the civic sense was fully justified. Could not public benefit be reward enough for an individual's actions?

Thus the concept of individualism as a self-sufficient constitutional value, which had its first glimmerings in the early 1500s and flowered most vigorously in the mid-1800s, had a century later run its course. It left behind a continuing emphasis on the importance of the individual, an emphasis which in the West no succeeding constitutional value could fail to incorporate, but by itself it was not sufficient unto the new day of large-scale industrialization and urbanization and their accompanying institutions. But if one concludes that the Western effort to erect individualism into a self-sufficient constitutional principle for a social order was essentially a search for an unattainable utopia, he comes back to face the question of the ethical basis for the use of coercion in society. What kind of a social *order* is wanted? What are the moral standards which both warrant and make less necessary the application of coercion? Social morality is the symbol of orderliness, and standardization of tastes a means for providing solidarity and unity without the use of force. But how much order should be sought, how much standardization can be imposed without sacrificing more of the individual's autonomy than is socially desirable? If individuals (in the aggregate) are not a substitute for society, neither does society substitute for the individual.

This issue has been nicely posed by the Australian political scientist, Ross Terrill, following an extended visit through Communist China. Everywhere he found a sense of nation-building pride and zeal, and subordination of the individual to the collective effort or "corporate design." The Revolution has been good for peasants and workers, but less clearly so for the freethinking intellectual. How can one strike, objectively, an overall balance as to its value for the "whole society"? Clearly there is no Benthamite felicific calculus to give us an answer. "Yet at one point we and China face the same value judgment. Which gets priority: the individual's freedom or the relationships of the whole society?" [19]

But that question is not one over which we possess some autonomous choice *as a society*. There *is* no "right" answer which we can expect to discover, all of us, by virtue of centuries or even millennia of social experience. The thesis of this book is that there is likely to be only *some* answer which has been embraced by a group with its own special vision, a group which given propitious objective circumstances comes to exercise a dominant role within a society, so that its answer becomes—as in China—the answer which is accepted for that time and place. Mao and his People's Liberation Army were the thruster group which made good in China. Would one dare to say that their views as to the proper place of the individual in China's society have become the constitutional order through the autonomous, reflective judgment of the whole population?

The Search for Social Order

The forms which the search for order have taken have been numerous. There has been a recurrent belief in the desirability of an "organic community" based on a "natural" hierarchy, characterizing such periods and places as feudalism in Europe in the Middle Ages, the Southern plantation system of pre-Civil War United States, the oligarchic rule in many countries of Latin America today.[20]

William James, in searching for the "enduring cement" that would hold a society together, pessimistically concluded that "So far, war has been the only force that can discipline a whole community, and until an equivalent discipline is organized, I believe that war must have its way." But his unwillingness to rest social order on a Spartan basis left him with the hope that man would become capable of organizing a "moral equivalent" for the military organization of society, which he thought might take the form of some kind of compulsory public service—what today might be thought of as a term of duty in the American Vista and Peace Corps of the 1960s. He was convinced that "surrender of private interests, obedience to command, must still remain the rock upon which states are built." [21]

On a more mystical plane, the American philosopher Charles S. Peirce, whose influence has been chiefly a posthumous twentieth-century phenomenon, argued that the individual was only a cell in the social organism, who could affirm his existence only by his relationship to an infinite community of inquiry, composed of all those past, present, and future who contributed to the inquiry after truth. The individual by himself was only a "negation" who could not escape ignorance and error. Only within the larger community, where the individual's efforts were disciplined and refined, lay hope for the discovery of the natural order of which man himself was part. It was the community, not the individual, that constituted an "end in itself." [22]

It is in the sphere of economic activity, however, that emphasis on the need for social order and integration has been greatest. There is, of course, the stream of utopian and ideological thinking, from Sir Thomas More and Saint-Simon down through Marx and Mussolini, which asserts the desirability of particular types of social order, standards of morality, and means of coercion. Without attempting even to distinguish among this vast literature, we can only note that the objective conditions which undermined individualism as a constitutional principle—in particular the expanded role of technology and the expanded scale of social institutions—have established a premise on the strength of which many have concluded that the "big" decisions have outgrown the democratic process and must be concentrated in the hands of a few technical experts. If this is especially the case in the economic sphere, it is not confined there. As Martin Shubik has commented, "The growth of numbers of people, amounts of knowledge, and speed of technology work against the individual being in a position to exercise free, reasonably well-informed, rational, individual choice concerning much of his destiny." [23]

The social system's technical requirements impose a certain burden on the individual to adjust *himself* to these needs, simply as a matter of furthering his own interests. We are back with John William Ward's twentieth-century redefinition of individualism as implying the individual's search for that role in society, or in an institution, where he can contribute most to its objectives. We can see the effects of this shift in the changing curricula of our educational institutions, which have become increasingly quantitative, scientific, and operational as Western society has found science and mathematics important to its economic and industrial growth. In countries which have experimented with national planning, there is a tendency for this molding of the individual to the system's needs to become more systematized. Long-term educational programing, for example, forecasts professional and educational requirements perhaps twenty years into the future, so that teachers can be trained in the necessary subjects and facilities can be planned to accommodate the flow of students into the stressed subject areas. Scholarships and fellowships are provided to lure young people into the wanted specializations.

Intellectual inquiry and economic interdependence have combined to place primary emphasis on the individual as simply a unit in a larger social system, the characteristics of which are partially discoverable through the natural sciences and partly controllable through the social sciences. In his curiously idyllic but "scientific" utopia, *Walden II,* psychologist B. F. Skinner has laid out the lineaments of a society which has discarded democracy as "scientifically invalid," since it fails to take account of the fact that in the long run "man is determined by the state." Based on a system of planning by experts, employing "positive reinforcement" (the rewarding of individuals for actions considered desirable), the system preserves a sense of freedom because of the absence of physical coercion. Individuals are conditioned to Spartan forms of self-discipline as well as to an acceptance of the limitations of their own physical and mental capabilities, thereby eliminating the competitive struggle and substituting cooperative relations. The objective is a cooperative society in which no one gains at the expense of anyone else. The theme is neatly summarized in the words of the chief architect of the system: "When a science of behavior has once been achieved, there's no alternative to a planned society. We can't leave mankind to an accidental or biased control. But by using the principle of positive reinforcement—carefully avoiding force or the threat of force—we can preserve a personal sense of freedom." [24]

To Skinner, speaking through his fictional planner, government for the benefit of all is not possible in a democracy, where the majority rules and the minority suffers. Issues tend to be decided yes or no, by counting the numbers. In a planned society, governed by experts, compromises could more often be worked out which would be reasonably satisfying to everyone.

But however gloved the hand of coercion, or under whatever terminological label, *someone* in authority, someone exercising hierarchical power, necessarily controls the individual whenever his role is written for him or decisions are made for him. The more scientific the plan, the more orderliness that is sought (freedom from chance, from the unexpected, from the unpleasant), the less room for individual idiosyncracy. "Of course, a technology which is subject to political and social controls can do wondrous things. But the very modes of thought and instinctive behavior required to develop and extend technology are themselves dangerous. They include a passion for order and logic, a disposition to discard that which is irrelevant to the necessary calculations, and a belief that technological advance is desirable for its own sake. . . . For the technological mind is shaped by the necessity to repress or discard the disorderly and the irrational which are, at our present stage of knowledge, fundamental to human freedom." [25] As Djilas has said of the Communist state-controlled system, discretion is out of place in a mechanism.

Congruence v. Divergence

The issue which thus emerges with respect to the constitutional value is how much congruence with the code of the larger society we demand from individuals and groups who have values and interests which are partially divergent. Some congruence is essential for social order, for the achievement of focal values, and whatever this degree of wanted congruence may be, it should be enforceable within the value code of the society itself. But no less than in the case of focal values there is an array of opinion within society as to the degree of congruence which can ethically be coerced. Even excluding the two extremes of those who believe the individual should be totally subject to the state and those who believe that he should be totally free, there is a spectrum of opinion as to the extent to which plans should be conformed to, orderliness maintained, standards and tastes enforced.

Particularly with the recognition that focal values have changed over the years, in response to changes in objective conditions and the thrusts of certain *components* of the society, how much system orderliness is compatible with possible future changes? How much is value conformity demanded to protect the interests of those who have become dominants, and who— quite genuinely, no doubt—see *their* order as what is best for society, divergence from which is contrary to the best interests of all?

This ineluctable question poses a peculiarly difficult problem for the social scientist. For him the pull in the direction of seeing society as an integrated system is a strong one. It satisfies his predilection for generalization, for theory and predictability. By concentrating on the forces making for equilibrium, the economist, for example, can more readily systematize and quantify his concepts. But once such a systems approach to human affairs is adopted, the social scientist cannot escape a definition of system purpose. What are the objectives, the grand design, the focal value of the social system which concerns him? It is necessary to know in order to understand and appraise the system's functioning.

Once the analyst has identified system purpose, he tends to evaluate all its component parts—all the subsystems and groups of which it is made up—in terms of the overarching system objective. From the viewpoint of the system with which he is concerned, the subunits should all be functionally oriented toward the overall purpose, not toward some more specialized or particularistic objective of their own. The purpose of the larger system thus controls his view of the desirable forms of behavior of the component groups. Any efficiency which is sought, whatever maximization is attempted, runs in terms of the system as a whole.

But it is precisely for this reason that an ethical choice confronts the analyst. If he is concerned with the system and its values, he applies a monistic standard, efficiency from *its* point of view, maximization of *its* present values. Any competing values of the groups of which it is composed are excluded. But this same system which he takes as given, representing a special set of values, partially compromised, which he would like to see operate more efficiently and more nearly achieve its goals and thus approach an equilibrium condition—that same system is always in danger if not actually in process of being fragmented and reassembled with a different configuration of economic and social relationships, responding to changes in the objective conditions and the relative abilities of thrusting groups to take advantage of them.

That continuing contest generates its own interest for the social scientist. If he responds to it, he finds himself looking at social issues and programs not only from the point of view of the system as a whole, as it is given, but also of its major contentious interests, and as to how it is changing. For him divergence of values and interests is as important as congruence, and there is no ethical basis for his esteeming one set of values more highly simply because they happen to be dominant at the moment other than as the means for the preservation of system order.

Whose Social Order?

There is no intention here of suggesting that the dominant group in every society seeks with the same degree of ruthlessness to stamp out views which run counter to its own values and interests. Like focal values, constitutional values differ among societies and within the same society over time. The constitutional values of different groups within the same society are also likely to vary significantly with respect to the permissible use of authority as well as the importance of order. Generally the desire for order is accompanied by an implicit desire for hierarchical forms, for status positions which are recognized by everyone, and functional roles which are accepted by those who are supposed to carry them out.

The excesses of thought and behavior committed in the name of nineteenth-century individualism provide no warrant for a pendulum swing that denies the importance of the individual even as against society, even as against system orderliness and purpose. The problem of constitutional values lies precisely in devising not simply a compromise or trade-off but a means of *relating* individual needs to social needs. The problem is not solved with false associations and ideological slogans, such as that under socialism the individual has no meaning, or that capitalism gives every individual a chance to make the most of himself. Individual and group autonomy is possible under socialism, and coercive controls can be strong and exploitative under capitalism.

The complexity of this ethical problem is enormous. It begins with the individual and his efforts at achieving an identity, which necessitates his assimilation of cultural values which are partly chosen for him but which he may partly and autonomously select, including, itself, the ethical value of the degree to which he accepts authority and the degree to which he attempts to free himself from its constraints. In some societies, such as the United States, there has developed a point of view that would make the "self-actualization" of the individual a kind of moral obligation. In other less developed societies with masses of uneducated and illiterate, often without meaningful activity and living on the ragged edge of subsistence, identity and "self-actualization" are submerged in Erikson's pseudo-speciation: one's life acquires meaning only through being a member of some group which views itself as superior to certain other groups.[26] Or the problem of identity may be resolved by living in a dream world—illusions fostered by such diverse means as drugs or movies or television.[27]

Moving beyond the individual, there is the constitutional problem of his relationship to the groups with which he associates himself. The organization of workers into labor unions may give them a greater voice in the conditions under which they work—greater autonomy relative to management—but at the same time subordinates the individual to the union authority. Self-government by any collectivity inevitably, as we previously noted, implies the individual's subordination to that collectivity, and requires a definition of the degree of autonomy for the individual within the group no less than of the group within its larger social setting.

That larger social setting imposes the most difficult problem of all. The more individuals who are bound together within a social system the less meaningful does self-government become, and the more serious the question of how much autonomy can be permitted to subordinate groups without subverting the social order. *Whose* social order, however, if *self*-government is chiefly a euphemism? Obviously the social order impressed upon society by its most dominant components. What gives acceptance to the coercive sanctions which they necessarily must apply to maintain the social order? Only the conviction by a large enough proportion of the population that the coercive sanctions which are in fact used are ethically justified because they serve larger interests than those of the favored few, because in this instance, as in the case of focal values, the dominants have managed to identify their own values and interests with those of society at large. Again, as in the case of focal values, this requires some accommodation of the hierarchical attitudes of other groups, including attitudes which have lagged from the past into the present. The more vigorously a focal value is asserted, the less compromised by accommodations, the more will the constitutional value come down on the side of social order at the expense of individual and group autonomy. The more diffuse—the less focal—are a society's style and objectives, the more permissive and less coercive are its constitutional values likely to be.

Notes

1. John Schaar, *Escape from Authority* (New York: Basic Books, 1961), p. 186.

2. Herbert Marcuse, "The Individual in the Great Society," in *A Great Society?*, ed. Bertram Gross (New York: Basic Books, 1966), pp. 58–80, especially pp. 72–77. In effect, the individual's total alienation—the anarchical *ideal* of total freedom—is rendered impossible by his *necessary* alienation through social controls not of his own making—a condition which, from one

point of view, is as trivial as man's dependence on food, but from another represents the tragedy of the human spirit which has occupied philosophers and poets throughout history.

3. Murphy, *The Dialectics of Social Life*, pp. 152–153.

4. Williams, *Culture and Society, 1780–1950*, pp. 239–240. Actually Coleridge's "clerisy" did not call for the revival of any preexisting class but for the national endowment of a new class dedicated to the preservation and extension of culture.

5. Ortega y Gasset, *The Revolt of the Masses*, p. 94. (Italics in the original.) In similar but less dogmatic vein, Thornton has commented that "The 'will of the people' means nothing if the people do not will anything in particular" in *The Habit of Authority*, p. 335.

6. Ortega y Gasset, *The Revolt of the Masses*, p. 70.

7. B. F. Skinner, *Walden II* (New York: The Macmillan, Co. 1948), p. 221.

8. Wilson, *In Quest of Community*, comments on this aspect of Royce's thinking on p. 164.

9. "The executive, the legislative, the investigating, the court, and the publishing bodies are one and the same." Djilas, *The New Class*, p. 89. In a moving statement following the detention of the biologist Zhores A. Medvedev, the Russian author Alexander I. Solzhenitsyn, himself out of favor with the authorities, published abroad a statement, "This Is How We Live," which read in part:

> "Without any warrant for arrest or any medical justification, four policemen and two doctors come to a healthy man's house. The doctors declare that he is crazy; the police officer shouts, We are the organs of force! Get up! They bend his arms back and take him to the madhouse.
> "This can happen tomorrow to any of us . . .
> "And there is no restraint of law; even the appeals of our best scientists and writers are bounced back like peas off a wall . . .
> "Even in lawlessness, in crime, one must remember the line beyond which a man becomes a cannibal.
> "It is shortsighted to think that you can live, constantly relying on force alone, constantly scoring the objections of conscience."—From *New York Times*, 17 June 1970.

10. The most eloquent statement along this line of which I am aware has been made by Adolf A. Berle, in *The Twentieth Century Capitalist Revolution* (New York: Harcourt Brace Jovanovich, 1955). With respect to the need for limiting the coercive powers of labor unions (already accomplished in part in the United States in the Landrum-Griffin Act), the most outspoken and objective critic has been Clyde Summers, as in his "Individual Rights in Collective Agreements," *Buffalo Law Review*, 9 (Winter 1960): 241.

11. As has been nicely developed by Bertrand de Jouvenel, "On the Evolution of Forms of Government," in *Futuribles I*, ed. B. de Jouvenel (Geneva: Editions Droz, 1963), pp. 96–105.

12. Jeremy Bentham, *An Introduction to the Principles of Morals and Legislation* (Oxford ed., 1876), p. 3.

13. Extracted from ed. John Bowring, *The Works of Jeremy Bentham*, Vol. 1 and Vol. 3 (Edinburgh, 1843), p. 301 and p. 43 respectively.

14. Karl Polanyi, *The Great Transformation* (New York: Holt, Rinehart & Winston, 1944), p. 141.

15. Henry Simons, "Some Reflections on Syndicalism," *Journal of Political Economy* 52 (1944): 1–25.

16. The quotations from Frank Knight are from his *Freedom and Reform* (New York: Harper & Row, 1947), p. 79. Italics mine.

17. John William Ward, "The Ideal of Individualism and the Reality of Organization," in *The Business Establishment*, ed. Earl Cheit (New York: John Wiley & Sons, 1964), pp. 77–112.

18. Wilson, *In Quest of Community*, p. 26. Wilson also stresses the acceptance of Darwinist evolutionary theory for this change of attitude.

19. Ross Terrill, "The 800,000,000," *Atlantic Monthly*, November 1971, p. 120.

20. With respect to the latter, Irving Louis Horowitz writes: "Democratic norms of political behavior come up against a feudal inheritance in which superordination and subordination are respected ingredients in politics. In the ideological sphere the argument between Catholic 'altruism' and Enlightenment 'egoism,' between medieval and industrial values, has never been resolved." "The Military Elites," in Lipset and Solari, *Elites in Latin America*, p. 158. Quoted with permission.

21. James, in Commager, *Living Ideas in America*, p. 646.

22. Wilson, *In Quest of Community*, pp. 41–42.

23. Martin Shubik, "Information, Rationality, and Free Choice in a Future Democratic Society," *Daedalus*, Summer 1967, p. 778. Shubik is optimistic enough, however, to believe that the computer, appropriately employed, can be made an instrument for preserving individual freedom.

24. Skinner, *Walden II*, pp. 219–220. Skinner has elaborated his thesis in *Beyond Freedom and Dignity* (New York: Alfred A. Knopf, 1971).

25. Richard Goodwin, "The Social Theory of Herbert Marcuse," *Atlantic Monthly*, June 1971, p. 84. The operationalist view that the individual can be treated as a functional unit in a larger system has been explored by Robert Boguslaw in *The New Utopians* (Englewood Cliffs, N.J.: Prentice-Hall, 1965).

26. In one of his more cynical asides, Barrington Moore puzzles why a tendency toward "snobbishness" and status distinctions seems to be pronounced even in some of the most "primitive" societies, and tentatively provides an answer which I fear has some claim to validity: "Though I cannot prove it, I suspect that one of the few lasting and dependable sources of human satisfaction is making other people suffer [by being made to feel inferior], and that this constitutes the ultimate cause." Moore, *Social Origins of Dictatorship and Democracy*, p. 338.

27. Dom Moraes has described how the masses of Bombay identify themselves with the film life. "The industry feeds them with dreams, to make them laugh or weep. They believe in these dreams more uncritically than any other audience in the world. They follow the stars with the attentive love of astronomers. To forget the squalid reality of his own life, a poor man will visit the cinema practically every day." "Bombay: Wealth, Shanty Towns, Speakeasies, Movie Aristocrats, Intellectual Admen and Death on the Trains," *New York Times Magazine*, 11 October 1970, p. 141.

6 / Distributive Values

Every society gives rise to certain advantages which are unequally distributed. It develops an economic organization out of which material advantages flow, a system of political authority out of which advantages of power accrue to some, a system of social relationships out of which status differences emerge. How these products of a society's organization get portioned among its people is the process which I call the distribution of the social advantage, thinking of the social advantage as a kind of Gross National Product not limited to goods but to all the valued aspects of social existence.

Since a society, in the face of changing objective conditions, orients itself around the values and activities of a class of thrusters who have been best able to take advantage of those conditions, and since, as we have seen, the thrusters who become dominants identify their personal interests and advantages with the preservation of a way of life they also see as desirable for society, there is no difficulty in concluding that they will structure the distribution of wealth, power, and status to their own advantage to the extent that this is possible. The accomplishment of this may take a bit of time, and a predecessor elite may have to be allowed to retain privileges which still shine with special luster because of cultural lag (a title, a coat of arms, an historic family seat), but the group which gives direction to a society benefits most from that fact.

The consequence is that as society becomes more systematically geared to the focal and constitutional values it adopts from the dominants, the inequality of reward gets built more systematically into the system. It becomes so integral a part of the social order that it becomes viewed as "natural" and something to be taken for granted. For example, among all Western nations (indeed, among most nations of the world) a continued rate of growth of the national product is posed as a national goal, from which all benefit. The achievement of a six percent rate of increase is looked on as a national accomplishment in which all share, not the gain of some special clique. Hence all are adjured to turn in a good performance, to work efficiently, since they themselves benefit from their own efficiency.

But just as Keynes pointed out the obvious but overlooked fact that the people who invest are not the same people who save, so is it equally obvious that the people who produce a bundle of goods are not the same people who consume it, so that for them to maximize their output does not necessarily benefit them directly. The efficient performance of the economy is geared to the benefit of some more than others.

In the effort to increase national output, some economists have become enamored of the idea of investing in "human capital" by increased appropriations to the educational sector. They have computed the rate of return on such educational investment, on the principle that the higher the return the better the investment. But it is not too extreme to suggest that the effect of the human-capitalists' calculations is to channel social investment (here in education) along lines which tend to serve those whom the economy as a whole already serves best. This does not mean that others—those who are educated—are not benefited in the process, but only that the economy is *structured* to yield superior returns to those in strategic positions. To the extent that the human-capitalists' rate-of-return analysis is based on price and income data deriving from the existing privileged distribution of power and property, the result can hardly be termed of equal benefit to all. The economic analyst who tots up the returns on social investment in education is performing the same accounting function on behalf of the existing system and its managers as the investment analyst who does the same for a business firm. Just as the latter entertains no illusion that the profit return he finds in the business accrues equally to "all" (workers, customers, suppliers, as well as owners), so need the economist have no illusion that the rate of increase he finds accruing to "society" accrues equally to all its members. Who would ever harbor such a naive notion? But the fact that we are still concerned with the overall objective as *social* objective, even though we know it is distributed unequally, reveals the extent to which inequality in the distribution of the social advantage gets institutionalized and accepted.

But to be accepted it must not affront people's sense of justice. Hence the basic ethical question inherent in the distribution of the social advantage: According to what principle *should* it be distributed? To what extent should certain members (who?) be allotted privileges denied to others? Does a more equal division of society's advantages somehow command stronger moral backing? How equal?

A perfectly egalitarian society is difficult to conceive and even to define. It would presumably require a completely status-free society, whose government and institutions gave no preference of any kind to any class, race, ethnic group, occupation, or to either sex, but reflected equally the interests of all, so that it made no difference who moved "up" or "down" (the very terms would have to be discarded), nor would the positions they moved to; the decisions made by anyone in authority (but what kind of authority?) would be without power to change anyone's condition. Under such an arrangement a society could hardly exist; it certainly could not defend itself.

But unless we are willing to leave the question of the distribution of the social advantage purely to "power," which would invite constant power plays and ploys and make for a degree of instability that Hobbes believed insupportable, we are driven back to the need for *some* form of justification for the distribution which takes place. Some ethical underpinning must be provided. Hence the need for a distributive value.

The distributive value is closely linked to the constitutional value and is often confused with it. Egalitarianism is thus often identified with democracy, which presumably treats each person alike, and both are contrasted with aristocratic and autocratic forms of government.[1] But this tends to confuse two sets of contrasts: on the one hand, the desire for social order (which *might* be linked with autocracy as a means of achieving it) versus the preference for individual autonomy, which is what we have labeled the constitutional value; and on the other hand, special privileges or an unequal share in the social advantage (which might be associated with aristocracy) versus equality in distribution. In both sets of contrasts, the hierarchical principle is likely to be involved, but in a different way. Political hierarchy (access to coercive power) runs counter to individual autonomy, while status hierarchy (access to privilege) runs counter to egalitarianism. As Guttsman has pointed out, English romantic thought embraced the basic tenets of the Enlightenment: freedom of thought, equality before the law—matters of constitutional principle—but it reacted vigorously against the egalitarian views of the French Revolution, a matter of the distributive principle.[2] Inequality among individuals can easily survive along with the autonomy of individuals, but to achieve equality among individuals may require the coercive power of the state.

Tocqueville had an almost mystical belief that the drive of history was in the direction of egalitarianism, which he defined—too simply—as the absence of inherited privilege. But he had no illusions that egalitarianism and democracy necessarily went hand in hand. In America, at the time of his explorations, they did, because of the special condition that a new country had been established distant from both the political and status hierarchies that characterized the old Europe, thus fostering both autonomy in the sense of self-government and equality in the sense of open opportunity for everyone. But the desire for equality among men was so strong, he believed, that the time might come when individuals would gladly give over the power of self-government to an autocratic national government which would ensure that all were treated alike.

It is probably a safe generalization that an emphasis on the constitutional value of social order tends to run counter to egalitarianism, since a social order can best be sustained when each one knows and accepts his place. No matter how fluid the system, no matter how much mobility it offers, the place which the individual occupies at the moment defines his position of superordination and subordination; individuals may move, but the authority and status structure remains.[3] It is a nice question whether a system in which each person was ruler for a day might be labeled egalitarian, but there is no question about a system in which roles are not impartially assigned but nevertheless carry with them a well-defined status. Although the Japanese social system has subtleties which often escape Western observers, it has been affirmed by many competent experts that in that country everyone is considered *not* to be equal but to have his defined place in a complex hierarchical order. His behavior is often not a reflection of his personality but is what his position calls for in the hierarchy, whether it be family, business, professional association, or any other association.

As we shall shortly see, it is an intriguing paradox that while an emphasis on social order and hierarchical authority tends to conflict with egalitarianism, an emphasis on the latter can lend support to hierarchical order as against individual autonomy. But we shall defer sampling that bit of political spice for the moment.

The manner of distribution of the social advantage has obvious consequences for the selfish interests of all, but it has social significance as well. The idea that a privileged leisure class is necessary to the advancement of learning and the arts, to the cultivation of intellect and taste, has been around for a long time.[4] I advert again to our perceptive friend of an earlier year, Alexis de Tocqueville, who pointed up the consequences for a society of elitist as against democratic institutions. His words are too eloquent not to quote:

Do you wish to give a certain elevation to the human mind and teach it to regard the things of this world with generous feelings, to inspire men with a scorn of mere temporal advantages, to form and nourish strong convictions and keep alive the spirit of honorable devotedness? Is it your object to refine the habits, embellish the manners, and cultivate the arts, to promote the love of poetry, beauty, and glory? Would you constitute a people fitted to act powerfully upon all other nations, and prepared for those high enterprises which, whatever be their results, will leave a name forever famous in history? If you believe such to be the principal object of society, avoid the government of the democracy, for it would not lead you with certainty to the goal.[5]

Ortega y Gasset would undoubtedly have supported him on this score. But Tocqueville did not view the cards as stacked in favor of aristocratic values, though he obviously shared belief in them himself. He saw good things coming out of the democratic constitutional system too, but of quite a different order—materialistic and quantitative. The contrast is remarkably similar to that which Nef made between the continental Catholic way of life, with its emphasis on beauty and quality, as against the Northern Protestant style of utility and quantity.

But if you hold it expedient to divert the moral and intellectual activity of man to the production of comfort and the promotion of general well-being; if a clear understanding be more profitable to man than genius; if your object is not to stimulate the virtues of heroism, but the habits of peace; if you had rather witness vices than crimes, and are content to meet with fewer noble deeds, provided offenses be diminished in the same proportion; if, instead of living in the midst of a brilliant society, you are contented to have prosperity around you; if, in short, you are of the opinion that the principal object of government is not to confer the greatest possible power and glory upon the body of the nation, but to ensure the greatest enjoyment and to avoid the most misery to each of the individuals who compose it—if such be your desire, then equalize the conditions of men and establish democratic institutions.[6]

Once again we observe the interaction between the three components of a social value system—the focal, constitutional, and distributive values. They do not compose a matrix in which all combinations are equally possible: certain combinations fall together more naturally than others; the content of one affects the content of another.

Allocating the Social Advantage: The Principle of Birth

Earlier it was said that the basic ethical issue underlying the distributive value was the principle according to which the social advantage was allocated. There are three quite separate principles which may be invoked: distribution according to birth (inheritance), distribution on the basis of competition and achievement, and distribution by means of political decision.

If distribution runs in terms of birth, this may take several forms. There is the notion of a "bloodline," according to which certain families which came into possession of advantages early in the life of a society pass these from generation to generation, usually undiminished by virtue of the rule of primogeniture, often enhanced through intermarriage. Such a nation of aristocracy is commonly based on land ownership, often originally as grants from the king by means of which he assured himself of a loyal following. It entails—or entailed, since it is no longer so true as formerly—

not only possession of material wealth and claims to personal services but also privileges under the law—sometimes exemption from taxes (as in prerevolutionary France and Russia), immunity from legal action brought by a commoner, monopoly over privileged positions in the government, church, and military. England was a society especially hospitable to such distribution of advantages by reason of birth well into the first half of the nineteenth century. While aristocratic privileges remain in many West European countries, they have been vastly diluted. In the contemporary world such enormous concentrations of privilege on the basis of birth tend to be confined to the underdeveloped areas, where popular governments have been frustrated by local oligarchs, and where modernization, industrialization, and nationalism have been undercut by regional potentates who prefer to rest on their traditional privileges.

But if the aristocratic principle of distribution has lessened its hold on the advanced countries, the principle of distribution according to birth has not disappeared altogether. The "old families" retain status, and by virtue of the right of inheritance of property they frequently retain wealth. Lloyd Warner, in his sociological study of "Yankee City," slotted such people into his "upper upper" class. Far more important than such lingering remnants of a faded aristocracy (and the much larger numbers of the middle class who inherit not status but wealth in widely varying amounts) is the manner in which birth has been negatively applied to deny advantage.

In the United States the blacks were, from the first, subjected to the grossest disadvantages—political, social, and economic—simply by reason of their being born black. There is no necessity of recounting here the details of a well-known sordid story. Suffice it to point out that discrimination had and has its own peculiar patterns in the North as well as the South. Typically in the old South blacks and whites, while segregated as to use of public facilities such as schools, washrooms, and waiting rooms, mingled much more closely in the neighborhood setting. The homes of blacks often backed up—alley-wise—to the homes of whites, throughout much of a Southern city. Long, ingrained conditioning kept the blacks in their humble place despite proximity. In the North the situation was substantially reversed. Public facilities were not formally segregated, but the blacks lived in their own restricted ghetto areas, bounded in physical as well as social space.

The civil rights movement of the 1960s was followed by a mass exodus of whites from the central cities as the blacks came pouring into them. The warning of the Kerner Commission has gone unheeded, and the consequences have been as it predicted: two societies are developing, the black and the white, separate and unequal. As Norton Long has pointed out, the suburb is the Northern means for achieving this result. "It has the advantage of being legal. If housing, education, jobs, and matrimony are to remain a charmed circle among formally equal citizens in an area of public goods, there is a powerful logic behind the existing metropolitan fragmentation and the basis for considerable resistance to the creation of really general governments." [7] Geographical localism again becomes the instrument for ensuring that the powers of a popular, heterogeneous-based, national government are not turned against those who are privileged by birth —in this case largely on a racial basis, with some ethnicity thrown in.

An even more pervasive caste system has (and still largely does) characterize India, especially in the rural villages.

In pre-British Indian society, and still today in much of the countryside, the fact of being born in a particular caste determined for the individual the entire span of existence, quite literally from before conception until after death. It gave the range of choice for a marital partner in the case of parents, the type of upbringing the offspring would have and their choice of mate in marriage, the work he or she could legitimately undertake, the appropriate religious ceremonies, food, dress, rules of evacuation (which were very important), down to most details of daily living, all organized around a conception of disgust. [8]

We can carry the effect of birth on the distribution of the social advantage much further than its support of certain bloodlines and its denial of others. In any society there are a variety of discriminatory practices designed to reduce the opportunity of participating in the things that society values, aimed against certain ethnic, religious, or language groups. Often such discrimination disappears in time, with assimilation of the minority. But its effect can extend over several generations, and indeed much longer, and since there is always some new disadvantaged group appearing to take the place of those who may be shedding their disadvantages, and since such attitudes can die down only to recur, birth operates to the disadvantage of numbers of people in most societies in their struggle for a share in the good things their society has to offer.

Since the vitalization of such discrimination operates to the advantage of those who are thereby placed in a relatively superior position, there is a tendency for family training to reinforce restrictive practices. Allison Davis has made a significant study of the way this "socialization" process helps to establish the child's class identity, creating attitudes which perpetuate notions of superior-inferior status. A social class system, he points out, such as characterizes most societies, restricts intimate associations to a limited group on the basis of a pattern of traits such as family position, education, manners, clothes, language, all of which tend to be hierarchically ranked. "Class training" by his parents and his peers ranges all the way from the choice of playmates to educational and occupational goals. His very conceptions of right and wrong—the ethical norms of the value system of his particular class—are drilled into him.[9] If such rigid forms of socialization seem to have lost some of their potency in the interval since Davis wrote, they have not disappeared altogether. If we include in the principle of distribution of the social advantage by virtue of birth all such widely distributed forms of discrimination, based solely on the accident of the class, caste, race, or ethnic group into which one is born, then we would have to conclude that this principle still has a good deal of vitality remaining in it.

The Principle of Competitive Achievement

The second major distributive principle is competitive achievement. In effect, this principle embodies the notion of the "self-made man." Any individual who can claw or climb his way to a position of advantage is entitled to the results of his own efforts. The contribution which young America made to this conception lay in its acceptance, as a necessary part of this principle, of the idea of equal opportunity in the competitive struggle. If some started the race with advantages from which others were excluded, the competition was clearly unequal and the results of the race could hardly be regarded as determined by relative abilities. The necessary condition for accepting competition as an ethical principle lies in equality of opportunity among those competing.

Clearly equality of opportunity is not possible in any precise sense. A poor immigrant is obviously handicapped relative to his counterpart from an established and prosperous native family. The person with good health has a better chance than the sickly. Some forms of discrimination are to be expected in any society, and to that extent the competition is rigged. Nevertheless, even taking all such considerations into account, if there is a fairly open society, a fairly general chance for any individual to show what he can do with his talents, and a fairly prevalent willingness that society's advantages should be distributed according to the results of such an open competition, then one can feel fairly satisfied that rewards are the result of personal effort and merit.

This has certainly been the middle-class creed in America, sustaining the encouragement given by parents to their children over many generations to study hard, work hard, and reap the rewards of wealth and public recognition. Tocqueville was impressed with the general concentration of every individual on making a success of himself, the expectation that everyone right up to the President would have to "make his own living," but at the same time he was somewhat appalled at the intensity of the competition, which seemed to leave men's minds filled only with their own rather than the public welfare.

One consequence of open competition is that, however equal the opportunities, the result must be inequality of condition. Those who win the competitions take the biggest share of the stakes. Andrew Carnegie put the matter succinctly in his gospel of wealth. God has endowed some individuals with larger talents than others. In free and fair competition, they must necessarily come out on top. The Horatio Alger formula of rags to riches, "Strive and Succeed," always left the hero in a position superior to those around him, as a consequence of his own merits.

There was, however, a curious ambiguity about this process. Did those who failed in the competition do so from lack of effort, so that they deserved to fail, or from lack of God-given talent, so that it was not really their fault even though it was their lot? The doctrine of individualistic self-reliance carried with it the corollary of no pampering of the indolent and improvident, a point of view which is necessary to make such a system work. On the other hand, it was unnecessarily cruel to consign to generations of poverty those who, through no fault of their own, lacked the means for making the most of such limited talents as they might possess: the youngster who had to drop out of school to help support the family, guaranteeing that his own children would have to do the same for him, for example; or the consumptive who was unable to secure proper health care and whose children inherited weakened constitutions; or the orphan who lacked proper guidance. These and other hardship cases lost out in the competitive race not through weakness of character but through circumstances of fate. To help them was not to undermine the system but to support it, to demonstrate its dedication to equality of opportunity.

Out of this regard for the "deserving poor" arose the middle-class notion of public service. This was an integral part of Carnegie's carefully conceived gospel of wealth: the efficient use of superior talents guaranteed disproportionate rewards, but those rewards were not to be used solely for one's own indulgences but as assets which God had given to him as steward on behalf of the social welfare. The emphasis on individual self-reliance was preserved: not the government, but the man of talents was to determine how society could best be served. And in Carnegie's philosophy that lay not in charity to those whose weakness of character had betrayed them but in props for those anxious to develop their own capabilities in the face of handicaps: libraries, free public schools, public health care.

Raymond Williams has insightfully described how a similar doctrine of service infused the British middle class. They were brought up, more than in the United States, to subordinate selfish interests to the general good, by various forms of public service. This was only a somewhat more genteel version of Carnegie's gospel, justifying itself on the ground of earned success and its accompanying obligation of service; more genteel in that it placed less stress on the competitive struggle, with the consequence that both success and service were on a somewhat less grandiose scale than Carnegie conceived of.

Williams points out, with considerable justice, that notwithstanding the "real personal unselfishness" which underlay the ethic of public service on the part of the successful, the philosophy was at root a justification for a system which distributed substantially unequal rewards. There was a "larger selfishness" which idealized or rationalized the principle of "distribution according to worth, effort, and intelligence" under which these "unselfish" people won the biggest stakes.[10]

Indeed, one could regard the formula of competitive success *cum* public service as an unconscious sop to conscience, grounded in the evident *inequalities* of opportunity which discriminatory practice of all kinds builds into any society—only Marx and his followers could believe that genuine classlessness is possible. Allison Davis has made the point tellingly, on the strength of his own empirical studies of the socialization process in the United States.

As the middle-class child grows older, the effective rewards in maintaining learning are increasingly those of status; they are associated with the prestige of middle- or upper-class rank and culture. The class goals in education, occupation, and status are made to appear real, valuable, and certain to him because he actually begins to experience in his school, clique, and family life some of the prestige responses. The lower-class child, however, *learns* by *not* being rewarded in these prestige relationships that the middle-class goals and gains are neither likely nor desirable for one in his position.[11]

This expectation of failure, which is institutionalized in the treatment of disfavored groups, builds up in the individual what Erikson refers to as "negative identity." If he is *not* expected to become anything of consequence, the identity which he builds for himself is based on that very absence of expectation. "If such 'negative identities' are accepted as a youth's 'natural' and final identity by teachers, judges, and psychiatrists, he not infrequently invests his pride as well as his need for total orientation in becoming exactly what the careless community expects him to become." [12]

With increasing recognition of the prevalence of inequalities of opportunity which get built into a society's system there has come a movement not to scrap the principle of distribution on the basis of competitive achievement, but to purify the system by removing as many of the inequalities as possible. The civil rights movement is an obvious manifestation of this effort, but a longer-standing tendency has been to rely increasingly on the general availability of educational opportunity as the great leveling device. This is unquestionably due in large part to the widespread belief that the future achievers will be highly trained specialists; the school leavers or dropouts are doomed to failure. Numbers of studies have stressed the correlation between education and achievement. The belief is prevalent not only in Western societies but virtually worldwide—in the socialist countries of eastern Europe, in industrialized Japan, in the underdeveloped nations. With education the chief determinant of success or failure, a society that believes in equal opportunity must give everyone the fullest possible chance at as much quality learning as he can absorb.

This contemporary notion of a "meritocracy"—a fluid intellectual aristocracy—has won widespread support, but it has also generated a growing antagonism. Intelligence and motivation are not equally distributed; simple availability of educational opportunity does not mean that all are in an equal position to take advantage of it. The benefits of social class and family environment cannot be removed simply by opening school doors. Mosca years ago made the point.

Qualification for important office—the habit of, and to an extent the capacity for, dealing with affairs of consequence—is much more readily acquired when one has had a certain familiarity with them from childhood. Even when academic degrees, scientific training, special aptitudes as tested by examinations and competitions, open the way to public office, there is no eliminating that special advantage in favor of certain individuals which the French call the advantage of *positions déjà prises*. In actual fact, though examinations and competitions may theoretically be open to all, the majority never had the resources for meeting the expenses of long preparation, and many others are without the connections and kinships that set an individual promptly on the right road, enabling him to avoid the gropings and blunders that are inevitable when one enters an unfamiliar environment without any guidance or support.[13]

The result may in fact be just the opposite of that which equal opportunity for competitive achievement calls for. Education can be made the screen through which are sifted all those who are to be allowed into the positions of privilege, to whom are distributed a disproportionate slice of the social advantage. As the numbers of secondary school graduates increase, the college degree becomes more important if the sifting process is to work. As college graduates multiply, advanced degrees become the prerequisite to preferred positions. Equal opportunity is formally maintained, but those who are disadvantaged at the starting line, who tend to be from the disfavored classes and groups, are screened out "without prejudice."

Ivar Berg has shown by empirical investigation how commonly business firms in the United States have established exaggerated educational requirements for many jobs. They thus create a screen through which they can sift out "undesirable" types.[14] A number of firms, at the height of the civil rights agitation of the 1960s, discovered that minority group members, especially blacks, were being systematically eliminated at the personnel office by types of tests which bore little relation to their employment. My own inquiries have led me to believe that if the present emphasis on formal education degrees as a condition of admission to certain types of jobs continues, especially in the managerial ranks, there is a danger that the United States could create a two-class society, one of college degree holders, the other of non-degree holders.[15]

Some have seen in the principle of competitive achievement a method by which the dominants of society can co-opt the ablest members of non-dominant families. It has been said that the building up of ladders for the ablest of society's suppressed groups to climb is simply a way of siphoning off their leadership, in support of existing values and institutions. Carlos Astiz has described how the Peruvian upper class was for long enabled to co-opt a rising middle class "of limited usefulness, with an indefinite role in the type of society which still exists in the country" by finding jobs for them in the government bureaucracy, some large business firms, and banks. There was a limit, however, to the number who could thus be absorbed. "The limit has been maintained in part, at least until recently, by a deficient educational system: most secondary schools are privately owned and quite expensive, and the few universities have complex admission requirements and practically no scholarships." [16] Once again education serves as a screen by means of which the apportionment of the social advantage is regulated and controlled.

Raymond Williams, in commenting on T. S. Eliot's conception of an "organic society," notes that to limit "the transmission of culture to a system of formal education is to limit a whole way of life to certain specialisms." He then adds:

What will happen in practice, of course, when the programme is combined with a doctrine of opportunity (as it now largely is) is the setting-up of a new kind of stratified society, and the creation of new kinds of separation. Orthodoxy, in this matter, is now so general and so confident that it is even difficult to communicate one's meaning when one says that a stratified society, based on merit, is as objectionable in every human term as a stratified society based on money or on birth . . . . It has even (because of the illusion that its criteria are more absolute than those of birth or money, and cannot be appealed against in the same way) a kind of Utopian sanction, which makes criticism difficult or impossible.[17]

Education as the institutionalized avenue of personal privilege implies a particular distributional value, opposed to "solidarity" or egalitarianism.[18] The radical apostate Ivan Illich has argued that the linking of status to educational attainment is simply an instrument for making the disadvantaged accept their lot on the premise that that is all they "deserve." "Individual citizens of all countries achieve a symbolic mobility through a class system that makes each man accept the place he believes he merits." [19] But even with free public education the poor can never afford the years of education that are a minor expense to the wealthy, because of the hardships of forgoing earnings during the years of learning. Moreover, the system places a premium on conforming to a graded curriculum whose content is controlled by those with the greater influence.

The distributive principle of competitive achievement, even when coupled with the general notion of equal opportunity, extended to the accessibility of educational opportunity, does no more than distribute the social advantage according to a principle which is inherently arbitrary. Its chief ethical justification lies in cutting a larger number into a privileged sharing of the social advantage, while maintaining *some* tie to personal responsibility for individual achievement—a tie which is questionable in fact but without some element of which any society would be lost.

The economist Edward F. Denison has pointed out that to spend community resources on those children who show greatest intellectual capability simply reinforces inherent inequalities. "Presumably we must take differences in natural ability as given, but no law of nature requires us to provide the most and best education to those already blessed with the greatest natural ability, and thus accentuate their initial advantage. If individuals *at all ability levels* benefited from equal expenditures for this purpose, the criterion of equality of opportunity might be regarded as met." [20]

Another difficulty with full acceptance of the self-reliance principle has been pointed out by Frank Knight. A system of distribution which is based on the contribution of the individual does not provide any very ethical foundation for the share of society's advantages which is accorded his dependents.[21] Unless we ignore their individuality and make them only an insubstantial reflection of the "head" of the household, presumably they have some claim to a share which is independent of his. To put the matter in the moralistic tenor of the self-reliance school, why should the overworked and harassed wife and her multiple children be denied some portion of society's good things simply because her husband is a drunkard and an idler? Or for that matter, because he is a person of limited mental or physical ability?

Political Decision

In part because societies have been unwilling to follow so harsh a policy, in part also because of different conceptions of society and the individual's relation to it, there is a third principle of distribution—by political decision. Revenues, political positions, and honors which are in the possession of the government are bestowed on others without necessary relation to their ancestry or their personal capabilities. The basis for such distribution may be the service which the beneficiaries have rendered to the dominants; political patronage is an ancient phenomenon. It may also be based on need.

In Camus's symbolic story, *The Fall,* the narrator, in prison, has just been elected by his fellow cell-mates as their "pope," a designation which carries an implication of equal regard for all. Nevertheless, he endeavors to obtain special advantages for his own constituency, those who have made him pope, particularly in the critical matter of the water allotment. Even within his own little group he finds that he cannot "maintain complete equality." He gives an advantage to this one or that, according to their condition or the work they are required to do. Like any dominant authority in real life, he bestows favors. Like any modern government, he redistributes income.

Indeed, with the spread of popular, representative governments, the pressures have been strong for redistribution of income from the wealthy to the less wealthy, and for the democratization of honors and prizes. Egalitarianism takes on a different meaning from that which the middle class supplied it, equal opportunity for achievement, and moves in the direction of equal condition. The argument is raised that equality of opportunity can in fact only be achieved when there is greater equality of condition. The equalizer is not only public education, it becomes income itself. Once the graduated income tax has implanted the principle of levying more heavily on the wealthy in support of public programs, which is to say to benefit the poor, there is no logical stopping point: the negative income tax is a perfectly rational extension of the principle, to supplement the incomes of the less privileged directly, and not only indirectly through government activities toward which they make little contribution but over which they have limited control. In the presence of popular governments, the principle of distribution by political decision, especially of equalization of advantage through the coercive authority of government, picks up a larger following.

We thus observe at least three major principles of distribution of the social advantage which may be called into play—the principle of birth, the principle of competitive achievement, and the principle of political decision. We may be sure that the distributive principle which the thrusters newly become dominants will favor is that which most favors them. But all three principles may conceivably be invoked to their benefit. If they cannot profit from the birth factor of ancient lineage, they may take advantage of the birth factor of their pseudo-species (as the WASPS in New England, as the Nordics in Nazi Germany). They can define achievement in terms of their own values and interests, so that rewards for achievement bolster their own position. The political decision can be used to buy support or silence opposition. Those who are unimportant to them and to their allies, or who are in conflict with them, can gradually be squeezed as to their share of the social advantage.

To the extent that popular representation has been spreading, in one form or another, as the most common form of government, one would expect that the dominants would be driven by the masses to political decisions favoring more and more equality in the distribution of the social advantage, in all its forms, economic, political, and social, and thus to their own disadvantage. There is some element of truth in this, but the picture is muddy.

It may be helpful to refer to the influential work of Professor T. H. Marshall to put the matter in perspective.[22] He believed that in the West generally, the last two centuries or so have seen an increasing equalization of advantage, which he viewed as a spread of citizenship rights, progressively, to additional sectors of social life. The eighteenth century saw the increasing equalization of the legal rights of citizens. (I would view this as the influence of the Enlightenment on the dominants—in England, to accommodate dissent; in France, first as the value of the thrusters who made the Revolution and then of Napoleon, who took it over, in each case with the hope that it would be a socially stabilizing value.)

The nineteenth century, according to Marshall, brought political equality, particularly as embodied in popular suffrage. (I would interpret this as the value of the rising industrial thruster group, with working-class allies, who sought changes in government policy to support their activities.) Then, in the twentieth century, came what Marshall terms the social rights, including the minimum wage, accident compensation, unemployment benefits, old age pensions, health benefits. (I would interpret this as the accommodation, by the industrial dominants, of the lower-middle and working classes to ensure their continued adhesion to the social order.)

If one looks at the matter in this light, then what we observe is not the continuous retreat of some privileged group before popular pressure, but a sequence of movements conceptually distinct even if not historically discrete. We see the retreat of a privileged landed aristocracy, the rise of a new thruster entrepreneurial class (the capitalists of Marx's strictures), their displacement in turn by a new thruster group who built larger and larger organizations on the basis of less and less ownership, and their accommodation of a mass electorate without significant loss of control. "Equalization" has taken place, but not as part of a single movement, not as the step-by-step backward movement of "the" upper class. It has been in part a consequence of attempted accommodation at different times by different dominants, in part the strategy of the thrust, again at different times by different groups.

The consequence of these several movements is to have created a large middle class with substantial stakes in the present distribution of the social advantage. Can equalization go farther, under popular pressure, without involving some redistribution *away* from the recent gainers, the lower-middle and working classes, *toward* others disproportionately disadvantaged and usually also disfavored, such as the blacks and the Spanish Americans in the United States, religious minorities in India and North Ireland, tribal minorities in some African countries, *some* demeaned and therefore disadvantaged group in *every* society? *Continued* equalization in the distribution of the social advantage is not likely to meet with general or majority favor. It would thus appear that past some point, where a majority of the population obtains a sufficient stake in the established order to feel aligned with it, the egalitarian principle is likely to run out of steam. The popular majority, instead of pressing for further redistribution, is likely to put on the brakes.

Brian Moore has painted a picture for Northern Ireland which could apply, varying the circumstances, to many other countries. A small number of Protestant elite, wealthy landowners and corporation board members, appropriate a disproportionate share of the limited fruits of the economy. Beneath them the battle rages between the Protestant poor and Catholic poor, the former desperately holding on to what little economic advantage their religious majority affords them, the latter bitterly pressing for some further share in the national pittance. The resident Catholic hierarchy encourages the militant faithful, but shies away from any drastic change which might threaten its own privileged position among the disadvantaged minority.[23]

The Ethical Issue

We have been dealing with something which I have termed the distributive value. It may seem strange to consider a person's or a group's demand for "more," or their holding on to a little more than others are clamoring for, a form of value. And of course it is not solely that by any means. Under the ineluctable scarcity condition, more for some means less for others, a straight pursuit of personal interests.

But beyond the satisfaction of one's survival needs, there *is* always the ethical question of whether more for me is "right" at the price of someone else's survival, or if not just survival, his welfare in some rather fundamental sense. The more we advance beyond subsistence, even considering the elastic nature of that concept, the harder it is to avoid justifying our "take" relative to that of others, of making a case for our satisfaction at the expense of the more needy or of some common (public) need.

Moreover, this sense of the need for ethical justification cuts two ways. As more individuals, groups, even whole societies secure advantages which loom large relative to the possessions of others, those who are the disadvantaged develop expectations which, while of course deriving in the first instance simply from personal interests, acquire an ethical backing which the wealthier have in effect handed them.

Unless one chooses not to justify his advantage on any other ground than that he has somehow obtained "title" to it, under a system which has conferred or recognized (has in fact *made*) that "title," he is driven to question the moral grounds for his share in the social advantage and to try to derive some principle which justifies to him and to others why his share is disproportionate—by much or by little—to that of others.

This ethical issue of course extends to the political decisions of governments which have a distributive impact. Since, in the view presented here, governments, while not wholly, are largely, reflective of dominant interests, they presumably reflect—not wholly, but largely—dominant values. At times the focal values of the dominants come in conflict with the distributive values of other groups within the society. Is the space program of the United States, so valued by its industrial and scientific establishment, "justified" in the light of the distributive needs of more "equal" housing conditions? Is the British government, still with aristocratic leanings, warranted in allocating $4 million worth of public funds to purchase a Titian that would otherwise leave the country, in the light of the social welfare needs of the submerged part of its population? The answer to those questions may be easy for the partisan, but on any objective (nonallied) basis there is no clear-cut answer.

Notes

1. For example, Mosca, *The Ruling Class*, p. 429.

2. Guttsman, *The British Political Elite*, p. 66.

3. It is on this ground that I find unsatisfactory Tocqueville's view that the condition of egalitarianism is satisfied by an absence of inherited position, and can be satisfied even under despotic governments. Any system which stresses social order, as a despotism would have to do, necessarily gives rise to positions of power and prestige which set some above others. The fact that such positions may not be inherited does not lessen the inequality to which the positions themselves—not the people who occupy them—give rise.

4. An interesting American expression of this view, in support of the Southern pre-Civil War social system, is contained in Wilson, *In Quest of Community*, p. 25.

5. Tocqueville, *Democracy in America*, Vol. 1, p. 262.

6. *Ibid.*

7. Norton E. Long, "Political Science and the City," in *Urban Research and Policy Planning*, ed. Leo Schnore and Henry Fagin (Beverly Hills, Calif.: Sage Publications, 1967), p. 254.

8. Moore, *The Social Origins of Dictatorship and Democracy*, pp. 337–338. Owen M. Lynch provides a good recent treatment on the subject of caste in India in *The Politics of Untouchability* (New York: Columbia University Press, 1969).

9. Allison Davis, "American Status Systems and the Socialization of the Child," *American Sociological Review* 6 (1941): 345–354.

10. Williams, *Culture and Society, 1780–1950*, p. 329.

11. Davis, "American Status Systems and the Socialization of the Child," p. 353.

12. Erikson, *Identity: Youth and Crisis*, p. 88.

13. Mosca, *The Ruling Class*, p. 61.

14. Ivar Berg, *Education and Jobs: The Great Training Robbery* (New York: Frederick A. Praeger, 1970).

15. Neil W. Chamberlain, "Manpower Planning," in *Frontiers of Collective Bargaining*, ed. John T. Dunlop and Chamberlain (New York: Harper & Row, 1967).

16. Carlos Astiz, *Pressure Groups and Power Elites in Peruvian Politics* (Ithaca, N.Y.: Cornell University Press, 1969), pp. 67–68.

17. Williams, *Culture and Society, 1780–1950*, p. 240.

18. *Ibid.*, pp. 328–332.

19. Ivan Illich, "The False Ideology of Schooling," *Saturday Review*, 17 October 1970, p. 68.

20. Edward F. Denison, "An Aspect of Unequal Opportunity," *The Brookings Bulletin* 8, no. 1 (1971): 7–8. Italics mine.

21. Frank H. Knight, "The Determination of Just Wages," in *Twentieth Century Economic Thought,* ed. Glenn Hoover (New York: Philosophical Library, 1950), p. 509.

22. T. H. Marshall, *Citizenship and Social Class* (New York: Cambridge University Press, 1953).

23. Brian Moore, "Bloody Ulster: An Irishman's Lament," *Atlantic Monthly,* September 1970, pp. 58–60.

7 / The Implicit Bargain

In the course of our investigation thus far, we have encountered multiple and diverse groups which jointly compose a society, each with its own particularistic value system built up over the years and incorporating focal, constitutional, and distributive values. We conceive of one or more of these groups responding to a change in the objective conditions confronting a society, with at times such thrusters rising to a position of dominance. They seek alliances and draw followers; they influence the adaptable and are accepted or ignored by the unconcerned. Gradually their values, like their influence, spread and become identified with society's values and interests. The extent to which a clear-cut definition of social values emerges is due to a number of factors, among which the most important are likely to be the degree of unity existing among members of the dominant class, the readiness of acceptance by others of the leadership of the new dominants due to the pressure of objective conditions (especially as these involve some crisis), and the extent to which the constitutional values of the dominants lean toward coercive use of authority to establish order.

But the clarity of social values is likely to be affected most of all by the necessity for the accommodation within the society of other groups, with their particularistic values. The specialized component groups of a society do not simply abandon their values in the face of dominant pressures: their values are, rather, *influenced* by the dominants, modified to reflect a greater congruence with those values which are becoming more and more recognized as central or common to the society. But the dominants, too, modify their values to make them more acceptable to those groups which are functionally of most importance in the successful running of society. A mutual accommodation takes place, but one which is oriented around the values of the successful thrusters.

The pattern of accommodation changes over time. Since there is almost always a lag of old values into the present, the thrusters who have newly acquired their position operate within a somewhat confused value framework. There are some exceptions to this. A revolutionary movement may mark a sharp break with the past, as in Russia. Or the physical separation of the thrusters from the former dominants, as the American mercantile interests were separated from the English landed aristocracy, may facilitate the growth of new values free of contamination by the old—though in that instance a hangover royalist component did create some muddiness.

Aside from this persistence of old values, the new but fledgling dominants are likely to be somewhat timid at first, insinuating themselves rather than asserting, making their usefulness felt more than their aggressiveness. This can be seen in Chekhov's superb example of a member of the rising entrepreneurial class in nineteenth-century Russia, Lopakhin of *The Cherry Orchard,* undermining the old landed aristocracy, exulting that he has bought "a property that hasn't its equal for beauty anywhere in the whole world," which he now plans to raze for a real estate development scheme. "I have bought the property where my father and grandfather were slaves, where they weren't even allowed into the kitchen."

Opportunism and even a certain craftiness may mark the early stages of the rising class. The early English industrial capitalists were thrusters as against the landholding nobility. In building their political position, they made use of worker agitation for political reform—an agitation in part stimulated by the very nature of the market system which the industrialists were busily creating. As political reform occurred, giving greater influence to the thrusting industrialists, they used that influence to strengthen their position not only against the aristocracy but also against the working class. Their value system became clearer and more pervasive, as so effectively portrayed by Galsworthy's Forsyte clan. But the increasing clarity of that value system, even granting the chiaroscuro effect of lagged values, creates its own opposition—in this case, organizations of labor, which require their accommodation through legal forms of recognition. Unions win the right to bargain collectively with corporate managements. Concomitantly with the spread and dominance of middle-class ("bourgeois") individualistic values goes the rise of the collectivist values of labor unionism, less pervasive, more particularistic, but with a modifying influence on the values of the industrial age. And both of these are set against a background of a continuing but declining value scheme of the old aristocracy, toward which both industrialist and workingman alike feel a peculiar nostalgia as long as it does not threaten their positions but adds a little romantic color to an otherwise drab scene.

The point which I should like to emphasize is that in this process it is not any overt bargaining (as between management and labor) in particular negotiations here and there, from time to time, which is the essence of the accommodation between dominants and other groups. It is an *implicit* bargaining with respect to the overall definition of social values and interests which is of the most vital significance. It is a series of loose negotiations between representatives of the chief interest groups affected, which may or may not occur on a face-to-face basis, but which result in a general understanding as to how the particularistic values of the lesser interests will be viewed by the dominants in return for the formers' acceptance of the essence of the dominants' positions. The "negotiations" may occur in the form of public statements of position, addressed to one's own constituency or supporters, perhaps even belligerent in tone, declaring what is demanded and hinting what may be conceded. It may occur in the form of legislative debate, or editorial comment by partisan newspapers or journals. It may come through personal conversations between highly placed representatives of the groups involved.

The Implicit Bargain and Dominant Interests

The outcome of such bargaining depends on the relative bargaining power of the groups involved, which in turn is a product of their aspirations (how strongly do they hold certain values and interests?) and the alternatives which are open to them (what if they do not make the concession which is being sought?). At one extreme, the dominants' values and interests may be clearly defined, and they can presumptuously ignore the accommodation which another group is seeking, either because that group is unimportant to them or because it has no alternative but to make peace on the dominants' terms. At the other extreme, the dominants are a loose alliance with partially conflicting values and interests, and they cannot afford to offend some group which is in a position to mobilize a potent opposition. Concessions will be made, and the resulting compromise will muddy all the more a system of values which was cloudy to begin with.

Generally speaking, the consequence of implicit bargaining is likely to be, over time, some lessening of the strength of dominant values and some supplementation with the values of other groups. Thus the effect of the implicit bargaining which has gone on in the United States between dominant business and subordinate labor, in the years since the founding of the American Federation of Labor in 1886, has been to substitute, in some degree, worker values (security and industrial civil rights) for business values (competitive rewards, pecuniary maximization). The value system gets a bit more confused as such implicit bargaining continues, but as long as the dominants remain so, it continues to reflect primarily their positions.

In his analysis of the ruling class, Mosca arrived at a conclusion which is highly relevant to this phase of our examination. As phrased by his English translator, Arthur Livingston: "The internal stability of a regime can be measured by the ratio between the number and strength of the social forces that it controls or conciliates, in a word, represents, and the number and strength of the social forces that it fails to represent and has against it." [1] The more comprehensive the implicit bargain, the more do the emerging values and interests become identified with the national values and interests, even though principally reflective of the values and interests of the dominants.

There is no implication here that every group in a society should ideally be included in the implicit bargain. We should not lose sight of those whom we have dubbed the unconcerned, who in some societies may constitute the largest proportion of the population. They are likely to be poorly or locally organized, without leadership, with little alternative but to accept the conditions which are imposed on them. We can recall that low status itself induces withdrawal from participation, one reason we can call these people the unconcerned. In underdeveloped countries where the mass is poverty-stricken, ignorant, submissive, and coerced, the implicit bargain can ignore their existence. In the United States prior to World War II the black population could be treated as virtually nonexistent in the implicit bargaining process: their aspirations had been checked for generations, and their alternatives were so insignificant they could scarcely be conceived. Why indeed should they be concerned about who ran a society which was unaware of their existence because it could afford to be?

At the same time, however great their coercive authority, the dominants cannot afford to make demands, even on those normally unconcerned, that are so repugnant to their particularistic values that they are inflamed into opposition. The Communist countries have experienced this reaction in their attempted collectivization of farms.

In countries which are in a state of unrest, where thruster groups are experimenting opportunistically in the face of changed objective conditions, and existing elites are seeking new alignments which will leave their position largely undisturbed, the implicit bargain may become an accommodation among several classes of interests, the actual dominance of any one of which is in question, and the homogeneity of whose values and interests is doubtful. Latin America offers a number of examples of this state of affairs.

Professor Moises Gonzalez Navarro, former president of the Mexican Historical Society, has provided his own interpretation of shifts in the implicit bargaining in that country over the last half-century. The thrust of the Mexican Revolution, presumably that of the exploited working class, especially its rural segment, was blunted by a conciliatory counterthrust from the rising middle class, especially its financial community. "The reconciliation between working class and middle class followed the pattern of

Porfirio Díaz's compromise with the conservatives and clergy: the government maintained the façade of a peasants' and workers' revolution, whereas the country's economic development confirmed the capitalist nature of the Mexican Revolution."

In a "series of mutual concessions," the financial interests were given a relatively free hand in the private sector and the Revolutionary Party inherited the political bureaucracy—except that by that time the latter had developed its own elite leadership whose growing economic and political advantages were supplemented by admission to the social circles of the traditional upper class. "Revolutionary phraseology continued to include workers' and peasants' slogans, but in practice the lion's share of the national income went to the capitalist pressure groups, even though at the same time state intervention in the economy increased considerably."

Small landholders improved their position, chiefly through government-financed irrigation projects, but large numbers of those without land or on unirrigated plots suffered. "In other words, the selfsame people who made the agrarian revolution, or their descendants, have little but poverty for their reward now that the revolution has passed into the industrial stage because it has been channelled through the capitalist system." [2] The implicit bargain represents a working relationship between two powerful groups which share dominance between them and make their accommodation with such others—for example, the labor unions—as are politically or functionally significant.

Robert E. Scott has sought to describe, in general terms which cannot apply in detail to all countries, the situation of political and interest-group fragmentation in Latin America which has prevented the rise of any cohesive industrializing thruster group. Instead, the traditionally dominant trio of large landholders, the military, and the church—still in an uneasy alliance, despite fermentation within each and differences of interest among themselves—manage to maintain a weak implicit bargain which limits how much initiative for change the central government can undertake. The best the traditional dominants can do is "to limit the speed and extent of advance in the political process by the challenging elites by setting up informal boundaries within which the government (usually personified by the president) may act quite independently but beyond which it steps only with great risk." [3] In some countries, such as Brazil and Argentina, the military has moved to assert its priority position. In others, such as Chile, a populist thrust from below has been undertaken. The situation throughout the continent is highly unstable. The implicit bargains shift but, in the absence of a cohesive thruster group, with its own clearly defined value system, or of a stable dominant group (since it is dependent on a shaky alliance), the situation remains one of unrealized opportunities in the face of changing objective conditions.

The Latin American experience should not lead us to substitute a theory of overt conspiracy among elite groups for the concept of an implicit bargain which I have been developing here. The dominants—if they do exist in a society, if indeed there is some identifiable dominant group or alliance instead of a condition of transition or instability—are simply the people who work together to make the society function in the way they believe it should, and who are able to impress their views on others by a variety of devices we have already considered. Behind them are bureaucracies to support their decisions. The dominants are not always in agreement among themselves, which may result in policy differences and a certain amount of infighting without necessarily affecting their privileged position.

At times government policies may actually run counter to dominant interests. This may happen for a variety of reasons, especially one which we shall explore shortly. Most basically the concept of the implicit bargain does not imply that the dominants always get their way, but that they are able to establish *more* of a kind of a social system which they prefer than any of the lesser groups can do, for the reason that their position in the implicit bargaining process is normally stronger than that of other interest groups: they feel more keenly the importance of making good their own value and interest objectives and believe more fervently that national interests are encompassed in the process, and their alternatives to the accommodation of any particular dissident group are more self-satisfying than the alternatives which the dissidents can contrive. On particular issues of greater sensitivity to a subdominant group, it may force accommodation on its terms. But that does not affect the overall position of the dominants as long as they are able to make good on what is most important to them. *Centralization* of purpose and of norms of conduct and methods of integration (that is, of values) is necessary if *system* objectives are to be won. If the dominants have managed to identify themselves with the system, this can only mean that the major system objectives will reflect their values. If the dominants are weak, system objectives become diffuse. The strength or weakness of the dominants, the primacy of their values within the society, is reflected in the unwritten terms of the implicit bargain which is worked out with the other groups whose influence, while secondary, still counts.

Pluralism and Discretion

The implicit bargain obviously cannot encompass all the relationships of a complex society (all of John R. Commons' "transactions," the whole of Clark Kerr's "web of rules"). It addresses itself only to a broad definition of how far different and even incongruent values will be allowed to coexist alongside values of style and national purpose, behavioral patterns and accepted uses of coercive authority which are recognized as primary. It constitutes a process by which, in the face of the following which thrusters-become-dominants have been able to build up, other groups with their particularistic value schemes learn, by trial and error, by probe and parry, how far they can carry nonconforming behavior before inviting repressive actions. As such groups, over time, learn to accommodate themselves to values and interests which gain generality of acceptance, they are likely themselves to undergo subtle internal shifts in their own values and interests which lessen the degree of divergence or incongruence with those of the dominants, so that the implicit bargain gains stability.

But whatever degree of divergent values and interests is tolerated by the implicit bargain, and whatever values (or actions reflecting values) are not even covered by the implicit bargain, leave room in the hands of subordinate interest groups for discretionary behavior. Since the implicit bargain can only extend to major system interests, this is likely to leave a good deal of room for maneuver and independent action on the part of such groups. The "middle class" of the urban bourgeoisie, in its early stages, was effectively excluded from the implicit bargain which ran between church and state, or perhaps it would be nearer correct to say that it was intentionally ignored. Although its value scheme diverged from prevailing values, it was tolerated because of its beneficial activities, and for the time tolerance was all that it needed and wanted. But this very exclusion from the implicit bargain allowed it a degree of autonomy that nourished its growth and permitted it to turn into a thruster group at a later time.[4]

Moreover, to the extent that the dominants lean toward a constitutional value of autonomy of action (for their own benefit), they necessarily extend this value to other groups, even of a competing nature. The consequence is likely to be a situation which political scientists have defined as pluralistic —that is, the presence of numbers of groups all enjoying some freedom of discretion (autonomy), a kind of parceling out of the sovereignty of the state among the constituent interest groups. This obviously would lead to value diffuseness, interest competition, and a sense of an "open" society.

For example, although we characterize nineteenth-century United States as "materialistic," under the influence of a competitive-achievement ethic, reflecting the influence of the industrialist class, we also recognize that the century was filled with a great deal of religious and spiritualist ("revivalist") activity which was felt even within the moneyed community,[5] that at least in the first half of the century utopian movements were rife and transcendentalist (other-worldly) thinking widespread in the intellectual community.[6] Labor unions, though subject to legal and institutional inhibitions, were allowed to survive. Such varied and cross-purposed activity gives strong support for the idea of a prevalent pluralism. One respected authority has thus commented of the United States: "We do not want full agreement on values; on the contrary, we hope for a rather full representation of the wide variety of values held by various groups in our society." [7]

But this is a point of view which obviously goes much too far and draws an unwarranted inference. Who is the "we" who does not want "full agreement" on values and who hopes for "rather full representation" of the array of values admittedly present in a society? The implication is that it is "everyone," all standing on the same footing, all asserting value equality or value neutrality. But this is patent nonsense. There are some values which "we" do not want to see represented and which tend to get excluded —"we" have shown little tolerance for the values of a Communist or fascist order, for example, and the very assertion which is made implies a broad agreement on a constitutional value which *excludes* hierarchical ordering and coercive integration.

The simple cataloguing of the number of special-interest groups present in a society, as though their very presence meant that they all "weighed in" equally, is a gross error. The inclusion of the leadership of certain large groups, such as the labor unions, among the "elites" of a country, as though they were equals in status with other elites is similarly a mistake. A dominant class—let us say the business leadership in the United States —can afford to accommodate (may even *have* to accommodate) other interests without thereby putting them on a plane of equality. Managements have learned to cope with all sorts of influence groups in the process of maintaining their *primum* position. Obviously they would prefer not to have had to make some of the concessions which they have had to make; they would have preferred freer discretion if it were possible. Still such accommodations as they have made have, on the whole, been a small price to pay for the continuity of a system in which they remain largely free to conduct their operations according to their own values and interests. In the implicit bargaining which has taken place over the years, there has been little question, except in time of crisis, as to who was the dominant interest around whose values and interests society's own values, interests, and activities were oriented. Calvin Coolidge was making no mistake when he affirmed that "The business of America is business." A Secretary of Defense under President Eisenhower was not far wrong in fact, if erring in public relations, in equating the country's good with the welfare of General Motors, and vice versa. Pluralism there is, but it is not a pluralism of equals. The implicit bargain reflects the inequalities present in the system.

Over time the implicit bargain tends to become institutionalized within a society, a matter we shall explore more fully later, so that the influence of the dominants is intruded into a number of the presumably "autonomous" associations which compose the pluralistic society. As Alvin Gouldner has observed, business interests in the United States

. . . exercise power, including political power, though not by voting and not by getting elected to office. They do it in these ways: primarily through their control of great foundations, with their policy-shaping studies and conferences and their support for universities; through a variety of interlocking national associations, councils, and committees that act as legislative lobbies and as influences upon public opinion; through their membership among the trustees of great universities; through their influence on important newspapers, magazines, and television networks, by virtue of their advertising in them or their outright ownership of them, which, as Morris Janowitz once observed, sets "the limits within which public debate on controversial issues takes place"; through their extensive and disproportionate membership in the executive branch of the government, their financial contributions to political parties, their incumbency in major diplomatic posts; and through their control of the most important legal, public relations, and advertising firms.[8]

Gouldner's summing up does not impute actual control by business over the institutions with which it is identified; it indicates only the extent to which members of the business community have had their values accepted as expressive of society's values, so that their membership, participation, and support is widely welcomed. The dominance of their position is also reflected in the fact that even conflicting groups—conservationist associations, consumer groups, and labor unions, for example—have had their own behavior structured by the initiatives of the business leadership. There is of course pluralism in all this—the very recital of the number of institutions involved confirms that—but it is a pluralism which is far from the self-controlled movements of autonomous units; it is the pluralism of the component units of a social system whose basic values, including its style and overall purposes, are reflective of a class of interests which still dominates the outcome of the implicit bargain, whatever the future may bring.

This institutionalization of dominant influence comes about quite naturally and normally. There is no plot to take over or infiltrate other organizations. As we saw in the first chapter, each group tends to develop its own leadership, which acquires stakes in the perpetuation of that group within which it has acquired preferential advantages. In a society which has come to accept, pervasively, the influence of a certain class or group, the leadership of *other* groups becomes based on a pattern of relationships it has established with the dominants. Thus the security of position of the various and multiple elites *within their own interest groups* generally tends to be built around the continuity of the dominant class, relations with which have been so structured that they emphasize the contribution of the multiple leaderships *to that relationship*. To put the matter slightly differently, every institution must develop its own leadership, and at the point in its history when that institution has found its place within the implicit bargain, and thus won a stable social position, its leadership tends to be co-opted into maintaining the system of relationships which have brought it to the top.

This process is nicely demonstrated in the relationship which has developed between the American labor union leadership and the business community. The heads of American unions have grown up in institutions which stress a collective bargaining relationship with individual corporations or industries, resulting in contracts of fixed terms and fixed duration. This is a system which by now is entirely congenial to business interests. The latter have learned to accommodate the process without serious loss to their dominant role. Whether the labor movement can gain more for its members by this route of individual corporate bargaining, rather than by the political process, is open to considerable question. But that issue is never seriously debated among the unions, since such a change of direction would clearly require a profound change in the type of leadership the unions would require, geared to different tactics and objectives. That it would be less palatable to management goes without saying. Thus the present pattern of organizational accommodation involves the incumbent union leadership and its successors in support of the continued existence of that system—to their own benefit as well as to that of management.

The Role of the Professional Politician

In the implicit bargaining process, the representatives of the interests involved may act on behalf of themselves. This seems to be largely true of societies which are more hierarchically structured, so that a relatively small number of individuals need be involved in the process. In most

Communist societies, for example, the party manages whatever limited bargaining may be needed.

But at times there is a need for a broker or mediator between two or more groups seeking a *modus vivendi*. In primitive and classical societies such a function was sometimes performed by a religious authority, a public figure of high moral stature, or occasionally a military leader. Weber speaks of the rise of the "lawgiver" function in ancient times, performed by some notable usually on an occasion when social tensions were high. He gives as examples the conflict generated when a warrior class began to become internally differentiated into a wealthy, powerful clique, on the one hand, and a debtor class, on the other, or when a rising commercial class, having acquired wealth, sought to challenge the preferred position of the old warrior nobility. In the first case a clearly dominant class was seeking to distinguish itself from inferiors; in the second, a thruster group was seeking recognition. In both cases a lawgiver's function was to mediate the conflict and to produce "a new sacred law of eternal validity," a little more explicit, perhaps, than what has been called here an implicit bargain, and presumably with an expectation of a somewhat longer life, but performing the same function.[9]

With the growing complexity of societies and the increase in the number of interest groups which had to be accommodated, the process of negotiating an implicit bargain among the relevant groups began to fall more and more to a specialized set of functionaries, whom we can call the professional politicians. In earlier days this may not have been a full-time role: there have been cases, for example, where members of the dominant landed aristocracy, whose sentiments might nevertheless dispose them toward a larger role for the rising middle class, might perform the mediator or brokerage function. These were hardly full-time functionaries but they certainly represent the first stages of the emerging professional political role. In time, individuals—usually those who, with the rise of popular democracies, embarked upon political careers—came to devote themselves wholly to the function. We sometimes think of them as independent individuals seeking the support of the populace, but if we dig below the surface we see that soon enough the politician seeking election had to make his terms with those who represented the dominant influence, and at the same time had to sell himself to a large enough number of voters to secure his election. This placed him in the position of feeling out what sort of a compromise would satisfy his dominant backers and still represent equity to other major interest groups and to the adaptable public. For some professional politicians the support of a thruster group might be more important, if the dominants already had a preferred candidate, but the politicians' requirement remained not much different: a formula which would satisfy their principal supporters, appeal to other interest groups and an ill-defined "public-at-large," and at the same time not so affront the dominant class that the latter would use their admittedly greater influence to sink them by fair means or foul.

This professionalization of the implicit bargaining process obviously serves to water down the power of a dominant class, since the professional politician, while weighing the balance of power as precisely as is within his capacity, has to find a formula which will be acceptable to a large enough voting public to win its approval. The implicit bargain in a system of popular representation must thus accommodate an amorphous public. Nevertheless, the disadvantage to the dominants is not as great as may appear at first sight. In the first place, they have presumably managed—by procedures which we have already examined—to have identified their own values and interests with society's, reducing the cleavage between the general public and themselves. In the second place, the art of the professional politician is to find a formula which can be so interpreted to variant groups as to appear to favor their views as against others, without actually giving away very much. Thus the extension of suffrage to the general adult population in western Europe and North America did not lead to any steady succession of populist governments, as had been feared by some and hoped by others. T. H. Bottomore has concluded that what seems to have taken place in the democratic countries up to the present time has been not so much a reduction in the power of the upper class as a decline in the radicalism of the working class.[10]

Nevertheless, the role of the professional politician has injected a note of uncertainty into the implicit bargaining process. The dominants are suspicious of his pandering to the public. Since to them the status quo is generally preferable to change, any program of reform addressed to the "public" is undesirable as a matter of principle. Andrew Carnegie expressed it with perfect simplicity, "Oh these grand immutable all-wise laws of natural forces," he exclaimed, referring to the popular application of Darwinian theory to natural (social) selection, "how perfectly they would work if human legislators would only let them alone!" [11] At the same time, populist causes have forever complained of being "sold out," unwilling to recognize that their limited quota of votes has seldom meant the margin of victory. But despite such continued maledictions directed against the politician, he is the indispensable broker in large, complex, diverse-interest societies.

This is true even in relatively underdeveloped societies which are at the same time large, complex, and composed of diverse interests. Robert E.

Scott has reported that in Latin American countries, politics has increasingly become "the responsibility of full-time, professional politicians, more or less neutral brokers" who try to mediate the relationship among the traditional dominants and the more newly formed interest groups of financiers, industrialists, professionals, associations of farmers, industrial workers, government bureaucracies. These groups do not wholly withdraw from the political (bargaining) process, but they tend to rely much more heavily on the politicians for effecting compromises "within the rules of fair play established by the political system," [12] a system which, precisely because it has established rules, tends to work in favor of the dominant interests.

Until recently, indeed, whenever the results of a Latin American election seemed to go beyond the bounds of "the rules of fair play" as understood by the dominants, their allies, supporters, and those who have been comfortably accommodated by the system, military intervention reestablished the desired social order. With few exceptions, genuinely populist governments could not be established through election majorities because the simple counting of votes does not constitute the making of a bargain. The dominant groups refused to be bound by results which did not have their acceptance. Irving Louis Horowitz has analyzed this situation at some length, arguing persuasively that this use of the military "as a means of national redemption" has tended to be endorsed not only by the landed oligarchs and conservative business elements but also by the middle class. The latter, including a large bureaucracy, fear that any civilian regime would "naturally and inevitably" reflect the interests of the numerically superior popular classes. "An informal bargain is thus reached which exchanges political democratization for fundamental integration of society along middle-class lines." [13] In effect, failure of the professional politicians, operating within a system of popular representation, to produce an implicit bargain acceptable to the dominants and their followers, leads to a substitution of the military as the broker-mediator, which designs an implicit bargain among all the organized interests, but customarily without reference to the unorganized and often unconcerned masses. In the Chilean election of 1970, which brought victory to a populist party, the question which racked the country until Allende was finally sworn into office was whether the military would intervene. That it did not do so was viewed as a major step forward for popular representation in Latin America.

It is the mark of a good politician, then, to secure election results which reasonably reflect the power structure of the society, unless he is prepared to push forward with a revolutionary movement. Otherwise, the interests which are in fact dominant, but which see themselves locked out of an election result, are likely to refuse their cooperation, on which successful functioning of the social system depends. The consequence is likely to be that despite the relative voting strength of those pressing for social and institutional change, the government elected will bit by bit make its concessions to those who can make things work.

But this is not the sole possibility in a system of popular representation. There are two others.

The professional politician who can effect an implicit bargain satisfactory to the dominant class, its supporters, the accommodated and the adaptables—that is to say, the professional politician who can win an election and operate within a framework which continues at least minimally to satisfy these groups, comes into possession of a residual discretion of his own. To the extent that he has ideas and programs which do not disturb the values and interests which are represented in the implicit bargain and which largely reflect dominant values and interests, he is free to embark on new initiatives of his own. As Wolfgang Friedmann has suggested, such residual powers (or as he terms them, a "reserve function") are more likely to be recognized in time of crisis, economic or military.[14] Thus Franklin D. Roosevelt could have his New Deal, Harry Truman his Fair Deal, John F. Kennedy his New Frontier, and Lyndon Johnson his Great Society as long as they operated within the premises of the implicit bargain which limited their discretion. Roosevelt pressed against the limit more than once, most notably in his effort to "pack" the Supreme Court. Kennedy brought a new style of American life, but died before he could test the possibilities of employing it in new focal directions, other than in such modest ventures as the Peace Corps. Both Truman and Johnson almost recklessly exercised residual discretion going far beyond the implicit bargain, the former in taking the United States into the Korean War and the latter by more deeply involving the country in the war in Vietnam. Neither so much disturbed existing institutional relations as stirred up passionate reactions to crisis situations of their own making. Truman was successful in winning support for his initiative, while Johnson was repudiated. In all these cases, the professional politician fell heir to—or seized on—a residual discretion which elevated his position beyond that of being simply a broker-mediator between the interest groups of his society.

There is a second major exception to the proposition that the professional politician must recognize the power structure of his society and act as faithful broker-mediator in effecting a working compromise (implicit bargain) among its component groups. He may play the demagogic role.

With the rise of popular representative governments and the potential for aggregating the votes of the adaptable and the unconcerned through specific and alluring appeals, there may be among the professional politicians some who are not content with simply mediating between the influential groups, on the one hand, and the dispersed and amorphous masses on the other. Some may grasp the chance (seize the opportunity created by the changed conditions of political organization, as themselves a thruster group) to try to mold the masses into a more cohesive following, *implanting* ideas of focal, constitutional, and distributive values which are designed to appeal to the many, and by so doing put themselves in power.

Such individuals need not be the popular stereotype of the demagogue —a Robespierre or a Hitler, a Huey Long or a Juan Perón; although charismatic appeal is an obvious asset, good public relations, a sense of timing, and a certain ruthlessness will serve as substitutes. As the *New York Times* once commented editorially, "If a candidate can spend enough money, can hire the right ghostwriters and television advisers, and can control the format of his public appearances, then he can invent a winning public personality for himself." [15]

Mosca believed that the demagogic appeal would always be addressed to the poorest (and therefore largest) component of the population, in the form of a redistribution of wealth in their favor.[16] But this is by no means the only possibility: the appeal may be addressed to the right as well as the left. It would seem a reasonable hypothesis that, given popular government, where there is only a small middle class the demagogic appeal will be directed toward the distributive value of egalitarianism. Where there is a large middle class and a prosperous working class, the appeal is likely to be toward the constitutional value of security, which means law and order, and probably controls over minority pressure groups. In either case, there is also the unattractive possibility that the appeal will be founded on the pseudo-value of ethnicism, racism, or some other "species"-differentiating trait. Hitler provides the supreme example, but other less revolting instances of the same phenomenon come readily to hand. In Bombay, to take one at random, in 1966 a "rather unsuccessful cartoonist," Bal Thakare, formed a new political party, whose name literally translates as "the army of Sivaji" (the latter a popular seventeenth-century warrior from the state of Maharashtra in which Bombay is located). The booming city has attracted to it, from the north, Gujaratis, Parsis, and Sindhis who are now popularly said to control all the city's wealth. It has also induced a flow of cheap labor from the south of India. The mass of the Mahrattas (natives of Maharashtra), whether or not they are, as reported, "unskilled and somewhat unambitious," nevertheless feel squeezed between these two classes from outside their home state. The platform of Thakare's party is Bombay for the Mahrattas—turn out the intruders. Riots have been staged by its followers, with looting and burning of shops of southern Indians, and mass rallies staged, with reportedly some 50,000 millworkers massing under the party flags and roaring their approval.[17] Hope for gain through a redistribution of economic opportunity and pseudo-speciation here go hand in hand.

But why, in such instances, is it not always the case that the demagogue's lance, even if he should be elected, is shattered on the rock of non-cooperation from the dominants? If the latter simply sat on their hands and refused to accommodate the politician, who would run the society's institutions? Will not the demagogue, simply to salvage his position, be forced into a bargain acceptable to those who really control society's workings?

The demagogue's effort is likely to be successful, it seems to me, only when changes in objective conditions have lessened the public acceptance of a long-established dominant class. When the dominants are still in the flush of a mission and a vision, the chances for an upstart demagogue to carry off the day are slim indeed. But if a dominant class has begun to question its own values, to hesitate in the exercise of its coercive authority, to accommodate dissident groups more readily, the chances for a successful demagogic move are vastly improved, and the refusal of cooperation by the dominants much less probable. Their own alternatives have declined along with their aspirations. Their bargaining power has ebbed.

It seems to me that the pluralistic society of the political scientists' dreams, where no group exercises dominance or provides purpose for a society as a whole but all pursue their particularistic values, is made to order for the demagogue—unless there is some "consensus" of values which has somehow held over from the past and which somehow retains its common appeal even in the face of particularism. This latter condition strikes me as rare indeed. If values are diffuse, because they are expressive of special-interest groups, the professional politician has a freer hand to put together a coalition based on an appeal to the self-interest of a simple majority, perhaps coupled with a suggestion of an ethnic or racial pseudo-value to give it some semblance of unity of purpose.

I also suspect that the phenomenon of demagoguery has played a greater role in history than we are generally aware, though I venture this opinion hesitantly. If we include among the demagogues those whom Eric Hoffer has called the "true believers"—individuals who are not simply contriving a mass following for their own advantage but who arouse a mass following behind some purpose that burns within them—we readily realize that the demagogue did not appear on the scene only with the appearance of popular representation and extension of political suffrage.

Is it possible, for example, that the Reformation can be considered the work of demagogues—Luther in particular, but some of his successors as well? Consider the period in question. From the fourteenth through the sixteenth centuries, the values which had characterized western European society were slowly disintegrating. Religion had been the great cement, and it still played a significant role for the populace. But the dominants of the time—the church authorities and the nobility of city-states and rising nations—appear to have lost the sense of purpose or mission with which they were once invested. They made and unmade alliances opportunistically, for plunder and power. The theme of religion was seemingly coming to an end even within the church: the papacy was looked on as a sinecure meant to be exploited. The materialism of the period was of an almost oriental richness—sumptuary rather than productive. Self-indulgence seems to have motivated the mighty more than mission. The period bears all the marks of diffuseness and disorder. Yet this is also the high tide of the Renaissance. It is almost as though that great flowering was intended only as an adornment for the vainglorious. As the church's religious interests waned, its secular interests increased. It competed with the heads of other states through war and alliance. To finance the profligate spending of its heads and to carry on its secular affairs, it was forced to raise vast sums from the working of its lands and to expand and encourage the sale of indulgences.

This is the period in which the Church's arrogance, secularism, and hypocrisy led to Savanarola's reforming crusade—and his ultimate burning at the stake. Did not a demagogue go there, in the form of a true believer? This is also the period when Luther, out of a background of mental torture and uncertainty, emerged as the flaming sword of righteousness aimed at the heart of the weakened dominants of the church. Cannot one conceive of the Reformation as a mass movement in which Luther sought to win a popular constituency away from the church, in effect to give every man a vote in this still very important respect of religious faith (every man his own religious authority) and to induce every man to cast that vote for his, Luther's, cause? As the contest continued, pseudo-speciation became rampant. Crusaders against "papists" and "heretics," wherever these were in the minority, aided the cause of unity.

I do not intend to minimize the religious significance of the Reformation in suggesting this construction, but simply to raise the question whether demagoguery, historically, is more likely to assert itself at those periods when, in T. S. Eliot's words, "the center does not hold," which is to say when the values associated with an established dominant class no longer retain their appeal in the face of changed objective conditions, when a period of diffuseness or actual disorder, of dissentient and contentious if not actually thrusting groups marks the social scene.

If demagoguery is not successful more often under such conditions, it may be due to the fear on the part of the masses that, however little they possess, even that little may be lost in any political upheaval. As Robert E. Scott writes of Latin American countries, "The truth is that the masses are too fearful and suspicious of change to welcome the destructive tactics of such [radical] leaders. This is by no means a rare attitude in poor countries where the marginal population has learned to survive under present conditions but has no reserve to fall back on in case an experiment in political theory fails." [18] Thus middle-class conservatism may lead it to embrace demagogic causes of law and order, of political hierarchy and populist repression, but lower-class conservatism may lead it to reject demagogic causes of egalitarian reform.

Continuity, Consistency, and Change

Let us return briefly to the implicit bargain before concluding this chapter. The basic terms of the implicit bargain change slowly, for the simple reason that the power relations within a society change slowly. Its "understood" rather than written form, its informal rather than formal nature, permit a certain amount of change to occur through interpretation by the professional politicians who come to office, even from different party backgrounds, without upsetting the accommodation of interests. As Bagehot commented of the period 1832–1868 in England, when office oscillated between Liberals and Conservatives, England was governed alternatively by the left center and the right center. This was scarcely surprising in the light of the similar class composition of the two parties.

Following the British electoral reform of 1868, the Liberal Party broadened its composition and appeal, while the Conservatives maintained their upper-class character. "Yet each remained an amalgam of social forces," and the Conservatives depended on working-class votes for their victories. The gradual decline of the Liberals was paralleled by the rise of the Labour Party, but also by the latter's *embourgeoisement*. Over the years both cabinet ministers and members of Commons show a persistently declining number of the traditional aristocratic and landholding classes and a rising number of the "new classes"—entrepreneurial and professional types, financial people, and labor union officials, reflecting the rise of the new dominants and their allies.[19] But until the traumatic impact of World War II, political policy showed no erratic swings; the terms of the implicit bargain changed slowly to adjust to the new balance of power within the society.

The basic similarity between the conduct of the Democratic and Republican parties in the United States has often been noted—praised by some as reflecting America's consensual stability, by others as foreclosing genuine choice. Both views miss the mark. The two parties are reflective only of a basic stability in the power distribution of the United States over time, except for such crisis periods as the Civil War and the Great Depression.

Even in the case of what appear to be major legislative innovations modifying the power position of parties to the implicit bargain— regulatory legislation imposed on business, for example, or controls over the internal policies of labor unions—their subsequent application normally proves to be much less affecting than had been supposed either by friends or foes. A nice example of this is provided in the passage of the Interstate Commerce Act, the implications of which alarmed Charles E. Perkins, president of the Burlington Railroad. He spoke out against the law and was minded to attempt to secure its repeal until calmed by the advice of Richard Olney, a corporation lawyer who—ironically but fittingly —subsequently became Attorney General of the United States. Olney wrote:

The Commission, as its functions have now been limited by the Courts, is, or can be made of great use to the railroads. It satisfies the popular clamor for a government supervision of railroads, at the same time that the supervision is almost entirely nominal. Further, the older such a commission gets to be, the more inclined it will be found to be to take the business and railroad view of things. It thus becomes a sort of barrier between the railroad corporations and the people and a sort of protection against hasty and crude legislation hostile to railroad interests.[20]

The early application of the Sherman Anti-Trust Act ran a similar course, though the unexpected succession of Theodore Roosevelt to the presidency and his intent to build a popular reputation on government oversight of business behavior gave it new vitality. In the Northern Securities Company case, the government brought a successful suit to dissolve a railroad holding company involving the interests of such tycoons as J. P. Morgan, James J. Hill, and E. H. Harriman. "The incredulity with which this attack was received by Morgan is reflected in the story that he suggested that his lawyer and Roosevelt's attorney general, Philander C. Knox, get together and settle the problem." [21] The essence of the story, whether true or not, lies in Morgan's treatment of the government's action as a breach in the implicit bargain which it would surely want to rectify. In any event, the Supreme Court subsequently returned to its more normal practice of watering down the impact of legislation which appeared to affront the implicit bargain by enunciating the "rule of reason" in antitrust measures. The traditional respect for the principle of *stare decisis*—that precedents shall be followed unless a case can be clearly distinguished—contributes to this stability in the application and interpretation not only of the law but also of the implicit bargain.

Thus the political process, as Arthur Johnson has pointed out, not only is designed to permit the establishment of new principles affecting basic relationships within society—the labor legislation of the 1930s, for example—but also to provide an outlet for popular emotions and importunate pressures of interest groups, an outlet which, in the event, may be more change-absorbing than change-creating.[22]

Nevertheless, the terms of the implicit bargain do change over the years, in response to changes in objective conditions, which, even if they do not bring a new thruster group to the fore, do affect the relative bargaining positions of the principal parties involved. It is the business of the professional politician to get a "feel" of such changes in relative positions and to mediate the modification of terms which they may call for. Thus a rebargaining of basic relationships can be conceived as always in process, in the sense of a reexamination or testing of their adequacy but not necessarily in the sense of a change in their terms.

The potential for a change in terms differs among the three components of the value system. It is most difficult to effect a significant change in the focal values, since this goes to the root of the social identity of many of the members of a society. It is significantly less difficult to effect a change in the constitutional value, since, for one thing, the inexorable pressures of specialization, industrialization, and urbanization have accustomed populations to a growing need for planned integration and a receding role for autonomous behavior even within the span of a generation. It is least difficult to secure a change in the distributive value, at least in societies which have achieved a measure of affluence, up to some undefined point short of equality.

Notes

1. Introduction by Arthur Livingston to Mosca, *The Ruling Class*, p. xix.

2. Moises Gonzalez Navarro, "Mexico: the Lop-sided Revolution," in Veliz, *Obstacles to Change in Latin America*, pp. 226–228. Quoted with permission.

3. Robert E. Scott, "Political Elites and Political Modernization," in Lipset and Solari, *Elites in Latin America*, pp. 127–128. Quoted with permission.

4. Gouldner, in *The Coming Crisis of Western Sociology*, p. 62, goes so far as to say that "from the standpoint of the feudal order's system of social identities, the middle class did not exist."

5. Perry Miller has described this superbly in *The Life of the Mind in America* (New York: Harcourt Brace Jovanovich, 1965), especially pp. 89–90.

6. The literature on American utopianism is substantial; a good brief reference is Maren Lockwood's "The Experimental Utopia in America," *Daedalus*, Spring 1965, pp. 401–418. Wilson's *In Search of Community*, which has been cited several times in this study, contains an excellent first chapter dealing with the transcendentalists.

7. C. E. Lindblom, in a review article, "Tinbergen on Policy–Making," *Journal of Political Economy* 56 (December 1958): 534.

8. Gouldner, *The Coming Crisis in Western Sociology*, p. 300.

9. Weber, *Economy and Society*, Vol. 2, pp. 442–443.

10. T. H. Bottomore, *Elites and Society* (New York: Basic Books, 1964), p. 35.

11. Quoted by Nye, *This Almost Chosen People*, p. 132.

12. Scott, "Political Elites and Political Modernization," in Lipset and Solari, *Elites in Latin America*, pp. 118–119. Quoted with permission.

13. Horowitz, "The Military Elites," in Lipset and Solari, *Elites in Latin America*, especially pp. 149–153. Quoted with permission.

14. Wolfgang Friedmann, "Corporate Power, Government by Private Groups, and the Law," *Columbia Law Review* 57 (February 1957): 155–186.

15. "The New Corruption," *New York Times*, 13 January 1971.

16. ". . . Once everybody has acquired the right to vote, it is inevitable that a clique should detach itself from the middle classes and, in the race to reach the better posts, try to seek leverage in the instincts and appetites of the more populous classes, telling them that political equality means almost nothing unless it goes hand in hand with economic equality and that the former may very well serve as an instrument for obtaining the latter." Mosca, *The Ruling Class*, p. 392.

17. Moraes, "Bombay: Wealth, Shanty Towns, Speakeasies, Movie Aristocrats, Intellectual Admen and Death on the Trains," p. 150.

18. Scott, "Political Elites and Political Modernization," in Lipset and Solari, *Elites in Latin America*, p. 127. Quoted with permission.

19. Guttsman, *The British Political Elite*, pp. 88, 92–95. Guttsman com-

ments of the period immediately following 1868: "It was thought that any deliberate attempt on the part of groups of politicians, or their leaders, to change the party structure through an alignment of Whig and moderate Conservatives would cause a dangerous imbalance of political forces, and would lead to 'greater violence in party warfare and the loss of that tacit understanding between leaders of both sides which has more to do with the smooth working of our complex political system than superficial observers, who only see the outside of public affairs, imagine' " (citing Lord Kimberly's "Journal of events during the Gladstone Ministry" [1868]), in *Camden Miscellany* 21 (1958): 1.

20. From James M. Smith and Paul L. Murphy, eds., *Liberty and Justice, a Historical Record of American Constitutional Development* (New York: Alfred A. Knopf, 1958), pp. 292–293.

21. Arthur M. Johnson, "Continuity and Change in Government-Business Relations," in *Change and Continuity in Twentieth Century America,* ed. John Braeman, Robert Bremner, and Everett Walters (New York: Harper Colophon Books, 1964), p. 197.

22. *Ibid.,* p. 217.

8 / The Philosophical Validation

The implicit bargain relates to the focal values of a society (its style, broad purposes, grand design), to its constitutional values (the importance of political order as against individual and group autonomy, and the appropriate use of coercive force in bringing the latter into line with the former), and to its distributive values (the extent to which differential privileges are recognized and accepted as socially justifiable). As we know, the implicit bargain centers around the values of the dominants, however modified or less exclusionary these become in the bargaining process. To a considerable extent this identification of the terms which will satisfy the prevailing power structure is engineered by professional politicians, whose own position is dependent on their effective exercise of a mediating function.

But the results cannot be left in so logically and emotionally unsatisfactory a state. What citizenry would care to believe that they and their society were responsive to dominant class interests? As we also know, the security of a dominant's position—unless it is to rely on naked force, which cannot sustain it for long—lies in its establishing its values as those which are best for society, in converting its class values into social values.

This requires more than mere assertion, especially in view of the fact that values and interests can be so easily confused. Dominant values—far from seeming to serve society best—may seem to be more self-serving. If in addition other values and interests have had to be accommodated in the implicit bargaining process, it is all the more necessary to couch the underlying values in terms of high purpose and evident morality.

This is what I shall call the process of philosophical validation. It tends to reinforce the original or evolving values of the dominants but in such a way as not to affront those with whom it may have had to compromise or those on whose adaptability it seeks to capitalize. This means that the terms of the philosophical validation must be broad enough to remove them from the realm of class values and warrant their being regarded as an affirmation of national principles, as part of the philosophical premises on which most members of a society will base their own identities.

Realistically, then, the philosophical validation is simply the *post hoc* rationalization or justification for social arrangements which have been promoted by a successful thruster group in the face of changed objective conditions. From this perspective, individualism did not start as a value which influenced the shape of institutions but emerged as a philosophical justification for a movement which was already underway and which required a greater emphasis on the constitutional value of autonomy if it was to be successfully pursued.

Class values—one expression out of the array of values characterizing a society—even when raised to dominant status by the vigor of a thrusting group do not possess any evident force of reason or justice or revealed truth. If they are to maintain a hold on men's minds and secure the dominants in their position, they must be validated by nonpartisan approval. They must be put in a form which lends itself to discussion, elaboration, exegesis. This can only be accomplished by intellectuals, philosophers, theorists, idealogues who capture in persuasive and enduring prose, etched in terms of morality as well as logic, general theses which are congenial to the value position which is in process of being established.

Such thinkers need not necessarily even be living at the time their views are given prominence. Very often some name of a person long since dead will stand out like a beacon symbolizing a point of view or way of life, his precise message at best vaguely understood but generally approved by the present population, even though most of them may never have read his works. Mention of John Locke produces certain instinctive favorable reflections on individualism and limited government among literate people in the United States, whereas Karl Marx is the U.S.S.R.'s counterpart. In either society the "other" name would be received with adverse connotation.

But the philosophical validation is not the work of one man, however towering his contribution. It is something which builds up over the years into a respected and venerated literature—in religious, ethical, and philosophical statements, in fiction and poetry, in judicial decisions and statesmen's formulations, from which come epochal phrases and ringing slogans. There is no single holy document, no unique intellectual source. Even in the heyday of the church's authority there were numbers of nonpapal affirmations of faith emanating from Augustine and the Venerable Bede, Thomas Aquinas and Bernard of Clairvaux. The works may come from different times and places, possessing both historical sanction and contemporary appeal. But collectively they constitute a body of work which, in its generality, provides a philosophical authority for the values which are being dominantly expressed.

As a compendium of intellectual, rational affirmations of a philosophical faith, they tend to have the abstract quality of the logician, which adds to the generality of their expression and saves them from undermining the compromises of the implicit bargain. Dealing with issues of social relations at their most fundamental level, they are also likely to contain enough of the obscure and even internally inconsistent to leave room for variant interpretation—ironically enough, like a politician's professions.

John Locke is perhaps as perfect an example of the philosophical validator as one can find. For many years scholars have assumed that his *Two Treatises of Government,* from which derive many of the great statements on individual liberty, the rights of property, and the limited role of government, were written expressly to justify the English Revolution of 1688–1689. Recently Peter Laslett has explored the external evidence available and made a masterly examination of the internal evidence of the documents themselves, concluding that although indeed they performed that function they were not written for that reason, but had been put to paper some ten years or so earlier, misplaced or stored during the period of Locke's "exile" from London during the preceding regime, then recovered, slightly edited for the changed circumstances, and published as a single book post-Revolution. Laslett comments of it, "It was at once a response to a particular political situation and a statement of universal principle, made as such and still read as such." [1]

The element of ambiguity which allows people of differing persuasions to find what they want in the authoritative text also applies to Locke. In the matter of property rights, for example, man had a "natural" and inalienable property right in whatever he invested with his labor, as long as it was no more than he could put to use for himself: here lay the basis for every man's independence of another, the material foundation of his individuality. But then Locke goes on to recognize the rising commercialism and the existing concentrations of wealth by according each man the right to purchase the property which others have "naturally" acquired, thereby undermining the foundation he had laid for individualism. "He is perfectly willing to contemplate the continuous or permanent appropriation of the product of one man's labour by another, a servant's by a master." [2] In spite of this and other inconsistencies and ambiguities, there has been little doubt about the general thrust of Locke's position, and many a historian has asserted that no other single thinker had a more profound influence on the shaping of American political philosophy. Indeed, one could agree that the very ambiguity of his position on property comported well with American ambiguity as to equality of condition and equality of opportunity—the insistence on the latter as being the true egalitarianism, even though it inescapably led to highly differentiated status and income positions. Locke's propertied individualism, rooted in nature, provided the basis for equality of opportunity, while his acceptance of the voluntary alienation of the product of the "natural" and inalienable right provided the basis for inequality of condition.

Locke *started* with the free individual existing in nature and mingling his labor with natural resources, to which he thereby acquired title—and in the process independence. The chief function of government was to protect the property rights which the individual acquired. The idea was immensely appealing to a pioneer society on an "unpeopled" continent whose members seemed to be in the process of doing that very thing. The philosophical validation made general the class values of a thruster group which was, at the time, fastening its attention not on unsettled land to be had by the sweat of one's brow but on wealth to be acquired by trading, financial dealings, and to a lesser extent manufactures, though these were still in an infant state. As the thrusters became dominants, the Lockean doctrine of individualism and freedom from social or governmental restraints served them well, but, embedded in the great founding documents—the Declaration of Independence and the Constitution—as well as embroidered in the writings of the intellectuals of the day, it also created a national identity that transcended class interests.

But not quite a national identity. The process of philosophical validation is nicely illustrated by the contrast between the doctrines which were winning acceptance in the North as against those in the South, where under different objective conditions different interest groups had acquired dominant positions. In the South, the great plantations, based on slave labor, could scarcely be justified by Locke's notion of the natural right of every man to acquire property—and the basis for independence—by mingling his labor with the soil. In the early years of the Republic, indeed, down until the wracking compromises of the post-Monroe era, the South could join with the North in espousing a philosophy which justified their separation from the mother country and the assertion of their own independence. Even in the face of slavery they could profess the basic right of individual freedom, by the simple process of excluding the blacks from membership in the society whose rights were in question. The North was party to this evasion in the Constitutional compromise—the implicit bargain, in this case made explicit—by which the black was, for political purposes, equated to three-fifths of a white man. The national judiciary upheld the basic compromise as a matter of principle in the Dred Scott case, in which—because Locke had made private property the cornerstone of individualism—the court felt compelled to affirm the slave-owner's property right in his slave.

But with westward expansion and the recurring question of whether slavery was to be allowed to spread, it became increasingly clear that the philosophy which validated the values and interests of the monied and manufacturing dominants of the North, however compromised, would not serve equally well for the plantation masters who had impressed a way of life on the South. Douglas Dowd has put the matter squarely.

For the southerner to convert himself to beliefs and behaviors which would support and comport with slavery required a concentration so intense that all else became secondary—including the process of capital accumulation. . . . Planters were of course interested in profits; so were medieval "businessmen" (as jarring a term as "southern capitalists"). But neither group approached the question of capital accumulation in the sense in which the northern manufacturer did. In the South, slaves were never *just,* or even most importantly, capital, any more than a Cadillac car is just, or even most importantly, transportation to the modern American. This was true because slaves *were* slaves, a fact of such enormity in America at that time that it could only be accommodated by dedicating southern society to its perpetuation. And this meant that economic development was relegated to the back of the mind of the southerner, big or small.[3]

Philosophical defense of the Southern position proceeded on two planes, which merged. One lay via the route of pseudo-speciation, which provided a sense of superiority and advantage to all whites, regardless of economic position, by investing them with special God-given qualities that set them apart from the blacks. Henry Hughes, a young Mississippian who in 1854 published his *Treatise on Sociology, Theoretical and Practical,* by a process of dialectical reasoning satisfied himself that the disunity between white and black men led to unity among the whites, where power and intellect were joined to preside over an organic society. In this way, "the maximum of civil power, wisdom and goodness is realized. All of one race are thinkers. This, by their vocation. They are mentalists." [4]

The other path lay through denial of the validity of individualism. George Fitzhugh in his *Sociology for the South,* published the same year as Hughes's treatise, sharpened the contrast between the "free society" of the North, with its philosophical origins in John Locke, and the organic society which the South had developed. Locke's fundamental mistake, said Fitzhugh, was in treating the individual as the natural unit, instead of the community. "The social body is of itself a thinking, acting, sentient being," which endows the individual with whatever significance he has. The North, like western Europe from which it had sprung, in making this philosophical error was speedily degenerating into a state of competitive anarchy, each man against the other, for whom the highest morality consisted of satisfying his greed. It could spawn no higher a cultural type than Benjamin Franklin, "low, selfish, atheistic and material." These were harsh words, but we may recall that only a few years earlier Tocqueville, but from a quite different perspective, had made judgments concerning the effects of economic competition on the individual's character which were not vastly different.

Fitzhugh then proceeded to a further conclusion which provided moral justification for his conceptual distinction. It was only in a slave society, where culture was something indigenous and integral to daily life and not an intellectual import, that the highest form of social life could be achieved. This was because slavery freed the superior class from daily toil and provided it the opportunity to cultivate tastes and minds. The parallel was drawn with Periclean Athens, which had under similar circumstances reached the pinnacle of civilization. Rollin Osterweis has interpreted this philosophical formulation as an ingenious attempt to identify the system of slavery with classical "democracy," at a time when democracy, as Tocqueville had so clearly seen, was on the rise.[5] But whatever the intent, the divergence from Lockean principles and the effort to erect an independent and more congenial philosophical validation for the values and interests which had grown up around the dominant planter class was abundantly evident.

The philosophical validation serves several needs. To Mosca and Weber there was a psychological need for those in superior positions to justify their privileges, and for those in inferior positions to be given a reason on the strength of which they could more readily accept their subordinate status. Mosca used the term "political formula" to cover such a dual-purpose justification, and conceived that it was originated by the ruling class itself. "And yet," he insisted, "that does not mean that political formulas are mere quackeries aptly invented to trick the masses into obedience. . . . The truth is that they answer a real need in man's social nature . . . of governing and knowing that one is governed not on the basis of mere material or intellectual force, but on the basis of a moral principle." [6]

Weber believed this "universal phenomenon" of the need of the privileged to justify their state to the less privileged was one of the functions of religion. "What the privileged classes require of religion, if anything at all, is this legitimation." [7] In times when "the class situation has become unambiguously and openly visible to everyone as the factor determining every man's individual fate," the justification evaporates and class struggle ensues. There is here an underlying similarity with Marx's superstructure of law, religion, and philosophy which justifies the advantages of the bourgeoisie, keeping the proletariat alienated in the face of its own exploitation, until the true state of affairs reveals itself by its very grossness, and the proletariat throws off, in one convulsion, both the myths and the power by which the bourgeoisie have maintained their position.

The philosophical validation of dominant values as social values, abstract enough to accommodate the results of the implicit bargain, must then justify and rationalize the distribution of advantages within society. "Thus, in American society a man who works hard ought to get ahead, does get ahead, and in getting ahead proves he has worked hard. By definition, then, a dominant stratification ideology justifies the distribution of power and rewards in the society." [8] But the philosophical validation must do something more than this. It is not simply soothing syrup for the advantaged and the disadvantaged. It is also a means of providing a philosophical identity which all—or most—members of a society can share, which helps to give meaning to their lives through commitment to certain points of view. The philosophical validation, despite its apparent looseness through ambiguity and inconsistency, at times can even constrict the behavior of those we call the dominants. The philosophy which served them best when they were thrusting for position may become something of a nuisance when they have attained and enjoyed power for a time. Nevertheless, as part of their very identities it may be difficult for them to disavow it. Because it has been invested with a deeper, symbolic, transcendant meaning, it has emotional power over them no less than over the disadvantaged.

Erikson has listed eight respects in which a society's "ideology" provides a set of ideals to its young people, assisting in their search for self-identity. We need not concern ourselves with the specifics of these, as they relate to the individual's effort at achieving some congruence with the world around him, providing a framework for his own developing sense of identity. But Erikson concludes that "without some such *ideological commitment,* however implicit in a 'way of life,' youth suffers a *confusion of values* . . . which can be specifically dangerous to some but which on a large scale is surely dangerous to the fabric of society." [9]

The transformance of class values into social values, even after the implicit bargaining process has broadened them to accommodate other values present in the society, is not complete until they have been validated by their embodiment, over time, in a philosophical formulation, which becomes part of the identity-consciousness of a society. This is not likely to occur if espousal of the philosophical position requires the acceptance of a negative identity—requires blacks, for example, to have to agree that they are racially inferior because they have not made it, as a class, in a society whose philosophical position affirms that whether a person is successful depends on his own abilities. But as long as the philosophical position is sustainable for most, helps to make logical order out of the multitude of discrete social phenomena surrounding them, and provides affective and effective support for their activities and ambitions, it performs a function which goes a good deal beyond that of justifying the existing distribution of the social advantage.

Despite Djilas' strictures on the formation of a new privileged class in Communist societies, chiefly Russia, which has manipulated the ideology to protect its own position, it seems more than probable that for most members of such societies his interpretation would lack persuasiveness. They may concede that some members of the Party bureaucracy had advantaged themselves relative to others, and be critical of this abuse of position. But to conceive that these few thereby had converted themselves into a privileged *class* would be another and more difficult matter. For the philosophical validation in such countries has long run in terms of a classless society—classless not in the sense of an absence of differential status and incomes (what society does not have these; they are too evident to be ignored) but in the sense of an absence of a special and privileged source of income, as notably inherent in private property. Djilas, to make his point to a Communist readership, had to argue that his "new class" of Party dominants in effect *created* a new form of property which it appropriated for its private use. "The ownership privileges of the new class and membership in that class are the privileges of *administration*. . . . The so-called socialist ownership is a disguise for the real ownership by the political bureaucracy. . . . In view of the significance of ownership for its power—and also for the fruits of ownership—the party bureaucracy cannot renounce the extension of its ownership even over small-scale production facilities."

Yet Djilas has to admit that not only are the rank-and-file of Communist society unlikely to regard such administrative monopoly as ownership, but a member of the new class would be unable himself to regard it in that light. Such a person believes only that without his leadership, society would flounder and fail. He identifies his interests with those of his society, "but he is not conscious of the fact that he belongs to a new ownership class, for he does not consider himself an owner. . . . Collective ownership, which acts to solidify the class, at the same time makes it unconscious of its class substance, and each one of the collective owners is deluded in that he thinks he uniquely belongs to a movement which would abolish classes in society." [10] If classlessness is known to be based on social ownership, and social ownership in fact exists, then it becomes difficult to persuade a people that somehow a new *class* has emerged. The social philosophy on which they have in part premised their personal identities denies it. Only if it were possible to convince them that ownership itself, *whether public or private,* has nothing to do with the existence of classes could one undermine the philosophical foundation of their identity, leaving them adrift in a sea of moral uncertainty. Realizing the difficulty of that route, Djilas has to choose the alternative of trying to persuade them that what was public property has been appropriated and made private, something which is condemnable *within* the Marxist philosophical framework. But I would venture a guess that his argument, to most Communists who know it, has the ring of semantic play, however much they may sympathize with his criticism of bureaucratic behavior. The latter, however, can presumably be changed without changing the system—or one's own sense of identity.

The Role of the Intellectual and the Pool of Philosophical Thought

Intellectuals do not constitute a class, in the sense of a homogeneous group. They are a category of individuals, often disputing among themselves, transcending national boundary lines and historical epochs. Some are aligned with genuine classes; others seek to support just causes; still others profess to be nonpartisan or neutral. Some, like Jefferson, Madison, Woodrow Wilson, like Gladstone, Lenin, and Nehru, have played dual roles by also getting into the public arena. Their views in the aggregate embrace the whole spectrum of possible values.

If the "great man" concept of history has any applicability, it is certainly in this area of idea innovation. From a Tolstoyan point of view one could readily argue that science and technology and even historical epochs (as distinguished from events) are not really the product of any individual; if someone had not made the discovery or taken the initiative, another would. But in the matter of philosophical innovation there is no "objective" discovery to be made, no objective conditions which make some intellectual initiative more probable than another. It is more akin to the realm of art, of poetry, or painting. We cannot say that if Rembrandt or Shakespeare had not happened, another would have done the same in their place, as might be said of Newton or Darwin.

Generally speaking, one can group intellectuals into two subcategories —those who look upon themselves as functioning in the scientific mode, and those who operate on a more speculative, metaphysical, or philosophical plane. Members of either category can wind up in support of the status quo or conservative causes, or in advocacy of radical reform. Until the nineteenth century, the philosopher type tended to dominate the scene, understandably enough. A Thomas More might advocate Utopian Communism, while an Edmund Burke would make an eloquent and persuasive plea for the preservation of tradition through a natural aristocracy.

Beginning with the nineteenth century, however, those who argued in the scientific mode came to the fore. Among these, the conservatively minded tended to look on society as simply one aspect of nature, hence a society simply by existing was necessarily subject to natural law. That this point of view could readily turn into a defense of the status quo is easy to understand. If an intellectual sets out to describe the functioning of a social system objectively, he takes the system as he finds it but also imputes to it a degree of orderliness and systematicity, simply because he is seeking to abstract from the whole of reality only those aspects which lead to the natural order he looks for. The school of logical positivists would go farther than this, arguing that the abstract concepts from which they build their system need not even approximate reality as long as they produce, deductively, conclusions which are in harmony with the order they believe they observe.[11] In any event, the intellectual is driven to construct as neat and tight a model as possible in order to permit predictable results, lending it in the process a kind of objective quality such as one might attach to the solar system, any departures from which can be explained away as frictions. The result is a kind of "natural order" explanation for existing social relationships. As Bertrand Russell has wryly observed of nineteenth-century English economics:

This science, in combination with the philosophy of Bentham and the psychology which James Mill learnt from Hartley, produced the school of Philosophical Radicals, who dominated British politics for fifty years. They were a curious set of men: rather uninteresting, quite without what is called "vision," prudent, rational, arguing carefully from premises which were largely false to conclusions which were in harmony with the interests of the middle class.[12]

In similar vein, Alvin Gouldner has interpreted Malinowski's anthropology—objective, descriptive, analytical—as constituting a defense of aristocratic patterns of behavior in an England which was disposed to ridicule them. No reformer,

Malinowski viewed native institutions from the standpoint of the aristocrat within the anthropologist, with a submerged sense of an affinity between the customs of the aristocracy and those of native societies: dinosaur called to dinosaur. This sensed affinity derived from the fact that both groups' customs were vulnerable to a popular criticism that could condemn each of them as archaic, outmoded, and useless. . . . Malinowski's emphasis on the functionality of *all* customs—his "universal Functionalism"—was a generalized statement of a narrower impulse, namely, to defend precisely those institutions that seemed devoid of utility to the middle class. . . . Indeed, Malinowski himself expressly drew the parallel between the "savage customs" of native peoples and "silly" English games, such as cricket, golf, football, and fox-hunting. These were not "wasting time," insisted Malinowski; indeed, an ethnological view would show that "to wipe out sport, or even to undermine its influence would be a crime." Aristocratic custom, style of life, and leisure, no less than native institutions, now had a common theoretical defense. Behind English Anthropological Functionalism, then, there was a hidden impulse to defend the aristocracy against a narrowly conceived bourgeois standard of utility, *in terms of a more broadly conceived standard of social utility.*[13]

One need not accept the characterizations of Russell and Gouldner in entirety to appreciate that the situations they describe occur frequently enough, and that social scientists who pride themselves on their objectivity are often in fact describing as "natural" social relationships which simply exist. Perhaps an even more forceful example is provided by Herbert Spencer, who translated Charles Darwin's evolutionary theories into a "natural" social system. The historian Russell Nye has said that Spencer's impact on American thought was probably greater than that of any other philosopher since Locke. He visited the United States in 1892, when his name was already popularly known, and became the most frequently cited economic authority of the decade. His appeal lay largely in the fact that since his version of economic reality was based on the new Darwinian biology, it could be said to rest on a solid scientific foundation. His system of economic thought rested on two laws, the "law of equal freedom" and the law of "survival of the fittest." Working from the evidence supplied by Spencer, the business community of the 1880s and 1890s constructed a solid, tight structure of laissez-faire theory on this new base. It was understood that the activities of the state in the field of business should be severely limited; that the law of supply and demand should be allowed to operate without hindrance; that wages should reflect the productivity of the worker; that competition in the marketplace was to operate under only the most minimal restrictions; that the primary responsibility for the workings of the economic system rested on "natural law." [14]

But intellectuals of a scientific disposition lend themselves to radical reform as readily as to defense of the status quo. With the spread of industrialism, intellectuals like Saint-Simon and Comte found in science and its applications man's hope for a brighter and more stable future; the subduing of nature in man's interests—the quest for "the mastery of chance," in George Grant's phrase—became for them the guiding principle. In effect, the proliferation of scientific and technical knowledge itself induced a compatible view of society as something to be explored, explained, and controlled ("engineered") in the same way. Since human beings are part of nature, their presently erratic (accidental) behavior can be controlled for the benefit of all—we are now prepared for Skinner's *Walden II*. Systems analysis and planning, in which people are part of the system and conform their behavior to its purpose, are seen as the means of overcoming otherwise intractable social problems. With science in the saddle, there is no problem which man cannot resolve if he puts the proper resources behind it. A school of sociologists has thus come into being which sees technological solutions as replacing ideological (philosophical) resolutions of men's most serious problems, and casts the technical expert as the dominant of the future, who impresses his scientifically validated (hence "neutral") values on society.

Throughout this period when science and its adherents were seeing the extension of a natural order into the increasingly complex industrial systems being developed, a very different attitude was being taken by the modern school of philosophical and metaphysical thinkers, who viewed the consequences not as man's mastery over nature but technology's mastery over man. From English and German romanticists came protests against the dehumanization of the work process and its social relationships. Samuel Butler embedded in the otherwise unremarkable *Erewhon* his remarkable satire which had technology evolving into a higher species, reproducing its kind and subjugating men to a servitor role, thereby beginning a line of attack, continuing into the present, that reifies technology and endows it with a will and purpose of its own.

In recent years, especially since World War II, the number of attacks on a technological dominance which society is seemingly incapable of resisting has grown apace. Marcuse argues from Marxist premises to the non-Marxian conclusion that, in either a socialist or capitalist society, technology has induced a way of thinking that leaves men intellectually and morally unfree, their only escape lying in a process of reeducation which is unlikely to occur because education itself is part of the system. Lewis Mumford, in an extraordinary survey of social evolution, combines the metaphysical and the historical to explain why men are now in thrall to "the machine," from whose power they can loose themselves only by a supreme act of will. Charles Reich and Andrew Hacker follow Butler more closely in reifying technology, investing it with a power which transcends its creator (as Karel Čapek, in *R. U. R.*), making it almost *super* natural, reducing men to being merely its "tenders."

In writings like these the technological system is made so *wholly* responsible for society's sad state that its critics find it necessary first to rest that system on a mystique quite comparable to the older religions: technology, like the God of the ancients, is viewed as a demanding, compelling, and all-powerful Force. It is responsible for all good and all evil. We have no control over it but supinely submit to its control (even though some, like Reich and Mumford, believe that man can transcend his God if he wills it passionately enough: the god of technology, which has subdued man its creator, can in turn be subjugated by the act of rejection, leaving man once more at the controls). This endowment of technology with almost supernatural power is necessary if the contemporary critic is to play a luminous role as heretic: he must first identify a dominant faith against which to rebel. That dominant faith is found in the prevailing view that if anything can be done, it will be done—our current version of "Thy will be done."

I have dwelt at some length on the intellectuals' role with respect to the values embodied in a "technologic society" partly because of its major contemporary interest but equally to illustrate the point that intellectuals are to be found on all sides of a value argument, or to put it more properly, distributed along the entire spectrum of attitudes toward the whole array of values represented within a society. There is in fact a pool of philosophical thought built up over the centuries which one can fish to extract something in support of virtually any set of values he may profess, even though all such supporting thought is not equally persuasive.

But which ideas are extracted, and which thrown back into the pool, does not depend on the persuasiveness of the ideas themselves but on their appropriateness to the time and the place. Ideas which were enunciated in the past and ignored may be taken up later when they serve a more immediate purpose. As Leslie Stephen put the matter with respect to England, "The logical strength and weakness of the various creeds which were struggling for the mastery during the eighteenth century, goes some way to explain the course of the intellectual history; but no explanation can be complete which does not take into account the social conditions which determined their reception." [15] Di Tella makes the point even more strongly with respect to contemporary Latin America and to underdeveloped countries generally. Given the prevailing internal and international conditions, reform parties in these countries find inappropriate and unusable political philosophies based on Western liberalism. Instead, they tend to adopt what suits their circumstances "from among the radical ideologies available in the world market." These are mostly variations of socialist and Marxist doctrines, blended with such nationalism and local ritualism as makes them more salable to the masses. "The word 'socialism' is now as malleable as the word 'Christian' and it is well on its way to becoming as useful

for ruling the masses as it once was for arousing opposition against them."
For more sophisticated elements of the population, particularly "underoc-
cupied intellectuals," there is a preoccupation with the concepts of Lenin,
Mao, and Castro. It is the capacity of such concepts "to become sacred
words, objects of a belief to which one is committed, that matters, not
their vulnerability to the criticisms of an Oxford philosophy don." [16]

Ideas in the philosophical pool can have indirect effects. The thinking
of one intellectual can have its impact on another, or on many others, supporting or building up a current of thought which in time commands wide
attention even though the originator was lost to sight when he was writing.
Stephen cites the case of David Hume, whose philosophical speculations,
published between 1739 and 1752, were ignored at the time. "His first
book 'fell dead-born from the press'; few of its successors had a much better fate." Yet within a short passage of time, the ideas contained in his
writings seemed to spread throughout English intellectual society. "A cold
blast of scepticism seems to have chilled the very marrow of speculative
activity." Stephen surmises that the explanation for the seeming paradox
of Hume's impact in the face of his evident lack of popular success lay in
two related factors: first, Hume influenced "a powerful though a small class"
of thinkers, who might be considered as the brain of the social organism;
and the effects were gradually propagated to the extremities of the system." And second, the spirit of the times was ripe for the reception of
such ideas.[17]

The ideas themselves are not likely to initiate a social movement. Ideas,
to be translated into action, require the intermediation of a thruster group.
But they can prepare the soil (men's minds) from which a thruster group
can reap a harvest of followers. They can reinforce the conviction of the
already or nearly committed.

The importance of the availability of such a philosophical validation of
dominant values lies, as we have noted, in the fact that it provides an abstract and moral basis for the acceptance of such values within the society
at large. It provides a mode of thought, divorced from any obvious expression of class values, to which "all men can repair." Without such a validation people would be forced to reconcile their own beliefs and those of the
dominants as best they could. The validation provides a common basis for
agreement, logically and emotionally persuasive, within the spirit of the
times, as this is given shape by the thrusters or dominants. Herbert Kohl,
in his critique of Wittgenstein's linguistic philosophy, comments: "If men
cannot agree in moral judgments or political judgments, Wittgenstein
shows perfectly well that they will not be able to communicate." [18] In this
sense, one can say that the philosophical validation invests a people's vo-

cabulary with common meanings that permit *meaningful* communication among themselves. We shall return to this matter later.

The selection of the philosophical validation from the pool of ideas is not generally undertaken by those who stand most to gain from it—that is, the thrusters or those who have become dominants. That would be to ascribe to them a degree of intellectual sophistication and breadth of knowledge not commonly found in men of action. Nevertheless, there are times when this is at least partly the case. In any large-scale movement there is likely to be at least one or more leaders who are also philosophers or ideologues. One thinks immediately of the period of the founding of the United States, on the one hand, and of the Soviet Union, on the other, as constituting examples when among the activists were men of great intellectual breadth and depth who contributed to the validation of the very course they were charting, in statements and affirmations sufficiently compelling, abstract, and charged with moral content that they continued to play a justifying role long after the values which they presume to justify have changed their substance.

But the more likely process of validation is that those intellectuals who perceive in certain thrusters the embodiment of the values which they themselves profess "attach" themselves to the thruster group—not crudely in the sense of performing a public relations job on its behalf, which would undermine the conviction they could carry to the public, but by providing the statements and affirmations which the thruster group itself adopts as expressive of its particular purpose while giving that purpose a larger significance. John Locke and Adam Smith are obvious examples here, and in a somewhat different way Karl Marx as well.

The expression of such views in support of new values is certain to evoke opposition from prevailing or contrary philosophies. Like the thrusters themselves, the ideas supporting them do not go unopposed. The opposition may come from intellectuals who have achieved a status and a stake in the existing scheme of social relations, and who reaffirm the old faith. John Maynard Keynes's *General Theory* constituted a tremendous intellectual endorsement of a change in political direction—a challenge to the existing constitutional value, with its emphasis on autonomy, and impliedly to the prevailing distributive value, which justified resulting inequalities of condition—and understandably it did not go without rebuttal from those who preferred things as they were.

That means not simply opposition from the dominants and their followers, who reap disproportionate advantages from the existing system, but also from intellectuals who have invested their lives in developing systems of thought supportive of the status quo, whether so intended or not. Joan

Robinson has commented on the pre-Keynesian preoccupation with static equilibrium, which was justified on the intellectual ground that to encompass in a single system of thought the interaction of the parts at a point in time, as well as their movement through time, would involve excessive complexity. "It was necessary," she writes, "for purely intellectual reasons to choose between a simple dynamic model and an elaborate static one. But it was no accident that the static one was chosen; the soothing harmonies of equilibrium supported *laissez-faire* ideology and the elaboration of the argument kept us all too busy to have any time for dangerous thoughts." [19] It is also understandable that many who contributed to the building of the economic orthodoxy were reluctant to discard it simply because one of their professional colleagues had uncharitably told them their ideas were obsolete.

If the thrusters' movement builds, just as its success draws along the more timid "little thrusters" or those who simply come later in time, so too with the providers of the intellectual validation. As what was once unorthodox, regarded by the prestigious intellectuals as faulty or misguided thinking, becomes more acceptable, it also becomes the means by which younger professionals can stake out new intellectual territory for themselves rather than continuing to explore old territory long since claimed by others.

In time, as the thrusters become dominants and the system of social relations to which they give rise becomes more firmly and clearly established, then that category of intellectual for whom system order and predictive theories are important can be counted on to produce the definitive abstract justification simply *because* it works as a system, predictably. The hard-to-escape sense of a "natural" order begins to make itself felt. Analysts in effect become trapped in the value premises and institutions of their time, losing objectivity.[20] The philosophical validation becomes a part of the general culture. It is transmitted from one generation to the next through the variety of institutional means which are part of the very system being validated.

Interpretation and Modification

Objective conditions change, forcing changes in the terms of the implicit bargain. As this occurs, the philosophical validation must be reinterpreted or modified to reflect the new circumstances. This can often be done as a matter of exegesis, without affecting the underlying "sacred" text, though from time to time it may require more serious amendment. Leslie Stephen describes the process succinctly.

The philosopher has a more refined procedure for softening the process of transition. The ordinary process is familiar in the history of law. Old rules which are too narrow or clumsy for the complex states of society are modified by judicial interpretation without avowed alteration. Legal fictions grow up without a recognition of their fictitious character, as the natural result of the attempt to bring a new class of facts under the old formula. The original nucleus is lost to sight under a mass of accretions and adaptations. Rationalizing is the same process in theology or philosophy. At each particular step it seems that the old rubric is being expanded or confirmed, and that its deeper meaning is being brought out by disregarding trifling changes in the letter; and though the initial stage of a theory may differ widely from the final, and even, in some most important cases, be almost its logical contradictory, the change at any given moment may be imperceptible.[21]

Moreover, the political authority of the system, dominants and professional politicians both, can effectively assist in this process of philosophical redefinition by choosing those redefinitions which best suit their purposes. The language which they employ, drawn from the pool of ideas to which relevant additions are always being made, develops a kind of imperialism of its own by appropriating certain meanings for key words and phrases—like freedom, individualism, self-government, social welfare— and excluding other meanings. The meanings it endorses are those which are operationally useful to its own continuity, reinforcing public attitudes of support. This is not always done with any conscious sense of duplicity; it may be accompanied by the best of intentions. The effect is there nonetheless. I have myself been struck with the philosophical implication which accompanies terms now current in the economic profession which appear at face value to be neutral and objective—terms like "human capital" and "manpower," which, however innocent the intent in their use, nevertheless subtly import into our thinking the idea of people as means rather than ends, of people as instruments for purposes defined by others, of people as tools for more knowledgeable tool-users, of people—like horses—as so much power to be tapped. These are terms which are literally made to order for the philosophical validation of a social *system* in which masses or aggregates of people are subject to the "guidance" of technical experts.

A philosophical validation which was appropriate for a thruster class on its way up may become reinterpreted and redirected once that class has comfortably established itself. Liberalism in its original formulation, which served the aspiring industrialists so well, became something of an embarrassment to the later nineteenth-century organizers of large-scale corporate activity until the problem was defined away by making the corporation an individual.

The most insightful analysis of this process of interpretative redirection which I have encountered comes from perhaps the greatest Polish sociologist of recent times, Stanislaw Ossowski, and I shall draw on it at length. Ossowski develops as a general principle that a thruster group—in a subordinate position when it makes its bid—tends to seek reinforcing strength in the underprivileged classes of its society, from people who, like it, seek change. But having attained privilege, the thrusters-become-dominants cut themselves off from the revolutionary themes, since these could only embarrass them by revealing how far they had departed from original principles—principles which would condemn their own privileges and justify their now-abandoned lower-class supporters in pressing for further reform. Two alternatives are open to them—overt rejection of the old faith, relying simply on the power which has come into their possession, or a reinterpretation of the old slogans. The first course is fraught with hazard, since the original ideals have probably already been institutionalized and are part of people's way of thinking. They constitute "a positive emotional capital" which it would be foolish to destroy. Fresh interpretation is the only wise course.

The new philosophical validation supports a conservative position, justifying the dominants in their advantages. But the old, original, revolutionary philosophy lives on in the minds of a few purists, who thus become the carriers of a continuing revolutionary impulse, a potential thrust which may or may not ever come to fruition. Ossowski cites several historical examples of this process at work.

When Christianity became the religion of the dominant Roman class, the derogatory term "peasant" (*paganus*) was applied to those who continued to profess the old religion. No attempt was made, however, to remove from the Gospels or other church writings those passages stressing equality and fraternity. In 313 A.D., the Synod, in a concordat with the emperor, agreed to condemn any of its members who appealed to the Gospels as a basis for refusing military service. ("Today," Ossowski notes in an aside, "this would be called a 'left-wing deviation.' ") "Christian doctrine, which had over the centuries been built up into the great system of Aquinas, became the mainstay of the new order, but all the passages of Holy Writ which might prove dangerous for the privileged classes, for the Church hierarchy or for feudal power, still retained their binding force." The sacramental sharing of bread and wine continued to be known as "communion," even after it had been transformed into a dispensation from the altar. On Maundy Thursday the bishop continued to perform the ritual washing of beggars' feet, "but this action did not involve any risk of lessening the gap which divided him from them nor help to make the relations between the Church dignitaries and the Christian population more democratic." In its official doctrinal interpretation, the Church justified such discrepancies between the teachings of Christ and its own practices on the grounds of the corruption of human nature, which rendered impossible the realization of the Kingdom of God here on earth.

"Thus," Ossowski observes, "when we view history in simplifying perspective we see Christianity being split into two main streams: the Christianity of the ruling Church, where the teaching of Christ protects the existing order from the dangerous aspirations of those who seek egalitarianism and freedom; and revolutionary Christianity, the Christianity of the mediaeval heretics and the peasant movements, where the teaching of Christ, drawn from the same books sanctioned by the official Church, leads to revolt against the privileged classes, the Church and State."

Then came the bourgeois revolutions—in England in the late seventeenth century, based in part on the revolutionary wing of the Christian movement, stressing individualism; in France in the late eighteenth century, based on a new secular egalitarianism. Once victory had been achieved for the thrusting bourgeoisie on these two fronts, "the revolutionary slogans became part of the civic catechism in the European and American bourgeois democracies." But then the same phenomenon occurred as had happened earlier in the Christian church. The democratic movement divided into two streams. One, the movement of capitalist democracy, continued to invoke the old themes while interpreting them in a manner which furthered the stabilization of a new order based around the now dominant business class. The other, continuing the revolutionary momentum embodied in the ringing slogan of liberty, equality, and fraternity, developed into Marxist socialism.

Ossowski is particularly interested in this latter stream, which presumably incorporates the values which were gradually being eroded by capitalist reinterpretation. Not surprisingly he finds that it too, like its capitalist counterpart, undergoes the same process of institutionalizing its doctrines in a form which is designed to stabilize the new order and to defend the privileged class—the "new class" of Djilas' writing, though Ossowski does not base it on any strained conception of a new "private property." The revolutionary dynamism of Marxian doctrine is transformed into state (which implies static) doctrine, based on the teachings of Marx, Engels, Lenin, and Stalin, "which," says Ossowski, "I have even heard referred to on occasion by the symbolic abbreviation 'MELS.' " "In the same way as the French revolutionary ideology of the threefold rights of man or the mediaeval teaching of the Gospels had done, so Marxism, in the period which was to be called the Stalinist period, split into a revolutionary ideology and an official doctrine, petrified in its intellectual content but flexible in its use as an apologetic shield for current policy."

If the church could justify its departure from original principles on the grounds of the corruptibility of man, the Marxist dominants had at their disposal the theory of dialectical development. A widening gap between principle and practice could be rationalized as a necessary step to reach the promised goal. "Using such an interpretation of the dialectical processes it was possible to strive for the attainment of a social order in accordance with the postulate of equality by combating egalitarian trends, even for instance by combating the feeling that emerged in periods of general shortage that the types of ration-cards issued to children should not be dependent on their parents' status. It was possible to strive to achieve a state of freedom by placing increasingly severe restrictions on it." Criticism of such measures could be silenced by reiterating the sacred thesis that social classes—privileged classes—can exist only in a society recognizing private ownership; the special advantages which some enjoyed under socialism were for the good of society rather than for themselves.

In the same way that the bishops had continued the ritual but meaningless washing of beggars' feet, any worker who had the opportunity to approach Stalin could address him as "comrade," and similarly "a charwoman or porter would be called 'comrade' by those who had unlimited bank-accounts, could shop at special stores and had access to special social services for themselves and their children." The original emotion-charged philosophical validation was retained, but the interpretation and application changed. "Equality" was preserved in form and doctrine, but not in practice.[22]

There seems to be an almost tragic inevitability to this reinterpretation of once-honored philosophical credos by a dominant and advantaged class to justify its preferred position. Examples from our own society remind us how little immune we are from this phenomenon. We have already had occasion to note the basically opposed value systems of the North and the South, and their accompanying quite different philosophical validations, which led in time to the Civil War and the emergence of Northern interests as custodians of national interests. At that point the dominant North was faced with the problem of how to apply its own philosophical validation to the blacks, whom it had freed partly as an act of war and partly as an affirmation of its own faith. The application should have led to racial equality, if it were to square with the ringing statements of the fundamental equality of men contained in its intellectual heritage, but clearly that was not acceptable to the whites of the North any more than to those of the South. Though rejecting the South's organic social order in favor of individualism, the North could support inequality among the races only on the strength of some implicit pseudo-value of purity of races, a pseudo-speciation based on an unexpressed belief in biological differences between the races even while according lip service to the doctrine of equality. As Gunnar Myrdal has said, "The race dogma is nearly the only way out for a people so moralistically equalitarian, if it is not prepared to live up to its faith." [23]

We have already had occasion, too, to note the changing content of the term "individualism," which was peculiarly a part of the American credo, as Tocqueville had observed. The philosophical validation for the defense of property under Locke—the securing of individual independence—gets extended to the corporation in the Dartmouth College case. Later the corporation inherits the rights of the individual by the legal fiction of making it a person, in the process acquiring vast powers over natural persons. "It was generally agreed after 1870," says Russell Nye, "that the chief aim of individual activity was to improve the economic or political condition of each person; there was much less interest in individualism as individuality, as self development, as personal distinction." [24] The constitutional value was reinterpreted to stress the advantages of institutionalized progress rather than autonomy. Individualism, by the turn of the century, was becoming construed as each individual's striving to find that role *within* the corporation (or other institution) where he was best fitted to serve.[25] The American society undergoes what has been called an "organizational revolution" but the term "individualism" is too sacred a part of the American canon to discard; it can only be given new meanings.

Or take the "Keynesian revolution," that upending of some of the old orthodox economic shibboleths such as the virtue of thrift and the tendency of an unregulated economy to approach equilibrium. Although resisted for some time by the keepers of the old faith, they were within a relatively short time able to incorporate it within the philosophical validation of the existing value scheme, slightly modified but triumphantly still largely intact. If unemployment could no longer be looked on as a natural purging of impurities in the economic body but was now regarded as a disease to be treated with preventive medicine, so much could be accepted in good grace. Even practical businessmen and professional politicians could quickly learn that fiscal deficits could be accepted without threat to the system. But above all, as Joan Robinson has pointed out, they learned that as long as the system could be kept at full employment, no questions would be asked as to the composition of the GNP. Its only importance was its size, as a guarantor of jobs for all, not its makeup, concern with which might have led to more public expenditure in place of private. Keynes himself had been concerned only with the former, the equalizing of saving and investment, *ex ante,* at the point of full employment, leaving everything else to the free play of economic forces.[26] Hence by embracing Keynesian unorthodoxy, one could gracefully accept a modification in the old constitutional values—a little more government authority in times of economic downturn—but also give them added strength by invoking the intellectual authority of Keynes himself against going beyond that.

Today we are going through another process of modifying the philosophical validation of system values in such a way as to recognize new needs but preserve old order. The "technological society" of abundance is under attack. Numbers of individuals, from youthful radicals to thoughtful professionals, have begun to raise questions as to whether the objective of growing material abundance is a desirable focal value—in part because it consumes resources which might otherwise be left for enjoyment in a natural state, in part because it contributes to pollution of the social and natural environment in a variety of ways we are only beginning to appreciate. The pool of ideas to which we referred earlier is acquiring more and more contributions questioning, on both fundamental and flimsy grounds, the American society's stress on technology as the key to growth, international influence, and the "good" life.

But the counter to this criticism is to recognize the need for coping with the effects of technology without questioning technology itself. President Nixon, in his State of the Union message of January 1970, argued that "The answer is not to abandon growth but to redirect it." The country could cope with the problems which technology created by turning to technology itself for the answers. The same inventive genius which had created the wonders giving rise to our contemporary problems could create new wonders which would solve them. One need not take issue with the President's approach to recognize this as a new interpretation of the traditional philosophical validation of the focal value of material growth. One can legitimately question whether in fact it could "solve" the problems posed. One need not condemn the desire of those in a dominant position to wish to retain that position, to continue to espouse the values which they identify with national welfare, and to continue to validate that position by such interpretations as can win acceptance; but one can recognize at the same time what is taking place.

The elasticity in interpreting a society's philosophical validation has been shown over the centuries, at all times and places. Its most frightening potential has been given fictional expression in George Orwell's "double think." But what is the alternative to such stabilizing and conservatizing reinterpretation of old creeds? In the face of changed objective conditions, original principles may become outdated and nonviable, and efforts to preserve them as conservative and self-serving as any amendment or modification.

The fact is that within any society there is a double movement which is always under way. On the one hand, the social system moves toward the reinforcement of its system characteristics—its purposes, its style, its norms, its coordinating authority—to make the system more workable. In this effort the conservatively minded intellectuals play their role by looking for order and consistencies and predictable relationships which conduce to a stable state. On the other hand, changes are inevitably occurring, so that the system must accommodate new forces and pressures, must compromise in the face of challenges, if it is to survive at all. In doing so it moves *away* from existing system order, muddying the neatness of its design. In assisting in this redesign the reform-minded intellectuals make their contribution.

Both these movements and types of validation are virtually inescapable. It is not a form of sequential dialectic but rather a type of counterpoint. *At the same time* the philosophical validation of a society serves to justify *both* resistance to change and accommodation to change, the first by interpretive use of "hallowed tradition" to rebut radical influences, the second by reinterpretive use of that tradition to rebut conservative influences.

Acceptance and Rejection

The philosophical validation is not accepted equally by everyone in a society. There may indeed be groups so peripheral that they do not recognize it or fail to understand its meaning. Others may accept some portions of the creed but withhold full support—accept, for example, an emphasis on individual autonomy but reject the substantial income differentials which others would view as a product of that autonomy.

In general, we may assume that the dominants believe in the philosophical formulation more intensely than any other group, only in part because it serves their interests best—in part too because it is the very depth of their conviction that has carried them to their positions of power. Those who have fared less well have less cause to believe deeply, both on grounds of interest and conviction. A recent study by three sociologists of attitudes of householders in Muskegon, Michigan, revealed not surprisingly that "the rich are more convinced than others that wealth is a result of favorable personal attributes" and "that poverty is the result of unfavorable personal attributes." In general, the wealthy believed that the poor did not work as hard and lacked ambition. The poor were disinclined to accept this evaluation and were less convinced of the effectiveness with which the doctrine of equality of opportunity was implemented.[27]

These results will raise no eyebrows, but the study also carries the suggestion that the disadvantaged see themselves not so much misled or duped as simply contained. They have acquired a belief in their own powerlessness within the framework of the system. Under the circumstances one would hardly expect them to give the same support to a philosophical validation which speaks in terms of equality of opportunity. They are more inclined to fall back on their own value systems to support their sense of identity. This is especially true of those whom the implicit bargain has ignored and hence to whom the philosophical validation has no real significance, as notably the blacks in the United States.

Along with those who only partially accept the philosophical validation, or who see themselves as not covered by it at all, there are some who insist on their own private, often distorted interpretation. Every society spawns splinter movements, some of which are, as the saying goes, holier than the pope. Thus there are right-wing movements which believe they embody the philosophical principles of American individualism or sanctity of private property more vigorously than the government; anti-Communist movements sparked by the fanaticism of a Joseph McCarthy; left-wing movements which press for a more extreme interpretation of freedom of speech or assembly than public officials will tolerate. These do not reject the philosophical formulations but only its interpretation or application.

Finally, there are other groups which refuse to accept dominant values as social ones, or to recognize the implicit bargain in which they are embedded. These profess contrary focal, constitutional, or distributive values. The same pool of ideas which gives rise to the dominant philosophical validation provides for such groups their own intellectual formulations, justifying their positions and seeking to provide a larger moral basis for a following. These ideas may serve to keep resistance to the dominant values alive or to create the ideology of a countermovement.

Depending on the nature of the prevailing constitutional value, some of this opposition can take place within the system's own institutions. To put the matter in reverse, to a considerable extent opposition to a prevailing system of values is limited by the institutionalized methods for its expression. In the West, the universities have been one chief avenue through which counter philosophies can be expressed and secure a following. As Lawrence Stone has said of them, they have "provided relatively safe havens of intellectual freedom in a heavily censored universe, from which can emerge new ideas and new facts which challenge both the existing social system and the existing set of values." [28]

Otherwise, opposition tends to find its expression in underground publications and movements, in "radical" art and theater, in random causes and protests. The possibility of maintaining any organized opposition, outside permissible channels of expression, is limited. The Communist Party has been little more tolerated in the United States than "revisionist" movements have been in Russia. But even within permissible limits, even in the absence of any continuing organization of opposition, there can be a cumulative effect of many voices speaking dissident views. Neighborhood caucuses urging decentralization of authority may lack only the galvanizing influence of a Mahatma Gandhi to gain greater political respect for their views, however misguided those views may be. The current movement against rational exclusivism—against the concept of Enlightenment man because it leaves out the nonrational aspects of life (feeling, fantasy, intuition, whimsicality)—can have its impact on attitudes toward formal education; the traditional appeal of learning which has brought ever higher percentages of American youth into ever higher levels of learning could conceivably be reversed.[29]

In the pool of ideas out of which emerge philosophical validations for such contrary points of view there are contributions by men of note supporting such protests. Sartre sees this as "a world where certain reconciliations are impossible and certain conflicts inevitable." To him, language and literature are for active use and engagement in "the world of ideological battles, where morality is a function of self-conscious political and religious allegiances . . ." [30] Marcuse in some respects affects the most radical philosophical posture of all. To him resistance is *always* warranted, since every event, every public policy, every value system, every philosophical validation, inevitably fails to mirror the whole of reality, inevitably excludes some part of the whole. What others exclude, what it is *policy* to exclude, it is his radical commitment to affirm. There are numbers of others—the list would be tediously long—who have lent their voices to philosophical positions supporting opposition to the prevailing public philosophical formulations.

This is nothing new. There have been other times and places when voices of protest were joined in a discordant chorus. It may all add up to nothing. On the other hand, even in the absence of any organized thrust to challenge the prevailing dominant position, one can conceive that the very dissonance created by many unorganized protests may create a sufficient sense of disunity to sap the effectiveness of an inherited philosophical validation. Particularly if the dominants are in some disarray within their own ranks as to whether some accommodations should be made, and with whom, or whether their values should be enforced, and how far, a kind of philosophical vacuum may be created. The value system becomes diffuse and uncertain. The terms of the implicit bargain are drifting. What is there to validate?

I venture no opinion at this point as to whether this is where American society is now. We shall come to that question in a later chapter.

Notes

1. Introduction by Peter Laslett to John Locke, *Two Treatises of Government*, rev. ed. (New York: Cambridge University Press, Mentor Edition, 1965), p. 91.

2. *Ibid.*, p. 118.

3. Douglas F. Dowd, "The Economics of Slavery in the Ante Bellum South: A Comment," *Journal of Political Economy* 66 (October 1958): 442. © 1958 by The University of Chicago. Quoted with permission.

4. I am drawing on R. Jackson Wilson's excellent study, *In Quest of Community*, pp. 23–26, for the material on Hughes and also on George Fitzhugh.

5. Rollin G. Osterweis, *Romanticism and Nationalism in the Old South* (New Haven: Yale University Press, 1949), pp. 94–95.

6. Mosca, *The Ruling Class*, p. 71.

7. Weber, *Economy and Society*, Vol. 2, p. 491; the succeeding quotation is from Vol. 3, p. 953.

8. John H. Rytina, William H. Form, and John Pease, "Income and Stratification Ideology: Beliefs about the American Opportunity Structure," *American Journal of Sociology* 75 (January 1970): 703.

9. Erikson, *Identity: Youth and Crisis*, p. 187–188. Italics in original.

10. Djilas, *The New Class*, pp. 46, 47, 56, 59–60.

11. This point has been discussed by Eugene Rotwein in his insightful essay, "On the Methodology of Positive Economics," *Quarterly Journal of Economics*, November 1959, pp. 554–575.

12. Bertrand Russell, *Legitimacy versus Industrialism, 1814–1848*, p. 79.

13. Gouldner, *The Coming Crisis in Western Sociology*, pp. 132–133. Italics in original.

14. Nye, *This Almost Chosen People*, pp. 130–132.

15. Stephen, *History of English Thought in the Eighteenth Century*, Vol. 1, p. 19.

16. Torcuato S. di Tella, "Populism and Reform in Latin America," in Veliz, *Obstacles to Change in Latin America*, pp. 52–53. Quoted with permission.

17. Stephen, *History of English Thought in the Eighteenth Century*, Vol. 1, pp. 1–2.

18. Kohl, *The Age of Complexity*, p. 128.

19. Robinson, *Economic Philosophy*, pp. 71–72.

20. Karl Mannheim, in *Ideology and Utopia*. (New York: Harcourt, Brace & World, Harvest Edition, first published 1936), p. 69, sees this as the manner in which "false consciousness" can arise—one's "total outlook as distinguished from its details may be distorted."

21. Stephen, *History of English Thought in the Eighteenth Century*, Vol. 1, p. 8.

22. Ossowski, *Class Structure in the Social Consciousness*, pp. 186–190. The whole of this remarkable book is well worth reading. It was first published in Poland in 1958, following the Stalinist thaw. Ossowski, who subsequently taught briefly in the United States, was barred from teaching in Poland under the Stalinist regime.

23. Gunnar Myrdal, *An American Dilemma* (New York: Harper & Row, 1962), p. 89.

24. Nye, *This Almost Chosen People*, p. 226.

25. Ward, in Cheit, *The Business Establishment*, pp. 77–112.

26. Robinson, *Economic Philosophy*, pp. 95–97.

27. Rytina, Form, and Pease, "Income and Stratification Ideology," pp. 713–715.

28. Lawrence Stone, "The Ninnyversity?", *New York Review of Books*, 28 January 1971, p. 22.

29. Marcia Cavell has provided a short and interesting account of this phenomenon in "Visions of a New Religion," *Saturday Review*, 19 December 1970.

30. Iris Murdoch, "Sartre," in *Writers in Revolt*, ed. Richard Seaver, Terry Southern, and Alexander Trocchi (New York: Frederick Fell, 1963), pp. 164–165.

9 / Institutionalization of Values

We have followed the course by which a thruster group, seizing on the opportunities provided by a change in objective conditions, may rise to a position of dominant influence within a society. As it acquires allies and followers, provides rewards for its supporters and wins over the adaptables, gradually its values are identified as those which are good for the nation. This process of identification of group values and interests with social values and interests is abetted by the accommodations and compromises which have been made in the implicit bargain, and by the philosophical validation which accumulates around the dominant values in a sufficiently abstract way to satisfy the terms of the implicit bargain and give a moral and intellectual justification to the whole.

But one thing more is needed—the transmission of those values and their validation from one generation to the next. This is something which does not just occur by virtue of a person's growing up in a particular kind of society. That is involved, but not only that. The values—and the interests which are so closely associated with them that sometimes they are seen as one—get built into the institutions on which a society must depend for its continuity, both in a political and economic sense and also in a psychological one. The values are not only absorbed but also transmitted.

This carries no implication that all the institutions of a society are faithful reflectors of a common set of social values, mutually reinforcing each other. Each institution—corporation, church, school, the military—has its own value system, its own focal, constitutional, and distributive preferences. In their uniqueness they necessarily display incompatibilities with each other. The amount of personal autonomy allowed by church, by corporation, by the army, in the definition of its constitutional value, for example, may be significantly different, even sharply contrasting, with the amount of autonomy fostered by family, school, or a profession.

Nevertheless, since they are all necessary functioning parts of the total society, they must also be compatible. In part this is achieved by emphasizing differences in the requirements of their functional roles: an army *has* to be run by hierarchical discipline, while a university relies more heavily on individual autonomy. Whatever their particularistic values, the institutions of a society must respect and reflect enough of the overall social values to maintain cohesion with the whole.

Despite this tendency toward some basic compatibility of values, institutional relationships are often in a state of flux. Changes in the objective conditions affect institutions differently. One has its functions diminished, while another may play an expanded role. Such changes in status affect an institution's sense of compatibility with the values of its society.

Moreover, an institution may be the instrument of a thruster group, intent on making a larger place for itself in society by modifying the latter's values. Even institutions which already represent the dominants of a society—the business firm in the United States, let us say, or the military of ancient Rome, or the church of the middle-ages—do not necessarily represent a unity of purpose. Within the dominant group there may be a smaller thruster class, more alert or eager to exploit changes which it sees as fresh opportunities, in the process modifying or reinterpreting the existing value system. Thus the rise of the nineteenth-century corporate "barons" or "czars" who organized whole industries, displacing small family enterprises, contributed to a shift in the American constitutional value without disturbing business hegemony. They invited partisan attacks from little and local businessmen as well as from farmers and consumers, and the government—bowing to popular pressure—made the semblance of a stand against them. But the new organizers were running with the tide; the opportunity they had seized was genuinely rooted in objective changes in technology and population. In this respect John D. Rockefeller was more in tune with the times than Theodore Roosevelt, the trustbuster, and J. P. Morgan with his visions of business consolidations was more farsighted than Louis Brandeis with his nostalgia for smallness. Without approving the consequences, one can see these as examples of institutional initiative which was not restrained by the need for institutional alignment with the values of the times. The changed objective situation in effect freed their hand. The same pattern can be seen in the institution of the Catholic Church, which in its rise from a struggling community of believers to a great imperial power had its own thrusters within its ranks.

Government As Institution

Of all the institutions in a society, government is the most pervasive. Except in totalitarian situations, however, the government is not itself the dominant institution. Its authority derives either from direct representation of the dominant interest (as Marx would have it) or from its performance of a brokerage role between the dominant interest and a larger public which cannot be ignored (as I would argue).

There are a variety of mechanisms by means of which the influence of the dominants can be filtered through the organs of government without an unseemly display of arrogance or power. First, there is the organization of the political parties themselves. Candidates do not so much volunteer their availability or draw a following to them by their own capabilities or magnetism; they are selected by the party leadership. Their qualifications— "reasonableness" of position, willingness to "recognize the facts of life," public image—are weighed not only in the light of how voters will respond but how financial backers will be impressed. The cost of campaigning is now so well known that the figures no longer shock. A committee established by the Twentieth Century Fund reported in 1970: "With the exception of incumbents in 'safe' districts, successful candidates for Congress must either be wealthy or have access to large sums of money. Challengers without such resources do run for Congress. Most lose." [1] Although funds are forthcoming from other interests than the dominant class of a society, the dominants, almost by definition, are those with the most to give, as well as the most to lose if they do not give.

In countries where there is no polarization of interests, dominant backing of more than one political party is common. In the United States, both Democrats and Republicans have their business supporters, even though they may not be equally favored. The consequence is that both *contesting* parties owe substantial debts of gratitude to the same supportive interest without whom they would not have been able to wage so effective a contest and whose support they hope to continue to enjoy.

Another instrument for the screening out of political actions undesirable to the dominants and for furthering actions favorable to them lies in the organization of the legislature. The several political parties commonly exercise effective control over the votes of their members and are capable of punishing deviation by such devices as loss of patronage to dispense, assignment to inconsequential committees, and simple ostracism. The British are even more effective at such party control than the Americans. Since party leaders, who exercise this power, can be expected to be more cognizant of the kinds of compromises and bargains which are needed to retain or secure party support, they can be expected to be less inclined to radical actions than many individual members.

The committee organization of legislatures can also be used to expedite desired actions and negate others. One of the most notorious of such devices is the requirement in the United States House of Representatives that the Rules Committee determine whether a bill shall be brought to the floor for vote. The chairman of the committee can himself make this decision unless he is overridden by a majority of his committee members. In December 1970, for example, Representative William M. Colmer, a Democrat from the Deep South, declined to permit referral of a bill which would have given the federal government power to enforce nondiscrimination in employment. The bill, he said, was vicious, and he had no intention of allowing the House to vote on it.[2] While the manner in which bills can be brought before or amended by a legislature exhibits considerable variety among countries, there is an underlying similarity in the existence of hurdles to legislation which is unwanted by the leadership or by powerful interests.

Legislation, once enacted, must be administered. For this there is a vast governmental bureaucracy, which does not change greatly in composition from one election to the next. In his scholarly study of *Class and Class Conflict in Industrial Society,* Dahrendorf sees this bureaucracy as filling roles of "political dominance" which "aim at the maintenance of existing institutions and valid values." Recognizing the skepticism with which many people might regard clerks, typists, minor officials—all part of the bureaucracy—as sharing in the exercise of such authority, he resorts to a parable to make his point. The illusion of a lot of faceless and relatively powerless bureaucrats is due to the organizational division of labor— specialization of function. It is akin to the manufacture of an automobile. Who makes an automobile? Is it the director who exercises nominal peak authority? The assemblyman? The welder? The foreman? The test driver? The file clerk? Clearly none of these has "made" the car, and yet we can scarcely conclude that "nobody" made the car. Cars are in fact being produced by an *organization* which includes all of these. The exercise of bureaucratic authority is similar, says Dahrendorf. "Nobody" runs the government machinery. There are thousands of individuals doing a variety of subordinate and seemingly unimportant jobs. But it is the collective result that counts. "All bureaucratic roles are defined with reference to the total process of the exercise of authority to which they contribute to whatever small extent."

But although the bureaucracy is in its totality the expression of the power of government, it has no substantive program behind which it puts its latent power. "By its monopoly of authority unaccompanied by independent substantive interests, the bureaucracy of the state is, so to say, the law of inertia of social development become real." The latent interests of the bureaucracies "aim at the maintenance of what exists; but what it is that exists is not decided by the bureaucracies, but given to them."[3] While

I would take issue with Dahrendorf's inclusion of the bureaucracy among a society's dominants, I do accept the inertial and conservative role he ascribes to it. It constitutes another filter through which actions inimical to the true dominants are screened out, along the lines we earlier had occasion to observe in connection with the regulatory administration of the Interstate Commerce and Sherman Anti-Trust acts. Much more could be said and documented on this score, but it would carry us too far afield.

Finally, there is another screen behind which dominant interests gain some immunity from the imposition of populist controls over their influence and interests—the judicial system. The legal process is almost designed to delay or thwart radical change. It is the medium par excellence for dominant challenge to legislation which distresses it. Years of delay can be purchased through a succession of appeals. The meaning of a law can be reviewed with such intensity that doubts can be implanted where once all seemed clear. Interpretations are made in the light of precedents —an appeal to the past—and with the meaning imputed to terms which has been given them by dominant usage—that imperialism over the language which we earlier noted.

None of this is to say that the powers of government are always addressed to the defense of dominant interests. The record clearly belies such a distorted conclusion. Objective conditions change; new thrusters appear and may have to be accommodated; the dominants accede to change, perhaps under the mediatory pressure of politicians who persuade them that it is better to give a little ground than to be pushed from the hill. Periods of crisis occur, when the dominants find themselves in disarray, their values seemingly betrayed, the philosophical validation a bitter irony. The Great Depression was perhaps the most vivid recent instance of such a disaster. But the brevity of time within which the old dominants, slightly chastened and with a fresh, more accommodating leadership, reasserted their commanding position within society and influence within the government following that crisis is testimony to the difficulty with which those in entrenched institutional positions are displaced.

Marx *defined* the government as the tool of the dominant class, and C. Wright Mills followed closely in this interpretation. Of course Marx and Mills were wrong in their crude identification of government with dominant power. If that were the case, the dominants could use the coercive powers of government as they chose, avoiding any need for accommodation or compromise. They would have no use for a political broker to mediate between them and the populist majority. They would have no occasion to be wary of the demagogue. Clearly no dominant is *that* dominant unless it encompasses all other institutions in totalitarian fashion.

Dahrendorf seeks to move away from this extreme position by according the government a role of independence in its own right.

Managerial or capitalist elites may be extremely powerful groups in society, they may even exert partial control over governments and parliaments, but these very facts underline the significance of governmental elites: whatever decisions are made are made either by or through them; whatever changes are introduced or prevented, governmental elites are their immediate object or agent; whatever conflicts occur in the political arena, the heads of the three branches of government are the exponents of the *status quo*. It is admittedly not sufficient to identify a ruling class solely in terms of a governmental elite, but it is necessary to think of this elite in the first place, and never to lose sight of its paramount position in the authority structure of the state.[4]

But Dahrendorf's formulation, too, seems to me to draw a film over the reality. He does not deny the possibility of an outside dominant influence on government, but he minimizes it in order to elevate the bureaucracy itself—the bureaucracy which, by his own admission, has no national purpose, no grand design, no sense of national norms, or style of conduct, no feel for the appropriate use of coercion to achieve coordination for needed objectives. It only does what it is told to do; it only seeks to preserve what already exists.

What such a construction neglects is that this inherent conservatism of the bureaucracy hits most vigorously at any thruster group. The dominants as a class, who enjoy disproportionately the advantages which society has to offer, want nothing better than the status quo. Changes in objective conditions may not allow them to retain that forever, but as long as they can forestall the effects by delaying tactics it does go on. In this respect the government bureaucracy, whatever its independent authority, exercises it on the side of those whose influence counts most at the moment.

From time to time reform governments will be voted in, and limitations will be imposed on some of the privileges the dominants enjoy, despite the makeup of political parties, the organization of legislatures, the administration of laws, and the interpretations of the judiciary. But to see such interludes as evidence of the basic independence of government, as though even in such reforms it is not limited by the dominants (if indeed they *are* dominants), is to miss the governor on the government.

In this sense, the incrementalists, who believe that government policy is made only by small adjustments, are basically right—for long stretches of time. As long as they concern themselves with an existing system of relations, it is difficult to take issue with them. It is only over the longer haul that their interpretation fails.

The Basic Institutions

If government, the most pervasive institution in a society, is not simply a tool for the dominants, there are other institutions which historically have peculiarly been their instruments. These are (1) the representative economic institution, (2) the church, and (3) the military. We call these the basic institutions.

In preindustrial societies, the representative economic institution is typically the large landed estate—the latifundium, a term which has come down from the time of imperial Rome and which is still current in Latin American societies. Landholding may head up to the state itself, which operates its lands through agents on a fee or contract basis, who retain whatever the surplus. With the breakdown of empire and the rise of feudalism, possession of land can be secured only through protective alliances with a more powerful warrior or "noble," to whom one cedes his lands, receiving them back in exchange for certain services, chiefly of a military nature but including economic contributions as well. Such a system of alliances extends down to the meanest serf and up to the highest noble, or king, of an indefinitely defined territory—all linked together through mutual rights and obligations, with title to the land resting ultimately with the king; his grants to supporters are conditional, but the rights exercised by those grantees relative to people living on the land are virtually absolute, limited only by custom and traditional obligations not always enforceable.

Relations between large landholders and the king have varied from country to country; the degree of absolutism invested in the head of the state differed significantly between preindustrial France and England, for example, while Italy was for centuries a country of feuding principalities, dukedoms, and papal states patched up with foreign alliances. But the principle that the land was parceled out chiefly in large territories under the jurisdiction of aristocratic families, who might organize and administer it as they chose, prevailed or at least persisted in attenuated form in Europe right into the eighteenth century. Even in the New World, large parts of both the North and South American continents were settled under grants of territory from European crowns, and the plantations of the American South and of South America were carry-overs from familiar European practice.

In these preindustrial societies, the large estate constitutes the major economic institution, and the values which are associated with that aristocratic form of organization filter through the whole of the society. Chiefly there is an emphasis on family loyalties, which carries with it a more local and particularistic, defensive and security-minded, hierarchically structured set of attitudes.[5]

By contrast, the dominant economic institution of industrialized societies is the corporation. The corporation was of course an instrument which was employed long before industrialization became the prevailing mode of economic activity—it existed in ancient forms, and continued under royal charters for specified purposes (the East Indian and African trading companies, for example) into the nineteenth century. There is no point in tracing here the stages by which there developed, in one country after another, some form of general incorporation procedure. First as family firms, embodying some of the traditional family loyalties and security-mindedness, then as public corporations based on increasingly rationalized and impersonal procedures, the corporation came to disseminate a different set of values from those based on the landed gentry.

As Karl Marx, Werner Sombart, and Max Weber saw most clearly, and as the English classical and neoclassical economists saw less apocalyptically, private profit-seeking in an industrial world, once let loose, has a kind of compulsive quality to it. The individual entrepreneur is driven to pursue profit for survival, whatever other values he may personally wish to accommodate. The idiosyncratic individual (like Robert Owen) and the family firm which feels its responsibility to the local community may mix nonprofit with profit objectives for a time, but sooner or later it gives way to the more single-minded and impersonal organization. This may be the result of crisis and failure, or of heirs who sell out, preferring to live in ease rather than continue the struggle, or simply inability to grow, until in time the firm fades away with a dissolution of assets.

It is not possible to identify any single set of values associated with "the corporation" as the dominant economic institution, since it has changed its form in response to changed conditions. It is customary to say that private enterprise breeds a materialistic preoccupation, a competitive drive to get ahead, and individuality. These were characteristics which Tocqueville observed in the United States of the 1830s. But the large corporate organization of today does not necessarily foster the same values, neither in the United States nor in other countries where it has developed. The large impersonalized bureaucracies which are characteristic of these modern corporations, within a largely urbanized and industrialized society, embody a different constitutional value which tends more toward hierarchical order than personal autonomy, and hence calls for a considerably different interpretation of the term "individualism" if it is still to be applied. Although there is continuity in its materialistic preoccupation, its order is more rationalized, organized, and impersonal, tending to "objectify" the individual. We shall have more to say about this in the next chapter.

The large corporation in an industrial society spawns a penumbra of other supporting organizations—not simply the smaller firms which supply it with materials and services or distribute its products but trade associations, specialized educational institutions, the public relations and advertising professions. It draws in other institutions and professions as supporters —not solely its supporters, but chiefly so—simply by virtue of its pervasiveness throughout the society. If one were to identify the institutional services of private lawyers, accountants, and engineers, for example, the majority in the United States would clearly be involved directly or indirectly with business. Finally, it gives rise to organizations which are designed to interact with it though on behalf of other interests, notably workers but also dealers and consumers. As we have already had occasion to note, the labor union gains its structure and function from its involvement with business. It has little independent purpose aside from that.

Societies which are in a state of transition from a largely agricultural and raw materials base, with a landholding aristocracy, to an industrialized type, more and more characterized by corporate organization (though not necessarily private), find themselves in a neither-here-nor-there position. The rising industrial class may or may not be a thruster group relative to the old aristocracy; it may be content to be accommodated. The new corporations may be associated with some of the landed families, or their managers may aspire to admission to the privileged circles. The values characteristic of them may be more reflective of the familial, protective, and conservative old order based on land than of the rational, aggressive, impersonal order based on industry. But however the relationship works itself out between these two economic classes, clearly they divide a dominant position between them in some fashion.

The second major institution which has served as a vehicle for a dominant group is the church. Here I speak primarily of the church in the West, though Mosca and Weber have made clear the importance of institutionalized religion in Eastern countries as well. It could hardly be otherwise. Until very recent times, and some would say persisting today, people have felt a necessity for some form of religion. Erikson has identified that need as the systematization and socialization of the "first and deepest conflict in life." It translates the "dim image" of each person's first parental protector into a collective image of a superhuman protector; it gives form to a vague mistrust of nature by giving it a "metaphysical reality" as a defined evil; it offers through rituals the periodic "collective restitution of trust." [6] Weber would add that it also provides a higher rationalization for a social order which distributes its advantages unequally.

Though some today deny the need for either religion or church, it is not clear what they would substitute for it. It has been argued that Western peoples are now tending to identify themselves with the machine[7] or with the social system of which they are part, which gives them direction and provides for their needs.[8] But whether this will prove sufficient, whether it will provide "that deep sense of specific goodness . . . which man needs in his relation to his principal source and technique of production in order to permit himself to be human in a reasonably familiar universe" [9] is a question still unanswered.

In any event, in the past the church was indeed a dominant institution in Western society. In the period of the Middle Ages it infused the whole of society with its specific meaning, making a social order out of what would otherwise have been simple superstition and coercive force. It continued such intellectual traditions as managed to survive and became the chief patron of the arts of architecture, sculpture, painting, and music. In the cult of the resurrected Christ and the intercessor Mother of Christ, the Virgin Mary, it institutionalized the sacraments which "officialized" a person's life from birth to death, and which gave meaning to both life and death. Through the steady accretion of secular power it became one of the great world imperial powers, making treaties and alliances, waging wars, and collecting tribute.

With the gradual decline of the church's influence following such debilitating events as the Reformation, the rise of the competitive nation-state whose king claimed divine right on equal terms with the pope, the spread of capitalism, and the growth and autonomous pretensions of science, the church ceased to be the dominant institution that it had been, but nevertheless retained considerable influence. In Protestant countries new religious organizations rose to fill the place it left vacant. In most Western countries, the chief exception being the United States, there was an "established church." Church officials were involved in affairs of state, either as makers or supporters of public policy. In Latin America the church gave its support to the landed aristocracy, just as the established church did in England. In the United States many a Protestant clergyman spoke up in defense of the "sanctity" of private property and the divine inspiration of laissez faire. If the church was no longer a dominant, it was the ally of a dominant.

A third major institution which has served the specific purpose of a dominant class has been the military. Particularly in periods when a society has been moving into a more settled agricultural state, with the burgeonings of an urban culture, has the military been of importance in protecting it from marauders. Its protective indispensability was readily turned into oppressive exploitation. Mosca points to Poland as an example of a country where the military, at first drawn from the agricultural population, gradually became a separate class. Using the coercive power of their military monopoly, the warrior leaders turned themselves into nobles and masters, appropriating for themselves an ever larger share of the produce until the peasants were left with nothing but their subsistence. Resisting, they were forced into virtual serfdom.[10]

An imperialistic society bent on world conquest must obviously accord a dominant position to its military organization. The style of the times, the society's grand design is bound up in that institution's leadership. In an earlier day its officers might be drawn only from the aristocracy to ensure unity of national purpose, while in contemporary times the military leadership might be overseen by party officials (Nazi, Communist) for the same purpose. But as a society expands in scale, industrializes, urbanizes, becomes more complex and sophisticated in all its institutional forms, the military, regardless of its monopoly of force, cannot effectively run a country by itself. Those in positions of economic influence can undermine any efforts at domination by simple noncooperation. The consequence is that while the military remains an important institutional base for a major interest group, it cannot do without civilian allies.

Latin America provides a continent full of examples of this phenomenon. There, as we have had occasion to observe already, the military operates as something of a "meddling mediator" among diverse interest groups, performing some of the same functions as a professional politician. The style of its operation differs among countries and over time. Several general types of military intervention have been identified: (1) the chief executive is a military officer, and with the authority of the armed forces behind him unites the country behind his leadership; (2) party politics continue to be a civilian affair, but the military maintains a supervisory role to ensure that order prevails; (3) the military stays on the sidelines as long as the traditional conservative forces retain authority, but intervenes to put down any radical movement; (4) the military exercises a veto power over which government takes office, thus acting as a political faction in its own right.[11] In general, the army in Latin America "views itself as the only force able to wield a national policy and enforce this policy on sectional interests through force of arms, if not by force of law. The armed forces believe themselves the stabilizer in a contest between social classes embittered by the gap between poverty and wealth." But the military does not itself have a policy or a capability for resolving the contest which it mediates. At most it can effect an alliance with those who best seem able to maintain economic order while accommodating modest changes. "It has enough power to prevent governments unfavorable to itself from exercising authority, but not enough to rule for any length of time." It "is strong enough to cancel democratic norms but cannot maintain political order for an extended period." [12]

Even in democratic societies, committed to constitutional political forms, the military cannot be regarded as simply another arm of government. It has a special status by virtue of the physically coercive authority it controls, which, while leashed as a matter of political philosophy, can always be unleashed in the face of changed objective circumstances or an intrusive event. In recent years numbers of people in the United States have expressed some uneasiness over the role of its traditionally nonpolitical military. Without attempting to build a catalog of charges which lend support to such qualms, we may simply note that official documents have revealed the extent to which the armed forces have intervened in matters of foreign policy, such as the extension of the Vietnamese war by policies calculated to force governmental acquiescence, and the provisioning of foreign governments with hundreds of millions of dollars of weapons on their own initiative, beyond any congressional authorization. The Central Intelligence Agency, a quasi-military organization, has been disclosed to have used both the U.S. Information Service and the Agency for International Development as cover for its espionage operations, undermining the effectiveness of their intended functions for its own ends.

On the domestic front the military, through its vast programs of arms contracts, has won the sympathy of a significant segment of American industry and of the labor force in those communities which are the beneficiaries. Hearings held by Senator William Proxmire in 1969 revealed that some 2100 retired military officers were then working for the hundred major defense contractors, and that there is a reverse flow of industry men to Pentagon positions, presumably helping to cement a community of relations between the military and industry. University faculties have been supported in research in a variety of fields, the social sciences as well as the physical sciences, by Defense Department grants. In the civil disturbances in ghettos and on campuses in the period 1967–1969, the army was later revealed to have kept under surveillance a large number of civilians who were "suspected" of possible subversive intent. And before the Columbia Broadcasting System had aroused Pentagon anger by its documentary television film on the military's vast public relations and propaganda programs, the *Wall Street Journal* had already disclosed, in the words of its own headline, that "Pentagon's Promotion of Its Own Activities Upsets Many Critics." [13]

This itemization does not add up to any suggestion of a military conspiracy to undermine civilian rule. For the most part, most of such actions were taken with the knowledge and support of at least some civilian members of the government, executive more often than legislative. The significance of these developments has been fairly put, I think, by Senator J. William Fulbright:

As we have developed into a society whose most prominent business is violence, one of the leading professions inevitably is soldiering. Since they are the professionals, and civilian bureaucrats refuse to challenge them, the military have become ardent and effective competitors for power in American society.[14]

Fulbright notes that the danger lies in civilian authorities adopting the outlook of professional soldiers, acceding to their expertise in the one thing in which they are most experienced, the use of force.

If we look for the values which are institutionalized in the military, the first to command our attention would be the constitutional value of hierarchical order, with a virtual absence of personal autonomy. Loyalty to the system is paramount. The erosion of this quality among the draftees of the war in Vietnam, the loss of discipline in the ranks, the willingness of subordinates to reveal embarrassing information to newsmen and congressmen, was of the greatest concern to the professional leadership. More than loss on the battlefield, which could be retrieved by subsequent victory, this sapping of the value core of the institution itself was a source of understandable alarm.

But in addition to this constitutional value, which is widely enough understood and accepted, there is the question of the military's focal value, which has less often been examined. I would venture the proposition that the same thesis value which has been said to characterize the military in Latin America is not peculiar to the culture of that continent but applies to military organizations generally: they view themselves as the instrument of "national salvation and redemption." [15] They constitute the shield of the nation against subversion or conquest from without or within, against foes external or internal.

Just how such a mission is to be interpreted depends on the character of the military leadership itself. The meaning will be one thing to a General Douglas MacArthur, who in carrying out his institutional mission was willing to challenge the President, and something else to a General Dwight D. Eisenhower, who was intuitively convinced of the need for a single chief executive, who could not be a man on horseback. The meaning will be still something else to a General Charles de Gaulle, who subordinated the civilian organs of government to the hierarchical austerity and personal loyalty of the army type of organization he knew best, for the glory of the France he loved like a mistress: his objective was clearly national salvation and redemption after the disastrous conduct of two world wars, and only secondarily, perhaps only instrumentally, was he concerned for his own place in history. And as against that towering, arrogant figure we may set the Lilliputian efforts of the military conspiracy against him, based on unwillingness to see national pride humbled by withdrawal from Algeria—another "surrender"—and which was willing to precipitate a civil war if necessary to prevent that ignominy.

Wherever one looks for independent actions of military leadership, whether of the General's plot against Hitler, which failed, or Nasser's plot against Farouk, which succeeded, or of Ayub Khan or Yahya Khan in Pakistan, or Suharto in Indonesia—one could continue with such a list till boredom set in—in each instance there is revealed a particular military conception of why "national salvation and redemption" demands military intervention.

Normally, in the so-called "stable democracies," the military's focal value can be realized within the framework of civil government. Responding to internal disturbances—the ghetto riots of 1967, for example—or to declared engagements with a foreign enemy, the military saves or redeems the nation *within* the overall social values, without challenge to other dominant groups or interests. But there is no rule of immunity which guarantees the democracies that in the face of changed circumstances the military may not become a thrusting institution, seeking to impress its values on society at large, forming alliances with or accommodating such groups as it needs for the sake of continuity, winning over the adaptable and the unconcerned with pseudo-values relating to national pride.

Senator Fulbright notes that the "Prize Essay 1970" in the semiofficial *U.S. Naval Institute Proceedings* of March 1970, presumably chosen by a jury of high-ranking naval officers, carried the title "Against All Enemies." Written by Captain Robert J. Hanks, commander of a destroyer squadron, who had also seen service in the Pentagon, its theme was that the *military* (my emphasis) must determine the nature and extent of external threats to national security and also the character of the response to them. Captain Hanks noted with concern the number of individuals, some in high places, like Senator Fulbright himself, who were seeking to curb the military, and labeled them as people who, whether or not with intent, would "so weaken this nation's defense as to place the United States in the greatest jeopardy in its history." With this observation, Captain Hanks forthrightly faced the conclusion to be drawn from it. While the external threat continues, "we now face an equally potent challenge from within." In concentrating on the external threat over the past thirty years, "some of us"—that is, in the military—"may have forgotten that we solemnly swore to support and defend the Constitution of the United States against all enemies, foreign *and domestic*." (This time the emphasis is the Captain's.) "If the United States is to be protected against efforts of those who would place her in peril—through apathy, ignorance, or malice—we of the military cannot stand idly, silently by and watch it done. Our oath of office will not permit." [16]

It would be wrong to read great significance into this essay with respect to possible future policies or practices of the American military. We shall return to that subject in a later chapter. I allude to this carefully conceived statement by a ranking naval officer, selected for special merit in a competition sponsored by a military journal, only to support the conclusion that the particular focal value pertaining to this basic institution is its conception of national honor, salvation, or redemption, in pursuit of which it is ready to mobilize its weapons of war, against enemies internal or external. In this respect the Latin American military establishments are distinguishable only for the frequency with which they have felt called on to exercise their independent judgment, within a cultural context characterized by rapid changes in objective conditions. In such a diffuse and uncertain situation, the military must "save and redeem" almost continuously.

We have been concerned with three basic types of institutions— economic, religious, and military—which historically have served as the instruments for thruster groups to achieve dominance within a society, to infuse it with its values, to provide it with philosophical sanctions. Each has its own particularistic values, differing in some degree from the values of the other two. But the point which I should like to emphasize is that there is a strong tendency for these three institutions to form a harmonious alliance among themselves, in which the congruence of their values is of greater importance than the divergence. At one time or place, one or another of these three institutions may outrank the others in dominance—the military in imperial Rome, the church in the Middle Ages, the landed aristocracy in England from Elizabeth to Victoria, the large industrial corporation in twentieth-century United States—but the remaining two have tended to serve as loyal allies and rewarded supporters, or at the least as tolerant if observant bystanders.

At times one class has combined two of these institutions within itself, as the feudal nobility functioned both as the military and the landed aristocracy, or as the Communist Party in Russia functions both as the industrial controllers and the interpreters of the religious (but secular) faith. Conceivably all three institutions could be combined within one governing class. In any case, however achieved, there is a strong tendency for them to effect a working alliance.

The necessity for this is clear. Without substantial congruence of values and interests among these three basic institutions, there is little prospect of social stability. If values differ significantly, they must be brought into closer alignment by one means or another. A few examples may be helpful in this respect. The Reformation, with its so-called Puritan ethic, was hardly responsible for capitalism. After all, capitalistic undertakings of some consequence had already been initiated in Catholic countries before Luther took to the pulpit, and they expanded in number and size in those countries after the Reformation had had its impact. But the type of capitalistic enterprise carried on under Catholic auspices was of quite a different order from that which the Reformation made possible. It was not so single-minded in its dedication to the turning of a profit; it was concerned with qualitative aspects of industrial activity, and could not have conceived of breaking up the family by making each member a separate unit of an impersonal labor market.

With the traditional church antithetical to such form of economic activity, it required a revolution within the church—a split so deep it never yet has healed—to create a new church with values which were indeed more congruent with the rising mercantile and industrial class, in effect two thruster groups calling to each other and making common cause. In England, the rise of the wool trade, with its potential for commercializing on village-populated agricultural lands, led to the enclosure movement and gave cause to at least some of the nobility to accommodate the rising commercial class, out of their own self-interest. The separation from the Church of Rome provided reason enough for the military to support the new national "independence" which was symbolized by the established Church of England, even if not by the dissenting Protestant sects. There is no need to involve ourselves further with English history to indicate the manner in which the value systems of these three basic institutions found their harmonious resolution, particularly as they were swept along on a tide of imperialism providing a sense of national mission in the pseudo-value of "the white man's burden," Kipling-style, which gave it popular appeal. (A century or so later "manifest destiny" would do the same for the United States.)

Another example of the necessity for some degree of congruence of values among these three basic institutions is provided by the contrast between Russian and Yugoslav communism. In Russia, centralization of economic authority has been the persistent theme. Even in the last decade, in which its industrial growth has driven it to experiment with some forms of decentralized administration, it has continued to operate under a comprehensive national plan which is binding on its individual enterprises. I have heard Russian economists themselves comment on the inherent difficulty of combining plan centralization with enterprise discretion; to them it is a technical problem which remains unresolved. This centralization of economic authority is accompanied by a Communist Party which essentially resembles Catholicism as to its orientation—confessional, authoritarian, and conformist, as it must be if its values are to be compatible with those of the economic administration.

Yugoslavia, by contrast, has adopted a gospel of decentralization. Its enterprises are autonomously run by workers' councils, which elect their own managers. The national plan, if it can indeed be called that, is chiefly indicative to the enterprises. (It is more substantially concerned with government investment in the country's underdeveloped areas, investment in enterprises which will, when functioning, be turned over to the workers' councils, and in undertakings which are necessarily national in nature, such as transportation and postal service.) In the face of this relative autonomy for industrial operations, its Communist Party has essentially followed the Protestant model—a preaching and teaching force, relying on prestige and persuasion rather than authority. Perhaps I have drawn too sharp a contrast between these two countries, but the basic difference, I suggest, is there. Once again, it illustrates the way in which the value systems of the three basic institutions must be in reasonably close alignment.

The significance of this fact is that the alignment acts as a conservative influence. Whichever of the three institutions may foster the dominants of the society, the other two tend to support it. The power relationship is cemented in the implicit bargain, and administered through a government bureaucracy which, as we previously saw, is also disposed toward maintaining the status quo. The professional politicians can deal with the adaptables and the unconcerned.

The Educative Institutions

All institutions educate people in one way or another, but there are two which are especially important in transmitting the values of a society—family and school.

The profound influence of parents on their children needs no restatement here. What is important for our purposes is that the parents themselves act as transmitters of the values of the society in which they have themselves matured, reflecting all the impressions and experiences which they have absorbed in the course of their own institution-surrounded lives. The Freudian terminology recognizes in the *id* all the individual's own instinctive drives, which in the course of time are subjected to the unconscious censorship of the person's acquired *ego*. The ego, in turn, is subject to the more traditional, deeply seated, and moralistic governor, the *superego,* which in effect is his bred-in recognition of the behavior his society expects of him.[17] The parents are the chief instrument for the building of the child's superego, which means that (in Freud's words) "what is operating in the superego is not only the personal qualities of these parents but also everything that produced a determining effect upon them themselves, the tastes and standards of the social class in which they live and the characteristics and traditions of the race from which they spring." [18]

In this early stage of a child's development, totally dependent as he is, feelings of shame and guilt can be played on to the point of exploiting his dependency in a way that can be psychologically authoritarian. But more subtle means are available, even though the parents may be unaware they are employing them: expressions of approbation, appreciation, affection, pride, or their negative counterparts, with respect to public figures, nationality or racial types, professional or vocational identities, religions, by means of which a young child accumulates a rather substantial stock of values which are characteristic of the particular society in which he is growing up. The type of literature brought into the household and discussed, parental reaction to entertainments and amusements, sex, and education—all have their impact.

David Riesman and Nathan Glazer follow the later Freud (though apparently with the belief that they are going beyond him) in giving less emphasis to the parents as neutral social conduits in the forming of the child's superego, than to all the influences which have gone into the shaping of what the parents themselves transmit. In commenting on the thinking behind their influential book, *The Lonely Crowd,* they have said: ". . . we saw modern industrial society as primary, and as having an impact on child-rearing through the parents as transmission belts for the social imperatives. Thus, the father, returning from the factory and the bureaucratic organization, shaken by the insecurity of modern industrial life, conducted himself vis-à-vis his children in such a way as to evoke a certain kind of personality in them. The link between character and society was forged in the home; thus forged, character went out again to meet society—very much the same kind of society." [19]

The same thought has been expressed by Hans Gerth and C. Wright Mills who, objecting to the traditional designation of the family as the primary agency in the child's character formation, argued that "The father may not be the *primary* authority, but rather the replica of the power relations of society, and of course, the unwitting transmitter of larger authorities to his spouse and children." [20]

Understandably, the values implanted in children vary according to the class status of their parents and associates. One of the earlier students of this subject, Allison Davis, whom I have already cited, empirically demonstrated the difference between lower-class and middle-class values with respect to such matters as physical aggression, sexual relations, recreation, attitudes toward school, institutional affiliation, and the effects which such variations have on people's subsequent behavior. He found that as a consequence of such class-determined trained-in differences, middle-class people exhibit a greater anxiety with respect to their total range of activities, and are "culturally motivated to suffer, to renounce, to postpone gratifications in order to achieve." [21] A more recent study by Melvin L. Kohn, *Class and Conformity,* reaches similar conclusions. Middle-class parents emphasize self-direction and internal standards for the guidance of one's behavior. Working-class parents stress externally imposed rules and responsiveness to authority. These attitudes are conspicuously correlated with occupational experience. Middle-class parents commonly are engaged in more complex work, requiring synthesis, coordination of other people or of processes, and the exercise of discretion. Working-class parents are more frequently found in supervised tasks, with settled procedures, where the exercise of discretion and the ability to resolve problems for oneself are less needed and hence not impressed on their children. Thus there tends to be some intergenerational transmission of class values.[22]

In recent years, more emphasis has been placed by sociologists such as Riesman and Parsons on the influence of peer groups on children's attitudes and behavior, to the extent that these almost at times seem to supersede parental impact. In the nuclear family, particularly if the mother is working, the child at an early age spends most of his time with his own age group, at school, in their own associations, on the streets. Aspiring to solidity with the group, he tends to conform to its standards. Nevertheless, the peer group itself is, to a large extent, "chosen" by the parents, in that its members are almost certain to be of the same race, class, and occupational status.

Lillian Smith, in *Killers of the Dream,* cites a Southern child as follows:
I do not remember how or when, but by the time I had learned that God is love, that Jesus is His Son and came to give us more abundant life, that all

men are brothers with a common Father, I also knew that I was better than a Negro, that all black folks have their place and must be kept in it, that a terrifying disaster would befall the South if ever I treated a Negro as my social equal.[23]

This is a clear expression of parental values. The same child, if associating with a peer group, might be disposed to challenge such white middle-class values as those involving sex, dress, language, and other forms of behavior not fundamentally affecting status distinctions. He would be much less likely to find any encouragement within his peer group—drawn from the same social class as his parents—to take issue with attitudes touching on the advantages of their common social status.

One of the saddest examples I have ever seen of the difficulty of modifying parentally inspired values, which in turn reflect the social environment in which the parents themselves are embedded, was displayed in a documentary film shown by the National Educational Television Network. A group of college "liberals" had come together for a protracted session. They were, at best, a synthetic peer group, put together to give a "cross section" of student life—Northern and Southern whites of varying ethnic backgrounds, blacks, orientals, some deeply religious, others unbelievers, but all outspokenly opposed to racial prejudice. They lived together and met in a series of unstructured sessions, where they explored the prospects for creating a world of fellowship markedly different from the world they had inherited from their parents. They started with high hopes, but as the days succeeded each other they gradually had to confront the numbing realization that they continued to carry the prejudices of their parents deep inside them, acting as a governor on their own emotions and actions, regardless of all the peer group activity which had gone on throughout their adolescent years. And those parental values reflected, in turn, all that the parents had absorbed from the society which had molded them.

The educational system of a society supplements the family as a transmitter of values, serving as a second major influence in the shaping of the individual's superego. Religions have long been aware of the importance of inculcating particular systems of belief in the child at the earliest possible age, building into him a governor over his own developing ego which reflects the values and interests of a larger community. In our own day we assume that governments of authoritarian societies will seek to control the minds of the young. I have seen some of the elementary texts from which Cuban children learn their alphabet, vocabulary, and sentence structure; they implant, along with grammar, specific attitudes toward work, the state, one's responsibilities to others, the evil intent of Yankee imperialists. We often forget, however, that this policy is characteristic not only of authoritarian governments but of societies quite generally. It is indeed one of the major reasons why any society considers it important to allocate resources to the education of its children. Marvin Leiner, who spent a year in Cuba studying its school system, relates that educators there freely admit their intention. When one of the officials of the Ministry of Education was asked at an educational conference in Italy whether it was true that the school system in Cuba was an instrument of the state, he responded (as he related to Leiner): "Yes, of course. Just as it was before the triumph of the Revolution, and as it is in present-day Italy." [24]

In similar vein Raymond Williams speaks of the ideal which has been built into the English educational system "of leading the unenlightened to the particular kind of light which the leaders find satisfactory for themselves." [25] And A. P. Thornton writes of nineteenth-century England: "The aristocrats supported a system that inculcated their own outlook into the sons of the middle classes, because it was in their interest to do so. The system did not allow for the parsing and analysis of principle; it was not designed to do so, but to uphold a culture, a habit of life, that did not primarily depend upon intellectual values at all." The writers whose works were filtered into the textbooks explained to young minds "how it had come about that England had reached its apogee in the Victorian epoch," and Thornton gives as his opinion that in the "long afternoon of that epoch" the explanation was accepted on faith. "George Bancroft," he notes wryly, "had once performed the same service for his fellow citizens in the United States." [26]

In pre-World War II United States, the dominant class consisted of the upper strata of business leadership, that class which has gone under the rather undignified but perhaps descriptive acronym of WASP—white, Anglo-Saxon, Protestant. Its values permeated the school system no less than had English aristocratic values in their homeland; the reason was not so simple as that of an attempted indoctrination in attitudes which would support the privileges of an elite group. That element was of course involved. But beyond that there lay a genuine belief, as exists in any dominant class, that its way of life represents the best interests of the country at large, and the instruction of others in those values is a social benefit. As we have had occasion more than once to observe, values and interests easily tend to become confused, for understandable reasons. A valued way of life depends on the continued influence of those who understand that way of life best.

Numerous studies of American communities have been made for a variety of sociological purposes. We can scarcely run through them all, but August B. Hollingshead's field investigation of "Elmtown," a small midwest town, is perhaps representative. After noting that "the school is the only tax-supported institution devoted exclusively to the training of young Elmtowners in knowledge, skills, and values cherished by the culture," he identifies those whose values in fact are "cherished." Although the seven-man Board of Education is nominally elected by and from the public at large, "in practice, the members . . . come mainly from the two upper classes and have to qualify under informal ground rules. Even to be considered for the Board a person has to be male, Protestant, Republican, a property owner, preferably a Rotarian, or at least approved by the Rotarians." [27]

That the situation has not changed markedly since the time of Hollingshead's study is suggested by a 1970 report by Joseph Lelyveld of the *New York Times* concerning Plainfield, Indiana, a town of 8000 just outside Indianapolis. When five high school teachers appeared wearing black armbands at the time of the first Vietnam Moratorium in October 1969, the school board was faced with public protests and demands for their dismissal. There was no disruptive conduct to complain of; it was purely a conflict of views. The board issued a policy statement that any teacher identifying himself with "any controversial movement" on school time could be declared guilty of misconduct and insubordination. Lelyveld reported:

As the community saw it, teachers were not paid to raise questions but to furnish the accepted answers.

"They don't teach good old American history like they taught it years ago," complained Dr. Gerald O'Neill, an optometrist whose waiting room is amply stocked with magazines of the Veterans of Foreign Wars and the National Rifle Association. "A lot of schools today forget the word patriotism. The kiddies aren't even told about Nathan Hale."

To Edward Whalen, president of the Plainfield First Federal Savings and Loan Association, the logical way to handle a teacher who called the community's values into question seemed no different from the way he would handle a teller wishing to question his bank's reliability.

"You say, 'I'm sorry, we can't use you any more.' It's as simple as that," he said.

Robert Hall, a Main Street insurance man who was returned to the school board at a recent election by a landslide margin, was asked if the board's policy barred teachers from identifying themselves on a "controversial" issue if their stand paralleled the community's—for instance, if they supported the President on Vietnam.

"No, of course not," he replied.[28]

That the Plainfield attitude is not peculiar to it is reflected in a poll undertaken by Louis Harris for *Life* magazine. Of parents questioned, 62 percent thought that discipline was more important than self-inquiry in the conduct of a school. Bayard Hooper, reporting for *Life,* commented that the parents knew "exactly" what they wanted from their tax-supported school systems: "Teach the kids to understand our existing values," they say; "discipline them to conform." [29]

Marcuse, resorting to his dialectical analysis, has argued that the school system in the West is another example of an institution which only partially comprehends reality, and is as significant for what it excludes as for what it includes. The *traditional* expression of "individualism" in the classroom fails to comprehend the possibility of the individual's developing his capacities *in his own way,* under changed institutional conditions. Thus, he concludes, the school system, like other institutions, must be viewed as conforming the individual, even though in an earlier period it was seen as the principal means by which the individual could liberate his uniqueness. Here it seems to me that Marcuse makes his point only by idealizing the "earlier" school system. Traditionally the view has been that *by* conforming the child to the values of his society one in fact liberates him for his own achievement within that context. School systems, neither in the past nor at present, have been expected to encourage points of view which release people from the governing superego which provides norms for the society as a whole, a style of life which, even if not actually shared by all, is viewed as desirable. Certainly until the recent urban concentration of blacks gave them some influence over local school systems, there was never any thought that they were to be exposed, in school, to materials questioning the philosophical validity of the system in which they were expected to find their roles. Quite the contrary, the educational system was intended to adjust those whom society classed as inferior to a way of life designed *for* them.

This doctrinal function of a public school system is especially characteristic of the lower grades of instruction. The upper levels (high school in industrializing societies, college and professional schools in advanced societies) serve a second function which we noted briefly earlier: they act as a screen to sift out those who will be permitted to go on to higher occupational status from those who will be encouraged to satisfy themselves with low-status employment.

Although educational reform in the United States in the nineteenth century had behind it the philosophical justification that it would serve to eradicate class distinctions by "pooling" all youngsters in the same school system, practice never approached the ideal. As Michael Katz has demonstrated, the high school very quickly became the instrument of the middle class. Few poor or working-class children made it into the new institutions. "For the middle class children who made up the bulk of high-school students, schools helped to maintain their status and position in the community. Schools were an entree for boys into business (though they taught little of major importance to enterprise) and for girls into teaching." [30]

Such educational sifting was even more pronounced in England. No provision was made for general secondary education well into the present century, though the Bryce Commission had made such recommendation in 1902. Instead, a form of scholarship support was provided for those who had, at an early age, demonstrated their fitness for higher education; otherwise youngsters were shunted onto an educational track preparing them for working careers. In France the *grandes écoles,* which constitute the *passe partout* for all the jobs of consequence in the society, are theoretically open to any student on a strictly competitive basis, but in practice they have served as a more easily justified screen to keep the lower classes out of prestigious positions, rather than as a device for letting them in.

In less developed countries the same process of class discrimination in the allocation of educational advantage persists into the present day. Sunkel has described the situation in Chile as of only a few years ago. There are different types of schools for different social classes. The ordinary primary school, designed for the low-income population, often offers only a few years of training, particularly in the rural areas, and children frequently drop out. Some few primary schools are attached to *liceo* which also provide intermediate education and are attended by middle-class children whose dropout rate is much lower. Private schools, enjoying a substantial government subsidy, show the lowest school-leaving rate. Not surprisingly, the bias built into such a system guarantees that only a few lower-income students obtain much of an advanced education—as of 1960 only about 2 percent reached the university, and these were normally to be found in the shorter, less professional courses. "Students of low-income origin are extremely rare in medicine, engineering, and other courses which take seven or more years to complete, and which maintain high academic standards." [31]

The system of slotting or tracking children of different levels of ability has received considerable support in the United States as a means of allocating public resources to those who can make most effective use of them. It is part of the gospel of meritocracy, and has received support from such eminent educators as James Bryant Conant, former president of Harvard. "I submit that in a heavily urbanized and industrialized free society, the educational experiences of youth should fit their subsequent employment." [32]

One cannot help wondering how a child's "subsequent employment" can be determined in advance, so that his education can be fitted to it. While their indictment may be somewhat strong, it is hard not to agree with Paul Lauter and Florence Howe that "tracking"—the system of determining the kind, quality, pace, and amount of a child's education on the strength of some indicator such as the "intelligence quotient"—"may assure the 'failure' of lower-class students," but "it allows the schools to 'succeed' in serving middle-class interests by preparing their children to fill the technological and professional needs of corporate society." [33] For the others, it is chiefly elementary literacy and value instruction which is their educational portion.

Nevertheless, for those children, of whatever class, who do make it through college, opportunities for more advantageous employment are opened up. One authority after another has testified that equality of education is a necessary ingredient to equality of opportunity. Even if the system is "rigged" so that fewer children from lower-income families are enabled to develop their intellectual capacities fully, but are screened out by the educational process itself, it remains true that higher education has been the principal avenue for such career advancement as does take place among their number. There is an interesting paradox here: lower-class parents tend to instill in their children the importance of discipline, of conformity to the rules, as we noted in the course of examining the family as the conduit of social values; they expect the public schools to reinforce these values. But the chief avenue by which children of lower-class parents are able to break out of this sense of hierarchical ordering and achieve whatever degree of autonomy the constitutional value of the social system permits lies in their working up the educational ladder high enough to *escape* conformism to some degree.

The higher educational system thus performs two functions: on the one hand, it constitutes one important means by which those whom the system advantages most, the dominants, their allies, and their principal supporters, are enabled to keep and enjoy those advantages; Norton Long has likened the college curriculum to a "gatekeeper" for the middle class.[34] On the other hand, it has served as the principal means by which the less advantaged can pass through the gate and be admitted to the inner circle. This co-optation of some of the more ambitious and talented (talented, that is, according to the standards the society imposes) acts as a safety valve for the system, permitting it to conceive of itself as an "open" system, free of hereditary classes or castes. Norman Podhoretz, in his disingenuous autobiography, *Making It,* relates the exhilaration he felt, fresh out of a Brooklyn Jewish background, at first exposure to the great minds in the field of English literature at Columbia University. This was what the world of the mind was all about. Then came the dawning realization that he was being accepted into that society "on good behavior," that is, as long as he conformed to the patterns of thought and conduct that went with a WASP-dominated culture.[35]

Pareto's "circulation of the elites" is not exactly a Ferris wheel, in which those who come to the top are constantly changing and everyone has the same chance to come to the top. There is an advantaged class whose members tend to stay within the ranks of the advantaged, with only a few departures, but from time to time the ranks open to admit a few exceptional outside individuals, who have in the process of winning the right of entry also acquired the values of those whom they are joining.

There are also varying degrees of association with the inner circle, so that more education permits a closer approach to those whom the system most favors, and some disproportionate sharing in its benefits. But in the very nature of the system, if education is to function as a "gatekeeper," the more widespread education becomes, and the larger the number of people who receive a college degree either by virtue of "open admissions," a lowering of standards, or more general economic support, the higher will become the educational requirements for the more prestigious positions. Otherwise, some new "gatekeeper" will have to be found to replace education in the selection of those to be admitted to the inner compound. We have had occasion to note this "receding egalitarian effect" before: the more equal (accessible) become the opportunities for attaining any given level of education, the higher (and therefore less accessible) will become the educational qualifications for the more advantageous positions.

The universities have thus typically served a conservative function in society. They have, as an institution, supported the existing system of values and sought to make it work more smoothly. Their major spokesmen have, frequently enough, contributed to the philosophical validation, as when President Charles W. Eliot of Harvard offered as his considered opinion that government's duty was chiefly that of "enforcing the sanctity of contracts and preventing cheating," and President Nicholas Murray Butler of Columbia gave as his view that "Nature's cure for most social and political disease is better than man's," so that a general policy of governmental nonintervention meant in effect allying oneself with nature.[36] The universities have ingratiated themselves with the dominant class with that remarkable phenomenon, the honorary degree, by bestowing honorific titles signifying intellectual and moral excellence on numbers of prominent businessmen and philanthropists (which is to say second-generation members of business families).

But it would be an error to regard the universities only in this conservative light. Along with this undeniable support for the prevailing social order, they have—more than any other single institution—harbored critics of the status quo. The tradition of intellectual independence, which is their virtue to be defended against all comers, has meant that at the same time its systems-developers and its theoreticians of the social equilibrium are refining their doctrines, as part of the philosophical validation, its radical critics (the "dialecticians" who are more concerned with what the system omits) are sharpening their challenges to the status quo. In a sense, this opportunity for the "circulation of ideas" is a necessary counterpart of the circulation of elites—a safety valve which by releasing pressure where it most builds up enables a society to function with a constitutional value embodying less coercion and more apparent autonomy, thereby justifying the relative independence which the dominant class desires for itself.

Notes

1. Reported in the *New York Times,* 9 June 1970.

2. *New York Times,* 3 December 1970. On the preceding day, the Rules Committee, by a vote of 7 to 7, had refused to clear, for consideration by the House, a bill providing for an independent consumer protection agency.

3. Ralf Dahrendorf, *Class and Class Conflict in Industrial Society* (Stanford, Calif.: Stanford University Press, 1959), pp. 297–300.

4. *Ibid.,* p. 302.

5. This set of attitudes, particularly as identifying Latin America, have been described by a number of writers. A good summary discussion is contained in S. M. Lipset's "Values, Education, and Entrepreneurship," in Lipset and Solari, *Elites in Latin America,* pp. 13–17.

6. Erikson, *Identity: Youth and Crisis,* p. 83.

7. *Ibid.,* p. 84.

8. Jacques Ellul, "Western Man in 1970," in B. de Jouvenel *Futuribles I.*

9. Erikson, *Identity: Youth and Crisis,* p. 84.

10. Mosca, *The Ruling Class,* pp. 54–55.

11. Horowitz, in Lipset and Solari, *Elites in Latin America,* pp. 148–149.

12. *Ibid.,* pp. 149–151. Quoted with permission.

13. *Wall Street Journal,* 13 November 1970.

14. J. William Fulbright, "The Governance of the Pentagon," *Saturday Review,* 7 November 1970, p. 22.

15. Horowitz, in Lipset and Solari, *Elites in Latin America,* p. 149. Quoted with permission.

16. Quoted by Senator Fulbright, "The Governance of the Pentagon," *Saturday Review,* 7 November 1970, p. 25.

17. If one wished to add to this psychological vocabulary the major terms which are missing and relevant he would include the *self,* which consists of our

reactions in a variety of situations, reflecting the interaction of id, ego, and superego; *I* as the conscious cognitor and evaluator of the self; the *ideal self* as the unconscious image we hold of the self we would like to be; the *ego ideal* as the ideologically oriented set of prescriptions and proscriptions affecting the actual functioning of the ego, somewhat more flexible than the superego; and *identity* as the conscious accomplishment of the ego, synthesizing all these manifestations of the individual. I have taken this terminology from Erikson. To avoid an excessively detailed journey into territory with which I am not well acquainted, I have restricted the analysis in the text to the terms which are most familiar and most relevant.

18. Sigmund Freud, *An Outline of Psychoanalysis* (New York: W. W. Norton & Co., 1949), pp. 122–123.

19. David Riesman and Nathan Glazer, "The Lonely Crowd: A Reconsideration in 1960," in Lipset and Lowenthal, *Culture and Social Character*, p. 434.

20. Hans Gerth and C. Wright Mills, *Character and Social Structure* (New York: Harcourt Brace Jovanovich, 1953), p. 34.

21. Allison Davis, "Socialization and Adolescent Personality," in *Readings in Social Psychology*, ed. T. M. Newcomb and E. L. Hartley (New York: Holt, Rinehart & Winston, 1947), p. 149.

22. Melvin L. Kohn, *Class and Conformity: A Study in Values* (Homewood, Ill.: Dorsey Press, 1969).

23. Lillian Smith, *Killers of the Dream* (New York: W. W. Norton & Co., 1949), p. 18, cited by Allport, in *The Nature of Prejudice*, p. 276.

24. Marvin Leiner, "Cuba's Schools Ten Years Later," *Saturday Review*, 17 October 1970, p. 70.

25. Williams, *Culture and Society, 1780–1950*, p. 238.

26. Thornton, *The Habit of Authority*, pp. 245, 262.

27. August B. Hollingshead, *Elmtown's Youth* (New York: John Wiley & Sons, 1950), especially pp. 121–128.

28. Joseph Lelyveld, "Patriotic Town Is Angry Over Teachers' Protest," *New York Times*, 29 May 1970, pp. 31–32.

29. Louis Harris, "What People Think About Their Schools," *Life*, May 16, 1969, pp. 23–40. The sample population on which the study was based consisted of 2500 students, parents, teachers, and principals of 100 schools in "representative" big cities, suburbs, small towns, and rural areas.

30. Michael B. Katz, *The Irony of Early School Reform* (Cambridge, Mass.: Harvard University Press, 1968), p. 91. Katz also notes (p. 92) that the high school served middle-class interests because they could spread among the public at large the cost of educating their own children.

31. Osvaldo Sunkel, "Change and Frustration in Chile," in Veliz, *Obstacles to Change in Latin America*, pp. 137–138. Quoted with permission.

32. James B. Conant, *Slums and Suburbs* (New York: McGraw-Hill Book Co., 1961), p. 40.

33. Paul Lauter and Florence Howe, "How the School System Is Rigged for Failure," *New York Review of Books*, 18 June 1970, p. 19.

34. Norton Long, "Local and Private Initiative in the Great Society," in Gross, *A Great Society?*, p. 85. In his "Report of the President" (Yale 1970–1971), Kingman Brewster notes (p. 24) that "the whole being of Yale in

the early decades of this century was devoted to the total collegiate experience for the development of Yale men. The classroom is never mentioned in *Stover!* The experience was designed to produce those fitted to lead a financial, industrial, and civil society dominated by an inherited elite. An appreciation of the amenities of life and culture, coupled with incentives and rewards for a public-spirited activism, served the maturing Republic well." Brewster's observation is a preliminary to his comments on the changes which are in process of taking place in the formulation of "Yale's purpose."

35. Norman Podhoretz, *Making It* (New York: Random House, 1967). Podhoretz is now editor of the Jewish monthly *Commentary*.

36. Nye, *This Almost Chosen People*, pp. 134–135.

10 / Continuity and Change: The Effects of Time

The notion that the vitality of a society and of its values tends to diminish over time, that it may give way to other more virile societies with more sharply focused values, is a theme which has been played on by many writers. "At first sight it might seem as though old age could never affect a people or a civilization," Mosca comments, "since human generations always reproduce themselves and each new generation has all the vigor of youth. Yet something that is altogether comparable to old age or organic debilitation does manifest itself in peoples." [1] In Schumpeter's analysis of social classes, harsh conditions and demanding tasks (comparable to Toynbee's "challenges") may inspire great deeds, giving rise to a great civilization, but the same level of achievement and the will which made it possible cannot be maintained, so that with the passage of time there comes decline. [2] Such life-cycle theses abstract from the causes of decline, making the latter a function purely of time.

I see no logical reason, however, why a dominant class *must* deteriorate, given its constant renewal from within and the co-optation of talent from without, given a flexibility which accommodates change through interpretation and rebargaining. Nor do I see anything like a "normal" or "customary" life span for a dominant class, without which the concept of its inevitable decline becomes meaningless. If one society's dominants can survive for a thousand years, while another's withers away within fifty, what are we left with except some conviction that all things must pass "in time," however long that may mean?

Thus except for significant changes in objective conditions or the impact of an external shock, a dominant group and the values it has spawned may continue indefinitely, the latter (the values) modified as necessary to accommodate other interests, philosophically validated and institutionally embodied. [3]

This is especially the case if membership in the dominant class is defined by institutional position, and access to such positions is open to those who meet certain criteria. In Western societies educational attainment has, as we have already noted, become the ladder for advancement into influential positions, not quite irrespective of one's social class position but significantly so. In this case it is not a dominant *caste* which continues, with membership defined by birth, but a class which is composed of the incumbents of certain institutional positions, by whatever route they may have reached those. The institution itself implants its value orientation by elevating to its leadership roles only those who confirm its traditions.

This emphasis on the continuity of a dominant class and its value structure suggests that a major shift in values occurs infrequently within a society, perhaps chiefly at a time of serious crisis or as a result of revolution, and that commonly value changes, if they do occur, are slower and more incremental adjustments to ongoing changes in objective conditions, chiefly in the form of reinterpretations of validated creeds not involving any major upheaval or rebellious contest.

This does not rule out some social dissonance, which at times may swell ominously in volume. If we remember the array of values present in any society, sheltered by groups or individuals, we can expect that from time to time circumstances will evoke an overt expression of conflicting values, but we can expect as well that, lacking any strong support from a thruster group, such dissonance will in time diminish and become absorbed in the interstices of institutionalized life. "Counter" movements—religious revivals and enthusiasms, student protests against the dominant culture, political agitations for distributive reforms—may emerge cyclically only to spend their force and subside.

Moreover, the fundamental, rock-ribbed philosophical validation (the "faith of our fathers") over time accumulates a penumbra of moralistic standards not essential to the value core, dealing with such matters as taste, esthetics, sex, privacy, language—standards of conduct which, while helping to define the style of an epoch and some of its norms, may not be vital in affecting a society's general objectives or its capabilities of integrated action. Changes in these standards can generate a good deal of heat, occasion profound pessimism, and sometimes evoke conflict, but they tend to be episodic, identifying periods which become popularly designated as "the Gay Nineties" or the "Roaring Twenties," "fin de siècle," or "the Age of Aquarius." At the time one may read genuine significance into such movements as signaling a transition to some new focal value, and at the time there is no certain way of disputing their potential significance, but more often than not these are only transient escapes from boredom or frustration, a kind of prolonged Saturnalia.

Indeed, one could reasonably argue that the longer a society perpetuates a value system, the greater the likelihood of its continued survival. More people acquire a stake in it, grow up in its traditions, are institutionally conditioned to accept it. Its very longevity seems to testify to a capacity for accommodation and interpretative adaptability which gives it resilience. Thus Talcott Parsons, for example, sees the American value system as basically unchanged from the past despite substantial changes in social structure.[4]

Threats to Value Continuity: Focal Values

If there is no logical basis for any biological or stage or life-cycle theory of social systems, there nevertheless are grounds for believing that the passage of time does have some tendency to affect their viability—not in the sense that they become "feeble with age," but that they lose their acceptability. The loss may be gradual and perhaps reversible; it may be sudden and complete. If one can speculate that the longer a system survives the more entrenched it becomes, one can also speculate that the longer it survives the more resistance and opposition it evokes. These are contradictory *effects* but not contradictory propositions. The outcome of such opposed forces cannot be predicted, but their existence can.

There are two forms which opposition to an ongoing system can take. One involves the sequence with which this study has been principally concerned, beginning with a change in objective conditions which provides an opportunity seized by a thruster group. But the decline of a dominant class and the erosion of the values it has implanted in a society is not necessarily simply the other side of the coin of a challenging, rising, thruster group. The former can occur without the latter. Changing conditions may undermine social values without respect to the effectiveness of new thrusts. This is something quite different from a metaphysical belief that the life juices of a dominant class somehow dry up simply with the passage of time, leaving only a decaying body behind.

As we noted early in this study, every society is host to an array of values, but only certain ones are selected and established as the focal values of a society. The other values do not simply go away: they remain the possession of particular groups or individuals who continue to nurture them, in some degree, even though conforming to the common norms. These become the *excluded* values, which may continue to have meaning for some elements of a society but are excluded from any influential role. The assets of the society, its physical and moral energies, are directed to the selected focal values, and the excluded values are either repressed, viewed with tolerant benevolence as colorful or idiosyncratic but harmless, or simply ignored. With the passage of time and the spread of dominant values, with their validation and institutionalization, the accepted focal values amount to a "litmus test" for compatibility with one's social environment. Their profession becomes a test of "patriotism," loyalty, even of spiritual or mental health. The individual who is unable to accommodate himself to such beliefs may be viewed as sick, perhaps requiring the ministrations of a priest or a psychiatrist, at the least in need of being "set straight" by friends or family.

But the longer the focal value is maintained with vigor, and the longer it thereby excludes alternative values, the more strain is it likely to set up within the system. Individuals who believe that the singleness of devotion to one value sacrifices other elements of value—perhaps even of greater value—become more restless, dissident, overt in their opposition. The expression of such dissidence by some encourages similar protest by others. The challenge to the focal value spreads. Carl Jung in his writings espoused the thesis that when certain characteristics or values, such as rationalism or secularism, get overstressed in a society, there is likely to be a swing toward compensating attitudes.

I do not want to suggest that such a dialectical response is commonly widespread, embracing a population at large. Quite the contrary: I would expect that the expression of opposing values is confined to a relatively small number of the more intellectually oriented persons, probably disproportionately composed of youths and young adults. As they make their views more widely known, they are likely to evoke a more dogmatic assertion of the traditional values from those whose interests are bound up in the existing order. What effectiveness it, the small nucleus, may have on the larger society is problematical, and a matter which we shall want to examine shortly. At this stage it is enough to point out that continued emphasis on certain selected values, and concomitant exclusion of the effective expression of others, sets up a condition which may lead to some contest of values.

We can observe the process at work, both with and without the presence of a thruster group, in the case of the decline in dominance of the Catholic Church in western Europe. In the Reformation countries, opportunities opened up by the collapse of church authority and the confiscation of church properties were seized on by a thruster group, which in time precipitated a change in focal values. Utilitarianism and materialism, and rationalism in their service, were all accorded greater social emphasis. In Tawney's words, "The general acceptance by thinkers of a scale of ethical values, which turned the desire for pecuniary gain from a perilous, if natural, frailty into the idol of philosophers and the mainspring of society—such movements are written large over the history of the tempestuous age which lies between the Reformation and the full light of the eighteenth century." [5]

In the Catholic countries of the continent no such thruster group appeared. Nevertheless, a waning of the religious focal value, which had rested with the dominant church, gave greater opportunity for the repressed value of materialism to receive more open expression; it did not initially emerge as a challenge, as in the Protestant countries, but it did over a more protracted period assert its position. The dialectical opposition inherent in this position received its most violent expression during the French Revolution, which turned on the church as savagely as on the nobility.

The trend away from spirituality, esthetics, and considerations of the quality of life and toward rational thought, quantitative interests, and utilitarian considerations had begun *before* the Reformation intruded its revolutionary impact. A dialectic reaction to the saturation of all social relations with a religious cast had already been under way before the advent of Luther, even in countries like France which did not respond to his mission.[6] The reaction in the Catholic countries, quite in contrast to England, was a renewed assertion of dogma. In the face of Luther's attack (which centered on the way that the religious focal value had been diluted with humanism, as well as on the church's claim to constitutional centralism), Paul III responded by seeking to restore some of the original purity of purpose and to stamp out heresy with the Inquisition. The excluded values, which had been seeping in out of laxity, were to be more firmly excluded.

We can take a more contemporary example. In Western industrialized societies, and most obviously in the United States, the focal value has become pecuniary wealth in the service of consumption. Economic aspirations have buried other valued objectives, quite explicitly and with the validation of the most estimable thinkers from the early years of the nineteenth century. We need only remember Bentham's strictures on pleasure as the only good, and his heavy-handed emphasis on consumption as not indeed the sole good but that good which was responsible for society's economic functioning.

But the dominance of this focal value has tended to evoke dissident reaction from those who believe that the excluded values should receive more attention. Indeed, we can go back to the preceding century to find ample early expression of this point of view. John Stuart Mill serves as a classic example. "I know not why it should be a matter of congratulation that persons who are already richer than any one needs to be, should have doubled their means of consuming things which give little or no pleasure except as representative of wealth; or that numbers of individuals should pass over, every year, from the middle class into a richer class, or from the class of the occupied rich to that of the unoccupied." [7]

More contemporary intellectuals have expressed reservations about the exclusion of nonmaterial values from Western, especially American, society. The sociologists Riesman and Glazer have said: "Young well-educated Americans today want more and different things out of life than their ancestors did: security and affluence enable them to want 'the good life' rather than the full dinner pail." [8] The historian Daniel Boorstin has commented: "When the getting of more and more comes to mean less and less, when more and more Americans begin to worry over the comparative merits of their increasingly elaborate automatic appliances performing evermore-trivial functions, is it any wonder that more and more Americans become skeptical of the salvation that lies in wealth?" [9] The economist Sidney Alexander has observed: "That wants are generated by the social process . . . in the profound sense of their dependence on the whole cultural matrix, certainly threatens the entire ethical basis of economics. . . . It challenges the principle that more is better, and opens up the question of what sorts of wants we should generate, what sorts of men we should make." [10] And the philosopher Erich Fromm, challenging the value of satisfying "artificially stimulated phantasies," has with heavy sarcasm said that "Modern man, if he dares to be articulate about his concept of heaven, would describe a vision which would look like the biggest department store in the world, showing new things and gadgets, and himself having plenty of money with which to buy them." [11]

The focal value of consumption is related to the ethic of work. Work in the contemporary value system is unimportant for any intrinsic satisfactions it may provide (they, if they occur, are so much gravy) but only because it provides the passport to the land of plenty. This concentration on work whose value is measured in money has also evoked its opposition from those who believe that other significant values inherent in work are thereby excluded.

Here again it is a simple matter to provide a sampling of the opinions of intellectuals on this score. The political scientist Norton E. Long believes that "we are beginning to see that a kind of spiritual poverty more desolating than the economic may be the unintended product of our outworn Calvinism. Serving the economy may no longer produce as a by-product in any humanly adequate sense the significant service of any humanly adequate god." [12] The Swiss philosopher Herbert Luthy, in the process of reexamining Weber's thesis of a Protestant ethic, observes that "the pursuit of individual gain has no meaning unless it culminates in enjoyment and stops there. By rejecting this enjoyment the effort is pursued without pause and without end, like the search for an impossible redemption." [13] The American economist Wassily Leontief, commenting favorably on the work of British economist E. J. Mishan, emphasizes that the technological conditions of production are not chosen with a view to enhancing man's enjoyment of life but only with the dominant requirement of industrial efficiency. [14] The French economist and administrator Robert Marjolin, while foreseeing that the basis for our material existence must remain mainly industrial, writes that "production and productivity are not ends in themselves. They must lead to a better and richer life. This is probably the greatest challenge facing us." [15] And Fromm, once again, voices an indictment of modern society on this count, in a summation put together by political scientist John Schaar.

Under present conditions, co-management and workers' participation would, most probably, mean only an acceleration of the present powerful tendencies toward materialism and what Fromm calls alienated consumption, for the workers have no conception of any moral or esthetic order beyond the present one. What has to be recognized is that the workers have been "corrupted," tamed. And they have been tamed to the harness of meaningless work not by the stick of hunger, but by the carrot of limitless consumption, by the vision of utopia offered by the ad-men and sold on the installment plan. Only if this fact is kept in mind can one explain the astonishing fact that organized business and organized labor have combined to make productivity, profit, and "full" employment—that is, work in its inescapable modern meaninglessness—the dominant and almost the sole aim and function of the community's internal political life. [16]

The various youth "counter-cultures" which have appeared in Western society since, roughly, 1965, ranging from purported revolutionary movements to rural "communes," have been symbolic of this protest against focal values—dialectical reactions against prevailing dominant values. Sated with consumption values, alienated by work whose only rationale is more consumption, dissident youths have sought to change or "opt out" of a society whose values exclude those they affirm. It would be patent nonsense to see in these limited and diminutive movements (however shrill they may at times become) the harbinger of a swift change in social values. The institutionalized values of a society are not so easily turned around by a handful of privileged and intellectualized protestants. But that is not necessarily to deny any importance to such protest movements. They may indeed fade away, a transient phenomenon which will go down in the history books as the "Restless Sixties." But it is also possible that they constitute evidence of growing strain in the social system, the audible escape of values which have been repressed—excluded—by the dominant values of our times. This is a possibility we shall come back to later.

The assertion of an excluded value poses an alternative to existing values, even though the alternative comes unsupported by a thruster group and hence incapable of making an effective challenge. But existing values may lose their potency for another reason, without even so much as the suggestion of an alternative on the horizon. This occurs when the philosophical validation loses its credibility.

We have previously noted that with changes in objective conditions, dominant values and their doctrinal expression must be reinterpreted to make them applicable. Individualism gets redefined so that it emerges in the mid-twentieth century as very nearly the reverse of where it began a century earlier: from constituting the island of privacy and the sphere of personal initiative which one can defend against others, it becomes converted into a conception of how a person can best relate himself to his social context. And yet such a reinterpretation, however much it may stimulate the ironic phrase of an unreconstructed philosophic curmudgeon, does not insult the intelligence of the general public. Naturally, if conditions change, values must adjust along with them, not by being tossed overboard but by sensible and reasonable construction, the kind of exercise in which the Supreme Court habitually engages, endowing hallowed traditions and honored phrases with new meanings which still possess some relationship —even if attenuated—to the original philosophic starting point.

But there come times when traditions and terms of value are given interpretations which are in fact an assault on a people's intelligence, when casuistical ingenuity serves only to destroy the validity it aims to preserve. That condition was reached in the United States, I believe, with the prolongation of the war in Vietnam. With all the vagueness of content of the inherited tradition of "democratic" values, that term still conveyed a sense of honorable political intent and relative achievement until credibility was strained and then snapped for many people, not only the young, by the public relations attempts emanating from White House and Pentagon to interpret the destruction of a people and the despoliation of a country as an act of preserving "democratic" freedoms. The Orwellian flavor of the interpretative phrases which flowed from the mouths of the highest political representatives served only to shatter, for numbers of people, nostalgic and residual beliefs in the philosophic content of what democracy meant. The "sacred truths" which were once held to be "self-evident," which had continued to maintain an apostolic quality even after they had undergone substantial surgical exegesis over the years, became blasphemies in the face of My Lai. I do not suggest that this was the case for a majority of the American population, but only that it was true in enough instances to weaken the value structure of American society. As in the case of the dialectical alternative, the credibility reaction may relate to only a relatively small number—certainly too small to have a direct influence on institutionalized values. It is only in concert with other value conflicts which we shall shortly investigate that some significance may attach to it.

It is always possible that such loss of credibility, like the profession of a counter (excluded) culture, may be a transient phenomenon, and that credibility may be somewhat restored with new political representatives and the passage of time. But credibility as to a creed, once shattered, is hard to restore, like loss of confidence in a person. Time may soften the sharp impact of the first revelation, but suspicion and skepticism remain: the fabric of belief has been permanently weakened.[17]

In the economic sphere something similar may be at work with respect to the primacy of private consumption as focal value. Aside from any dialectical assertion of counter-values, there may be simple disillusionment with the philosophical view inherited from English thinkers that private wants are insatiable, and that satisfaction of such wants is the *summum bonum*. In a society whose cities are gradually dissolving into slum stews, in which millions are trapped like chunks of meat, the credibility of the private-consumption thesis is being contested by more and more intellectuals, however much it is still adhered to by suburban dwellers.

Thus the dialectical process—the resuscitation of long-excluded values —and the loss of credibility in what was once viewed as philosophically valid can raise seed clouds of doubt with respect to the continuity of traditional focal values. Both expressions are almost certain to be confined, in their first manifestation, to small groups, primarily intellectuals, who certainly do not merit classification as thrusters.

Time and Constitutional Values

Just as in the case of focal values, so too is it possible for the passage of time—not aging in the biological sense, the false analogy which we have rejected, but history in the sense of an unfolding of events—to erode constitutional values. Changes in objective conditions characterizing a society may force either the centralization or decentralization of hierarchical authority within a given political unit, with an attendant weakening in the acceptability of the mix of authority and autonomy. Here the result is so dependent on the specific content of the political order and philosophical traditions that we are reduced to considering two quite general cases. Let us consider first the pressures making for centralization of authority in mature industrialized countries.

In such political units, changes in all our four categories of objective conditions are creating strong pressures for the placement of increasing authority in the hands of the executive branch of government. Advances in science and their technological applications have gone beyond the capacities of individual enterprises to carry out effectively in enough instances —atomic and nuclear energy, space and communications developments, transportation—to raise expectations that the scale of future advances will increasingly involve central governments. Support for further progress in these areas comes more and more frequently from government appropriations, with government direction. The scale and complexity of economic activity has grown to the point where management of the economy to avoid or soften unemployment and inflation has become accepted even by those conservative forces which fought such government intrusion only a decade ago. Public economic planning is now no longer the ritual advocacy of left-wing liberals but the cautious proposal of reflective businessmen. The growth in numbers of population and their concentration in metropolitan centers have raised problems of housing, congestion, physical safety, health and hygiene, and education—all transcending the political capabilities of local governments and requiring integration through central mechanisms—social planning on a scale comparable to economic planning.

The intricacy of these problems, the frequent crises which they precipitate, the necessity for expert judgment and prompt action throw responsibility for decision and action increasingly on the executive rather than the legislative arm of government. Just as the large corporation operates effectively through its management, subjected only to periodic review by its board of directors, the trend in government is toward decision and action by the executive, tempered by accountability to the legislature.

In government as in the case of the large corporation, central management cannot permit itself to become overloaded with multifarious problems of varying levels of significance and so must decentralize discretion in those matters where central policy can be effectively elaborated at lower levels in the organizational hierarchy. Decentralization thus proceeds hand in hand with centralization. But the movement is scarcely a proportional one: it is the major decisions which create the style of the times, provide the grand design, establish the instruments for coordinating the subordinate units, and these are taken over by the center; it is the subsidiary and effectuating decisions which get pushed down to local levels.

At least two consequences of interest to us flow from this centralizing tendency. In those societies, principally in the West, where social values have stressed individual autonomy, the pressure of objective changes runs counter to this traditional value. Granted that the movement began long ago and gathered momentum at the turn of the present century with the increasing scale of private operations—the rise of the large corporation, the mass university, the amalgamated labor union. The reinterpretation of individualism allowed us to see these institutions as individuals, and to wrap them in the same mantle of autonomy which we accorded to real persons. We continued to speak of the "private" society, using the term to distinguish it from the public province of government, dismissing as ideologic heresy Marx's insight that organizations grown to such size, so dependent on and influential over major sectors of society, could hardly be described any longer as "private." And whatever was private was autonomous, subject of course to limited regulation where this revealed itself as necessary but nevertheless resting on a foundation of immunity from public direction, secure in the exercise of its own discretion. The autonomy which was preserved was, to be sure, less that of the individual than that of the organization; the discretion which made it a "free" society was less that of the citizen than that of its mass organizations. But this change in the objective conditions of Western society could be made compatible with the inherited philosophical validation, and it did not confront the dominant business class, as a class, with a challenge to its position. Private enterprise— whatever its scale—was equated with individual autonomy, and the traditional values retained their strong supporting role.

But this continuity of traditional values is now threatened by the centralizing tendencies of government, which in its coordinating and goal-setting roles intrudes on the autonomy of the private enterprise, requiring its conformity to rules and objectives determined outside the organization. The professional politicians who nibble away at corporate discretion cannot ignore the very real remaining corporate power; public plans must reflect enough of business interest to win its support. It is also conceivable that a new class of businessmen may learn to use a more powerful government to their own benefit. But whatever the outcome, the fact remains that circumstantial pressures are undermining traditional constitutional values, and moving societies which have stressed privacy and autonomy closer to the other end of the authority spectrum, toward hierarchical decision-making. No amount of theorizing about pluralism or veto groups or participatory planning can disguise the fact that the tendency is toward central decisions, controlling subordinate units, not because that result is necessarily wanted by power-bent politicians but because social conditions push them inexorably in that direction. And this undermining of old constitutional values obtains whether or not there is a thruster group on the horizon to view this as an opportunity on which to seize for its own advantage.

A second consequence of this development also lurks in the background, with a potential for disrupting the value cohesion of a society. Lord Acton's aphorism concerning the evils of power has impressed itself on the Western consciousness, sometimes with misleading results. The fact that power can be abused has led even very intelligent men to the conclusion that therefore power should be obliterated. This totally unsophisticated political point of view in fact became the foundation for a very sophisticated school of economic theory, which saw in competition—the more the better—the avenue of escape from the dilemma Lord Acton had proposed. Perfect competition, the ideal, guaranteed that all economic power would be drained from the system. Moreover, economists of this persuasion tended to believe that the free, competitive economy was the cornerstone of genuine democracy; each voter was free to choose from among numerous political competitors, beholden to none because of his economic autonomy. This view continues to enjoy substantial support, even if the philosophical formulation has been somewhat adulterated.

But political power, an essential ingredient of social organization, cannot be so easily dispensed with. In an earlier chapter we examined Ossowski's incisive analysis of the manner in which an ideology, once come to power, divides into an administrative ("ruling") class which institutionalizes and compromises the original doctrine, and a radical class which continues to pursue the purity of the initial conception and thereby makes itself a subversive force. He illustrated his thesis, it will be recalled, with reference to the development of the Christian and Communist creeds. Ossowski's model helps to illuminate the process by which accession to power leads to corruption. Those who come to power riding an ideology which has emerged from radical or opposition beginnings are faced with the necessity of making decisions and taking practical actions which *must* in some measure be wrong or unjust. The possession of office—authority, discretion—*requires* decision in the face of ignorance, doubt, ambiguity, conflict, and as a consequence it cannot escape being at times abusive. The abuse may be unintended; it may be willful; it may be viewed as "the lesser of two evils," which still leaves evil inherent in the decision. But those who administer a once-righteous cause *necessarily* debase it in time simply by the exercise of discretion, and every set of values *must* be cheapened simply in the process of being applied.

These observations are not intended as an extraneous bit of philosophical platitude but rather to suggest that, with the centralization of authority and discretion in the executive arm of a national government, the scope of discretion broadens and the exercise of discretion becomes more focused, more isolated, more assignable to particular people. They become the carriers of the values which a society purports to express, and their *necessary* failures of judgment are more likely to be spotlighted as failures of those values. Whether through action or inaction, they are more likely to be seen as compromising or prostituting the traditional values which have served as social cement. This danger may be muted by effective reinterpretations of the philosophical validation, or by open admission of error, inviting forgiveness, or by skillful use of public relations, but the number of occasions on which discretion must be centrally exercised in important matters renders a society's value system more and more susceptible to disbelief. The occasion for loss of credibility in social values increases, it seems to me, with the centralization of authority, particularly in a society composed of nonhomogeneous elements. And this, again, is without respect to the presence of a thruster group advancing an opposing creed.

I shall be briefer about the contrasting decline in dominant values in those countries, the less developed ones, which have suffered colonial rule over a long enough period to have had indigenous values snuffed out with the dissolution of the old dominant class. Thrusters in the form of local allies of the colonial masters, adopting their values, took their place. With the new wave of nationalism which swept the world following World War II and the concomitant decline of imperial control, many of the new nations were left with a dominant class reflecting the values of their former masters, entrenched and institutionalized but largely inappropriate under the changed conditions. India is an excellent case in point. The consequence was often a vacuum of national values which was partially filled by a revival of local values and pseudo-values. Here the movement has been from the hierarchical authority exercised in the name of former colonial powers toward the other end of the authority spectrum, emphasizing local autonomy. Once again this was without necessary respect to a thruster group. A movement such as Gandhi's may have provided an important momentum for independence, but in its emphasis on a revival of traditional village culture—"a return to an idealized past," in Barrington Moore's phrase [18]—it offered no vision of a future way of life, in the introduction of which strong-willed thrusters would lead the way.

India cannot, of course, be taken as "typical" in any strict sense, but it is perhaps not stretching too far its relevance to other decolonialized nations in pointing out that disunity arising from local pseudo-speciation has been more frequently the case than national unity supported by common social values. Perhaps the reason lies only in the shortness of time in which to spawn a thruster group strong enough to fill the gap left by the departed.

There is yet another way in which changes in objective conditions may undermine the credibility of the constitutional value. If we assume that every society must manage some combination of hierarchical authority and individual autonomy, the issue then becomes one of where the emphasis will fall.

Societies which have stressed personal autonomy—the free-enterprise societies—have had to face the reality that such freedom gives license for the strongest to rise to positions of dominance, in the process limiting the autonomy of others. Unrestricted competition breeds monopoly. The less regulated or controlled a society, the greater the opportunity for private agglomerations of power. American antitrust and fair-trade legislation is based on this premise.

It is the weaker, poorer, less-advantaged members of a society who least benefit from personal autonomy and who most espouse hierarchical authority. Only through government protection can they hope to escape the depredations of the strong. Only through government authority can they hope to secure some redistribution of the social advantage in their favor. "Soak the rich" has always been a popular rallying cry for populist causes.

Under these circumstances, it is understandable that the most ardent advocates of personal autonomy are those who feel secure in their strength. Society thereby becomes a field open to their exploitation. To the extent that they can include enough allies and beneficiaries in their successes, they can maintain support for the constitutional value by which they benefit. To the extent they fail—as temporarily in the period of the Great Depression—or neglect a large enough or strategic enough component of the population, they create a reaction from the weak and neglected, a political reaction supporting stronger hierarchical authority more responsive to the masses. The contemporary emphasis on social expenditures for welfare purposes, for example, represents a lessened respect for the principle of autonomy.

But hierarchical authority is not automatically exercised on behalf of the masses. It can be used, for example, either to foster egalitarianism, as in Cuba, or to repress egalitarianism, as in Pakistan. "Collective or community control," which is the only hope of the underdog, can also be used against him. Minor concessions made with great fanfare can mask the manipulation of government authority for the benefit of the already privileged. Especially when large populations are involved, the idea that governments are "responsive" to the wishes of "the majority" loses much meaning. Who are the majority? It is obvious nonsense to respond with

"51 percent." The figure by itself is empty of content. One has first to pose an issue to which a population responds, but there is never just one issue; there are countless issues, and with respect to any one of these the division of numbers may be vastly different than with respect to others. Votes can only be cast for persons, as votes of confidence, and it is these persons, the professional politicians who are elected, who must decide the issues, which means that they must mediate the implicit bargain, out of which the disadvantaged, with limited bargaining power, are likely to receive only token concessions.

When there is a shift toward hierarchical authority and away from autonomy, the same forces which felt most comfortable with their freedom are likely to regroup and reassert their strength in a different manner to assure their continued dominance. Indicative planning in France has been hailed as a major victory for participatory collective decision-making, involving as it does some 3500 representatives of business, labor, government, and the public, but there is more than a suspicion that the large corporations and trade associations have learned quickly how to dominate the commissions which have been established. Collective bargaining in the United States has been, with considerable reason, hailed as a major achievement for the collective control by workers of their working conditions, but it took little more than a decade for managements to learn to live with it without sacrificing any significant advantage.

On the one hand, the constitutional value of autonomy may have relatively limited worth to those whose discretion is repressed by others asserting their own uninhibited strength. On the other hand, the hope that the constitutional value of hierarchical authority will be exercised on behalf of the repressed and disadvantaged may prove a delusion if that authority is captured by the already strong. Under the circumstances, the *form* of government may appear to have little significance to the depressed portion of the population, or to radical elements looking for fundamental social change. The result may be a loss in the credibility of the very philosophy of representative government. Representative of whom becomes the crucial issue.

I am not suggesting that this is an inevitable accompaniment of growth in the size of populations, but neither is it fanciful conjecture. The issue of the "appropriate" form of government has been with us since the time of Plato, and a continuing aspect of that issue has been the effect of size of population. One line of thought has held that self-government is possible only with small populations. That idea has become less and less voiced as national populations have swelled to the hundreds of millions.[19] How do we dare to question, even to ourselves, whether self-government is really a meaningful concept under such conditions, when we have been bred on that principle? What constitutional value are we prepared to put in its place?

But to the extent that the doubt gnaws that self-government has any substantive content in large societies, we cannot evade the corollary question: Who does govern? The "people"? Interest groups? Professional politicians? None of these answers carries any conviction. What are we to believe—those of us in the United States who have been brought up on the philosophical validity of the paramount place of personal autonomy, those in the U.S.S.R. who have been brought up on the philosophical validity of the paramount place of collective decision? Constitutional values, like religious ones, may be open to contemporary question as generally spurious. Credibility is strained to the breaking point. But we cannot live *without* some constitutional value, even if it invites our disbelief. Perhaps Aristotle was right, after all, even if trivially, in believing that forms of government must succeed each other as each loses its acceptability, and Mosca, in asserting that in *each* form of government there is always a ruling class and a class that is ruled, was simply elaborating on Aristotle, rather than denying him as he thought.

But the point I am making at the moment is that the passage of time, which requires the expression of some constitutional value, may belie that value in the very process of applying it, increasingly undermining confidence in its philosophical validity. Its acceptability and effectiveness then diminish, even in the absence of any challenge from a thruster group.

Time and Distributive Values

Finally we come to the corrosive effects of time on the distributive values of a society. Even if we assume that a dominant class has succeeded in distributing social advantages—economic, social, and political—among enough of a population to secure acceptance for its principles of privilege, there are forces at work militating against the indefinite continuity of these principles. Once again these are linked to changes in objective conditions.

One of the most important of such changes is in the numbers, composition, and location of a population. When we think of the pressures of numbers on resources, we tend to think in purely Malthusian terms, a simple ratio which yields an estimate of per-capita subsistence, declining over time since people increase faster than nature's yield. But if we remember that a society's resources are not distributed equally among its people, such a simple arithmetical ratio tells us very little. The average GNP of a country tells us nothing about its distribution. There are the advantaged and the disadvantaged, and all those in between.

Moreover, the resources which are distributed include a wide range of goods, from food to space, and of other advantages, from jobs to education. The essence of the population problem lies in the relative fixity of certain of these resources—not for the population as a whole as much as for certain components of it. If urban congestion increases, the relative fixity of urban space affects everyone adversely—but some more than others. The wealthier residents can compensate for the reduction in per-capita ground space by resorting to luxury apartments, a second home in the country, more frequent vacations. Less privileged groups, though also increasing in numbers, will be confined to more or less the same geographical space, with more families to the housing unit, more persons to the room. The Malthusian effect is concentrated on them. If the pressure of numbers of children on educational facilities increases, the wealthy can resort to private schools and tutors. Those unable to afford such provisions must accept more intensive use of class space and teacher time, with an inevitable deterioration in quality.[20] If a racial or ethnic group, or a caste, has been confined to a limited range of menial jobs, and its numbers increase, the competition will be intensified among this disadvantaged class for such jobs as are available to it. If at the same time technological advances have reduced the need for jobs, either on the same or on a higher level of skills, the struggle will be exacerbated: the exclusion of the lower class from upper-class jobs will be tightened, to protect the privileges which the upper class enjoys, while the opportunities in lower-level jobs diminish.

All peoples cannot turn changes in circumstances—political or economic—to their advantage. Those who simply receive the impact of change, unaware of its implications or uncertain how to react to it, may face constricting conditions. Thus a study of agrarian unrest in Latin America found that peasant organization in Bolivia, Brazil, Mexico, and Peru, among other countries, occurred in areas where agricultural modernization had been introduced in a kind of watered-down version of the English enclosure movement of an earlier day, leading to deterioration in the conditions of the peasants affected. Landholding patricians, expanding commercial crop cultivation for export, had evicted peasants from land or usurped communally held lands or attempted to increase labor obligations or refused to mitigate hardships. The consequence had been to promote peasant radicalism.[21]

As we earlier noted, the disadvantaged may seek relief in a movement toward increased hierarchical authority at the expense of the autonomy of the privileged. Those who are protesting their circumstances may see government as the only instrument of remedy. Thus some spokesmen for the Catholic minority in Northern Ireland have called for England's assumption of full responsibility. If the political situation is in fact intractable, they ask only that England make them wards of the state, supporting them in a position of economic dependence.[22] In the United States some members of the black minority, long shut out from competition on an equal basis for jobs, education, income, and other amenities, have turned to demands for a fairer share on a "no-contest" basis. Distribution by quota, without respect to any form of qualification or contribution, is seen as the only means of avoiding discrimination.

Thus in the face of changes which redistribute disadvantages as well as advantages unequally, pressures can be expected to well up from below from those who find their position deteriorating. In some cases the deterioration may be absolute, in other instances relative. At one time a differential advantage may be accepted which at another time, in the light of changed conditions such as demonstration effects through improved communications, is no longer tolerable. Although pressures from the advantaged for a restoration of eroded privileges are by no means unknown, the more common phenomenon is agitation for a more egalitarian distribution —that persistent movement noted by Tocqueville.

But such pressures will *always* be stopped somewhere *short* of egalitarianism. If we think of a society as a pyramid of people, with the dominants at the peak, the most disadvantaged at the bottom, and the rest of the population distributed between, we can conceive of this broad middle stratum (the middle class) as seeking to narrow the gap between the top of the pyramid and itself. It will endeavor to remove upper-class privileges demeaning to it, and to create paths for "upward mobility" for its members, as the sociologists would say. But this same middle-class stratum will be equally anxious to preserve distance between its position and those at the bottom of the pyramid. It will endeavor to maintain a status distinction and an economic advantage relative to the classes it considers "beneath" it.

The numbers and abilities of those in this middle class can be expected to force concessions from the most privileged groups. With respect to the upper and middle strata, then, the movement is toward a more equal sharing of advantages. But the combined weight of the upper and middle classes is more likely to be effective, even in a society with universal suffrage, in resisting pressures from the lowest, most disadvantaged groups. Only when conditions in this bottom segment have deteriorated to the point where they invite radical, militant, disruptive action is there likely to be any significant amelioration in the form of a redistribution of income. Prior to such acts of desperation one can expect sporadic reforms based on humanitarian impulse, welfare activities of a voluntary and "public service" nature, which are either temporary or minimal in nature. Even in the face of rebellious behavior, or in anticipation of it, there will be at best Bismarckian reforms which seek to draw the sting of revolt, acts of appeasement which provide a sense of improvement in conditions while still maintaining the relative positions of advantage.

Even socialist societies, which are ideologically closer to the egalitarian principle, have found it necessary to create a structure of privileges, as we noted previously, justifying such departures from equality as being in the interests of society as a whole and distinguishing them from the privilege structures of private-enterprise societies on the ground that they are not class-based (which is to say based on private property ownership). In every society thus far there have always been the disproportionately advantaged and disadvantaged.

On what principle, then, is the distribution of the gross social advantage to take place? Clearly the distributive value cannot be converted into a simple exercise of power without forfeiting any basis for its general acceptance. Relative advantages and disadvantages must be justified and rationalized in order to satisfy a sense of "rightness" on the part of both those who benefit and those who do not, in order to ensure coherence and relative harmony within a society, and avoid perpetual class antagonisms and social disorder.

As we earlier noted, there are basically three distributive principles— by birth, by competitive achievement, and by political decision. The principle of birth, of inherited privilege, has lost most of its appeal in the face of middle-class egalitarianism. The principle of competitive achievement is increasingly refused by the lower classes (the disadvantaged, as we now call them), who more clearly perceive that such a principle simply validates their inferior status. There remains the principle of political decision. Thus country after country has been sent in search of an "incomes policy," some formula by which its economic product might be apportioned acceptably to all.

With rapid technological change reducing the need for the services of some people—"obsoleting" them, in the jargon—the issue of the relationship between work and income has been pointedly raised. If consumption should become less of a focal value, reducing the need for output; if automation should within some decades reduce even further the need for workers, the question of whether or how work opportunities could be distributed among the members of a society, and the relationship of work to income, would be troublesome indeed. What must one do to deserve a share in society's output and privileges, and how much of a share?

But without respect to such future problems, we can conclude that generally, in the case of distributive values, as in the case of focal and constitutional values, the passage of time and the intrusion of changes in objective conditions serves to discredit them. Those who find themselves in deteriorating positions are unwilling to accept the result as philosophically valid by the old standards. Those remaining in positions of advantage are driven to stratagems of repression or concession to preserve those advantages. If repression, then social cohesion is lost. If concession, then a chain of other claims and pressures is set in motion as individuals and groups seek to maintain a relative standing.

In sum, over time values are made vulnerable by changes in objective conditions and the intrusion of unpredictable events. The disintegrating influences may not be strong enough to invalidate existing social values but they are likely to weaken their validation. Values can be preserved for a time by reinterpretation and modification, but they cannot last forever. There are long-term elements—dialectical upgrading of excluded focal values as existing ones are overfulfilled, cumulative judgmental errors of hierarchical discretion by those wielding institutionalized power, loss of credibility in both focal and constitutional values, resistance to relative deprivations which have lost any satisfactory rationalization—these all serve to erode the prevailing value structure, whether or not a substitute set of values is challenging. Value diffuseness, value disorder, even value anarchy are then entirely possible.

The end of church hegemony in Europe provides an excellent illustration of this effect of time. The long-standing denial by the church—in doctrine if not always in practice—of the value of material accumulation became too extreme for the more ambitious. Worldliness, humanism, luxury penetrated the church itself, giving rise to some internal dissidence. The values it sought to exclude became more strongly asserted. The hierarchical power it exercised invited arbitrary and abusive judgments as well as corruption, evoking the savage attacks of the puritanical Luther. Its stand against the autonomy of the individual affronted a rising class of intellectual inquirers, and again aroused Luther to deny the very basis of church authority. Concomitantly, the unrest generated by the struggles over these focal and constitutional values gave opportunity for groups of peasants, particularly in Germany, to protest the excessive inequalities built into the distributive principles of the time. They were no longer willing to accept the philosophical validation that these were part of a divine order. The prevailing value structure was thus subjected to pressures and strains from a number of sources. On the continent, however, the structure —though weakened—survived for another two centuries, though with considerable disorder. In the northern Protestant countries, attack on the prevailing value structure was more vigorous. A new thruster group emerged, and in time gave birth to a radically altered set of values.

Notes

1. Mosca, *The Ruling Class,* p. 369.

2. Overton H. Taylor has discussed this aspect of Schumpeter's thought very perceptively in his *Economics and Liberalism* (Cambridge, Mass.: Harvard University Press, 1955), pp. 291–293.

3. Robert A. Nisbet advances a very similar view in *Social Change and History* (New York: Oxford University Press, 1969). For him, changes occurring *within* a social system are only casual or minor readjustments. The system operates to perpetuate itself; its functional relationships get tinkered with to improve performance. There is no immanent force which makes them less and less sustainable. Any major changes in the social system come from outside it. Here he falls back on the concept of the "intrusive event" offered by the historian Frederick Teggart, to which reference was made in a previous chapter. "I am suggesting that when we come down in our analysis from the abstract wholes such as mankind and civilization, within which, by definition, all change *must* be internally based, to the social behavior of human beings, considered in time and place, significant change is overwhelmingly the result of non-developmental factors; that is to say, factors inseparable from external events and intrusions." (P. 280) Tensions, conflicts, dysfunctions within a system at best provide the materials of potential change, but if any change is in fact precipitated from them it is due only to an intrusive event which builds on them. Tensions have gone on in many countries for decades and even centuries without leading to significant social change, Nisbet argues.

I would myself go a long way down Nisbet's road, but there is, I think, a class of change-making factors which are internal to a *society,* even though not necessarily related to its *system* functioning. I refer to those circumstances which we have designated as "objective conditions." Population changes, for example, can occur within a society for nonfunctional reasons, reasons which are not deducible from any modes of behavior prescribed by the system. A new knowledge authority may arise from within a society no less than it may be imported from outside. And even though technological changes and political adaptation may be functions of a society's values, there is no guarantee that they may not provoke serious internal problems leading to radical reconstruction.

But with that modification I would associate myself with Nisbet's conclusion that any "stage" or "life-cycle" theory of social change is a purely metaphorical construct.

4. Talcott Parsons and Winston White, "The Link Between Character and Society," in Lipset and Lowenthal, *Culture and Social Character*, pp. 100, 103.

5. Richard H. Tawney, *Religion and the Rise of Capitalism* (Baltimore: Penguin Books, 1947), p. 227. Note here Tawney's emphasis on this change of attitude among "thinkers" and "philosophers"—a small intellectual coterie.

6. Nef, *The Conquest of the Material World*, pp. 223–231.

7. John Stuart Mill, *Principles of Political Economy*, Ashley ed. (London: Longmans, Green & Co., 1940), p. 749. Williams, in *Culture and Society, 1780–1950*, provides an excellent survey of other exponents of this minority point of view in England.

8. Riesman and Glazer, in Lipset and Lowenthal, *Culture and Social Character*, p. 432.

9. Daniel J. Boorstin, "Tradition of Self-Liquidating Ideals," *Wall Street Journal*, 18 February 1970.

10. Sidney Alexander, "Human Values and Economists' Values" in *Human Values and Economic Policy: A Symposium*, ed. Sidney Hook (New York: New York University Press, 1967), p. 110.

11. Erich Fromm, *The Sane Society* (New York: Holt, Rinehart & Winston, 1955), p. 135.

12. Long, "Local and Private Initiative in the Great Society," in Gross, *A Great Society?*, p. 87.

13. Herbert Luthy, *From Calvin To Rousseau* (New York: Basic Books, 1970), p. 9.

14. Wassily Leontief in a critical review of Walter Heller's *Perspectives on Economic Growth*, in the *New York Review of Books*, 10 October 1968.

15. Robert Marjolin, "Major Economic Problems of the Free World in the 1970s," *The Conference Board Record*, November 1969, p. 15.

16. Schaar, *Escape from Authority*, pp. 276–277.

17. Stephen has referred to this phenomenon in somewhat different language. "There are [however] times when the emotions take side with the intellect; when the old symbols have become for large classes associated with an oppressive power, and have been turned to account for obviously degrading purposes by their official representatives." *History of English Thought in the Eighteenth Century*, pp. 16–17.

18. Moore, *Social Origins of Dictatorship and Democracy*, especially pp. 370–378. Moore's summation is worth quoting: "Many Western liberals, distressed by the horrors of modern industrial society, have found Gandhi a sympathetic figure, especially for his stress on nonviolence. To me this sympathy merely seems to be evidence for the *malaise* in modern liberalism and its incapacity to solve the problems that confront Western society. If one thing at least is certain it is that modern technology is here to stay and will before long spread throughout the rest of the world. It is perhaps equally certain that whatever form the good society may take, if it ever comes, it will not be that of the self-contained Indian village served by the local artisan symbolized in Gandhi's spinning wheel."

19. I have discussed this matter at some length in *Beyond Malthus: Population and Power*, Chapter 5.

20. A poignant illustration of this is provided by a novice public school teacher who reported his experience in the *Yale Alumni Magazine* of June 1970: "The fact is that no more than a handful of my 170 students will ever escape their depressing environment. There is no room to grow in the poverty-stricken ghettos of North Philadelphia. Blocks and blocks of row houses pour legions of children into the streets and schools to play together in packs so tight that every person has to develop amazing personality defenses just to give himself breathing space. Thus even conversation is often hostile, boasting, and aggressive. And energy can never be harmlessly exerted in open space; rather it is always directed toward other people so that during a day a class will make itself more and more volatile until explosions of fights and yelling ease the pressure. It hurts to fail to teach these children. School should be one way to escape the ghetto; instead it is one of the conditions of the trap."

21. Stavenhagen, "Marginality, Participation and Agrarian Structure in Latin America," pp. 78–79.

22. Moore, "Bloody Ulster," p. 62.

11 / Continuity and Change: Thrust and Riposte

When can a change in values be said to have taken place? That seemingly simple question is in fact not easy to answer. We have noted more than once that incremental changes in values can come as a matter of accommodating (and quieting) dissident or pressure groups; reinterpreting traditional values may be a means of adjusting to changes in objective conditions without losing control. If we treated each such minor modification as a change in values, we would have to conclude that social values are always in the process of change; we would have to retract our earlier conclusion that there is some tendency to a continuity of values.

On the other hand, alterations in the structure of values may continue over so long a period, or occur so frequently, that at some stage there is little resemblance to the set of values which marked the beginning of that "epoch." When this occurs, surely we have to admit that a fundamental change in values has taken place, even if by an incremental process. But how many incremental changes add up to a fundamental change? Are we really playing with meaningless conceptual distinctions?

The view which I would argue is that a fundamental change in values occurs only with the rise of a new class of dominants, when a thruster group has made good. It may accomplish that feat as the end result of a succession of incremental changes, as notably in England in the transfer of power from a landed aristocracy to an industrial elite. Revolution is not an essential ingredient of thruster success. But however gradual the change, at some point a new class emerges to put its different impress on a society.

This position intrudes a second and related question. The composition of a dominant class does not remain static but changes, incrementally, over time. If, for example, we consider that businessmen have constituted the dominant class in the United States throughout its history, clearly the composition of that class altered radically following the Civil War and particularly after the turn of the century. The local owner-manager who had inherited his position gave way to the national industrial magnate who achieved his position not through inheritance but by entrepreneurship and financial manipulation, and he in turn yielded to the professional manager who capped a career by being tapped for the top spot by a small group of insiders who controlled the ownership-proxy machinery. Are we here confronted with a change or continuity of dominants?

A dominant class necessarily changes its composition and tactics over time. We can expect that new blood coming up from within recognizes and seizes opportunities that carry forward and enlarge upon the objectives of its predecessors. But such insurgents, while they may joust and compete with others in the dominant class, do not endanger the dominance of the system which that class has established. They work within the system, in alliance with its more traditional class associates. Perhaps we can best label the phenomenon of a significant movement from within a continuing dominant class as involving "inside thrusters"—a group as distinguishable from pure thrusters as, say, a reform movement is from radical change. We would then say that a reinterpretation of values, preserving the continuity of the dominant institution, occurs under the impetus of an inside thruster group, while a more profound modification or substitution of values calls for a thruster group external to the existing dominants.

Alliance for Change

A thruster class is seldom strong enough in its own right to carry the day against the incumbent powers. It must rely on support from *below,* from a mass following somewhere down in the social pyramid, where changes in conditions have created unrest. I am using the term "mass" here in a purposely vague way, since its meaning depends on historic context. It may conceivably be an undifferentiated population of peasants in a two-class society; it may be an urban proletariat in a developing economy; it could be an ethnic or racial minority which constitutes a significant "lump" of undigested population within the larger society; it could conceivably be simply the "poor" or most disadvantaged members of a society who share a common misery in a variety of settings, rural and urban. The prime considerations are that it possesses numbers and social wounds.

The mass may be present before the thrusters appear on the scene, or vice versa. Which comes first is an empirical, historical matter, of no special concern to us. The facts important to us are that the thrusters require a following to give themselves bargaining power with the dominants, and the mass requires leadership to give it direction, organization, and plan.

The importance of leadership to a mass seeking changes in its conditions has been underlined by many observers. The peasant organizations in Latin American countries which have sought amelioration of their conditions have tended first to attempt peaceful, legal means and only on encountering rigid resistance have resorted to more radical forms of action. It is at this time that they particularly feel the need for leadership and outside assistance. A study conducted by Gerrit Huizer found that leadership tended, in the initial instance, to come from inside the peasant group, but that these were not typical peasants. They tended to possess charismatic personalities, determination, and some previous "modernizing" experience in such forms as education, urban background, or life abroad.[1] But it is difficult for peasants, even with such leadership, to develop permanent organization, and if their leaders should be co-opted by "the system" the movement disintegrates. Similarly, Barrington Moore has commented that it is the absence of organization and leadership which has so far permitted the dominant class of India to check radical movements for change among industrial workers and peasants alike.[2]

What is necessary, then, is some symbiotic relationship between a thruster-leadership group and a mass following. Examples of this sort of working relationship are numerous.

Moore has provided a fascinating interpretation of the French Revolution as a contest between a weakening but still dominant class (the monarch and nobles, and some bourgeoisie who had been drawn in—"feudalized"—by their dependence on the monarch) and an alliance of more independent (though not very aggressive) bourgeoisie and the working mass. Moore sees "the Revolution as composed of two quite different but interrelated revolutions fought by these two latter quite separate but allied forces. There was thus the bourgeois revolution, which involved town merchants and small landholders, both of whom felt insecure in the face of the feudal claims of the nobility, which was pressing them more insistently in order to grind out the larger sums needed to keep up with the life at court. There was also the radical revolution, composed of a larger number of landless or virtually landless peasants and—increasingly—the sans-culottes of the cities, the proletarians and lesser artisans.

The nobility at first refused any concessions, but its more liberal members prevailed and concessions were offered. At this stage, as Moore sees it, the bourgeois "revolutionaries," their property claims assured and their political position improved, would have been willing to settle, perhaps leading to some form of democratic or constitutional monarchy, as in England. But the radical revolutionaries, hard-pressed by rising food prices in the cities, forced the hand of their bourgeois allies, obliging them to continue the struggle or to face the prospect of losing out on their property rights, so nearly won, to the extremists who were preaching redistribution of wealth, egalitarianism, and communism. It was only as the army turned back the promonarchical forces at the borders, and could then be used to bring the radical revolutionaries under control, that gradually the bourgeois revolutionaries regained the upper hand, creating the conditions under which capitalism could emerge in France free of both feudal restraints and radical attacks.[3]

Thus the mass was necessary to the bourgeoisie, even though their interests were as much antithetical as common. There was, in fact, a collaboration among people of competing interests in which each used the other. This is, perhaps, a more typical than atypical situation. The opposition to existing values, and to the dominants whom they most benefit, comes from many sources. Their opposition is by no means always to the same thing. Their interests are by no means always compatible. Yet no opposition group, by itself, is likely to be strong enough to have its way. Some alliance is necessary, though it may have to be built around disparate objectives and interests.

In general, as we have noted, protests against focal values are likely to emanate from those who feel that other (opposed) values have been too much excluded. For the most part, this means that such protests will come from the intellectuals, from the more creative and ambitious classes, who are less concerned with the material desire for "more" (the distributive value) than with something that the existing value system cannot provide. If a thruster group emerges, it will be from this class. Conversely, the mass—which will include the more disadvantaged—is less likely to be concerned with changing social objectives but only with receiving a more equal share in whatever society is producing.

It is not surprising that so much of the student opposition of the last decade should have come from the affluent whites; after all, they were in a position to argue that the focal value of consumption had been overachieved and were therefore most prepared to assert the excluded values, which to them were more exciting precisely because they were not to be had. But I do believe that the element of affluence has been somewhat overdone in the analysis of why such youths rebelled. It was not only the rebelliousness of affluent youth but of college youth; the intellectual thrust is, I think, as important as the fact that they were well fed. Similar challenges were being made in other industrialized countries, always from the college groups. While one may argue that college is simply an assembly place or staging ground for the young, or that it is more likely to be the affluent who go to college, these arguments do not convincingly discount the intellectualist element of such youthful leadership.

Nor is it surprising that on many American campuses the radical whites and the radical blacks found it difficult to make any effective alliance. The former were seeking a change in focal values. The latter, who still identified themselves with their own racial minority, were more interested in a redistribution of the social advantage without respect to focal values. The white youths became absorbed in environmental issues. Blacks saw these as obstacles to the achievement of greater equality on the consumption front; they wanted not more parklands but more housing, not less industry but better jobs in industry. Both were opposed to "the establishment," and their efforts often supplemented each other, but the liaison was uneasy.

Despite these different objectives and the suspicions they engender, outside the college campus, in society at large, the blacks—that mass, though minority, group—cannot hope to effect fundamental distributive changes by themselves. They depend on an alliance with some thruster group which can provide the necessary leadership. The charismatic leaders which the blacks themselves can provide are, like the peasant leaders of Latin America, susceptible to co-optation, and in any event are often unable to obtain entry to the right quarters, or to win over supporters from among the dominant class itself, or to influence the relatively advantaged—blacks and whites both—who are fearful of losing status if the black mass gains in status. If a white thruster group has other—focal—objectives, and is interested in advancing its own position within society by seizing on such opportunities as changing objective conditions permit to "make a new nation" in which it will play a larger role, these are simply the terms on which the disaffected blacks must purchase its support. If the black mass comes to believe that it cannot effect distributive change except by alliance with some front-running thrusting group, it may thus get drawn along behind new focal values in which it is not especially interested—as long as these do not threaten its own egalitarian objectives. For, after all, the militant blacks in the United States seek more consumption largely because that is the standard by which their status is now measured, but if what gnaws at them most is inequality, rather than lack of goods, they may be prepared to shift their focal value, along with others, as long as they are guaranteed more equal status.

An alliance between thrusters and a mass is, then, what is essential to any fundamental change in social values. Along with the French Revolution, the Russian Revolution provides an instructive example. Here the thruster group was a small band of refugee intellectuals with a clear vision of where they wanted to go. The working masses were willing to be led. The symbiotic relationship was quickly established. The argument that the Party leadership was only acting in the interests of the masses justified its autocracy. The argument was false only in the exclusiveness of purpose which it attributed to Lenin and his followers. They did seek to advance the welfare of the masses, but they also sought to advance their own position and power, identifying the latter with the former. They rationalized their power by the use they made of it, but they were tenacious in holding on to it against any challengers. Leadership—control, power—was itself a prize and privilege which in its nature only few could share; it certainly could not be shared with the masses. Dominance was sought ostensibly, and to a degree in reality, as a privilege which was needed by a few to benefit the many, but dominance was also sought for its own sake, and to avoid being dominated by others. With the passage of time the values of the Party dominants became validated and institutionalized. That the validation and institutionalization stressed different constitutional and distributive values from those of capitalist countries does not mean that the process by which those values were impressed on the society was any different. It was not the masses who overthrew the czarist regime, but a thruster group with a mass following.

So too in China. The decay of the central regime, the exploitation of the peasantry by local marauders and warlords, were the twentieth-century end result of a longer-term erosion of the upper class and the social values they had established. Despite this diffuse and disordered situation the peasants were unprepared for any sustained action on their own part. Barrington Moore, who has investigated the matter, writes that he has seen nothing that would indicate that the peasants "were about to organize or do anything effectively of their own accord." [4] Like the Latin American peasants, their own leadership, when it did emerge, was too personal to outlast the individual. They had to turn to the outside for any sustained, organized leadership. The Communists under Mao were the thruster group. But the alliance between these two symbionts took time to develop. The thrusters, in truer Marxist pattern, first sought their following in the urban proletariat, without success. The intrusive event which finally sparked the Party-peasant alliance was the Japanese occupation. In the almost half-century since that took place the old dominants of China have been discredited and confined to a few islands, and a new set of dominants, with markedly different values, has taken their place. The change could not have occurred, however, without a mass backing. In turn, the mass backing does not negate the necessity of a definable thruster group which, while providing the intellectual and moral leadership necessary for others, sought advantage for itself. How can one—or a group or class—lead and dominate unless it believes in its own superiority? And seeks to ensure the perpetuation of its position, justified by the service it renders to others? Just so would a group of businessmen justify their running American industry as contributing to the welfare of society, and deny that another group (a government agency or a workers' council) could do the job so well.

The potential for this symbiotic relationship between thruster and mass in developing countries has been noted by a number of writers. Torcuato S. di Tella has described the situation with respect to Latin America. On the one hand, there is a group of discontented intellectuals and persons with above-average education who find limited opportunities in the traditional society, dominated as it is by the old oligarchic families and their institutional allies. These discontented—incongruents, di Tella calls them—are sometimes joined by impoverished aristocrats who have lost their social status and wealthy businessmen who have been denied one. These tend to support an industrializing and modernizing program. Although their actions and programs have been tentative, they provide the ingredients of a potential thruster class. On the other hand, there is a mass which has acquired a desire and expectation for an improvement in its position, without knowing how, or feeling it necessary, to earn that improvement by their own economic *or* political effort. "Groups lacking sufficient economic or organizational power demand a share in both the goods and the decision-making processes of society." Following Gino Germani, di Tella refers to this as the "disposable mass," "larger and more demanding than any Louis Napoleon would have dreamed of." These two disparate classes—the incongruents, with the thruster potential, and the disposable masses—complement each other. "Their social situations are different, but what they have in common is a passionate hatred of the *status quo*." [5] Conceivably a symbiotic relationship may develop.

A somewhat similar potential has been noted by John Waterbury in Morocco. He notes the rise there of underemployed, restless, and educated members of upper-class families, who seek some larger role in their society. "Without them, there would be few spokesmen for those victimized by economic stagnation. Without them, grievances could pile up indefinitely for want of those who could exploit them, articulate them, and use their weight as as a lever or hammer to attack the incumbent elite." [6] Here too there is at least a speculative possibility that these challengers of the present dominants may turn into a thruster group spearheading a movement for modernization which will use the uneducated and untrained masses as its bargaining power.

The Moroccan case suggests what has historically been common enough. The mass following has at times been used by the thrusters simply as a tool to prize open a situation for its own benefit, following which the tool—mass interests—has been lightly discarded. This is scarcely surprising. As we earlier noted, the thruster group is more likely to be interested in focal values. They are more likely to be intellectuals and even to derive from upper-class backgrounds. They are not so much the disadvantaged who seek a more equal share for themselves as the discontented who seek a more important role, a larger scope for their efforts. The mass, their bargaining weapon, is, on the other hand, concerned with a more equal share in society's output, rather than a shift in the direction of its objectives. With such disparate interests one can readily understand that once a thruster group has managed to make good in its assertion of new values, it will seek to benefit from its improved status by securing disproportionate advantage for itself. Its erstwhile allies, with their rallying cry of more egalitarianism, will be bought off with mild reforms, and old colleagues in arms will be co-opted with governmental position; the mass following will be only incrementally benefited.

This was largely the situation in nineteenth-century England, when the rising commercial and industrial middle class used the populist movement as the tool to secure an improved position for itself. It pried open the doors of privilege which had been partially closed to its members, but not wide enough to permit its working-class allies through those same doors. The latter had to be content with concessions. The story has been carefully documented by W. L. Guttsman, who shows that the first Reform Act of 1832 made relatively little impact on the composition of government, but the second Reform Act of 1867 evoked a marked change. "The Cabinets of the period 1832–68 were . . . still predominantly aristocratic in character, and even Radical pressure did not change this fundamentally." But beginning with Gladstone's administration of 1892, "men of middle-class background [by whom Guttsman means "the sons of businessmen, professional men, managers, administrators and the like"] form at first a significant and later a predominant part in the personnel of the top layer of the British political elite." These "new men" in British politics were also increasingly put in charge of government departments with large administrative functions, while sinecures, along with the prestigious foreign and empire affairs, remained aristocratic prerogatives. Working-class representation was scarcely discernible until the period of the Great Depression and the war.[7]

Raymond Williams has commented on the difference in the constitutional values of business (middle-class) and working-class components of nineteenth-century reform movements in England. The former stressed society as a neutral ground for the cultivation of the individual in his own interests; the latter emphasized social and collective control of the individual in the interests of all. The distinction was somewhat blurred by the idea of "service"—public obligation undertaken by the individual voluntarily

—as put forward by bourgeois moralists. The idea of "service" muted the individualistic philosophy and made it more acceptable to the working class. In addition, British imperialism converted the nation-state into a single entity contending against other such entities, and undercut any working-class conception of an international community. Within this nationalistic framework (individualism extended into the international sphere), the "service" area which blurred the sharpness of the constitutional design took the form of "the white man's burden." [8]

A nearly parallel version of this English experience seems visible in contemporary Latin America. Luis Ratinoff has observed: "By gaining the support of wider social sectors [the working-class masses], the middle-class parties and leaders brought pressure to bear on the groups traditionally in power, and paved their own way toward greater participation in decision-making and in the handling of public affairs. . . . The 'workers' movement' and the 'people's movement' were watered down in time into compromises with the different demands of the existing order, and were converted into middle-class movements." [9] On the whole, however, Ratinoff's Latin American middle class is less clear as to objectives and more opportunistic as to tactics than its earlier counterpart in England.

In some ways the classic expression of the use by an intellectual thruster group of the masses as a tool was given by Selig Perlman. [10] In large part a reflection of his own flight from a European Marxist background, to some extent the consequence of his observation of the functioning of the American labor movement as typified by the American Federation of Labor's "business unionism," Perlman believed that capitalism (and labor) could thrive only in those societies where "organic labor" refused to listen to the siren songs of an intellectual group seeking to reform institutions along their own preconceived lines. To the latter, whose paradigm is a dedicated Communist thruster group, labor is simply an "abstract mass" to be used in executing their social designs. From a quite different perspective, Barrington Moore, whose iconoclastic views have ruffled some academic feathers, comments more sweepingly, embracing capitalistic and communistic societies alike: "On this score it is well to recollect that there is no evidence that the mass of the population anywhere has wanted an industrial society, and plenty of evidence that they did not. At bottom all forms of industrialization so far have been revolutions from above, the work of a ruthless minority." [11] But they could succeed, we would add, only because they rode on the strength of a mass which believed it would benefit from a change.

But if the thrusters can use a mass to their own advantage, it is also true that sometimes a dissatisfied mass can *create* the opportunity for thrusters actually to emerge. The very existence of widespread dissatisfaction may constitute a change in objective conditions which can be seized as an opportunity. By putting themselves at the head of a mass movement, such thrusters seek to create new positions of power and influence for themselves. This may be true of even the most social-minded of individuals: we have noted before that thrusters and dominants both have the capacity of believing that the advantages of position which accrue to them also benefit society as a whole.

It is always hazardous to project a genuine thruster group out of a contemporary enthusiasm, especially if of small dimensions, but it is at least conceivable that the ambitious, restless, social-minded college graduates of today, of whom the "poverty lawyers" and "public-interest lawyers" are perhaps the most visible, and of whom Ralph Nader is the archetype, may be a new thruster group created by a disadvantaged mass, an alliance which conceivably could create them as a new dominant force within American society, reflected in a fundamental rather than incremental change in social values. I would myself be skeptical of that possibility, but I would not want to rule it out.

If, in addition, we remember that among present dominants there may exist those who see a different future for themselves, and who are willing for that reason to break with their present institutional interests, these add possible additional leadership for such a mass following. The existence of the disadvantaged mass may itself evoke its needed leadership: demand creates the supply. Thus in a number of countries where traditionally the church—Catholic and Protestant alike—has been the ally of a dominant class, we find expressions of a radical movement within the church hierarchy. In some developing countries, where the army has long been the ally of the traditional dominants, some young officers have created a "military leftism" which sees national salvation and redemption emerging from populist causes. Even young business executives in the United States have been known to become disaffected and seek to realize their own values through the opportunities offered by dissension, racial conflict, and environmental decay.

This is certainly not intended as a prediction, for the United States or any other society. I cite the potential only to underscore that a thruster group and a mass are symbionts, each relying on the other, and—as in the case of any alliance—they may sometimes emerge from unexpected quarters. If the thrusters pursue a successful course, creating a momentum which adds new allies and wins the tolerance of others, their growing strength will be recognized by the professional politicians in the hammering out of changes in the implicit bargain. Intellectuals will always be available to create a philosophical validation. But the road of a thruster group is not easy. Before its new set of values can displace the old (even allowing for a long-lagged retention of or continuing affection for the old, in a diffuse relationship), the existing class of dominants, whose influence extends through all the basic institutions, must be persuaded or made to concede—not necessarily to surrender abjectly or collectively or even to remove themselves from their positions, but to recognize a new superior authority. Such a rare shift of power and values can occur only if the objective conditions are propitious.

Resistance to Change

The resistance powers of an existing dominant group are partly psychological—how much it *wills* to resist change, how deeply it is still committed to a way of life as well as a preservation of interests. This is an historical matter. But assuming will and commitment, there are three tactics which dominants can employ to preserve their position: co-optation, concession, and repression.

Of these three co-optation is by all odds the most to be preferred. The basic institutions of society are preserved by admitting into their upper ranks those talented individuals from whatever class or background who otherwise, thwarted in their ambitions, might become fomenters of opposition. Mosca makes this admission of new blood into its ranks a necessary condition for the continuance of the ruling class. Pareto sees in the "circulation" of elites the means of avoiding class rigidities to which a society would otherwise succumb. The institutions carry on, with such adaptations as changes in objective conditions may seem to require, but the class of people who occupy the institutional positions do not necessarily carry on as a closed caste. The business firm continues to play its dominant role in society, but it recruits its managers from a meritocracy of talent. The hurdles to be jumped may still exclude unwanted components of the population, but they are lowered enough to admit some of the bright, eager, and ruthlessly ambitious young men from lower- or middle-class backgrounds along with those who are born with advantage. The upward mobility of talent demonstrates the openness of the society and constitutes a rebuttal to those who argue that opportunity is monopolized by the favored few.

The English aristocracy employed this device much more effectively than their French counterparts, as Tocqueville pointed out. Writing of late eighteenth- and early nineteenth-century England, he remarked on the absence of any caste system, so that commoners and nobles might intermarry or carry on a common business. Tocqueville exaggerated the degree of social fluidity, but the essence of his point remains:

The reason why the English middle class, far from being actively hostile to the aristocracy, inclined to fraternize with it, was not so much that the aristocracy kept open house as that its barriers were ill defined; not so much that entrance into it was easy as that you never knew when you got there. The result was that everyone who hovered on its outskirts nursed the agreeable illusion that he belonged to it and joined forces with it in the hope of acquiring prestige or some practical advantage under its aegis.[12]

If this openness of class (abetted in large part by the custom of primogeniture, under which only the eldest son inherited title and privileges while younger sons and daughters were left more or less to make careers for themselves) did not suffice to curb the thrusting industrial middle class indefinitely, it did so for a long time. Other reasons were present as well, but certainly the mixture of social fluidity with social snobbery bought the aristocracy at least a century of grace.

In contemporary Latin America the co-optation of a middle class before it has made up its mind whether it wishes to thrust is now preserving, again if only for a time, the dominant position of the landed oligarchy. Observer after observer has commented on the phenomenon of patronage, or clientalism, and its effectiveness in blunting opposition. Ratinoff comments: "The degree of dissatisfaction in the middle classes depends largely upon the opportunities open to them for improving, or preserving, the positions they have gained. If the system provides a reasonable degree of satisfaction for such aspirations, the middle classes tend to model their behavior and standards on those of the traditional social elite." He then adds: "In this sense, the diminished rigidity of social inequality can only have the effect of preserving traditional strategic institutions and of subjecting the functioning of new institutions to their limitations and possibilities." Scott has similarly remarked that "Too many members of the challenging elites [thrusters, in our terms] have adopted the ruling groups' elitist norms and conservative tendencies and have sold out their followers in the popular organizations." [13]

The United States provides an extraordinary case of the successes and failures of co-optation as a means of preserving a way of life. Businessmen have constituted the dominant class over the years, but clearly some have been more influential than others in impressing their values on society. On the whole, the most influential segment of business leaders has been the White Anglo-Saxon Protestant. In fulfillment of its constitutional and distributive values, competitive access to privileged positions has presumably been kept open to all comers, but in practice it was the exceptional individual outside the WASP community who made his way to the top. Robert Dahl, in his study of New Haven society, *Who Governs?*, has, for example, shown how the large Italian subpopulation, though eventually admitted to political position, was for long largely excluded from top business posts; I recall myself, in doing field work in New Haven about 1950, the stir created by the elevation of the first Italian-American to a vice-presidency in one of the major corporations.

World War II constitutes something of a watershed in this respect, though in part it is only a convenient peg for dating the changes which were taking place. From one point of view, a greater degree of genuine co-optation began about this time. In E. Digby Baltzell's analysis, wartime expansion led to an influx of other ethnic groups into the business community. The old WASP leadership retained its hold on top positions in the large corporations (which continued to absorb some of the old family firms). The newcomer "ethnic" businessmen tended to organize new, smaller, and less prestigious firms, though some were admitted to upper-class status. The old WASP values were assimilated, but modified, in the process—a process which Baltzell dubs the "democratization of plutocracy." [14] From this perspective, co-optation was relatively successful.

From another point of view, however, it can be argued that the seeds of *failure* of co-optation, planted prior to the war, began to sprout about this time. The involvement of the old dominant class (the WASP) in civic interests, which had earlier followed naturally from their local business involvement, was largely dissipated by their shift of interest to the national corporation, a shift accelerated by the wartime expansion. The national corporation due to its nature was less concerned with local (civic) involvement. Concomitantly there occurred an efflux of the same business leadership to the suburbs. This left the large cosmopolitan cities as spoils to be fought over by minority groups, with their more particularized values. There was an almost total absence of co-optation of leaders of these groups into the still-dominant business hierarchy. The consequence was a diffuseness—some would say almost an anarchy—of values in the large urban centers.

There is a form of co-optation which shades subtly over to the use of concession as an instrument for preserving position. The dominant class may adopt the symbols of a protest group and muddy the question of how much opposition actually exists between established institutions and challenging minorities. At the same time that Charles Reich was celebrating the youth movement which was to bring the "Greening of America," one of whose symbols was its casualness of dress, the local branch of my Manhattan bank sprouted cages of colorfully attired tellers, dressed in everything from flaming blazers to micros, from headbands to bell-bottoms. Had the youth movement taken over the bank, or had the bank taken over the youth movement?

The swift commercialization of "revolutionary" culture, another aspect of this symbolic co-optation, has been perceptively analyzed by Elenore Lester.

What has happened is that in the past few years the media have developed an insatiable appetite for this kind of material. It relates well to the atmosphere of excitement and novelty that advertisers seek to create around their products. To a public which has become acclimated to the idea of permanent cultural revolution, going out to make a revolution is something like going out to buy that revolutionary new detergent, Total Pure. New is good. Revolution is better. In a consumer society in which obsolescence is as vital to existence as rain was to primitive man, only stasis is frightening.

Everybody wants what is new and revolutionary—the plugged-in housewife who turns from our latest-model vacuum cleaner to a participatory media experience at the Electric Circus; the church parishioner who participates in an "environmental eucharist" created by an Off-Broadway playwright who blindfolds worshippers for "turned inward" feelings and leads them from basement to bathroom, where their sins are flushed away; the advertising-agency man who visits an experimental workshop at New York University's School of the Arts and finds: "It certainly makes you stretch your mind and imagination. It would take your mind off things after a day at the office—in fact, it's just like a day at the office." Of course, the New Theatre performing its rituals of out-with-the-old-in-with-the-new has society's blessing to create a new counter-culture every day.[15]

This is culture co-optation with an effect very similar to the co-optation of individuals of a different class. The established institutions swallow what is designed as protest and make it their own. The potential for sublimating protest in conformism was suggested by the political scientist John Schaar more than a decade ago:

Everywhere the call goes up that one should have what he wants and do as he wishes. In its purest form, this tendency is expressed in Existential philosophy, with its unwillingness to see man subjected to loneliness and meaninglessness. In its most morbid form, the tendency appears in the economic realm, where man is regarded as a creature of desires whose main right and purpose is the consumption of more and more goods and the enjoyment of more and more pleasures.[16]

The forms of protest thus dissolve into the pleasures of consumption. The challenges of the discontented can be adapted for institutional use. The expression of an unsatisfied value is transformed into a market for goods. New "life-styles" can be packaged and merchandised. Blue jeans, the symbol of austerity in a period conscious of poverty, are styled and tailored for sale in high-priced boutiques. Che Guevara outfits are sold in Ivy League shops.[17] The phenomenon underlying the symbol does not go away, to be sure, but its significance is somehow diminished by indiscriminate and nonsignificant use. Symbolic co-optation robs the fraternity of its secret handshake, its membership identification: everyone becomes, ostensibly, "friendly" and "feeling."

The second instrument for preserving dominant position is concession. This is a bargaining ploy in the implicit bargaining process. Agreement on one's terms can sometimes only be achieved by moderating those terms. The concessions may be illusory—not so much the bread and circuses to distract the masses as seemingly genuine remedial social policy which, however, somehow never gets executed. Land reform in Latin American countries has become a classic example. But the concessions may also be real, robbing a protest movement of enough of its objectives to undercut its zeal and diminish its following. Here the Bismarck social reforms are the classic example, beginning with the industrial accident insurance law of 1884.

In the debate preceding the 1889 old-age and invalidity pensions act, the value of social insurance as a means of attaching the worker to the existing order again came to the forefront. In a speech before the Reichstag, Bismarck reasoned that pensions would not only reduce discomfort among the laboring masses but would also directly tie their income security to the stability of the state. "I will consider it a great advantage," he said, "when we have 700,000 small pensioners drawing their annuities from the state, especially if they belong to those classes who otherwise do not have much to lose by an upheaval and erroneously believe they can actually gain much by it.[18]

In England only a short time earlier, William Morris, hoping for a change in social values, had anticipated Bismarck's *Realpolitik* in wondering whether "The tremendous organization of civilized commercial society is not playing the cat and mouse game with us socialists. Whether the Society of Inequality might not accept the quasi-socialist machinery . . . and work it for the purpose of upholding that society in a somewhat shorn condition, maybe, but a safe one. . . . The workers better treated, better organized, helping to govern themselves, but with no more pretence to equality with the rich, nor any more hope for it than they have now." [19]

In societies which are characterized by numerous specialized institutions —the pluralist societies of the industrialized West, for example, and even those which, while still industrializing, are well along the way—the opportunity for countering or anticipating direct challenge by minor concession is improved. The satisfaction of the limited objectives of those groups with the most bargaining power may cause them to drop out of the opposition.

The American labor movement, for example, is on the whole a willing supporter of business institutions, from which they have bargained substantial benefits. Few individuals would be more appalled at the prospect of political radicalism directed at the integrity of the corporation than the labor unions. It would cast them on an unknown sea, with no objectives of their own and no independent sailing ability. In any showdown with corporate power, the business leadership, barring any egregious mistakes of its own, can count on strong union support. Contrariwise, no radical group contesting corporate dominance can expect the labor establishment as an ally.

This phenomenon is not confined to the United States. Anabal Pinto has written with respect to Latin America that "a breach develops between militant trade unionism, restricted to economic objectives or those affecting the internal affairs of certain firms, and strictly political attitudes. Taken as a whole, the organized workers and the party leaders closest to them tend to take a narrow view of socio-economic problems in general, including development." [20]

Even when concession has not tamed a union membership generally, the union leadership—which enjoys its status precisely because the movement it heads has been built to operate within the established system—is likely to exert a moderating influence. In 1968, at the time of the worker uprisings in France, which had occurred with a spontaneity that troubled the official union leadership, an astute French observer commented of the latter: "They have built up solid organizations designed to oppose the regime *within the framework of its institutions.* They remain steadfastly on the side of law and order and tremble at any call to armed insurrection which would sweep them away along with the regime. They did not want to create agitation but to quell it and keep control over their restive troops." [21]

Similarly with other interest groups. The more a society is fragmented into special or functional communities, the easier it is for the dominants to make pacifying concessions to the stronger groups, perhaps even as a temporary expedient, without actual abdication of any power and advantages which cannot be recouped in time. The theme that "we advance together" implies no change in the order of the ranks.

Outright repression is the third principal instrument by which a dominant class can sometimes maintain its privileges, at least for a time. Repression need not take the form of physical restraint; it is more likely to consist in regulations and rules inhibiting the freedom of activity of dissident groups. Nevertheless, the effectiveness of such restraints must ultimately depend on force, and modern totalitarian regimes have demonstrated the ruthlessness with which such force can be applied. In his effort to collectivize Russian agriculture, Stalin (according to Djilas, who is backed by other authorities on this matter) threw millions of peasants into labor camps.[22] There can be no doubt that, officially or unofficially, torture has been resorted to in contemporary Brazil and Greece in an effort to silence radical opposition. The Pakistan government in 1971 undertook massive military and punitive actions against their recalcitrant Bengali population with calculated cruelty and unrestrained vindictiveness. The point is clear without reference to other numerous cases which might be cited.

However effective such direct application of force may be in the short run, it is at best only a delaying action. As Bismarck commented with respect to worker alienation and socialist agitation, "With mere police measures the problem cannot be solved." [23] The causes of dissidence or resistance are not touched; repression, by ignoring those causes, permits a bad situation to deteriorate further and inflames an already present sense of injustice. Repression works best when it is accompanied by the other devices of co-optation and concession, draining off potential resistance leaders and conciliating large enough segments of the population to reduce the size of the opposition. Thus in the advanced industrialized societies, which have spread their material benefits rather widely throughout the population, it is not just a small privileged upper class which feels a stake in the status quo; it is a large and influential leadership, more or less open, strongly entrenched in the major institutions, and supported by a sizable proportion of the population which has acquired enough status and material benefit to be fearful of losing these in any radical shift.

As I observed in a previous study of population pressures, even those members of a disadvantaged group who have made their way out of it are just as likely to be found on the side of continuity of the existing system, even though it discriminates against the group from which they derive at least some part of their identity. Blacks who have secured an education, a good job with middle-class income, and have been able to move into newly opened areas of good housing are likely to resent and resist the infiltration of lower-class blacks into their preserves.[24] Upper-class Indians who have inherited British status following independence are just as likely to resist democratization. Having made one's way with difficulty up the ladder of privilege, one does not like to have an escalator installed for the general public.

The effort to contain those who would alter the value structure and its supporting institutions thus has many adherents. It is scarcely surprising, then, that a public opinion poll taken by the Columbia Broadcasting System in 1970 showed that 76 percent of the population opposed allowing any group the freedom to organize protests against the government. Smaller majorities would have favored restricting other forms of criticism of the government, freedom of the press, and double jeopardy, and would have supported preventive detention.[25]

This fear of losing through any radical social revision what one has gained goes very far down in the social structure. The more desperate the poverty, the more valuable is some small perquisite, and the more vital is some small dribble of income, the cutting off of which would spell disaster. Latin American poverty is notorious, but Robert Scott has nonetheless concluded, on the strength of his own investigations, that even when populist leaders have been co-opted by the establishment, their followers accept such defection with little protest. "In time, of course, more dedicated and frequently more radical leaders appear in an attempt to displace the betrayers, but surprisingly few of these potential political innovators succeed. The truth is that the masses are too fearful and suspicious of change to welcome the destructive tactics of such leaders. This is by no means a rare attitude in poor countries where the marginal population has learned to survive under present conditions but has no reserve to fall back on in case an experiment in political theory fails." [26]

We have now come full circle. From an initial position which stressed the inertial forces of continuity, we moved to examine the strong forces, operating over time, which serve to undermine the position of an existing dominant class and the social values which it represents; but, continuing on, we recognized the means by which a determined class of dominants, even in the face of such opposition, can maintain their institutional hold on a society, with some modification of their advantages and their values, to be sure, but still retaining the dominant power. The conclusion which emerges is that continuity is at least as probable as change.

The fact is that there is no basis for a general theory of value change. We can delineate the ingredients in the process, but we are utterly incapable of prediction. The historical situation is compounded of ongoing changes in objective conditions, intrusive events, the response of existing dominants, of thruster groups, of various masses, all of which can arrange themselves in unforeseeable patterns. The result may be continuity, or fundamental change, or disorder or anarchy, or a stalemate.[27] This impenetrability of the future does not foreclose attempts to identify the principal forces at work and to act on the basis of one's judgment, but such attempts must always be accompanied by a recognition that others are doing the same thing, and that their actions—like one's own—are modifying the very premises on which action is based.

Notes

1. Gerrit Huizer, "Report on the Study on the Role of Peasant Organizations in the Process of Agrarian Reform in Latin America," mimeographed (Geneva: International Labor Office, 1969). Some of Huizer's findings are reported in Rodolfo Stavenhagen's "Marginality, Participation, and Agrarian Structure in Latin America," which itself is a perceptive and informative essay.

2. Moore, *Social Origins of Dictatorship and Democracy*, p. 388. It is interesting to note that Tocqueville too believed that a mass could not, on its own, effect significant changes in its condition. It required a leadership which he believed must come from some members of the ruling class who were ready to detach themselves from their peers and put themselves at the head of a popular movement.

3. *Ibid.*, pp. 40–110.

4. *Ibid.*, p. 221.

5. Di Tella, in Veliz, *Obstacles to Change in Latin America*, pp. 49–50. Quoted with permission.

6. Waterbury, *Commander of the Faithful*, p. 319.

7. Guttsman, *The British Political Elite*, Chapter 4, especially pp. 75–78. Thornton, too, in *The Habit of Authority*, p. 236, remarks on the way that reform played to middle-class advantage but excluded working-class representatives: "Harold Laski once calculated that between 1867 and 1884, 60 per cent of Cabinet ministers were aristocrats by birth, 67 per cent were graduates either of Oxford or Cambridge and 60 per cent were products of public [upper-class] schools. Between 1885 & 1905 the picture did not greatly change: 58 per cent were aristocrats, 83 per cent were graduates and 65 per cent were from public schools. Of the House of Commons itself, sitting beneath this aegis, 'perfumed by the presence' of aristocracy, Bagehot remarked in 1870 that it represented the plutocracy, just as the Lords represented the aristocracy, of England. The main interest of both these classes, he added, was identical: they wished to prevent or mitigate the rule of uneducated members. 'Sensible men of substantial means are what we wish to be ruled by.' "

8. Williams, *Culture and Society, 1780–1950*, pp. 325–327.

9. Luis Ratinoff, "The New Urban Groups," in Lipset and Solari, *Elites in Latin America*, pp. 70–71. Quoted with permission. Ratinoff notes that this middle class at times supports drives to enhance the position of a country on the world scene, increasing home-front unity. At other times it espouses a policy of government interventionism, ostensibly on behalf of a mass following, but with a recognition that the expanded bureaucracy resulting would provide it with its own sphere of privileged position.

10. Selig Perlman, *A Theory of the Labor Movement* (New York: The Macmillan Co., 1928).

11. Moore, *Social Origins of Dictatorship and Democracy*, p. 506.

12. Alexis de Tocqueville, *The Old Regime and the French Revolution* (New York: Doubleday Anchor Books, 1955), pp. 88–89.

13. Ratinoff, in Lipset and Solari, *Elites in Latin America,* pp. 68–69 (quoted with permission), and Scott, "Political Elites and Political Modernization," in *ibid.,* p. 126 (also quoted with permission). In some countries co-optation has taken the form not of admitting *individuals* to dominant positions but of alliances between the dominants and a potential thruster *group.* Barrington Moore has generalized that, in developing economies, a coalition between influential segments of the landed aristocracy and an emerging but still unaccepted commercial and industrial elite has been a crucial factor in perpetuating traditional institutions and privileges. (Moore, *Social Origins of Dictatorship and Democracy,* pp. 184, 371)

14. Baltzell, "The American Aristocrat and Other-Direction," in Lipset and Lowenthal, *Culture and Social Character,* pp. 268–291.

15. Elenore Lester, "The Final Decline and Total Collapse of the American Avant-Garde," *Esquire,* May 1969, p. 78.

16. Schaar, *Escape from Authority,* p. 234.

17. The following editorial, entitled "Let Them Eat Bullets," appeared in the *New York Times,* 11 December 1970:

> "Why not a gas mask as a pocketbook? Or a food stamp as a chic design for a brooch? Or the replica of an atomic warhead to make an amusing hat? None of these fashion fantasies is more offensive than the new fad of the cartridge belt, apparently designed to give 'relevance' to women's stylishness.
> "When the cartridge belt was first worn by armed student militants during a campus revolt, the public was justifiably shocked, both by the symbols of violence and by the depth of fear and frustration reflected in the display. The decadent chic, in turn, mirrors society's pathological lack of comprehension and compassion. It debases tastes and life-styles as it transforms the implements of extremist revolutionaries into toys for the rich."

18. Gaston V. Rimlinger, "Social Change and Social Security in Germany," *Journal of Human Resources* 3 (Fall 1968): 414.

19. Quoted from Williams, *Culture and Society 1780–1950,* p. 157.

20. Anabal Pinto, "Political Aspects of Economic Development," in Veliz, *Obstacles to Change in Latin America,* p. 28. Quoted with permission.

21. Sanche de Gramont, "The French Worker Wants to Join the Affluent Society, Not to Wreck It," *New York Times Magazine,* 16 June 1968. Italics mine. De Gramont also applied his comment to the leadership of the French Communist Party.

22. Djilas, *The New Class,* p. 57.

23. Rimlinger, "Social Change and Social Security in Germany," p. 412.

24. Cleveland's public housing program broke down in 1970 partly for this reason. Plans for constructing low-income housing met with hostility from both white and black middle-class families in whose neighborhoods the new units would have been placed. The director of the housing authority commented: "When blacks make it into the middle class, they start to act just like whites when it comes to public housing." *Business Week,* 18 July 1970, p. 28.

25. *New York Times,* 16 April 1970.

26. Scott, "Political Elites and Political Modernization," in Lipset and Solari, *Elites in Latin America,* pp. 126–127. Quoted with permission.

27. The latter potential has been most effectively set forth by Karl Polanyi in *The Great Transformation,* where he conceives that a social deadlock has emerged in mid-twentieth-century Western societies from an inability of the old dominants to control and of the two thruster groups he sees emerging, one from the left, one from the right, to make themselves effective as yet.

12 / The International Context

The political unit within which we have thus far pursued our search for social values has been the nation. But no nation is indefinitely able to withdraw into its own shell, cutting itself off from intercourse with other nations, even though some have done so successfully for a time—Japan is the notable example—and others have adopted more or less isolationist policies. In centuries past, the "world" of any nation was likely to be rather circumscribed: even an Alexander missed two continents and barely touched a third, and the Inca nation had a very limited "international" horizon. But today no nation can escape the impact of virtually every other, at a minimum through the effect of decisions reached by international bodies broadly representative of the organized world. Our effort to uncover the source, persistence, and change of social values can hardly stop at a society's national borders; extranational influences cannot be ignored.

We shall find, however, that we can deal with this phase of our investigation in shorter compass, since the same set of concepts which we have developed thus far can be made to serve in the larger setting.

We start from the premise that there is always some roughly identifiable set of relationships existing among nations. At periods, particularly prior to the fifteenth century, a number of relatively discrete sets of relationships could exist contemporaneously and lack regular commerce or connection with each other. Even so, it would be possible to identify the regions within which empires, alliances, networks of reciprocal relations composed a more or less discernible international system, and we could then say that, collectively, these several systems described the world order of that time.

In some periods disorder has been the rule: Europe, following the disintegration of Rome and before the revival of town life and commerce in the late tenth century, was a mosaic of disjointed fragments, composed largely of feudal and self-sufficient enclaves. International contact, to use that term loosely, consisted chiefly of limited trading and much armed conflict, offensive on the part of some peoples, defensive on the part of others. Still, we could describe the international relations of that region at that time in just such terms, as a weak and unstable system. The point is simply that insofar as historical records permit, in the same way that we can identify the social, economic, and political relationships *within* societies, we can also identify some relationships *among* societies.

If we pass over the earlier and less-developed centuries and come down to more modern times, we can the more readily discern such systems of international relations. Since the age of the great explorations, and particularly with the emergence of England as the greatest imperial power of modern times, we can speak quite realistically of a structure of international authority. This first tended to take the form of a centralization of power, backed by military might, in the metropolitan countries of Europe, later joined by the United States. This structure of authority built up its own institutional forms to secure its position, including an international monetary and banking system, organized market relationships which cast certain nations in the role of materials suppliers and others as materials finishers, internal government and administration systems in the dependent nations which could be most effectively overseen by the imperial powers, systems of education which produced an indigenous elite whose careers depended on furthering the metropolitan interests, and status systems which emphasized the superiority of the ruling power (a form of pseudo-speciation).

Where do values fit into this picture? Let us think, for the moment, of the international scene as simply a very large society. Just as the smaller national societies with which we have been preoccupied can be disaggregated into a number of component groups, whether along ethnic, racial, functional, or some other lines, so too can we conceive of the larger international society as composed of a number of subpopulations, in the form of nations.

At any point in the world's history, whether within a region or the world as a whole, some country or group of countries exercises a dominant position in organizing that system (or systems) of international relations to which we have just referred. It will have succeeded in effecting alliances with other nations, it will have won the acceptance of still others which believe they can benefit from the relationships it is introducing, and it will have met with tolerance or indifference from the larger number of smaller nations which in any event feel unable to affect the situation. The values of the dominant power or powers will be intruded into the dependent nations, in part accepted voluntarily by those who seize upon this change in the objective conditions for personal advantage, in part spread through incorporation into the basic institutions, and in part taught in the educational system. Arnold Toynbee has put the matter pithily. "A way of life is not itself alive. It is not self-propagating and not self-perpetuating. Accordingly, when we find a common way of life holding a world-state together, we must look for the human agents who have been the bearers of this unifying way of life in its spread over the face of the Earth and in its transmission from one generation to another." [1]

For many, perhaps most, of the subject populations it will not be a matter of accepting the dominant values *as* values so much as accepting them as rules of conduct which must be followed to assure security of existence. Just as many component groups within a national society maintain, even if only weakly, their own particularistic values while conforming to the dominant social values, so the component nations of a world order continue to nurture, even if with diminished fervor, their particularistic values while conforming to the dominant prescriptions more or less imposed on them. In time, however, as the domestic dominants become more closely aligned with the international dominants, the latters' values become more and more absorbed. They validate an accepted way of life. Then, by the process we have examined at some length, the value structure of the local dominants, reflecting imperial preferences however modified to accommodate the indigenous culture, gradually seeps throughout the society.

The intrusion of dominant power values into dependent societies springs in part from a missionary zeal, at least with respect to focal values—a desire to cultivate in others the same preference for a particular way of life which fires the breast of the dominants. In the matter of constitutional and distributive values, however, in the very nature of the relationship there is an emphasis on hierarchy—the sphere of autonomous development allowed the dependent nation is limited—and on status-based privileges for the metropolitan citizens. (We may recall from a much earlier day how the Apostle Paul, when arraigned by the hostile Jews, invoked the privilege of an appeal to Augustus on the strength of his Roman citizenship.)

It is scarcely surprising in view of this appropriation of the social, political, and economic advantages which the dependent society gives rise to, that the interests of the dominant power become confused with its values, and policies which are adopted presumably in conformity with the latter in reality serve the former. The "white man's burden" is shouldered partly out of some sense of focal value, however misguided, but the burden is borne willingly because it is a valuable burden. America's "manifest destiny" to bring the benefits of individualism and self-government to all peoples, whether they wished them or not, may have been touched off by a missionary zeal, but the "destiny" which was "manifest" was helped along by strong measures because it served dominant interests. The institutions which the superior power spreads it does so as a reflection of its value structure. (The United States supports education in underdeveloped lands, in furtherance of its constitutional and egalitarian values.) But those institutions, planted abroad, likewise serve the dominant power's interests, just as they do at home. (The education which the United States spreads is of a utilitarian nature, useful to its corporations domiciled abroad.) [2]

The world, then, is a larger theater within which some change in objective conditions creates the opportunity for a thruster nation to seize (just as with a thruster group inside the nation), carrying with it its own national value system, spreading the latter to the other nations which it comes to dominate in the course of its thrust, making such accommodations as are necessary to secure its position, institutionalizing its values, winning special advantages for itself so that interests and values become difficult to distinguish, preaching its philosophical validation to the rest of the world as a supporting religion or ideology. Thus the British seized the opportunity presented by an age of maritime exploration and their own lead in industrial development to colonialize half the world. An accommodation was worked out with their continental contenders following the Congress of Vienna in 1815, facilitating the export of its institutions, so that the nineteenth-century phase of British expansion depended less on the military presence and more on free trade, a gold-based system of exchange, transfers and protection of private property wherever located, all leading to the economic dependency of unindustrialized nations but receiving a theoretical justification in the doctrine of comparative advantage, which proved that both the dominant and subordinate trading partners were better off. Military power lay behind acceptance of the institutional order, to be sure, but the power could be held in reserve. The institutional order functioned very well without military command, particularly after enough of the colonials had been educated to the rules, and had come to accept them as valid.

It is difficult for a single power, whatever its size or strength, to organize the whole of the world around its interests. The theater of action is too great. The numbers of peoples to be contained are too many. Nevertheless, as the nineteenth century demonstrates, a concert of powers, all subscribing to compatible even if not identical value systems, may be able to effect a limited number of interlinked networks. The Western powers who assembled at the Vienna Congress, whatever their nationalistic particularities of values and interests, had enough in common to maintain world dominance jointly for a century, broken only by occasional internal squabbles of no major importance. The rise of a major thrusting nation—the U.S.S.R.—following World War II created an effective competitive world power. Seizing on the opportunities created by the power vacuum in eastern Europe, it was able to establish its dominance in that sphere. It likewise offered an alternative relationship to smaller, less developed nations seeking escape from dependence on the old Western bloc. Two world systems came to coexist in uneasy tension where previously there had been only one. The values and interests of each conflicted; security for each seemed to depend on relative strength. With the rise of a third thruster power, mainland China, new possibilities for a realignment of nations and a reshaped world order have emerged.

The world—the so-called international community—thus clearly does not conform to any Wilsonian ideal of a number of autonomous societies each with its own freely expressed social values and institutions, any more than a national society is composed of a large number of autonomous groups and individuals operating independently according to their own value codes, without respect to each other. There must be some system of international coherence which emphasizes certain major themes of the times, and which operates by certain constitutional and distributive principles, however inchoate these may seem. But because of the numbers of peoples involved, the extended geographical spread, the diversity of cultures, it is less feasible to establish a single cohesive set of values internationally than it is nationally. The latter is difficult enough: we recognize the compromises and concessions, the diffuseness and disarray of values even within a single society; how much more prevalent that condition within the world order. But just as we can generally define some value structure within a society, however weak its hold, which traces back to some dominant group (possibly one passing from the scene) and perhaps also to a thruster group rising to take its place, so too in international relationships. Whatever coherence we descry—and there must be some—does not simply emerge from a consensus of autonomous nations; it traces back to some dominant nation (whether now strong or weak) around which some group of nations is clustered, and perhaps to some thruster nation, to which another group of nations relates itself.

The dominants and thrusters are there because, in their day, they have seized on opportunities created by changes in objective conditions, whether in terms of a new knowledge authority, economic organization, population shifts, or political organization. Some changes may even be engineered expressly to create the opportunities for a rise to greater world influence. This is all the more likely by virtue of the fluid boundaries of the political unit, resulting from mergers or dissolution.

Europe in this respect constitutes one of the most interesting contemporary theaters of action. Even before World War II there had been those who decried its organization into culture-bound and historically separated national units. These may have been appropriate to a stage of the world's history when a nation the size of England or France or Spain could exercise dominance over others, spreading a way of life to large geographical areas. But in the modern world, dominated by giant nations such as the United States, the Soviet Union, and potentially China, the individual nations of Europe become more and more dependent, old dominants which are being thrust aside. Ortega y Gasset lamented the mediocrity into which Europe had fallen—a nest of small nations, lacking vision, saddled at one extreme with old and weak aristocracies whose only purpose was to preserve as many of their privileges as possible and at the other extreme with politically emboldened but vulgar masses whose only object was "more" to consume. Any largeness of vision could emanate only from great leaders, but these would come to the fore only if the stage were large enough to invite their involvement. Hence his appeal for a united Europe which would provide the scale necessary for new world leadership—not of a materialistic or militaristic but of a moral order.

Ortega y Gasset may be faulted for some of his prejudices, but his conception of the relationship of national scale to international values, via the intermediary of a thrusting or dominant power, is difficult to deny. The later conception of Jean Monnet, which led to the formation of the Common Market, followed in that spirit. The present slow but persistent effort to fashion some workable form of federalism—a new "nation"—out of that alliance may ultimately lead to a fresh European thrust. Failing that result, one can only expect a continued decline in European influence on world affairs, with a possible divisiveness of interest and diffuseness of values in those countries, for reasons we shall shortly explore.

One conclusion to which we are almost unavoidably driven by the foregoing observations is that some substantial size is necessary for a nation to make its impress on the world scene. Numbers of population alone do not, of course, confer this capability of dominating other nations; there must be a level of economic development, a stability of political organization, and a thruster group which has become dominant and has impressed on its own society a sense of purpose and cohesion. But if numbers alone do not confer world influence, the latter is impossible without them. At the same time, the larger a nation, the more difficult it is to achieve that form of government we have come to call democratic: responsive to its citizenry, protective of individual liberties, mindful of free assembly and the right of protest, involving the people in government of their own affairs. Indeed, the term "self-government" becomes empty of content in the large society. The latter may have the power to turn politicians out of office, to force them to placate its heterogeneous population with policies acceptable to the majority and not wholly unacceptable to the organized minorities, but this is something quite different from self-government.

But what is the alternative to nationhood on a large scale? The alternative is to forgo any significant influence on the system of international affairs, which increasingly molds the internal policies of individual countries. If the United States were to disaggregate into its separate states, and the Soviet Union into its constituent republics, so that each of these became an independent nation, with its own administration, its own foreign service, its own military forces, its own economic relationships, the diffused influence of those numerous states and republics would be as nothing compared to the consolidated influence of each of these two great nations as they exist today. Thus a large society confronts an unhappy political imperative. To secure its own way of life, to preserve its own value structure, to protect the interests which build up around it as a dominant power, it must remain large and powerful. But in doing so it unavoidably moves toward a constitutional value which requires hierarchical control, internally, and mutes the opportunity for the autonomous development of individuals and groups.

Every employee of a large corporation knows the reality of that dilemma. To influence the policy of his corporate world, he builds up his own political representative—his union. This is his instrument for achieving industrial democracy. But to be effective, that union must be coextensive with the corporation, which means that it must usually operate on a national scale. But in operating on a national scale, it passes beyond the worker's control. Policy is made at its national headquarters—centralized policy, since it applies throughout the company. The chances for the individual worker to affect union and company policy become more and more remote. He may vote against his national officers and reject negotiated agreements, indicating displeasure, but that is hardly what we mean by democracy, industrial or otherwise. His influence over working conditions extends only to his local plant, and then only if it is not too large and if the conditions in question can be distinguished from conditions in other plants, so that no precedents are set. This is the price he must pay if the worker society to which he belongs, as a collectivity, is to have anything to say about the major conditions governing his employment. What alternative is there? To dissolve the national union into its local compartments, closer to his control, would leave him and his fellow workers without any influence on national corporate policy, robbing local control of most of its meaning.

The analogy to world order is clear. International policy is largely a product of dominant nations. Their values and interests are impressed on the other nations within their orbit. But the price their citizens pay for this influence over others is less influence over their own internal affairs. Paul could benefit from his citizenship in imperial Rome, but he could have no voice in framing its policies.

Some small countries may find it feasible to remain outside the orbit of any dominant power, largely preserving their autonomy—as long as that is compatible with dominant interests. Little Sweden may pursue her "middle way," the envy of many a larger society because of its independence and affluence, but little Sweden can do so because her values and interests are compatible with (and thus protected by) those of the dominant Western, American-oriented bloc. If the United States were to become enfeebled, and western Europe dissolve into internally divided small countries, Sweden would have a much tougher time preserving her autonomy. If a nation wishes to secure its own values within the international system, it requires size and power. If it cannot provide these on its own, then it depends on an alliance with, or the benign power of, some other major political unit.

Stephen Enke has posed the problem in commenting on the argument that military expenditure is wasteful and should be diverted to other purposes. "If the United States had no military power and hence lessened international influence, can we be sure that this course would be costless in terms of other values? A large fraction of our defense expenditures may be buying us important national objectives even though we cannot adequately describe them." [3]

Thus, in the very nature of the present world order, we stand to sacrifice our traditional values in the process of preserving them, whichever route we follow—the path of neutrality and peace or the path of world power. We cannot preserve them against the divergent interests of other thruster nations without maintaining our power, but power requires size and centralization of authority inimical to the constitutional values which are part of our identity.

Thrusts across National Boundaries

Every society is—more or less—a seat of contention. The existence of common social values, which lay stress on unity of purpose and norms of conduct, is accompanied by an array of divergent focal values, however muted these may be. Common social values override and exclude divergent ones, rendering them ineffective, but these latter do not die: they often remain sheltered, dormant, or latent within the bosom of some group, potential with life if given some nourishment. Their expression may be tolerated as merely insignificant if confined within the bounds permitted by the constitutional value. There may even be brief periods when the excluded values enjoy a temporary fashion, subsiding of their own accord because they arouse only a weak, passing, and limited response, perhaps helped off the stage by official or unofficial impatience with their denigration of a way of life in which most people have an investment and involvement. Thus the recurrent religious revivals of nineteenth-century America and the utopian drives for cooperative workshops and communities of the same period quickly languished in an increasingly commercial and corporate environment, even though the values represented did not perish but simply went underground or found expression in literary and scholarly texts, where they created no offense.

Contention over distributive values is more persistent, and is likely to drag in with it disputation over the appropriate constitutional values, since these can be used to defend or attack the prevailing distribution of social and economic advantages. But we have been through all this before; it is enough to remind ourselves, for present purposes, that any society always contains within itself the seeds of divisiveness.

In moving to the international scene, we encounter within a nation new possibilities for dissenting or thruster groups to increase their effectiveness. If they have been severely and continuingly frustrated in their efforts to secure greater recognition for their positions, they may have little compunction in seizing whatever opportunities the international situation provides to obtain aid from one of the world powers, either dominant or thruster. With a disaffected, intellectualist, aspiring leadership ready to provide the thrust and effect the tic with the foreign power, with a dissatisfied and disadvantaged mass disposed to provide weight to the effort, an opposition may be created which requires the domestic dominant group to offer concessions, perhaps even to agree to an uneasy coalition, or to face possible revolutionary insurrection. For its part, a world power may covertly support a cause which gives some promise of prying loose a country adhering to a competing or alternative international bloc, thereby strengthening its own position.

If at first this possibility sounds overly calculated and more romantic than realistic, history readily supplies us with a plenitude of examples. Without recourse to ancient, medieval, or renaissance ages, we need only recall the numerous instances of internal subversion—"fifth column" activity—which have occurred in the last few decades. The United States has earned a reputation for supporting conservative governments against leftist coups (for example, Korea in 1949 and 1950), just as the Soviet Union has been identified with support of such attempts (for example, Greece in 1947). At times the roles have been reversed, with the United States lending its weight to conservative coups against leftist governments (as Guatemala in 1954), and the Soviet Union strengthening leftist governments against conservative assault (Cuba after 1961). When division runs deep within a country, and there is a dedicated but frustrated thruster group around which opposition can coalesce, it attracts the self-interested support of one of the international powers in a divided world.

But this is not the only way in which domestic dissension can have international repercussions. Within some geographic, linguistic, religious, or ethnic cluster of countries which have pursued their separate national paths, thruster group may reach out to thruster group, across national boundary lines, in an effort to reinforce each other's insurgency and in the process to establish some larger political unit. The advantage of this lies in simultaneously providing a larger stage appropriate to a larger vision (a new focal value) and in enhancing the new nation's influence on the world scene. From one point of view, the American Revolution constituted such a united effort by thruster groups in the separate colonies against the mother country. Unity in Germany and Italy was achieved only over strong opposition from leading factions in the smaller principalities which were being supplanted. From time to time there have been pan-Slavic, pan-Arab, pan-African insurgencies.

A third threat to the security of incumbent governments is the possibility of a rebellious secession of a cohesive and dissatisfied group. If frustrated in its effort to alter government policy along lines conforming more closely to its values and interests, but not strong enough to mount an overthrow of the government, its best alternative may seem to lie in establishing itself as an autonomous political unit. Since such a move is almost certain to be opposed by the government, the activist group may find it expedient to look to an outside power for assistance. In recent years the theater in which this act has been played out over and over again has been Africa, which has become divided into smaller and smaller units. Asia, too, has experienced fragmentation in the face of the divisive pulls of religious, language, and ethnic groups which have sought greater constitutional autonomy for their own development. Thus East Pakistan (Bangladesh), found its champion in India in its contest with the mother country. In all such instances the external support derives from countries which stand to benefit from the division.

In the light of the potential danger of such opposition and subversion, the dominants of a country can sometimes secure their position by alliance with, or at least orientation toward, one of the dominant world powers. In the face of growing internal pressures or of actual insurrection, dominants can expect help in maintaining their position. Economic assistance may come partly in the form of military aid. Technical experts can be counted on to advise. Sponsorship and support for a disputed position can be expected in international councils. Something of a protective mantle is spread around them.

The greater the potential for domestic disunity, the greater becomes the threat of outside intervention, and the more dependent become a country's dominants on outside support. The presence of dissatisfied and thruster groups constitutes a continuing danger to the nation's position, a continuing invitation for the coalescing of its internal and external opposition. Thus the strength of a country's social values becomes a major factor in effecting and maintaining internal unity and coherence. Where this cannot be achieved through the devices of co-optation, concession, and subtle restraints, it may be sought through an appeal to some form of pseudo-speciation—the effort to submerge genuine internal differences in a false sense of unity against a common foe, an appeal to nationalism as a matter of pride in one's "kind," to patriotism as a cult.[4] Opposition to the government then becomes identified with treason, and political repression is justified in terms of national independence or national welfare. Speaking of the former colonial dependencies, Minogue comments that the new nationalist leaders, who commonly are the younger, European-educated but European-disaffected elite, "present their political struggle as one carried on by one homogeneous society against outside oppressors"—the former imperial power. "But they then have to admit that these outside oppressors have internal allies—stooges, traitors, tribal and traditional habits of thought—in short, *all that resists the national leadership*." [5]

But if this is true of the smaller weaker nations, it is also true of the nation that exercises or aspires to world dominance. It may be tolerant of divergent opinions within its society, in line with its constitutional values, as in the United States, but it cannot afford to be so tolerant of divisive actions as to weaken its internal unity, on which depends its international influence. "Politics stops at the water's edge" was a fundamental proposition in American history until shattered by the war in Vietnam. When internal disunity and deep divisiveness spread within a great power, as they have in the United States, its position of world influence is decidedly weakened. Its allies become unsure whether it can deliver support when needed; its international opposition questions whether it can move decisively if challenged. Its position is nibbled away at the edges, and if not checked the bites become bigger, until it is challenged to "put up or shut up," to demonstrate either its strength or its weakness.

In the face of such a threat to its position, the major power no less than the minor one is likely to resort to the pseudo-value of nationalism. Can a once-proud and dominant country be relegated to an inferior position without eroding the pride of each of its citizens, including those who have been the fiercest critics of its values? If it is America's "manifest destiny" to rule the world, is it not just as well to be an American citizen? If *some* nation is to build a world empire, had it not best be one's own nation? If *some* way of life is to be imposed on the international order, is it not preferable that it be one's own way of life? In arguments like these lies the power of pseudo-speciation, and if indeed there are some groups so disaffected as to be unmoved by such nationalistic appeals, their intransigence then becomes the warranty for their suppression. Internal unity becomes restored either by papering over class or racial or religious division with the veneer of national oneness or by containing forcibly those who would subvert the "common" national interest.

In these days the phrases "national dominance" and "subordination" fall sourly from our lips. Most people, it seems, would like to embrace the position that through some form of orderly world government, individual nations can live at peace with each other, each developing autonomously its own way of life, coming together in representative assembly to agree on such rules of common conduct as are necessary for international comity and commerce. But this, as we have already noted, is a utopian vision. Even should an effective world government be established, as surely will occur in time, it must respond to all the forces to which governments have always responded. There will always be dominants and thrusters, depending on those who see and seize some opportunity in changed world conditions, and these will leave their impress on the world society. The process may take place with less violence and more political intermediation, with more implicit bargaining, but some nations will always wield more influence than others in the matter of values and institutions, and in the interpretation of the implicit bargains.

Time and International Values

Just as the social values of a nation may decline over time, with the decline of a dominant class, so too in the case of the values underlying international relations. As in the domestic case, this may be due either to the intrusion of a new thruster nation, providing an alternative to which other nations may orient their positions, or it may be due to the erosion of dominant values even in the absence of a thruster. Periods of international disarray, involving a weakening of bonds linking subordinate nations to a major power, or a disintegration of a world system into looser blocs on a regional, ideological, or some other basis, may occur without the presence of an identifiable thruster nation.

Such an erosion may take place with respect to the focal, constitutional, and distributive values, collectively or severally, as we noted in the case of a single society. Nevertheless it does appear to me unlikely that the present dominant focal value—materialistic advancement, economic growth —is likely to be displaced on the international scene in the foreseeable future. The chief challenge to a focal value arising from the passage of time, as we noted in the previous chapter, comes from a cumulating belief that the values which have largely been excluded should be accorded greater weight. If, for example, consumption has been almost exclusively emphasized, then the nonmaterial values may take on the luster of strange, if not forbidden, fruit. The economic principle of a diminishing marginal rate of substitution applies even as between values: the greater the emphasis on consumption, the less important is each increment of consumption satisfaction and the greater the interest in the nonmaterial values which consumption-concentration tends to exclude.

Now the focal value which characterizes the present world order reflects the dominance of the relatively affluent and materialist nations, especially the United States and its Western allies, and the U.S.S.R. And conceivably materialism may be losing some of its appeal *within* those countries, particularly among the intellectual leaders, providing some challenge to prevailing philosophical validation (going back to Locke, Smith, and Bentham in the one case, to Marx and Lenin in the other). But to the rest of the world, to whom the values of the dominant powers have been spread, even to those Eastern societies which we tend to classify, crudely, as "spiritual" or nonmaterialistic, the grinding, omnipresent force of poverty—in contrast to the affluence of the West—has served to strengthen the appeal of materialism. After all, such nations have a long way to go before a consumption-mindedness would submerge them in a surfeit of goods, distracting their minds from other competing focal values. Hence the subordinated nations, whether oriented toward the United States or to the U.S.S.R., have tended to respond readily enough to the focal value of materialism which the dominant powers have championed. It is only that these lesser nations wish to share more equitably (or more equally, in any event) in the distribution of the world's material advantages—a distributive rather than a focal value. Thus it would appear to me that whatever may be the movement away from consumption values within the dominant powers, this focal value which they have seeded in the world at large is still flourishing. And I find it highly doubtful that either the United States or the U.S.S.R.

could move toward a lessened emphasis on consumption and manage to carry their poorer supporters along with them—unless, indeed, they were to engage in a redistributive program (embrace a distributive value of world egalitarianism) on a scale which would be difficult for their own populations to accept. After all, what is the point of being a dominant nation if that carries no material advantage with it?

But does this embody a contradiction, that the dominant powers are in fact trapped in a value structure by the very nations they dominate? To a degree, I suspect this paradox in fact exists. For in the eventuality that either or both the United States and the U.S.S.R. should undergo a value revolution, I would expect that new thruster powers—Japan or China, for example—would continue to pursue the focal value of materialism with even greater assiduity, since with material wealth would come world power, with increased industrialism would come the potential for military might. The pseudo-value of race and nationalism (all the stronger for having been trampled on by the white Western nations) would presumably strengthen their thrusts. Thus for the present dominant nations to move toward a form of asceticism-*cum*-charity (unlikely though that prospect is) would mean their vacating their seats of international influence to rising powers who embraced the focal value which they themselves were in the process of abnegating. Whatever the path of international power politics, then, whether the present dominants retain their dominance or new thruster nations join them or thrust them aside, I see the focal value of materialism persisting.

This does not mean that the passage of time may not modify the way in which that value is expressed by today's dominant powers. Conceivably it may be reinterpreted and refined. Thus I would expect that we shall become more concerned with environmental effects, less attracted to consumer foibles, fashions, and extremes, and less competitive among each other and with other nations on a consumer standard. Nevertheless, the focal value of materialism will remain firmly front and center, at least for some time to come. My belief on this score is based more on international than on domestic considerations.

It is with respect to the constitutional and distributive values that I would expect greatest erosion to take place with the passage of time. The principle of self-determination has been held out by the Lockean West and has even won some semblance of acceptance from the Marxian powers (who regard "people's" governments, however established, imposed, or maintained, as representative). But the credibility of this philosophical validation has been worn thin by repeated repression of populist movements, whether from right, left, or center. Imperialism has been given expression both subtly and crudely, militarily and economically, even by those who have disavowed it. "The idea of American Responsibility can only be understood as a projection of the regular and systematic expansionism of our economic and political institutions—a feature of our society which dates at least from the 19th century. American troops, for instance, have made those trips to Cuba and the Dominican Republic before—a number of times. They have also pursued the American Responsibility in Asia for at least a hundred years. They have been intervening in the Philippines, China, Manchuria and Siberia for more than two generations." [6] The catalog might be lengthened considerably. Russian intervention has been even more blatant, as in Hungary in 1956 and Czechoslovakia in 1969. In all such cases the good faith and credibility of the imperial powers is called into question.

The continuing play of power by those who are at the center of the international stage serves to undermine credibility in the value structure of the dominant powers. As we noted in the case of national governments, the exercise of power cannot be escaped by those in authority, but in its very nature and however well-intentioned its use, it must be exercised at times on the strength of inadequate information, with judgment which by hindsight can be considered "inexcusable," and in situations which cannot avoid doing harm to innocent parties (the "lesser of two evils" circumstance).

When this occurs on a world scale, the consequent effects (the "corruption" unleashed by power) are at times almost bound to be on an equally monumental scale. If the idealistic and ebullient young nation described (at about the same time) by Alexis de Tocqueville and Domingo Faustino Sarmiento, subsequently president of Argentina, is hard to recognize in the dogmatic and self-righteous United States of today, perhaps the chief difference lies in the fact that in the intervening years it achieved dominant world power—and episodic corruption *necessarily* goes with the exercise of vast power. Since it is hard to admit error, a nation generally resorts to self-justification, and the corruption is compounded into conceit. The result is gradually but cumulatively to erode respect for the power-wielding authority and the values for which it presumes to stand.

Finally, in the distribution of the world's advantages, inevitably a disproportionate share accrues to the dominant powers. Following Gunnar Myrdal's principle of "cumulative causation," which can be given the rough meaning that economic effects reinforce themselves, the wealthier and more powerful countries continue to build on their wealth and power, while the poorer and weaker countries find it difficult to avoid a further deterioration of their circumstances. There comes a point at which the gap separating the advantaged nations from the disadvantaged becomes too great to justify by any ethical standard; to accept any validation of the differential status would be too hopeless and too degrading for the underprivileged. No philosophical principle would seem to justify so small a portion of the world's population enjoying so large a portion of the world's wealth as is actually the case. Only the historical use of power—the seizure by thruster nations (and hence of thruster groups within those nations) of opportunities offered by changes in objective conditions—offers an explanation. But history and opportunism, while they may explain, cannot be converted into a philosophical foundation for existing privilege. Thus the distributive value, with whatever philosophical underpinning it may possess (such as the principle of comparative advantage), ceases to legitimate existing international relations. Just as domestically societies have been driven in search of some principle by which to justify the distribution of advantage (an "incomes policy" in the economic sphere), so internationally the search is on. Time has the effect of eating away at the value foundations of a world order no less than of a domestic social system.

But again as in the case of individual societies, the international dominants have powers of resistance. If the passage of time threatens their dominant position, with or without a challenge by other rising powers, there are means by which they can move to maintain their position. There is no need to detail here procedures for containing international dissidence which are basically similar to those employed on a domestic front. They reduce to three: Through co-optation, a thruster nation is admitted to the club and allowed to share in the benefits. This is particularly valuable if that nation wields influence over a bloc of countries less susceptible to the dominant power itself; this is the basis for a "sphere of interest" policy, the acceptance of another nation's hegemony over a piece of the world which cannot otherwise be easily held in check. The search for a "detente" between the United States and the U.S.S.R. provides a present example. Obviously before long some accommodation must also be made for China and Japan. By enlarging the circle of the favored nations, dominance is diluted but not lost.

Concession constitutes a second device for maintaining position. If the disadvantaged nations band together in an expression of resentment over their share of the world's wealth, a program of "foreign aid" or "technical assistance" may temper their wrath. Just as a redistribution of wealth has occurred within the affluent nations, which have all become "welfare states," redistribution can occur within the international "community." The egalitarian principle is extended a little further, but its effect stops far short of actual equality. Advantage continues to be distributed disproportionately, but less blatantly so.

As a measure of last resort, national status may be defended by military might. A dominant nation is such because it possesses power to compel others to accede—substantially—to its ways, and is prepared to use that power. This is the defense which a succession of American Presidents gave to their country's involvement in Vietnam. If it failed to honor commitments to defend that nation against Communist aggression, what countries now within its orbit would continue to give credence to its readiness to use the power it possessed on their behalf, if the occasion arose? The value of power would be lost by irresoluteness as to its use. As Benjamin Ferencz, who served as executive counsel at the Nuremberg War Crimes Trials, summed up the meaning of the so-called "Pentagon Papers" dealing with the Vietnam intervention: "Our motivation and policy was to avoid Communist control of South Vietnam at all costs and to demonstrate our ability to have our way in world affairs." [7]

To defend its status as a dominant world influence, a nation must be prepared to support its position by might. The problem for it is not whether military or other repressive action is justified at all—that question is resolved affirmatively when it assumes a dominant role. The problem lies in determining when such action is the most effective means of maintaining its position. As domestically, so internationally is Bismarck's view the appropriate one, that more is to be gained by inducement than by repression, by providing positive reason for the action wanted rather than negative reason for an action not wanted. B. F. Skinner would surely agree. But inducements may be effective only if the one to whom they are offered realizes that they are made from a position of strength and is willing to be induced rather than invite stronger measures. The cost of refusing the concessions must be greater than the cost of accepting them, even if they do not measure up to aspirations. There is an implicit threat from the side of the dominant power that the refusal of its assistance will deteriorate the relation between the two, the dominant and the weak, and that alternative efforts by the latter to break out of its luckless position are likely to be undermined or thwarted if not comporting with dominant interests. That implicit threat, to be effective, must be backed by a recognition that big governments can and will act ruthlessly, when provoked, to preserve their international interests.

Thus the process of value continuity and change which we observed in the single society extends into world relations, adding significantly to their fluidity and complexity. The social values within a nation are affected by the values exported and supported by the dominant power or powers and injected and extended by any thrusting nations. The world is not an anarchy of values, any more than is a nation, but as in a nation the unity, diversity, or diffuseness of values differs over time, as does their strength or weakness. Changes come with major changes in the principal objective conditions. Since changes in objective conditions affect nations differently, and unpredictably, changes in the values underlying world order come not continuously, in some smooth transition, but epochally, and usually with spasms of disorder.

Notes

1. Toynbee, *Change and Habit*, p. 150.

2. Thus Malcolm W. Browne, reporting on student unrest at Del Valle University in Colombia, quotes one student: "Our main quarrel is with gringo imperialism. Yankee aid is spent on our universities not for the benefit of the Colombian population but to produce technicians to operate the gringo-owned factories." *New York Times*, 3 April 1971.

3. *Journal of Economic Literature* 9 (September 1971): 844, in a review of six books dealing with industrial conversion from war to peace.

4. In reporting on his visit to Cuba, J. H. Huizinga, roving correspondent for the *Nieuwe Rotterdamse Courant*, expresses his admiration for the moral basis of that society. "After ten years, the 'reign of virtue' that every revolution knows still holds sway in Cuba . . . To [Lee Lockwood, another correspondent] no starry-eyed observer, Cuba represents 'the only attempt in the entire world to test the proposition that it is possible to construct a society . . . by placing ethical values first.' " But then Huizinga, on further observation and reflection, has second thoughts. "My doubts only began with the discovery of the fierce hatred that forms the counterpart of their passionate idealism." Che Guevara preached " 'relentless hatred of the enemy, impelling us over and beyond the natural limitations that man is heir to and transforming him into an effective, violent, selective and cold killing machine.' And Fidel shows himself as a good hater. When he comes to talk of 'American imperialism,' it is as if Dr. Jekyll makes way for Mr. Hyde, so ferociously does he rant about 'the universal enemy, the enemy of mankind,' whom it is 'my true destiny to fight.' " J. H. Huizinga, "Three Faces of Castro's Cuba," *Interplay*, June 1970, pp. 20–21.

5. Minogue, *Nationalism*, p. 154. Italics mine.

6. Gar Alperovitz in a review of *Intervention and Revolution*, by R. J. Barnet, in the *New York Times Book Review*, 24 November 1968.

7. From a letter to the editor of the *New York Times*, 18 June 1971.

13 / American Values: Past and Present

We stand now at a point in time when there is widespread speculation over a possible change in social values. While prediction in any scientific sense is not possible, the preceding analysis does lay the basis for a reasoned judgment. In this chapter I shall consolidate some of the earlier scattered comments with respect to the values in America's past and sketch in where we seem to be now. In the following chapter, I shall venture some opinions with respect to possible futures.

The Past

America's colonial period was largely shaped by the values of a pioneering thruster group emigrating from England. Of necessity, simply as a matter of survival, its efforts were largely concentrated in agriculture and to a lesser degree in trading. As Mosca has observed, in the absence of any crystallized institutions there quickly developed a spirit of individual enterprise, uninhibited by inherited social class status. Inevitably, however, a patrician class evolved—more prosperous, more intellectual, more public spirited, a group of "natural aristocrats," as John Adams would have it, out of whose number came the "founding fathers."

Their views, built into such philosophical validations as the Declaration of Independence, the Constitution, the Federalist Papers, stressed the constitutional value of individual autonomy and self-development, with a minimum of government controls. After all, prizing as they did their own freedom of action they believed it equally good for all others; seeking—like others—their own advantage, they believed with Locke that security of property was the mainspring of economic motivation. In terms of the distributive principle, they had no qualms in asserting equality of opportunity for all, with no inheritance of privileged position. Though divided on the issue of whether the vote could be trusted safely to every male adult, even those who favored property qualifications were agreed on the desirability of affording everyone a chance to acquire property. The desideratum was a

273

nation of equals, even if nature itself frustrated the fulfillment of that ideal by endowing some with less talent and ambition than others.

The Puritan doctrine of salvation through work (the full use of one's talents, whatever these may be) and the "covenant with God" which linked spiritual and material development compatibly formed the focal value. Obviously such generalizations did not apply equally to all colonial settlements, but they can be taken as broadly representative of those who were to play the most active leadership roles.

Such a system of values gave full opportunity for the majority of the population to seek their subsistence and possible wealth on the abundant land. It also gave full opportunity for the numerically smaller but more economically sophisticated commercial, financial, and manufacturing interests to begin the building of fortunes in the growing cities on the eastern seaboard and, before long, in interior towns as well. The natural aristocracy of the Revolutionary and pre-Revolutionary period gave way in the early nineteenth century to the thrusting business interests.

By the time of Tocqueville's visits, he could readily foresee the rise—out of conditions of equal opportunity—of business magnates who would organize the efforts of a multitude of workers—not Marx's proletariat, but a prosperous "middle-class" citizenry, perhaps somewhat stunted in their intellectual and cultural development by their preoccupation with money-making and getting ahead on the job. The growing ascendancy of business, while evoking some protests as to its behavior, brought no concerted movement for radical reform. The variety of cooperative and associationist schemes which dotted the American landscape in the mid-nineteenth century were short-lived. They provided no thrust. If business interests were acquisitive, this only reflected the spirit of the times. If they were sometimes exploitative, they were also demonstrably successful in developing the country. If businessmen were occasionally overweening in manner, they were, after all, self-made, and barred no one from following their path.

Concomitant with the decline of the eighteenth-century patricians and the rise of a dominant business class there occurred the advent of the professional politicians.[1] These effected the implicit bargains that made concessions to labor on public education and suffrage, to farmers on easy money, internal improvements, and land policy, and after the Civil War to Populist movements with respect to regulation of railroad rates and milling charges—concessions which hardly touched the power of business.

The Civil War removed a challenge to the increasing business-based value system, and at the same time provided a stimulus for expansion in the size of markets and establishments. General incorporation laws permitted the incorporators, rather than the state, to define their own purposes, in the pursuit of which they were accorded privileges respecting their financial and fiduciary status. "The new style of corporation statutes in effect judged that corporate status had no social relevance save as a device legitimized by its utility to promote business. The obverse of this judgment was that regulation of business activity was no longer to be deemed a proper function of the law of corporate organization. The function of corporation law was to enable businessmen to act, not to police their action." [2]

By the judicial construction of the corporate charter as a contract and judicial extension to the corporate entity of the privileges and immunities guaranteed to a "person" under the Fourteenth Amendment, the growing business institutions retained the same freedom from government intervention which the received doctrine of individualism had preserved for the natural individual.[3] Freedom of contract was interpreted as precluding any interference with the "voluntary" agreement between two consenting "individuals"—such as corporation and worker.

"More and more Americans were coming to measure all things with the yardstick of economic fulfillment. This made it possible for the Right to argue that Liberal democracy and laissez-faire capitalism were really one and the same thing, which in turn made it possible for the business community to defend itself against the heirs of Jefferson with Jefferson's own words, to celebrate the struggle against social reform as a last-ditch stand for human liberty." [4] The significant consideration here is not—or not only—that business interests were able to carry off this reinterpretation of values as a matter of self-interest, but that such an interpretation found widespread acceptance. It was not a case of business forcing its values on a reluctant public, but of identifying national interests with business values.

The growth of the national market in the latter half of the nineteenth century, the opening up of the West through the cooperative relationship of American troops and railroad barons, began the transfer of the locus of power from community institutions to national. The national corporation superseded the local family-held manufacturing operation, a process which continued down through World War II. National labor unions were formed to provide a complementary relationship. National trade associations became the basis for coordinated political and economic activity.

By the turn of the century financial management, through the devices of the trust and the holding company, had given rise to pyramids of power. But throughout this period of the consolidation of business into larger, more hierarchically structured units, governments—city, state, and federal —continued to operate on the constitutional premise of noninterference with business. Occasional legislation such as the Interstate Commerce and Sherman Anti-Trust acts, unenthusiastically enforced as they were, constituted exceptions rather than evidence of a changing rule. As late as the 1920s, Herbert Hoover, as Secretary of Commerce, preached a vivid gospel of individualism which drew its inspiration from the traditional philosophical validations.

The identification of business methods with religious values hardly flagged from the time of Calvin to the time of Calvin Coolidge. The nineteenth century heard its great preachers support individualistic competition as divine law. Thus Henry Ward Beecher identified God's intent with the American doctrine "that it is the duty of the Government merely to protect the people while they are taking care of themselves—nothing more than that." [5] Local ministers followed suit. The chaplain of the Scranton City Guard, a citizen's militia which was organized for the protection of life and property during the violent strikes which swept the nation in the depression year of 1877, was equally certain of the Lord's will. "Competition, and not selfish combination, is the essential foundation upon which the whole structure of industrial society must stand, in a free country, and under true Christian civilization." [6] The twentieth century produced even more imaginative connections between religion and business. Bruce Barton, a widely respected figure in the field of advertising, authored a book that portrayed Christ as a great chief executive. "Nowhere is there such a startling example of success in leadership as the way in which that organization [the brotherhood of the disciples] was brought together." Moreover, Christ had grasped the most fundamental principles of getting one's message across. He could serve as a model to any aspiring advertising man. "Jesus had no introductions. A single sentence grips attention; three or four more tell the story; one or two more and both the thought and its application are clear." "The absence of adjectives is striking." "Jesus used few qualifying words and no long ones." "Finally, Jesus knew that any idea may have to be repeated." [7] His philosophy was the foundation of modern business.

Business support of military ventures in the period up till World War II, and military reciprocity, is too tangled and complex a story to be attempted here. The "merchants of death" theme was persistently played on, and by others than Marxists. But however much business may have profited from war-oriented production or the expansion into foreign markets under such direct military auspices as those provided by Commodore Matthew C. Perry in Japan, it was clearly no simple case of a business conspiracy to lead the country down a shell-torn path. Americans had long displayed a chauvinistic zeal. A belief in the nation's "manifest destiny" to carry its values (including the focal values of materialism) around the world already existed in the first half of the nineteenth century. It was regarded as divinely sanctioned if not ordained, and there were numbers who were willing to accelerate God's will by military crusade if that were necessary. In the face of such a general missionary zeal, it is latter-day scapegoating to portray business as the source of American jingoism. But what is equally clear is that the value structure of the society—its emphasis on competitive materialism as the *summum bonum* and God's test of a chosen people—lent itself to this application.

Thus we have in the American past a nice illustration of how the values of a society, plastic in their earliest stage because still largely free of institutionalization, were given their form by a thrusting business class which soon became dominant, and which drew along with it as allies the organized church and the military. The necessary implicit bargains were presided over by professional politicians, making such concessions as were necessary to ensure continued agreement on fundamentals. The growing government bureaucracy performed its administrative and interpretative functions with a regard for precedent and convention which helped to preserve the situation as given.

The depression of the 1930s was perhaps the only serious challenge that the American business system had to face. With a collapse of the economy went a collapse of confidence in business leadership. Incipient demagogues and radical reform programs won substantial followings. Although the government intervened in economic affairs as it had never done before, although perhaps more significant regulatory legislation was passed in a decade than in all the nation's prior history, and although workers organized on a scale never previously achieved and even "seized" a number of industrial plants, in the end no thruster group emerged and there was no upheaval of values. Incremental changes were made, and traditional values were reinterpreted. The implicit bargain gave greater recognition to labor interests.

It is one of those unanswerable questions of history whether more significant changes may have come had not World War II intervened to unify the nation and eliminate persisting mass unemployment. Whatever one's speculations on this score, at war's end it was clear that business had recovered its old élan and prestige.

The Present

The United States is still a business-dominated, industrial-oriented society. For all the talk of a postindustrial, service-centered economy, for all the strident challenges of functional and nonfunctional interest groups such as organized labor and the blacks, business leadership still retains the strongest decision-making power. This is not to say that its influence is as great as it has been in the past, or that it may not feel itself beleaguered. It says only that American society still reflects the values associated with the business class more than any other set of values in the contemporary value spectrum, and that a business point of view is still largely expressed by the nation's government and institutions. It is not to say that business generally gets its way or that it is happy with the present state of affairs— economic, political, or social, or that it may not view its status as deteriorating. It is only to say that no other cohesive interest group, with a more or less clearly understood set of values and objectives, has as much strength in the implicit bargaining process, and that as a rule the professional politicians cannot hope to win office or manage office without its support or assent.

THE FOCAL VALUE

We should expect, then, that American society still places primary emphasis on private consumption and material welfare as its focal value. One need only open his mind and eyes and ears to assimilate the impressions registered in a single day in an American city to become convinced of this preoccupation. David Potter contributed the insight that the one institution which the United States uniquely originated, on a level of importance, he believed, with such institutions as church and school, was advertising.[8] Of course its historical antecedents can be found, but in terms of modern advertising, which surrounds a citizenry with ever-present appeals to buy, so that each person is scarcely ever out of range of its impact during his waking hours, no culture conceived of such an institution until the United States in this century.

Some analysts have seen in corporate advertising a baneful instrument for the control and manipulation of consumer tastes, robbing the consumer of his autonomy. When such an indictment implies that the large corporation can create an assured market for its own products, however "unneeded" these may be, the criticism goes wide of the mark. What is most significant is that advertising *in the aggregate,* without respect to the particular products which are being promoted, constitutes a form of continued indoctrination in the value of consumption, no different in its effect from the repeated rituals of a theocratic society. It fosters a consumption-mindedness, makes consumption the focus of what life is all about, extending its influence pervasively to all aspects of society.

Service-buying has of course increased enormously in the period since World War II, in other countries as well as in the United States, but it is material consumption which is particularly crucial. Many services are related to or dependent on the output of the great industries, preeminently the automobile industry. Thus in the 1971 recession, the President, to encourage consumption, recommended the elimination of the excise tax on automobiles, not because more automobiles were "needed" by the public —indeed, automobile congestion, pollution, and disposal were high on the list of urban problems—but because, as presidential advisers pointed out, an increased sale of 100,000 cars would mean an additional 25,000 jobs. *Time,* in reporting the move, added that "one out of every six U.S. jobs is directly or indirectly linked to the auto industry." [9] Repair services are of course directly dependent on a prior sale of material goods. The travel and recreation budget has been expanding, but a large part of travel costs involve mechanized transportation, accommodations, and related facilities. Education and health increasingly call for expensive equipment. Services will of course play an expanding role in consumption patterns, but any notion that the future lies with the proliferation of many small and personal enterprises, eroding the influence of the large industrial corporations, is simply misguided. It is inconceivable that any economy could grow and remain great or prosperous without a substantial industrial base: the concept of a *post*industrial society is economically disingenuous.

The importance of maintaining high-level goods consumption has, if anything, increased, and new mechanisms to undergird it have been forthcoming. Whereas not many years ago consumer credit was something that commercial banks frowned on, they now compete with each other in urging individuals to borrow against future earnings for present enjoyment. The credit card smooths the transaction process. The shopping center is becoming the nucleus of community life in newer suburbs which are planned along those lines. As one architect explains the concept, "We are using the economic and social potential of a regional center to create a real community center. We view our centers not only as retail environments, but as part of a larger community environment." [10]

The current reinterpretation of the American focal value has divorced material abundance from the work ethic. In earlier years work, although undertaken only for the promise of material reward, encompassed the idea of developing one's talents, however modest these might be. In contemporary life that Calvinist view has been all but abandoned. Work has become more and more simply the putting in of time on activities that carry little meaning. This loss of meaning is due in part to the historical process of fractionalizing operations into segments without any immediate relationship to the whole process, a technological matter, but in part also—a newer phenomenon—due to the lesser consequentiality, the greater triviality, of the products to which the production process is addressed. This trivialization of consumption and production is directly correlated with the spread of affluence. It is perhaps most blatantly acknowledged in the Christmas season, when we have become accustomed to seeing advertisements of frivolous objects "for the man who already has everything."

This phenomenon, to the extent it does exist, creates a frustration which runs deep in terms of values. Work is undertaken only for the goods it will buy, but the pleasures of consumption—while still real enough for most people—for others are wearing thin. Nevertheless, the consumption ethic is still pervasive. Even if the fetish of goods begins to lose its magic, what is there that works better? So the New York State Lottery appealed to the subway-riding masses: "Our $1 lottery can make you $100,000—think of what you can do with the money." And individuals for whom work has become a dull but necessary routine must find some justification beyond mere survival for pursuing it, a justification which in contemporary society is most readily available in buying goods. What else is there?

Indeed, it is a reasonable surmise that the emphasis on consumption as life's major satisfaction, on consumption as a way of life, will become more insistent even if more subtle. If automobiles are recognized as polluters of the environment, this requires the addition of antipollution devices to "purify" their purchase: consumption of goods is not curtailed but increased in the process. If garbage and rubbish disposal becomes a problem, "compacters" appear on the market to reduce the week's household droppings to a small cube. A way of life is not lightly discarded or demeaned; on the contrary, if subjected to attack, it is defended the more vigorously. The solution to the problems of industrialization is more industrialization, as President Nixon advised the nation.

But the dialectical opposition to an entrenched focal value—the assertion, by a minority, of values which have been largely excluded—is clearly making its appearance. On the one hand, it comes from a youthful, intellectual, upper-middle-class group of dissenters who find goods less and less capable of supplying "meaning" to their lives. If they do not "drop out"—an extreme form of protest which has lost its popularity—they have substituted other kinds of activities as the focus of their well-being. Interpersonal relations have become more important to them; encounter groups —not only the highly publicized, professionally conducted enterprises, but smaller, more informal, less sophisticated but more intimate and sometimes more intense associations—have proliferated. The search for intimacy with others, or at least the sense of its need, has increased, particularly among the young, and cannot be satisfied with goods.

Another form of opposition comes from some working-class youth. In the Detroit automobile factories, absenteeism has become a major problem. In 1971 it was reported to average 8 to 9 percent on midweek days, and around 15 percent on Fridays and Mondays. "A great many of the workers who stay off the job are younger workers who feel that they can make enough money in three or four days to meet their needs." [11] A vice-president of Ford Motor Company has predicted that employees in the years immediately ahead will be even less willing to put in "full time" on dirty, uncomfortable, monotonous jobs, shedding the commitment to work which has been considered one identifying characteristic of an advanced industrialized nation. The reverse labor curve which economists have associated with underdeveloped countries is making its presence known in the United States: at higher rates of pay, some workers supply fewer hours of work. They prefer the pleasures of leisure time (or escape from working time) to the pleasures of more consumption.

That choice has, of course, been made repeatedly in the past, on a social basis, as customary hours of work have declined with rising productivity. The 72-hour week gave way to the 60-, 54-, 48-, and 40-hour week, and is still on its way down though more in terms of additional holiday and vacation time rather than fewer hours per week. This historical phenomenon has not, however, been associated with any resistance to the values of the system; it has not required a defiance of the system of industrial discipline. In some respects, it reflected the need for more free time in which to enjoy the pleasures of consumption. In contrast, the new phenomenon does embody defiance of industrial order; it reflects individual rejection of the self-discipline on which industry has depended, the commitment of the individual to the work process with the consequent subordination of personal idiosyncratic preference to common standards. It is as though the individual soldier in the ranks were to decide for himself when he would rise and when he would fight.

The dilution of the work ethic has taken one other form worth note. In the face of concentrated poverty, with racial overtones, in the cities, there has been a startling acceptance by many in business and governmental circles of the need for income grants unrelated to work. The goal of full employment, embraced in national legislation in 1946, has already been abandoned as public policy. It is plain for all to see that few people in responsible positions expect that this country will ever again be able to provide jobs for all who want them. But with this pessimistic conclusion comes the necessary corollary that those who do not work must nevertheless eat. Indeed, they must do more than merely survive on a subsistence diet; they must be able to consume at some standard of minimal decency if open unrest is to be avoided.

The consequence is that the provision of jobs has given way to the provision of income, under a variety of welfare measures which are in process of being dignified in formal programs of a "negative income tax" or federal "income supplements," as a matter of legal right. Consumption remains the focal objective, though in this case divorced almost completely from a work ethic. The focal value is reinterpreted from consumption through work to consumption through income however derived.

There is another form of resistance to the American focus on private consumption which has gained ground among intellectuals in recent years —the belief that public consumption is more important than private, that the increment to national income could more usefully be spent on environmental improvement, general health programs, the upgrading of education, and other such public endeavors. For many years orthodox economists resisted such advocacy on the ground that the individual could be better expected to know his own wants and preferences, and that no satisfactory scientific standards existed for establishing that, in the aggregate, tax dollars spent by public officials purchased as much satisfaction as private dollars spent in the market. It took some years before an economist of the stature of Alvin Hansen could assert to his fellow economists that he could not prove, but that he *knew,* as a matter of faith, that the marginal dollar spent on public goods would purchase greater satisfaction than the marginal dollar spent on private goods. John Kenneth Galbraith pursued the argument further in *The Affluent Society*. A small but significant cadre of professional economists, with some lay following, adopted a doctrinal belief in the desirability of public consumption rather than more private goods.

But the prospect for any imminent shift in focus was laid to rest in 1964. In the tax legislation of that year the Keynesian thrusters were in effect co-opted by business. The President's Council of Economic Advisers under Walter Heller won acceptance for the idea of the "fiscal dividend" —the concept that the growth of the economy generated additional governmental income which had to be allowed for either in the form of reduced taxation or higher public expenditures in order to avoid "fiscal drag." But which form was more desirable—tax cuts for private spending, or tax-rate stability with public spending? Out of "practical politics" the first option was chosen. The concept of the "fiscal dividend" was radical enough for business to take; it would be too much to ask it to swallow, in addition, the preferability of public over private spending. Economist Jesse Burkhead has commented: "Thus tax reduction, undertaken for purposes of stabilization and growth, reduced the possibilities for altering the composition of output and the distribution of income. It was tax reduction that transformed the fiscal revolution to the fiscal-counter-revolution. . . . Tax reduction can appropriately be called commercial Keynesianism." [12]

The importance of this victory for the traditional class of business dominants hardly needs stressing. The government may be an outlet for goods, but it is not as pliable a market as private consumers. Business would become more a dependency, less the controlling influence. We shall have occasion shortly to reexamine this conclusion, but it is easy to see how it would be persuasive to an older generation of business leaders. The importance attaching to the primacy of private markets was underscored by the chairman of General Motors, James Roche:

This delusion—that the consumer cannot trust his own free choice—strikes at the very heart of our free competitive system. The system is founded on the conviction that in the long run the consumer is the best judge of his own welfare. The entire success of free enterprise can be traced to the vitality it gains by competitive striving to satisfy the discriminating customer. To destroy the concept of consumer sovereignty is to destroy free enterprise. If the consumer can be convinced that he really does not know what is good for him—and this is what the critics try to do—then freedom leaves free enterprise.[13]

The point which I am emphasizing here is not the strength or validity of the dialectical opposition to private consumption as focal value. I refer only to its emergence. It would be in error, I believe, to conclude that such resistance constitutes any present threat to the focal value of the present business-oriented social system. It does, however, have some significance as a challenge. It is obliging the business dominants to defend their position and even to counterattack, as they have not had to do since the grim days of the Depression Thirties. The ruling value of private consumption still rests secure, but perhaps not as easily as in the past.

There is one other aspect of the American value structure which warrants at least passing reference here. The nineteenth- and early twentieth-century doctrine of manifest destiny, under which the United States felt a duty to export and even at times impose its clearly preferable value structure wherever possible, gave way after World War II to a successor policy of cold war and containment. It was the mission of the United States, as the only remaining "power" in the Western world, to defend Western values (as most vigorously expressed in its own institutions) around the world. The inevitable confusion between values and interests persisted. It would be excessively cynical, however, to assume that only interests were involved. The struggle would not have been carried on with the same intensity—in the Middle East, in the Far East, in Berlin, in Latin America—if there had not been a profound conviction that the country was fighting to preserve a way of life, a set of values. Destiny might no longer seem so manifest in decreeing the American pattern for the world at large, but it remained an objective still worth fighting for.

THE CONSTITUTIONAL VALUE

We have been speaking so far of the focal value. If we turn to the constitutional value, we find that major changes in two categories of objective conditions facing the United States have had the effect of moving it along the spectrum away from individualism and autonomy toward hierarchical control and systemic order. The first of these is the increasingly technical nature of our industrial processes and the increasing specialization of all forms of work, accompanied by a growth in the size of organizations. The second is the growth in the size of population and shifts in its concentration and composition. These two changing conditions tend to reinforce each other.

As we noted previously, there has been both an absolute and a relative increase in the amount of white-collar and personal service-oriented work, which conveys (especially in the professions) the suggestion of a growing individual autonomy in the American economy. Even within the large and concentrated industrial sector it is sometimes argued that greater opportunity now exists for the expression of personality than in the smaller, family-centered corporations of the past. "The internal structure of any corporation today is less hierarchical, more dependent on the interplay of many wills, many power centers; information has become the corporate lifeblood. Persuasion and communication are replacing mechanical routine." [14] The modern corporation, it is said, has transformed and democratized the idea of elites by opening up opportunities at the top to all those who can advance on their own merits.

The initial plausibility of this conclusion dissolves on closer inspection, however. What has happened is that the hierarchical controls have become more sophisticated, less blatant, more positively than negatively reinforced, in B. F. Skinner's formulation. We have become far more "systems" conscious, with a realization that a clearer definition of the system constrains the individual components to perform the role within it for which they are cast. The freedom to rise in the corporation, the autonomy of the small entrepreneur or professional, is circumscribed by a social system which may lie less heavily on one's consciousness but which nonetheless largely controls his movements. The more specialized are people's functions, the more dependent on the system do they become to integrate them with other specialized components.

Even the professional, who for so many symbolizes individual autonomy, tends to get caught up in the orderliness of the system. Medical doctors become involved in national health programs or with private but highly institutionalized insurance systems. The private teacher or tutor has all but disappeared. Lawyers, scientists, and engineers increasingly work within the confines of corporate or government "game plans," their "independence" preserved in their own minds by the premise that they are value-neutral, unconcerned with the objectives of their client (to whose wishes they can therefore bend without feeling the pressure placed upon them). Indeed, value-neutrality has become the chief refuge of the professional in contemporary times, held fast to since it so neatly preserves the fiction of autonomy at the same time that it trivializes the nature of that autonomy. As two eminent sociologists have expressed the matter blandly and bluntly, *"For the individual* it becomes increasingly indifferent what the "goal" of the employing organization may be, in the sense that the social structuring of his role can be treated as, to a substantial degree, independent of that goal." [15]

The status of the individual is defined by his relationship to "the employing organization," whether one speaks of the seniority standing of the manual or clerical worker or the hierarchical authority of the manager. If individuals are free to rise within the organization as far as their abilities (for which we often use education as the surrogate) permit, their abilities are defined in terms of the needs of the organization. These needs are spelled out in short-run, medium-term, and long-run plans and budgets, which are binding on the members of the organization, identifying an expected performance—often measurable—for which they are held accountable.

That all of this weighs more or less lightly on many people, so that the above description might seem forced and pejorative, is in large measure due to the increasing sophistication in the way that people are related to the system. In terms that have gained widespread currency, Theory X (relying on command and obedience) has given way to Theory Y (emphasizing discussion, persuasion, consensus).[16] Sensitivity training, pioneered by social psychologists, has been enthusiastically taken up by both private and public organizations; it aims to make the individual more conscious of the reactions of others to his behavior, hence less obstructive to organizational purpose. In 1969 the National Industrial Conference Board, a research organization geared to the interests of enlightened business, published a study on how business firms were seeking to integrate the behavioral sciences into their operations. "Behavioral science's chief aim is greater productivity through optimal use of human resources," it asserted, and then proceeded to make clear its conception of personal autonomy within such a behavioral-science-managed system.

In terms of objectives:

The reasons why companies have sought to integrate behavioral science findings into their management are many and varied. But in most cases they are seeking to change the basic climate of the organization by the creation of: open and free-flowing communication; increased productivity through concerted group effort; participative decision making; improved superior-subordinate relationships; integration and improvement of human and economic objectives; and enriched job content and individual freedom as motivational factors.

In terms of accomplishment:

The companies expressing the most satisfaction with their behavioral science programs are those that do not view them as programs at all. Instead, they see them as a completely different way of improving and managing the enterprise. These firms are trying to impact the total organization by applying behavioral science principles at all levels. Their behavioral science applications extend beyond trying to develop managers. Instead, they encompass every facet of the company's operations in terms of meeting such objectives as long-range planning, career development, productivity, and profitability.[17]

This statement illuminates the relationship between personal autonomy and system organization as it has developed within the contemporary large-scale organization. The operations of the latter cannot be left to chance or personal idiosyncracy. Increasingly it calls for planning and controls in the achievement of clearly identified objectives. But the individual plays his role in achieving those specified objectives within a framework of social relations which create the illusion of discretion and individual freedom. Or perhaps it would be more accurate to say that individual discretion and autonomy are bounded in ways which are more ambiguous (participation, consensus, persuasion, communication, "brainstorming," integration) and so permit a sense of independence, but an independence which is in fact ineffective. The group activity and committee decision-making which is characteristic of large-scale organization allows the individual to "participate" as vigorously as he chooses, but the "shared" decision which emerges is firmly embedded in limits which the organization, the system, defines.

If hierarchical authority *within* the corporation has increased with increase in size, the legitimacy of that authority—its representative character—has been subject to more vociferous attack. Consumer groups, conservationists and environmentalists, civil rights leaders have recurringly questioned the placement of authority in the hands of virtually independent and self-designated managers who are motivated primarily by private rather than public interest. This attack on corporate autonomy has so far been less than successful, even though it has obliged managements to be more public relations minded.

Nevertheless, the corporation is not immune from external controls over its autonomy in the form of requirements which the *larger* social system imposes on *it*. This is not simply because the operations of the economy have become more interdependent. After all, the free competitive market exhibited, at least in theory, the highest interdependency one could imagine, so that within the Walrasian system not a price could change, of product or factor, without setting in motion a train of repercussions. The change that has occurred is that major decisions increasingly take place in large-scale organizations, both private and public, whose size has conferred a degree of power over others in the pursuit of self-defined goals. It is the existence of these diffused pools of power which invites—indeed, requires—some form of conscious coordination if overall (system) objectives are to be achieved.

This has perhaps been most clearly and overtly demonstrated in the French planning mechanism, which is "indicative" only, relying for its effectiveness more on the internal logic of the system than on the coerciveness of government. Whenever public objectives (housing, wage-price stability, pollution control, employment, racial tolerance, transportation, education—the priorities change from year to year but there is always something of urgency confronting the public) assume critical importance, whenever social objectives like these demand official attention, they require a coordinated effort for their solution. In some instances laws may be passed to assure the desired result, but as often it is administrative measures or executive "guidelines" which are called into play. With varying degrees of explicitness, these become "le plan" in France or "the game plan" in recent American terminology, and impose a logical even if not a legal compulsion on those whose actions they are designed to affect. Behind the logical, nonlegal compulsion may rest varying degrees of punitive and coercive power which help to make the logic persuasive. Even when there is some resistance to the system program, the knowledge that the outcome—the achievement of the desired public objective—depends on each person's playing his role, so that "sulking" not only destroys the game for everyone but threatens public obloquy toward the recalcitrant, exerts a strong pressure to conform.

At the same time that we can thus identify a movement toward a firmer structuring of public and corporate objectives, shifting the emphasis away from individual autonomy toward hierarchical order, we cannot suppress the contrary feeling that the youth cults of recent years and the growing *lack* of order in major urban centers, especially in the United States, give evidence of greater individual autonomy, amounting almost to license in some cases, or freely granted public permission to reject the compulsions of society ("cop out" or "go on welfare"), in other cases. This is where the changes in population distribution are having their effect.

The youth cults have been variously explained, but one common ingredient appears to have been an emphasis on independence from "the system." In dress, sexual relations, educational interest (or lack of interest), use of time, the message was "do your own thing." In some instances conformity to a cult simply substituted a different source of compulsion, but the dominant theme was personal autonomy. We shall examine the significance of this attitude more fully in the succeeding chapter. Suffice it for the present to say that to some degree the theme was a short-lived one, a brief but violent revolt which spent itself against the established institutions and then fell back exhausted. But to some unmeasurable extent it did make its impact, and introduced a greater measure of idiosyncrasy into society which added to its color without significantly changing its structure. The new areas of autonomy were for the most part trivial. The increased use of drugs which accompanied the youth phenomena I would attribute to disaffection with the focal value rather than a search for autonomy or self-development. Far more significant than the youth movements as a rejection of the legitimacy of hierarchical order has been the eruption of racial disorder.

The post-World War II concentration of blacks and Latin minorities in the major cities, with the consequent white exodus to the suburbs, about which so much has been said that no more need be added, has increasingly made those cities hostages of a segment of the population which has never been integrated into their institutions or into the social system generally. The shift toward firmer hierarchical structuring within both corporation and society affected them little, since they were so little a part of those structures. The cities began to become a field of exploitation for those who themselves felt exploited, particularly the young among the minority groups, who felt unmotivated by an educational system designed to fit them into an economic order which was not prepared to receive them except on demeaning terms, if at all. But it was not only an undisciplined core of the young or a lawless element who struck out at a society they regarded as hostile. Studies subsequent to the riots of 1967 clearly revealed that in many instances blacks of above-average income and education were venting a pent-up rage at discriminatory treatment. Such anarchistic developments —some episodic, some endemic—as have occurred in urban society are not, however, reflective of particularistic social values held by a racial minority in opposition to dominant social values: they are simply a rejection of the latter values, more akin to the expression of a "negative identity" such as Erikson postulates for those from whom nothing more is expected, the self-fulfilling expectations as to black performance held by the dominant whites. The concentration of such rejected population in the urban centers creates a mass phenomenon, but it constitutes no organized expression of divergent *values,* unless it is the pseudo-value of racial speciation. It is more a conflict of *interests.*

Racial tensions undermining stable civil relations have been imported into the urban-based plants of companies employing unskilled and semi-skilled labor. As the populations of the cities have changed in composition, so necessarily have the labor forces of their large-scale industrial and commercial establishments and their service and governmental agencies. The consequence has been a lessening both of self-discipline and imposed discipline in the work environment, as alienated blacks resist the authority of a system which they believe has always discriminated and continues to discriminate against them. Absentee rates have increased, the quality of workmanship has deteriorated, responsiveness to supervisory authority has declined.[18] The undercurrent of antipathy and conflict between black and white workers has exacerbated any normal problems of organizational discipline. Attitudes formed outside the plant, reflecting white resistance to a new black assertiveness, are reproduced in the corporate setting.

Within a society which is, nationally, overwhelmingly white, the consequence has been to stir up sentiment for an assertion of stricter control over individual or group actions threatening disturbance of the established order. Youthful white protesters against the Vietnam war were swept up in this condemnation of vociferous and violent protest, but with de-escalation of the war the blacks remained the principal target of champions of the existing institutions. A nationwide poll undertaken by the Columbia Broadcasting Company in the spring of 1970 concluded that a majority of American adults were willing to limit some of the basic freedoms guaranteed in the Bill of Rights. Interpreting the results of this and other symptoms, James Reston gave as his opinion that "a great many people now seem willing to choose order at the expense of some of their liberties, or at least at the expense of somebody else's liberties." [19]

Thus the apparent emergence of greater license and individual autonomy in the cities of the United States is not expressive of any constitutional value, either by society at large or any subordinate groups. It has only served to elicit a growing sentiment that systemic order needs reinforcement at the expense of individual discretion. The urban phenomenon provides no exception to the generalization that the present period exhibits a shift away from individual autonomy toward a more highly structured social order, responsive to the greater need for coordination of specialized activities in the service of public objectives—some new, some old—and to the problems posed by the growth of population and changing composition of the cities.

With the growth in scale of organizations, private and public, the very meaning of the term "self-government" comes into question. How can large numbers of individuals with conflicts of interests and some divergence of values effectively "govern" themselves? How can they even be effectively "represented" when, given their numbers, they have no contact with their representative, and he cannot conceivably represent equally the divided views of his constituency, and his own influence in a legislature grown to the size of a conference depends on such considerations— irrelevant to the concept of representation—as seniority, financial backing, friends and family, not to mention physical stamina and persuasive power?

Under such circumstances the role of the professional politician in molding opinion becomes of greater importance, and public opinion can be molded by a variety of devices which smack more of the marketplace than of intellectual conviction. To the extent that the feasibility of self-government or genuinely representative government recedes, the reliance on the authority of those in public position—hierarchical authority— increases.

This heightened reliance on government as the coordinator—the manager—of the economic system as a whole obviously undermines the autonomy of the corporation. Its discretion is limited by its linkage to the larger system, which more often than in the past is likely to define objectives binding or at least influencing corporate management. But the relationship is not one way. While leaders of the corporate community may continue to complain of government intervention, their complaints are now less convincing. They have themselves become persuaded of the need for governmental coordination if the economy—which is their base of power —is to prosper, and moreover they are themselves still the strongest influence on national policy. If their organizational autonomy has thus been attenuated, this has been necessary for the reinforcement of their position.

Their dominance may be somewhat diluted, but no other interest can contest it.

THE DISTRIBUTIVE VALUE

In the area of the distributive value, the same racial redistribution of population has likewise had its impact. Among the majority population associated with the dominants—white middle-class America—the theme of equality of opportunity is still pervasive. The surrogate for this value has increasingly become equality of educational opportunity, since educational attainment so directly affects job opportunities. The plums of society should be awarded to those demonstrating the greatest merit on the objective basis of intellectual and skill achievement, without respect to race, ethnic origin, or religion. Meritocracy is thus equated with egalitarianism.

The mass substitution of blacks for whites in the Northern and Central cities following World War II has eroded this interpretation of America's egalitarian creed. The concentration in such urban centers of black and Latin minorities who—for disputed reasons which need not concern us here—are unable to take full advantage of "equal" educational opportunities has led to a parallel concentration of frustration and unrest. Since the civil rights agitation of the mid-sixties this has resulted in a rapid acceleration in welfare programs designed at first simply to alleviate conditions of distress but increasingly regarded as a "rightful" participation in society's advantages. The traditional conception of equality of opportunity began to acquire a gloss that this objective could be attained only with greater equality of actual *condition*. Children in slum areas, without adequate food, health, housing, and cultural facilities could scarcely be expected to avail themselves, on an equal basis, of the opportunities which American society afforded. Hence some remediation of their lower standard of living was essential to permit realization of the egalitarian distributive value. A greater equalization of actual economic condition was necessary to the equalization of opportunity. Aside from the massive increase in welfare loads, this interpretation led to expanded municipal payrolls, often federally financed, which included a growing proportion of the new population. Private employers were importuned and administratively required to increase the proportion of minorities in their labor forces. In the case of both public and private employment, prior hiring standards were diluted so that the meritocracy principle would not constitute a bar to expanded employment.

The net result of these several measures was some improvement in the minority share of total income, but not by enough to extricate large numbers of the new urban residents from what was defined as a condition of poverty. Many of the Southern rural poor moved to Northern and Central cities where they remained poor even though at higher levels of income. The cities replaced their wealthier white populations with poorer black and Latin ones, in numbers which created a political problem, requiring redistributive concessions. In effect, the dominants and their middle-class allies sought to retain their "earned" advantages by "unearned" concessions to the disadvantaged, who were becoming more vocal in their protests. The distributive value was pulled and mauled a bit, but not discarded. A notion of some minimum floor to income—a more contemporary variation on the minimum wage theme, but no longer related to employment—began to win acceptance as a foundation necessary to justify retaining the principle of equality of opportunity.

Aside from the question of appropriate income shares under conditions of inflation (the issue of wage-price relations, which has become endemic since World War II), a more fundamental distributive question has thus emerged: On what basis should individuals or families, employed or unemployed, be tied into the national income stream on a continuing basis? The need for some income policy other than "market share" has been registered, but what that policy should be—a political issue—is being answered on an ad hoc, makeshift basis. The dominant business value relating distribution to competitive effort and market success cannot be abandoned within the framework of existing institutions, but—like the constitutional value—it has been modified in order to preserve it. *Above* some basic individual or family income level, some "standard" equality of condition not yet established on a national basis but clearly to be expected, the egalitarian principle continues to refer to access to opportunity. And this, despite the effects of meritocracy (in part because of them) is at best a relative matter. In George Orwell's undying phrase, "Some are more equal than others." How could it be otherwise?

THE IMPLICIT BARGAIN
AND THE PROFESSIONAL POLITICIANS

The terms of the implicit bargain have shifted in recent years, so that dominant interests are no longer as strong as they once were. More concessions have had to be made to supporters, such as organized labor, and to dissidents, such as the blacks, in order to satisfy the former and contain the latter. The political unit in which the professional politician has had the greatest difficulty in effecting accommodation has been the large city. The changing racial composition of the metropolitan centers is placing greater political power—in a number of instances which will be steadily increasing, *majority* power—in the hands of racial groups which are nationally a minority, the blacks and Latins. In the summation of the Kerner Commission report:

The Negro population is growing faster, both absolutely and relatively, in the larger metropolitan areas than in the smaller ones. From 1950 to 1966, the proportion of nonwhites in central cities of metropolitan areas with one million or more persons doubled, reaching 26 percent, as compared with 20 percent in the central cities of metropolitan areas containing from 25,000 to one million persons, and 12 percent in the central cities of metropolitan areas containing under 250,000 persons.

The 12 largest central cities (New York, Chicago, Los Angeles, Philadelphia, Detroit, Baltimore, Houston, Cleveland, Washington, D.C., St. Louis, Milwaukee, and San Francisco) now contain over two-thirds of the Negro population outside the South, and one-third of the total in the United States. All these cities have experienced rapid increases in Negro population since 1950. In six (Chicago, Detroit, Cleveland, St. Louis, Milwaukee, and San Francisco), the proportion of Negroes at least doubled. In two others (New York and Los Angeles), it probably doubled. In 1968, seven of these cities are over 30 percent Negro, and one (Washington, D.C.) is two-thirds Negro.[20]

Since the time of the Kerner Commission's report, the proportionate increase of the nonwhite segment of the population has increased in the major cities. The presence of this politically important and economically disadvantaged group cannot be ignored by the urban politician. He must accommodate it as best he can. But the financial resources of the cities have been dwindling with the exodus of the middle- and upper-income whites, whom the blacks have displaced. The major cities are thus left with a population requiring more public assistance, but less revenue to redistribute. State and federal subsidies have relieved some of the pressure, but these legislatures are controlled by the whites, who are increasingly located in suburban areas outside the black central cities, and generally indisposed to subsidize massively the cities they have fled. Hence the underlying pessimism of the Kerner Report. "The nation is rapidly moving toward two increasingly separate Americas. Within two decades, this division could be so deep that it would be almost impossible to unite: a white society principally located in suburbs, in smaller central cities, and in the peripheral parts of large central cities, and a Negro society largely concentrated within large central cities." [21]

The influential role of business and its middle-class supporters, while still the most significant single force, has thus been declining in the major cities, which have become maelstroms of racial tension. There the professional politician, if he is to hold office at all, must be responsive to those who are seeking a radical change in the distributive value. But outside the large central cities the dominant role of business and its allies remains firm enough that the professional politicians in state and federal governments, in their brokerage role, must recognize and respect it. The United States is still a business-responsive and business-oriented economy, not because "big business" is able to bludgeon any opposition into silence, but because the values and interests of the largest proportion of the middle-class population are strongly supportive of the social values which business represents.

If the professional politicians and the administrative bureaucracies appear generally to look with special favor on business interests—in a range of matters running from resource use to tax advantage, from regulatory actions to support of failing corporations, from availability of tax lists for advertising purposes to support for industrial research—this is not because business has bought these favors with campaign contributions (though that is a factor not to be wholly ignored). Nor is there any implication here that business always has its way: clearly one function of the professional politician is to make whatever concessions and accommodations are necessary to maintain a workable system. Environmental controls and consumer interests can be taken into account—but with a "rule of reason" that avoids business hardship and provides time for adjustment. Poverty and race relations can be recognized by administrative orders even if their enforcement is uneven and slow-paced.[22] But politicians and bureaucracies recognize the weight of business in the political balance because the business system itself has a constituency which is basically loyal even if occasionally critical.

INSTITUTIONALIZATION AND ADAPTATION

The ways by which the corporate system has entrenched its position in American society are manifold. Large numbers of the working middle class are convinced—and casual international comparisons support their conviction—that they have "done better" under American business leadership than their counterparts abroad have fared. Others higher in the income scale depend for their livelihood on jobs peculiar to a competitive business system, such as those in corporate finance and advertising. A sizable proportion of the population have savings invested if not directly in corporate securities then in mutual and pension funds, which are based on corporate securities. Nonprofit institutions such as churches and private educational institutions have endowments which are partially invested in corporate securities, and they derive additional current income from corporate grants or individual gifts from corporate officials. The same corporate officials sit as members of directing boards of philanthropic, religious, and educational institutions.[23] The educational system, while opening opportunities for education at all levels to a higher proportion of its school-age population than any other country in the world, has structured that system largely in terms of practical, applied forms of instruction, preparing students for entry into a business world. It pioneered in the establishment of professional schools of business administration, and until recently as many as one-sixth of its male collegiate undergraduates were enrolled in such courses. Stanley Hoffman has argued that the emphasis on utilitarian knowledge, "the triumph of specialization under the guise of professionalism, the undermining of general education," has led to "a growing dependence of the university on the 'knowledge market' outside, that is, both the industries and the government." [24] The orientation of intellectual inquiry along "objective," "value-free," and technically based lines has meant the creation of a cadre of intellectuals prepared to enlist their expertise in whatever service would employ them as technical experts, which in effect has most often meant serving the existing business system, which alone can offer such employment on such a scale.

It should be emphasized again—the point needs stressing—that none, or very little, of such business hegemony has been the consequence of any overt plan to dominate society, or any conspiracy to divert potential opposition. It follows from the profound belief by the business dominants in the values for which their class stands, in the identification of those values with the welfare of society as a whole, and in their ability to convince others of the validity of that conception. If in recent years, for reasons we have already examined, there have been signs of more restiveness under that value system and a disenchantment with some of its apparent social and environmental consequences, such signs are by no means reflective of widespread opposition to or alienation from business leadership. In some degree this is due to an increasing business acceptance of the principle of "social responsibility," an almost undefinable concept partly compounded of a responsiveness to public opinion and political pressure (as in the matters of minority employment and environmental improvement), partly of the contemporary American counterpart of the British elite's sense of "service," mitigating the impression (and reality) of self-interest by self-conscious attention to disinterested "public" causes (such as support for opera, special museum showings, and educational television programs).

By such sensitive reaction to societal pressures and public relations mindedness, the business system changes in ways which *it interprets* as necessary or desirable for the preservation of its dominant position—never in ways which fundamentally depreciate its interests or reveal a vision of a future society much different from that of the present, except for the beneficial impact of technological changes in which it expects to pioneer.

There is perhaps one further exception: in the large corporation there is probably a clearer realization of the growing role of government in the overall management of the economy, and of the unhappy necessity for that larger role. The function of the professional politician and the government bureaucracy in maintaining the economy on an even keel through maintenance of aggregate income and avoidance of inflation, in representing American interests in international economic relationships, in fostering programs of domestic welfare which will palliate pockets of dissent, in taking the initiative in major scientific or technical projects beyond the scope of even the largest corporations—these and other governmental roles have been recognized and accepted, however grudgingly, by an increasing number of business leaders. But in accepting the government's role, they have not themselves abdicated. They clearly expect to be influential over government's decisions, treating government as a necessary but not very dependable ally in the preservation of their own interests. If in the process, this necessitates some diminution of their erstwhile autonomy, it also extends the potential *scope* of their influence. If the total social and economic *system* becomes more emphasized, casting them as components of that system, subordinated to its somewhat shadowy objectives, at least there is no other single force as capable of giving definition to those objectives—and hence a definition generally compatible with their own interests. This is a less sharply etched version of Galbraith's "new industrial state." Like a good pedagogue and publicist, Galbraith has simplified his case in order to make it more easily comprehensible. The reality is less clearly defined. The number of businessmen who see this relationship in any systemic sense is, as far as I can gauge, quite small, and the number who consider it desirable even smaller.

In sum, at the present point in time, the large corporation remains the dominant influence on American values, but that influence, while still pervasive, has been threatened and diluted—in part through the new organization of radical social conflict along racial lines, concentrated in the cities, requiring a political solution the nature of which is not yet clear; in part through the increased functions of political authority in economic and social integration, which, while subject to business influence, must also deal with conflicting or alternative interests; in part (perhaps much the least part) by an intellectual and youth challenge to its focal materialistic value, which has so far registered an impact containable within the "social responsibility" doctrine.

This modification of the position of the business dominants has had some effect on the structure of social values. America's present social values are thus focally materialistic, as in the past, though with some modest concessions to qualitative considerations and a diminished emphasis on the related value of work; constitutionally more hierarchic, stressing social order and integration over individual autonomy, and distributively more egalitarian than in the past, though more in affirmation than in practice. But overall what is involved is reinterpretation and incremental adjustment, not fundamental change.

Notes

1. Richard Hofstadter writes of the "Regency" politicians of New York State who came into prominence about 1830: "Lawyers, often without enough practice to keep their minds and energies fully occupied, they were also the friends and associates of the small-town businessmen and small-scale bankers. They came from a social class for which the perquisites and connections, the marginal advantages and limited prominence of small offices were much esteemed as means of making one's way toward the top." He adds that they were "outside and somewhat at odds with the older aristocratic leaders, estranged from political leadership by inherited wealth and position or personal brilliance and glamour. They thought that negotiation and the management of opinion were better than leadership and deference." *The Idea of a Party System* (Berkeley, Cal.: University of California Press, 1970), pp. 241–242.

2. James Willard Hurst, *The Legitimacy of the Business Corporation* (Charlottesville: University of Virginia Press, 1970), p. 70.

3. Hurst notes in *The Legitimacy of the Business Corporation,* pp. 62–63: "Constitutional doctrine defined both by the United States Supreme Court and by state legislative practice emerged to limit legislation which would subvert the organizational integrity of the business corporation or the functional integrity of the distinct body of assets with which it worked." It was the Dartmouth College case of 1819 which gave this conception its most explicit statement. Although addressed to an educational and nonprofit institution, its most important application soon came to be to business corporations, which were playing "a rapidly growing part in the economy, in great measure because their charters gave them operational utilities similar to those which [Chief Justice] Marshall's opinion noted as making the college an effective, continuing instrument."

States reacted to the decision by making provision for "reserve clauses" in corporate charters, enabling the legislature to modify or even repeal the latter. But such clauses had something of a reverse effect, contributing "to extend the concept of legitimacy to cover private as well as public power by asserting, as they did, the state's continuing authority to supervise the character of the private corporations it sanctioned." But such supervision was seldom forthcoming. "In practice state legislatures were conservative in wielding their reserved powers without the consent of those interested in a corporation." Legislative inaction, in the face of the explicitly reserved power to act, thus conferred an aura of legitimacy on private corporate activities.

Hurst, like other authorities, also construes as judicial lawmaking the Supreme Court's interpretation of the due process and equal protection clauses of the Fourteenth Amendment "to embrace corporations' transactional ability and assets as 'liberty' and 'property' of persons." He notes (p. 66): "These readings of the Fourteenth Amendment materially extended the legitimacy which the law conferred on private corporate power and at the same time substantially curbed the legitimacy of government regulation of corporate behavior."

4. Clinton Rossiter, *Conservatism in America,* 2nd ed. (New York: Random House, 1962), p. 130.

5. Quoted by Nye, *This Almost Chosen People,* p. 133.

6. Samuel C. Logan, D.D., *A City's Danger and Defense* (Scranton, 1877) p. 327. In the text, Dr. Logan had this sentence set in capital letters for emphasis.

7. Bruce Barton, *The Man Nobody Knows* (Indianapolis: The Bobbs Merrill Co., 1924; rev. ed. 1956), pp. 30, 93–97.

8. David Potter, *People of Plenty* (Chicago: University of Chicago Press, 1954), Chapter 8.

9. 30 August 1971.

10. Quoting Morton Hoppenfeld, "Shopping Centers Grow into Shopping Cities," *Business Week,* 4 September 1971, p. 36.

11. William Serrin, "The Assembly Line," *Atlantic Monthly,* October 1971, p. 66.

12. Jesse Burkhead, "Fiscal Planning—Conservative Keynesianism," *Public Administration Review* 31 (May–June 1971): 339. Burkhead credits the phrase "commercial Keynesianism" to Robert Lekachman's *Age of Keynes* (New York: Random House, 1966), p. 287.

13. James M. Roche, "An Address to the Executive Club of Chicago," published and distributed by General Motors, March 25, 1971. Roche was arguing against governmental regulation of advertising and quality standards, but his comments apply with equal force to public spending as a substitute for private spending.

14. Max Ways, "The Crisis of Success: Material or Mental?", *Conference Board Record,* July 1971, p. 37.

15. Parsons and White, "The Link Between Character and Society," in Lipset and Lowenthal, *Culture and Social Character,* p. 107.

16. The terminology derives from the late Professor Douglas McGregor, but the message has been conveyed by countless others.

17. Harold M. F. Rush, *Behavioral Science,* "Highlights for the Executive," (New York: Industrial Conference Board, 1969). Quoted with permission.

18. Serrin, "The Assembly Line," pp. 66–67, describes the effects of racial tension in the Detroit automobile plants.

19. *New York Times,* 19 April 1970.

20. "The Concentration of Negro Population in Large Cities," *Report of the National Advisory Commission on Civil Disorders* (1968), Chapter 6, Section 4.

21. *Ibid.,* "Conclusions."

22. On the day that the House passed a bill extending the life of the Office of Economic Opportunity, also incorporating "a vast new program" of day care and other services especially benefiting children of poor parents, an O.E.O. official commented: "The war on poverty is turning out like the war in Vietnam. It's disappearing little by little—so slowly that no one will be able to say exactly when it died. Or criticize the President." *New York Times,* 8 December 1971. The bill, even then threatened by presidential veto, removed from the O.E.O. the controversial legal aid for the poor, and contained innumerable Congressional limitations on how its funds should be spent.

23. A Yale University Study Commission on Governance, appointed by Yale President Kingman Brewster, submitted a report in 1971 which found that "a problem with the Corporation [the governing body of the university, consisting of 19 trustees] has been its homogeneity and its consequent intimacy with some parts of society to the near exclusion of others." It went on to comment: "Judging by the character of the group, they must have repeatedly cut the search process [for successors] short by turning to men sufficiently close to them in social origin, career, age, school affiliation, and the like to make the choice of successor fairly easy.

"It also appears that, in selecting successors, the successor trustees have undervalued the importance of scientific, educational, and research leadership in favor of financial, business, and administrative leadership."

24. Stanley Hoffman, "Participation in Perspective," *Daedalus,* Winter 1970, p. 187.

14 / The Future of American Values

What does the future hold with respect to possible changes in social values in the United States? If there is no basis for prediction, in the normal scientific meaning of that word, we can nevertheless discern a limited range of probability based on the foregoing analysis. But along with these prospects foreseen within the range of probability there is inescapably an indefinite number of unforeseen prospects which may determine the future, as a consequence of what Teggart named the "intrusive event." These lie outside our analytical framework. For our purposes we restrict the future to the remaining years of the present century. There appear to be three "most likely" lines of value evolution.

Scenario One

One distinct possibility is a gradual winding down of business dominance without a concomitant rise in any other source of commonly held social values. The necessary consequence would be value diffuseness and increasing disorder, or to put it another way, value particularity and group divergence.

The causes of this condition would presumably trace back to an increasing erosion of business influence as a consequence of the three opposing forces referred to in the preceding chapter, accompanied by a withdrawal of other interest groups—functional and nonfunctional—into more cohesive and insular units as a means of self-protection. Differences among groups would be stressed to heighten the sense of identity and exclusiveness, increasing the potential for intergroup conflict at sensitive points of contact. Former commonalty of interests with or dependence on the business dominants would steadily decline. The position of the once powerful would be subjected to increasing criticism and decreasing respect. A residue of the old values would still survive in the basic institutions, supported by those whose personal interests were bound up most closely in them, but the acceptance of those values in society at large would be more and more attenuated.

The three principal sources modifying business influence we identified as the changing urban composition, the augmented powers of the central government, and an alienation and withdrawal of intellectuals and youth. Let us consider the possible developments in each of these which might contribute to value diffuseness in the near-term future.

An unarrested decline in the major cities would have the consequences against which the Kerner Commission warned. The flight of the whites would continue and perhaps accelerate. Black isolation would become more complete. The black populations of the metropolitan area, in their isolation, could become more internally integrated, as a minority group in a hostile society but with a political base subject to their control which could be used as leverage to pry open greater equality of condition. Nevertheless, to use this leverage effectively would require a *degree* of cohesiveness within the black community which it would be difficult to achieve. It is more likely that members would become divided among themselves, breaking down into subgroups stressing different interests. There may be the upper-class blacks who would see the cities as a cultural foundation on which they could build a more indigenous and self-respecting component of the larger society—an opportunity to be seized as a "little thruster" group which could, however, never aspire to dominance. There may be others, more militant and immediate in their aims, who would see the cities as a seized prize, spoils to be exploited for whatever temporary advantage they could bring. Still others, more anarchic and despairing, might view the cities as the remnant of a hostile culture on which their rage and frustration could be vented, as objects to be despoiled, ransacked, and vandalized vindictively. Other elements might also be present. Their respective strengths could be expected to vary from city to city. In whatever combination, they would constitute a direct challenge to the sanctity of private property comparable to expropriation by foreign governments, heightened by the fact that it occurred within the society of the dominants themselves.

The second factor which could dilute the influence of business is the assumption by central government of augmented responsibility for effecting a workable integration among competing groups. This would not be the same thing as the presently increasing role of government in managing the economy, recognized by a growing number of business leaders as necessary and hence accepted by them as long as they can effectively influence the policies which government, as economic manager, adopts. This would be something quite different. The lessening influence of business, whatever concessions the urban blacks might be able to wring from an unwilling society (or alternatively whatever demonstration the blacks might provide of the impotence of that society to govern its own cities) could be expected to make other contentious groups, even former allies, such as organized labor, more assertive. The possibilities are apparent in the automobile industry, where workers are disinclined to work as hard or as many hours (the absentee rate rises dramatically) but demand higher rates for the hours worked so that their consumption does not suffer proportionately. Discipline falls off, and attempts to reenforce it are counterproductive. Business becomes more and more simply one among a number of contending interests, which government holds together by mediation. This is not very far from the pluralists' dream, but it is more likely to turn into a nightmare, as government responds more and more to ad hoc pressures and crisis situations, requiring makeshift accommodations and bargains which set in motion "me too" demands from other groups not similarly accommodated.[1]

Centralization of social power in the government, in this fashion, would result in short-run "planning" without much other purpose than simple continuity. For example, to the extent that environmental constraints required governmental regulation and limitation of production (and hence of consumption), as some believe is possible, the distributive value would be brought under further pressure. Centralization of power would represent neither consolidation of society around clearly defined objectives nor effective leadership. It would constitute a "Mother Hubbard" of a government, inward-looking, concerned only with keeping unruly offspring in some semblance of order.

Nor would this decline and diffuseness of values, the weakening cohesiveness of the society in the presence of the divisiveness of its constituent groups, be lost on other nations. American influence on world order would inevitably decline: world power cannot be exercised from a weak national base.

A third impetus to the waning influence of the business sector might derive from the withdrawal from "business society" of numbers of individuals, particularly among the young and the intellectuals, who under other circumstances could be expected to be major contributors to the vitality of a people. Among these would be the ones who were turning away from a consumption-saturated society toward some of the excluded focal values, indulging in private or communal intellectual retreat and nonmaterialistic life-styles. They might continue to live within orthodox society without being a member of it, piecing together a modest living out of occasional jobs, inheritance, free-lancing, sharing, or public welfare programs, in order to build a life more self-styled than is compatible with institutional existence. Another group might consist of those who, rebelling against institutional discipline, found their refuge in drugs—a problem which America's friendly Swedish critic, Gunnar Myrdal, has speculated may soon become more intractable even than race relations.

A proliferation of those whom the business values had alienated, on any substantial scale, would detract from the philosophical validation of those values. Even in smaller numbers, if they included articulate and intellectually gifted critics they could constitute a viral attack on self-confidence, contributing to the philosophical doubts of others. Of the three forces weakening the business position under Scenario One, I would expect this to be the least potent, but this is not intended to downplay the significance of contagious ideas, particularly if objective conditions—such as a deteriorating environment—should give substance to the ideas being spread.

If one simply extrapolates present tendencies, then, a foreseeable possibility is a continuing decline in the capacity of the business sector to provide a value core generally acceptable to American society. Once dominant, business would retreat into a position of one interest group among others, even if its bargaining power remained a little stronger. It no longer would constitute the nucleus around which other groups would orient their activities. Value diffuseness and value competition would be more the pattern. A loss of social cohesiveness and national influence would be the consequence.[2]

Scenario Two

A second possibility for America's value future lies in the rise of new thruster groups, spearheading a movement which, in time, might undermine the established dominants and their associated values. I have previously argued that any genuine change in values, the substitution of new values for old (in contrast to the reinterpretation of old values as a means of keeping them alive) must come through the rise of a new dominant class. Is there on the horizon, then, the visible sign of any approaching thruster group, gathering momentum as it charges?

The decade of the sixties saw the rise of a number of challenges to the prevailing value system. Every observer can construct his own catalog of these protest movements. Without claiming comprehensiveness, I would suggest that they substantially reduce to three sometimes overlapping categories.

1. The anti-consumptionists are basically opposed to the present materialistic focal value. This group includes those who, dialectically, have moved toward the sensual, mystical, emotional, spiritual, non-

accumulative values which have been largely suppressed in the institution-alized culture. The "hippy" is a fading symbol of such enthusiasms. The emphasis is sometimes on "joy," "love," fellow-feeling and sharing, some-times on a "return to nature" and an ascetic attitude toward one's needs, sometimes on the creation of individual worlds of fantasy and ecstasy, con-trasting with the world of objects, as notably in the drug culture.

I would dismiss this group as lacking the potential for a thruster move-ment. However sincere may be the beliefs of individuals subscribing to this faith, I see no grounds for their accumulating a growing following which would threaten the prevailing consumption orientation. But more impor-tant, the very nature of their diffuse creed fails to provide the basis for any alternative form of social organization. Persons of this persuasion may contribute—perhaps significantly—to the lessened dominance of business values, but this effect belongs in Scenario One. It is not the stuff of which a thruster group is made, with the strength to impress its values on the whole of a society.

There is a second constituent group among the anti-materialists which has greater likelihood of making its impact. This is the environmentalist, anti-growth movement, which attacks a consumption-centered society, for which a constantly growing GNP is a visible and necessary sign of prog-ress, as despoiling the natural environment at a rate which quite literally threatens disaster. From an initial concern with conservation of nature it has moved to a greater concern for the conservation of human life and civ-ilization. Foreseeing the exhaustion of certain primary resources, the irre-versible pollution of major bodies of water, the possibility of cumulative de-terioration of land and air through the abuses of a technology-using consumption-preoccupied world population, and an approaching Malthu-sian debacle of staggering proportions, this group includes a number of re-spected scientists who have buttressed their convictions with impressive analyses.

If this group of anti-growth environmentalists is the seed of a genuine thruster group, they would indeed be the carriers of a revolutionary change in social values. Aside from the obvious rejection of the contemporary focal value, they would necessarily embrace a constitutional value veering markedly toward firm social control over individual actions, even in areas now considered inviolably private, such as the right of human reproduc-tion. They would likewise thoroughly disturb present distributive values, since the egalitarian principle, if pursued, could be achieved only through redistribution in the absence of further economic growth, through a pro-cess of leveling down rather than of catching up, and this on an interna-tional as well as a domestic basis.

Indeed, acceptance of the environmentalist argument would bring with it an upheaval in social values so great that it is hard to imagine a society embracing them voluntarily. Acceptance would have to come not through the path of persuasion but from the exigency of circumstance. If the consequences of pursuing the present focal value of consumption prove to be as catastrophic as predicted by the environmentalists, it is conceivable that the resulting change in objective conditions may induce support for their cause. If such a trend should develop, however, it would have to mobilize around some identifiable thruster group. "Concerned scientists" might supply the ingredients for public policy aimed at control of individual behavior, both in terms of rationale and means (Barry Commoner plus B. F. Skinner), but there are no obvious focal or distributive values around which they might coalesce. A negative policy of opposition to material growth puts nothing affirmative in its place, either in terms of a *summum bonum* or an ethical base for distribution of the social advantage, including a fixed level of GNP. On such issues it is already apparent that they are likely to speak with different voices. In the absence of a common value structure and identity, I cannot visualize the environmentalists as true thrusters, as anything more than a pressure group. In the face of the monumental challenge to existing values inherent in their anti-growth theme, it seems to me most likely that their strictures will be partially accommodated in policy changes by existing dominants, with the general support of a middle-class population which does not want to believe in the necessity for any more drastic change in its way of life. Whether in a longer run the pressure of objective circumstance will force change, under the aegis of some as yet unidentified thruster group, remains an open question; I am highly dubious that anything of that sort will occur in the next twenty years or so.

2. A second theme represented in the protest movements spawned in the sixties deals with the constitutional value, stressing the desirability of individual autonomy and self-development. "Do your own thing" became the motto, referring to everything from dress to sex, from vocation to avocation. Encounter groups gained popularity as a means for the institutionally inhibited person to release his "inner" self and discover his "true" identity. "Who am I?" became the burning question for innumerable latter-day Socrates, more out of *Weltschmerz* than intellectual probing.

This group need not detain us long. It clearly is the opposite of any thrusting movement, turned inward on self rather than outward to society. Some of its members have been co-opted by an adaptable establishment, as we earlier had occasion to note. Others continue their preoccupation on a part-time basis, while coexisting with the social order which troubles them.

Still others have "dropped out" of society for varying periods of time, subsisting as best they might. Closely related to the anti-consumptionist "love" and "nature" cults, they may weaken the hold of existing values simply by rejecting them, but they constitute no assertive force for positive change.

3. A third protest concerns the distributive value and is most effectively embodied in the civil rights movement, challenging discriminatory treatment against minorities and women. Here the emphasis is on greater equality or equity of treatment: the two are not always distinguished. As such, it does not challenge materialistic focal values directly; it is interested in obtaining a greater share in "the good life" as already defined. Moreover, there is little cohesiveness among the principal carriers of this protest: blacks, Latins, women, and the welfare population do not make common cause even though they share a common grievance. None of these constitutes a revolutionary class in the sense of seeking to represent the interests of society generally within an altered framework of values.

At best, this mass of the discontented constitutes a potential bargaining power which might be mobilized by some smaller thruster group. If, for example, one can imagine the environmentalists developing an affirmative program, seizing on the deterioration of the human habitat as an opportunity for the promotion of a new order, one can also conceive their enlisting the support of the disadvantaged in achieving their cause. The latter might provide the critical mass needed for the former to make their challenge effective. This possibility has, I think, virtually no chance of realization. Not only is the essential thruster group missing from the scenario, but the "mass" is itself too fragmented in interest.

In short, however vehement the protest movements originating in the sixties and continuing into the present, none of them conforms to the image of a thruster group seizing on changing conditions as the opportunity for asserting a fresh vision of a society in which it plays a leadership role, carrying others along with it as allies, followers, opportunists, or adaptables.

One substitute for a thruster group does exist—the emergence of a professional politician or political party based on a demagogic appeal to discontented "masses." As we previously noted, such a movement could lean either to the left, encouraging a prospective majority which viewed itself as disadvantaged to embrace the distributive principle of greater equality, or to the right, promising a potential majority alleviation of social pressures threatening their present position. In the United States, too many people have a substantive stake in the existing distribution to risk the chance that they might do better under a more egalitarian government. Resistance to increasing the amounts of public assistance under present and proposed welfare programs is indicative of the probability that redistribution has leveled downward about as far as it can go in the foreseeable future. The large working population which looks on itself as middle-class would almost certainly expect to lose rather than gain under an egalitarian program. As for a demagogic appeal to a conservative majority which is apprehensive over possible loss of status and vaguely uneasy about festering social problems which threaten enjoyment of present advantages, there are other more likely alternatives.

One of these consists of our second possible scenario for the future, based on the emergence of an *inside* thruster group. By this I mean the gradual rise to positions of corporate responsibility of a small leadership group who aim not at replacing business as the dominant institution but in refashioning business in a significantly different pattern so that it can remain dominant. In this respect it would be the most recent descendant of such corporate inside thrusters as those who, in the period following the Civil War, began turning business into a national system under increasingly specialized control in contrast to the former family-owned and locally oriented institutions of the early part of the century, and the more recent thrusters who have converted national business into international enterprises.

Let us call the new inside thrusters "social technocrats," to suggest the flavor of their orientation. The "social" in the term does not imply some mystical or emotional conversion to a sense of social responsibility, stemming from the heart rather than the head, but a recognition that a continuing emphasis on the privacy of their operations may cost them their present influential position. They recognize the rise of a new set of objective conditions—new systems of technology calling for the organization of resources on a larger scale than even a large corporation can manage by itself, systems which must be more fully integrated across political, geographical, and industrial boundary lines (transportation, waste disposal, education, housing, crime control as examples). They see these as requiring the same efficient management of resources and people, but on a larger scale, as the old production techniques, which begin to look more and more antiquated, however automated they may be, by reason of the narrow context in which they operate (privately, almost anarchically; economic, instead of parts of an embracing social system). Hence also the technocratic aspect of the thrusters' orientation—a reliance on highly developed economic and engineering efficiency, tempered as need be, but no more than need be, by political and organizational compromises to secure the assent of those who must work the system. Thus social controls are part of the management problem, not in any crude sense of coercion but within a framework in which people are given the sense of participation. This is achieved not by arbitrary command but by the compulsive effect on people of being made part of an orderly plan for the achievement of results which are recognized as socially desirable, so that the requirements of their role stem more from a social contract (of a kind Rousseau never conceived) than from a private employment contract.

In achieving such a social-political-economic system, the corporate managers themselves obviously assent to a larger role for government as the initiator and coordinator of the system as a whole. Central planning becomes not something to be fought but the essence of the system. The autonomy of the large corporation is sacrificed to the national plan, just as in an earlier day the autonomy of the family corporation gave way to the authority of the national corporation. In the process, the new inside thrusters achieve greater power for themselves, a larger sphere of operations; they view the changes in objective conditions as opportunities to be seized and taken advantage of. They can view matters in this light because they see the national plan as an extension of their own operations; the more positively they use government authority as an instrument, the more capable they are of achieving their own objectives. Social objectives become a market to be exploited for corporate advantage, as long as these can be structured within a framework which basically reflects present social values, somewhat modified and reinterpreted. Since a national plan is nothing that can be put together by popular vote or even by legislative logrolling, it relies heavily on experts for its design and managers for its execution, and business can supply both. Professional politicians react to public pressures, transmitting the pressures registered to the national planning group, predominantly composed of business interests, for incorporation into the overall design.

What a challenge for such an inside thruster group! As a professor in a business school, I can easily visualize the sparkle in the eyes of young people training to be corporate executives in such a mold—unloosed to throw corporate assets behind the realization of society's real and pressing wants, freed from preoccupation with peripheral and problematic private wants based on inducing people to continued private consumption beyond any point of rational need. And corporate profit into the bargain! And continued eminence of the business management sector as well! Who could ask for anything more?

Eli Goldston, president of Eastern Gas and Fuel Associates, has written the script for those who wish to play out this scenario. He begins by recognizing that present social problems, especially those centering in the cities, have shown themselves to be beyond the reach of bureaucratized and underpaid civil service administrations. They are also immune to the efforts of autonomous business corporations. What is needed is a closer working partnership, "a conspiracy in the public interest," he says, citing Andrew Shonfield. Moreover, he is optimistic that such a view is gaining ground. "The newer attitudes we need are becoming common among big business leadership, and private business can now be drawn into participating in the solution of many current social problems."

This "superseding of public administration" by private business activity will operate with the traditional profit motivation, but now fitted to public objectives. "The entrepreneurial thrust, if encouraged, guided, and controlled by the public agencies of our society, may represent the only permanent solution to the urban problems that have clearly overtaxed the capacity of our public agencies. It offers the best hope that the deprived and neglected parts of our society can be swept into the mainstream of our economy."

Recognizing the importance of changing objective conditions, Goldston argues: ". . . strong forces are pushing business to face the major problems of our society, and ways exist to encourage and control business participation. Today's highly professional manager, eyes focused on profit performance, operating with excellent controls and within strict rules in the glare of a public scoreboard, needing growth opportunities, and not limited by conventional business boundaries, may be the most promising recruit for solution of the crises in our public service." [3]

Goldston is, I believe, too sanguine as to the number of "big business leaders" who already hold the view he espouses. On the whole, the present generation of corporate executives is more likely to view such a prospect as one to be avoided rather than seized. A lingering suspicion of government as the enemy of business autonomy—an addiction to a constitutional value of independence from government control—is far more pervasive. But one need hardly expect that overnight a dominant class will be converted into inside thrusters; the very terminology suggests the unlikelihood. What would the new thrusters be "inside" of, if the old edifice disappeared? More realistically, we can say that a very few top business leaders would now champion such a new scenario, but that as objective pressures build, their number—particularly from the rising generation—can be expected to increase.

Goldston envisions the need for government to hold out a carrot to tantalize business into responding to the opportunities he sees. But that is hardly the conception of a thruster group. I would myself expect the rising thrusters to assert aggressively the need for their services, and to prod the government into such legislative policies as may be necessary to win their objectives.

Perhaps the closest approach to the potential of this collaborative relationship between government, as system manager and coordinator, and business, as the effective instrument in the achievement of system objectives (each influencing the other), has been reached, though far from perfected, in France. Within the framework of a national plan, in the drafting of which are involved representatives of both government and industry, economic and social targets are jointly agreed upon. Theoretically, the labor unions are involved too, but practically they have had little influence except as exerting external political pressures. Theoretically too, the French legislature approves the social objectives and the plan as a whole, but practically the unwieldy Assembly can do little more than provide the broadest sort of directives for the guidance of the experts and register approval or disapproval for their work when completed. Its influence is roughly equivalent to that of the board of directors in a large corporation, neither significant nor insignificant.

One observer has explored this aspect of the French system in some depth. He concludes:

The *économie concertée* defines a partnership between the managers of big business and the managers of the state. It provides big business with the active participation and support of the state while keeping broad participation politics away. From the perspective of big business, the *économie concertée* is the most satisfactory reconciliation of its potentially conflicting wants: big business needs the active participation of the state in the management of the economy, but it fears opening economic administration to popular participation.[4]

The national plan is the focus of this collaboration, prepared by a number of commissions representing major sectors of the economy (the vertical commissions) and a smaller number of horizontal commissions dealing with problems such as manpower and capital needs which cut across the sectors. All these commissions are dominated by representatives of government and business; a few labor members may sit in, but their influence, as we noted, is miniscule, in large part because they simply do not have access to all the operating data on which decisions must be based, in some degree because they are unused to dealing with the technical issues involved. The plan is not binding on business; the term used to characterize it is "indicative." It suggests what can be accomplished *if* all cooperate in its execution.

Its appeal lies in its basic core of order and control, its aura of intellectual elegance and sophistication, its modern, scientific mystique, and its apparent freedom from ideological commitment. The plan represents an attempt to take charge of events, an effort to shape the nation's future. In the political and ideological vacuum in which the new generation of ranking civil servants lives, it is the ideal instrument for an enlightened, nonideological elite to lead the nation; it is also an ideal retreat from the vagaries and vulgarities of Parliamentary politics and ideological commitment.[5]

Ever since the initiation of the French planning process there has been dispute as to its effectiveness. Despite its presumed voluntary character, does the government actually possess powers of enforcement (in the form of access to capital funds, preferential rates of taxation, subsidies, favorable depreciation schedules, placement of government contracts, and other such devices) so that what appears as voluntary with business is actually more binding on it? Or are the government's powers so limited, in a private enterprise economy, that big business only responds when it is to its interests? The answer falls somewhere between.[6] In such a collaborative arrangement, the private firm surrenders some of its autonomy as part of the political bargain. What purpose would a plan serve if it did not have some compulsion over those subject to it? On the other hand, the large enterprise has its influence on the plan, which it uses to its own advantage. Why else should it participate in the arrangement? As Earl Cheit has summarized the matter: "In broadest terms, the Plan's objective is to bring economic power under political control, a point clearly understood by American executives operating in France. 'At home we think about autonomy,' one told me. 'Over here we look for influence.' " [7]

The potential reward to large-scale business for its involvement in the national plan has been suggested by François Perroux, perhaps France's most distinguished economist and a member of the Conseil Economique et Social which reviews the plan: "Monopolies in France and Europe are gaining in strength. They create *both* supra normal profits and innovations. The Plan which develops and depends on them cannot at the same time attack them. It does not possess the means to discriminate between their positive and negative effects." [8]

The comment by Perroux foreshadows where public objection might be brought to bear on an economy guided by social technocrats. However effective they might prove in moving on problems which could be alleviated by public consumption and capital projects, one can anticipate some protest against profit-making at public expense, at private fortune-building out of public misfortune, at private gain from public need. The price of such an arrangement might well be a limitation on the rate of profit allowable on publicly financed projects, and this in turn might discourage business participation if it had more profitable opportunities in the private consumption sector. The only alternative would seem to be for government to *require* business participation in public production, under a profit ceiling, as in wartime. But such an alternative would jeopardize business support, creating a condition which would cease to look like opportunity even to the most imaginative of inside thrusters, and drive the government into a more radical posture than it is likely to find support for among a generally conservative electorate.

Nevertheless, ways around this difficulty could be found. If the new breed of business thruster can be satisfied with a profit performance a little but not very much less than corporations have enjoyed in the past, a product mix that blended public and private consumption might be entirely acceptable to it. Such sacrifice as was necessary would be made primarily by a dispersed army of stockholders, while preserving to business management the position of dominance which it now enjoys. There may be some necessity initially of protecting participating corporations from the raids of more opportunistic managers, who would see a larger potential profit than was being realized with the given assets of the participating corporations. In time one would expect that this problem would take care of itself. The increasing proportion of GNP being allocated to public consumption would accord those companies meeting such demand a larger absolute profit, even though the profit rate may be less than for companies operating solely in the private sector. After all, a 5 percent return on a billion of sales is to be preferred over an 8 percent rate on a third of a billion, and one could assume that growth to a larger scale of operations would depend increasingly on how effectively a company geared itself to the national plan.

And what would be the impact on social values of a successful thrust by such a group of social technocrats? Remarkably little. It would preserve private enterprise and the present distribution of advantages with relatively little change. The necessary modification of values, interests, and institutions would actually be much less than appears at first encounter. The focal value of materialistic consumption would persist, though with a larger component of public as against private goods, and tempered by the rising concern for environmental effects. The social technocrats are hardly likely to sponsor a vision of the future which is not based on an increased capacity to produce.[9] The present *summum bonum* is likely to remain very much in place, with some easily justified modification in the nature of the output. As for constitutional values, we have already noted the gradual shift toward a more hierarchic form of control, stressing social order. The social technocrats would do no more than fit into that tendency; indeed, the alternative to the loose system of planning which they would bring with them might ultimately be a more highly centralized system of controls. If the French experience thus far offers any lesson it is that national planning under private enterprise necessarily leaves a large measure of autonomy to the individual firm in carrying out generalized public objectives.

In terms of the distributive value, there might be some slight move toward an increased egalitarianism flowing from the higher level of public expenditure, but this would depend, among other things, on the tax structure, the rate of profit on government contracts, and the wage-price structure, none of which is easily predictable. Nevertheless, given the fact that the power balance in society is not likely to be greatly altered, one need not expect any major modification in the distribution of the social advantage.

On this analysis, the kind of business-based social technocracy pictured here would seem to commend itself to a class of inside thrusters. The objective conditions would appear to lend them support. Nevertheless, there are good grounds for questioning whether this scenario will in fact be played out. One consideration is whether the public—that amorphous mass—would be willing to accept what might prove to be more visible business dictation of social objectives. A second is whether corporate business leadership would fear that a loose form of central planning under its sponsorship might be only a way-stop to tighter controls under a broader-based political supervision.[10]

A third and perhaps the most crucial question is whether such an arrangement would in fact provide any solution to major present problems, particularly that of racial division in the cities. Business managers, whether private enterprisers or social technocrats, are not magicians, and planning in itself carries no guarantee that racial tensions can be planned away. Public programs may be instituted, with or without private business support, but there remain the issues of whether the growing minority populations of the major American cities will accept being planned for, or whether they will want more active participation not only in the program design but also in the business execution, and whether—if so—the major corporations will see their own autonomy and dominance diluted not only by popular government but also by minority demands.[11] Would it not be preferable to let government wrestle with the problem of the central cities, without involving business in a social confrontation for which it is ill prepared? Is it really so clear that business leadership cannot continue along its present path, gradually and independently adapting itself to changed environmental conditions as it always has, supported by a majority of suburban-based whites whose chief anxiety lies in preserving a way of life that white America has made and would like to enjoy? Who wants political planning anyway, except those whose intent lies in changing inherited values and subverting the interests of those who support those values?

Despite these psychological deterrents, the technocratic development seems one distinct possibility.

Scenario Three

As we saw in an earlier chapter, a dominant group whose position is threatened can respond with concession or with repression. Scenario Three is based on the latter. In the face of objective conditions which create pressures for changes in social and economic relationships, there is resistance to change. But those who resist are not only the business leaders but middle-class white America as a whole, who feel the success that was theirs slipping out of their grasp. The values of business are their values, and they have no wish to change them, except insofar as it is necessary to subordinate the constitutional value of individual advantage to a more cohesive and defensive national authority, temporarily, in order to preserve what they have.

To understand the rationale for this attitude we must remember that we are not attempting to chart the course of American values under present conditions, but for a future a decade or two away. And Scenario Three is based on the speculative possibility that by that time the challenges to the United States on the international scene will have become aggravating to national pride. Its ability to impress its values on the world order will have been sharply curtailed in Asia, Latin America, and Africa. On all three continents one might anticipate a wave of nationalization of American-owned properties, until little was left under American control. But this— whatever the measurable dollar loss—would be only the symbol for the unmeasurable loss of influence and friendship. The old stereotypes of Yankee—and racial—imperialism would be revived and burnished; the heady new stereotypes of native independence and self-assertion would provide the affirmative contrast.

In Europe one might anticipate that the revulsion from the United States would not appear in so extreme a form. Racial antipathies would be lacking; ethnic ties would be stronger. The uncertain need for a military ally under rapidly changing world conditions would dictate the strategy of maintaining ties which could be strengthened if need be. Nevertheless, too close a linkage might prove more of a handicap than an asset in building relations with the rising new nations. Moreover, past memories of American economic superiority, its brash *nouveau-riche* overlordship of the old and truer European aristocracy, its crude assertion of material power as a substitute for wisdom, experience, and culture—these might continue to rankle.

If such diminishment of American prestige and position in the world seems more pessimistic than the prospects warrant, perhaps perspective can be restored by recalling that no nation which has imposed its will on others by virtue of its might, either military or economic, has been loved for its efforts; even when its acts have been garbed in charity and hope— as in the Marshall Plan following World War II—they necessarily create in others a sense of dependency which is unconsciously resented and consciously thrown off when the opportunity arises. With the passage of years since the destructiveness of World War II has come the rebuilding and rejuvenation of economies, so that industrial growth has proceeded at a rapid pace in a number of strategic areas of the world. If Herman Kahn is excessively simplistic and ebullient in hailing Japan as the coming superstate of the twenty-first century,[12] he is nevertheless pointing in the right direction.

The restrained assessment of foreign views of America's declining world position *as of the present* by Max Frankel, Washington correspondent of the *New York Times,* is suggestive that the United States faces, at best, an uncertain path leading into unfamiliar territory where new dangers lie in store for it, without any assurance of assistance or even sympathy from those whom once it could summon to its aid.

In Britain a high-level planner wonders whether a rapidly accelerating flow of history had not brought America to the condition of Britain 20 years ago, yielding an empire while denying it and fighting futile rear-guard actions all over the world while waiting for its perceptions of its role to shrink as much as its power.

In Japan a defense official confides that references to the American "nuclear umbrella" would no longer be permitted in official papers and statements. This will be a modest but clear step, he says, toward adjusting rhetoric to the new reality—the end of certainty about American protection and the beginning of maturity as Japan contemplates the three nuclear powers around her.

In India, even in the midst of war [with Pakistan], an editor finds time to project his resentment of Americans and Europeans for not taking their instruction on Asia from Asians. India is destined for power and dominance on the subcontinent, he observes, and the big-power club cannot close the doors until China, then India and perhaps Nigeria, in Africa, have arrived.[13]

Thus at the peak of national affluence, when more Americans would possess the means and time of traveling to all ends of the earth for pleasure, they would find themselves everywhere less welcome, more coolly treated or disregarded, perhaps even insulted. American business would more often find doors closed against them. The standard American reaction to such an imagined prospect—"they'll be glad enough to take our dollars"—is only indicative of the very American image to which the rest of the world would be reacting. The "ugly American" syndrome would prevail.

Deprived of that love and approval which they desire and to which they feel themselves entitled, Americans might be expected either to force their country's presence on the world, out of its sheer might and out of a sense of "right," making temporary alliances wherever shifting world conditions made this advantageous to others, or—less plausible—to retreat into a fortress America, impregnable and self-sufficient. It seems highly unlikely that the majority of Americans would simply sigh in resignation or accommodate themselves, in a new world order, to the values and interests of rising thruster nations such as China and Japan. They would find it too difficult to adjust to any image of themselves other than as "Number 1." [14]

Nor is this so surprising. Very early in this investigation we discovered the importance of the political unit, notably one's country, in helping to form one's sense of identity. The point is nicely and simply expressed in the response of a retired Pittsburgh painter to an inquiring reporter: "If America falls behind it makes a difference in the way I feel about myself." But along with this understandable derivation of one's identity from the values and characteristics of his society there goes also the less laudable value which Erikson refers to as pseudo-speciation, the view that somehow one's own people (Americans or Chinese or English) are a superior species, so that to be "set down" by others is demeaning and intolerable. The "master race" psychology manifests itself in varying degrees, but Americans are not immune to the virus. The designation of its South Vietnamese allies as "slopes" or "gooks" is only a recent crude indication that white Americans esteem other nationals—and especially other races—less than they do their own.

If the possibilities envisaged in Scenario Three materialize, then, we may anticipate that Americans will be induced to stress the continuity and preservation of their old values, as the values of a superior people, and to regard them as something to be defended against any threat from other peoples. If the rising nationalism in other continents and the growing power of thruster nations of another race suggest encirclement, there is only one response worthy of a proud people. They will depend on themselves for their own security: in a world of rising antagonisms and few friends, a military buildup is the only recourse.

It may seem unthinkable that a country which today is sick of the protracted war in Vietnam and which has given evidence of wanting nothing so much as to extricate itself from military adventures should turn around and embrace a rising new militarism. But if one thinks again, this does not seem at all improbable. For one thing, there would have been a lapse of a decade or two between the present war weariness and a future militant-mindedness. The moral disgust which today many feel over a "dirty" involvement which strikes them as having no personal significance could easily give way to a sense of personal insecurity and fractured identity in a world which treats them with disdain. Should Gulliver tolerate Lilliputian efforts to pinion its strength? It is almost predictable that in these changed world circumstances the same generation, many of whose members, on college campuses in the last few years, have accused their country of befouling its honor in countless Vietnamese villages, would bring to the fore new spokesmen who would accuse their country of having failed to wage that war vigorously enough, to a successful conclusion. The Vietnam war may then be regretted not because it occurred but because it was lost. The humanitarianism of today's doves will be seen as misguided and naïve, no substitute for the rational *Realpolitik* championed by the more farseeing hawks.

This outlook by a frustrated people would not call, at least in the beginning, for any shift in values. As already noted, it would emphasize defense and preservation of the traditional values. The focal value of material production and a rising GNP would undergo some shift into military output, but this could be accommodated without serious strain on the economy: full employment would be assured. To manage such a high-production economy would require some controls—of wages, prices, profits, allocation of materials—but these we have already begun to accustom ourselves to. Political decisions, as we have had occasion to note, are playing a larger role even now alongside "impersonal" market decisions. The business dominants might be expected to consider a loose system of controls, under a familiar hierarchical order, less threatening to their own established position than a more managed order, with uncertain objectives, under a class of social technocrats. A public military market overlaying a private consumers' market is hardly unfamiliar territory. Dow Chemical officials could probably be regarded as spokesmen for the business community generally when they declared:

Our position on the manufacture of napalm is that we are a supplier of goods to the Defense Department and not a policymaker. We do not and should not try to decide military strategy or policy. Simple good citizenship requires that we supply our Government and our military with those goods which they feel they need whenever we have the technology and capability and have been chosen by the Government as a supplier.[15]

This posture is a more comfortable one for business than becoming involved in Goldston's program of contracting for projects of social amelioration, such as rehabilitating the cities. The military make policy in their own field, which does not intrude on business's sphere of authority. Fluid exchange of officers between industry and the defense establishment contributes to a comity of relations. The two combined present a phalanx behind which American prestige as first in the world—first in productive and military power—rests as secure as the changing world makes possible. If a military-industrial complex emerges as a reality rather than a potential, it would do so in defense of America's "liberal" social values, except that the nineteenth-century pseudo-value of manifest destiny and its twentieth-century version of making the world safe for [American] democracy would metamorphosize into keeping the hard, cool flame of Christian civilization burning in the face of winds of change from hostile hordes.

Given the power of this military-industrial alliance, the professional politicians would have little problem performing their brokerage function. No significant opposition could be expected from the white majority, whose national identity is at stake. Protests might arise on some administrative aspect—the equity of wage-price arrangements, for example—but is less to be expected on the matter of military preparedness. A nation does not take chances with its future if it has the capabilities of securing itself. Military budgets would expand, but so would jobs and incomes. Science and engineering would again be directed to advanced weapons systems, and value-free scientists and technicians could happily pursue their intellectual bents. Opportunistic alliance would be sought with countries we once condemned as threatening to our values, but with which we would then share the common objective of preserving power and prestige. The most likely candidate in this respect is the U.S.S.R., largely white and Western like ourselves, with whom we have been carrying out a quasi agreement during the painful learning experience of the cold war,[16] and whose sphere of influence would then be threatened not by us but by the same forces threatening us. With these two powers aligned, in all their military and economic might, what combination of thruster nations could successfully challenge a reasonable facsimile of the existing world order?

National defense policy hammered out along these lines has good prospects for winning widespread acceptance as a way of life over an indefinite time span. What reasonable alternative is there? A gradual winding down and loss of world position, as in Scenario One? A preoccupation with domestic problems, as in Scenario Two, when the threat is as much external? Numbers of acute social analysts have observed that "militarism" is not confined to military men, but is often found in its most virulent form among civilians—and politicians who find an external enemy a convenient inducement to domestic unity.

But this last objective—internal unity—suggests the weakest point of Scenario Three. No nation can present a convincing posture of strength which is unable to maintain order within its own jurisdiction. If we project present trends for a decade or so into the future, there is little that suggests anything other than a steady deterioration of America's major cities. The decline in "law and order" which has been so remarkable a phenomenon of the last decade could be expected to continue unabated into the future. Racial division would become more pronounced as the cities reflected a higher proportion of blacks. "Black consciousness" would assert itself in ways offensive to the white majority residing *outside* the cities. (Newark has already supplied relatively trivial instances of this: a black-dominated Board of Education prescribing the "black liberation" flag to be flown in all public schools where black students are in the majority, a group of black activists seeking control of the city's only community-oriented radio station.) The proportion of young blacks in the cities will rise even more than the rate for all age groups as a consequence of the higher black birth rate. Among this group would be concentrated the effects of lack of job opportunities or other useful employment of their time, lack of motivation to address themselves to improving their education in a society which continues to discriminate against them, lack of any reason to acquire habits of discipline when living by one's wits on the streets is a more exciting and productive form of activity, and lack of respect for a society which they have learned to scorn and to treat as an appropriate field for exploitation. How does one cope with such a massive breakdown of the rules which make society possible? As more and more of those who are financially able escape from these urban traps, the decline of the cities will accelerate. Whatever a reluctant Congress might do in terms of appropriating funds for the cities, money by itself cannot restore the civic amenities.

But what of the possibility that the divisive issue of race can be resolved by white voluntarism? The response to the Kerner Commission's report already lays that hope. The prospect that white Americans, as a class, will give up their economic and social advantages over black Americans, as a class, is highly unrealistic. If we include the Latins among those discriminated against, then, roughly speaking, four out of every five members of the population gain from discrimination, and it would require a conversion of souls and denial of self-interest unprecedented in history for them voluntarily to abnegate that advantage. There is not even any agreed upon way by which one could begin to remove the disabilities which have been created. Where would a society start—with jobs, education, housing, health—when all are involved? How does it build motivation when credibility has been lost? How can deeply rooted and institutionalized attitudes be removed within a time span acceptable to both those giving up their special advantages and those impatient for a new order? Within any foreseeable future, domestic tranquility would surely have to be achieved by a different route.

The United States would thus confront the unhappy situation that at the very time its influence was ebbing in the world order, and when it felt a pressing need to shore up its sagging position by military preparedness and a show of might, its credibility would be undermined by events occurring within its own borders, by the virtual abandonment of its major cities to a state of chaos and anarchy which it seemed incapable of controlling, as though a malignant virus were destroying it from within, creating a domestic disunity disastrous to an effective international presence. The internal developments pictured here may seem overdrawn, but there are ample grounds for conceiving of this course of events as a realistic outcome of present tendencies.

If indeed these prospects were borne out, a viable order could not be restored to the cities simply by a flow of more money for public services and private relief. It would require an economic rehabilitation and redevelopment on a scale which would be possible only if it involved the great corporations, and before that a control of crime and corruption of a degree of rigor which would necessitate some external police authority, capable of carrying out what local political officials cannot.

The inability to achieve these results through normal political channels might well elicit the imposition of some form of national military government in the cities—not merely a temporary "calling out of the Guard," as in the civil disturbances of 1967, but a more permanent form under federal forces. It is here that one might expect the military to assert its functional role as the instrument of national salvation and redemption—not in the sense of its seizing control on its own initiative, not in the sense of establishing a military dictatorship, but in the more "correct" procedural sense of responding professionally and efficiently in the discharge of a duty which would be assigned to it by the national civil authorities. It could be expected to undertake this duty with dispatch and determination in view of the integral relation to its international mission: restoration of order at home would be a prerequisite to its effective influence on world order.

Once again such a potential development might seem like disaster-mongering to a people which has learned to abhor military rule as a breakdown in government, but in fact a breakdown in government is essentially what would be involved. The prospect envisaged would not have appeared at all unlikely to that percipient philosopher-observer of the American scene in 1835, Alexis de Tocqueville, who viewed American cities even then, though of no great size (New York had only 200,000 inhabitants) as the gathering place of displaced peoples, immigrants and freed blacks, who had little stake in the society which surrounded them. "As inhabitants of a country where they have no civil rights, they are ready to turn all the passions which agitate the community to their own advantage." At that time, rural America could ignore the unrest and rioting in the few large cities as an evil not much affecting them. "Nevertheless," wrote Tocqueville, "I look upon the size of certain American cities, and especially on the nature of their population, as a real danger which threatens the future security of the democratic republics of the New World; and I venture to predict that they will perish from this circumstance, unless the government succeeds in creating an armed force which, while it remains under the control of the majority of the nation, will be independent of the town population and able to repress its excesses." [17]

Clearly such a military form of government in the major cities would have a racial overtone, but white America would presumably be prepared to accept that fact, if not complacently at least with no more concern than it has shown in bringing about the locational and economic racial division which would have led to this unhappy denouement. But it is also conceivable that if the deterioration of the cities had proceeded far enough, a majority of the blacks would also welcome a restitution of social order, on which any economic gains in the cities would have to be premised. In those cities in which they would constitute the majority residents, they would presumably also constitute the majority victims of the economic and social fracturing.

The extent to which blacks as a class would be benefited or exploited under a military form of urban government depends on several unpredictable variables. One need not automatically assume that the South African pattern of repression would be imposed on black communities. It is equally arguable that in those major cities where blacks had come to constitute the bulk of the population, the potential danger to them from a local authority unresponsive to diffuse political pressures might itself induce a more cohesive, effective, and responsible political organization among the blacks. And that a military government, less committed to racial prejudice than to the effectuation of its professional mission, might hammer out an implicit bargain with the responsible members of the community according to which the latter might find more opportunities for self-development and even self-government than in the chaotic framework of cities without effective political and economic power.

Whether even the military could reclaim the cities to a viable order would depend on their finding support for necessary programs on a national scale. Urban order would not be established simply by putting men in uniforms on the streets. It would call for economic and political programs integrating the urban centers with the rest of the country, instead of leaving them isolated islands sinking under the weight of their own human debris. Thus the military would soon enough find that to carry out the mission assigned them would require their becoming more deeply involved in social and economic policy, exercising influence in Congress in these areas just as they have in the more traditional military areas. They could be expected to develop their own economic specialists, capable of arguing the needs for the cities more effectively than the politically fragmented and shorter-term city mayors under present political arrangements.

In short, we would find—under this scenario—the military emerging as a genuine thruster group, not because it lusts for power but because changing objective conditions would have provided a richer field of opportunity for the exercise of its role. Both on the international and domestic fronts, events would give greater weight to its monopoly of force as an instrument for national redemption and salvation. The events in question would not have been created by the military as the vehicle for their rise to greater power, but, if we are dispassionately analytical, those events would nonetheless constitute the opportunities on which the military would seize—out of a sense of their mission and its associated values—to carry through their vision of the form of society appropriate to the circumstances, impressing on the society those values to which they, as a functional group, are deeply committed. The easy identification of their own group values with national values which we earlier observed to be characteristic of a thruster group would apply here. The confusion of group values and group interests, with protection of the latter seen as necessary to advancement of the former, could likewise be expected.

Nor need one expect that a military thruster group would set itself against the old business dominants, attempting to displace them. Why should they, when they could make such effective use of them in the provision of the military plant and equipment which would be needed, and when values and interests of the two groups are not in fact that radically opposed to each other? It would be much more likely that a working alliance would be effected, just as between military and church in an earlier day. The military-industrial complex, which has been so often regarded as a kind of sinister conspiracy for the furtherance of special interests, would emerge as a welcomed leadership class, drawing to itself other allies and supporters such as the scientists and technologists, whom so many have seen as themselves a rising thruster group, but which I would view as simply a neutral tool lending its usefulness to whichever class is capable of asserting its dominance. Larger numbers of "little thrusters" and opportunists, of adaptables and tolerants, of admirers of power and success would form a base of support.

And what would be the values affirmed by the new leadership class? If the earlier thesis prevails, that a genuine shift in values emerges *only* with a new thruster group, responding to the opportunities provided by a change in objective conditions, then we could anticipate the possibility of a significant modification in America's social values. I would see this as occurring along the following lines.

In the area of focal values, there would be a movement away from preoccupation with private consumption (personal accumulation, ostentation, distinction) toward a doctrine of austerity for the benefit and rehabilitation of the nation as a whole. Such a doctrine would permit a diversion of production to military preparedness, on the one hand, and to the vast domestic reconstruction that is needed (in housing, transportation, urban redevelopment) on the other hand. This shift of the focal value from private to public needs, from fad and fashion to austerity, would have several appeals. It would continue to give greatest importance to material production, even though the composition of that production would be altered; thus the allied industrial dominants would have their interests protected, though at the price of renouncing the primacy of a consumer market which they could more readily control. But the recognition that national and social needs were to be given priority over private and sometimes frivolous consumer interests might also be expected to appeal to the idealistic and consumption-sated intellectuals and youths who on their own would have little prospect of asserting alternative values. It would be ironic but by no means improbable that the successor generation of the contemporary anti-militarists might find in a program of military austerity, directed to an almost mystical notion of national redemption, a soothing substitute for materialism—even though material production remained the basis of the system.

In the area of constitutional values, the shift would be more predictable and more sweeping. A military thrust could not occur without the assertion of the hierarchical forms of control on which military organization depends. Military government in the major cities would be almost certain to undermine present constitutional values of individual autonomy as embodied in the Bill of Rights. The instrumentalities for military control have already been put in place, even if on only a modest basis. The extension of military surveillance into all walks of civilian life, usually with the support, if not instigation, of civil administrations, is now well known. Reliance on informers, wiretapping, mail inspection, and a domestic intelligence network has expanded within the recent troubled years. In the face of protests from civil rights groups and influential congressmen, the Department of Defense purports to have dismantled much of this apparatus, but skepticism persists among the critics. Links with other intelligence agencies, such as the F.B.I., C.I.A., local police departments, and private credit agencies have been established. In these relations with a civilian population the military has thus already developed a considerable experience on which to build.

In the conduct of these activities, we could reasonably assume, I think, that the military would not be guided by any concepts of self-aggrandizement but by the effort to perform its mission of national salvation effectively. Like any thruster espousing certain values, it would believe those values could best be preserved by protecting its own organization against subversion and opposition. What would be important would be the acceptance of such protective activities by a population which sees them as necessary for the achievement of a focal value in which it has come to believe. Beyond that, there is the need for a philosophical justification of the constitutional pattern laid down.

The rudiments of that philosophical validation are not difficult to discern, even though they may derive from sources now viewed antithetically. It would, I presume, follow somewhat this formulation: The problems of social organization which confront contemporary society can only be managed through centralization of control. But centralized control precludes traditional concepts of democracy: *self*-government is an illusion. Some dominant power always lies behind the central controls. The notion of individual autonomy, of privacy, of independence of opinion and action is confined to a shrinking field of relatively minor and local matters. The major decisions are made not by any public, or a majority, or a constituency, but by a small control group representative of certain values and interests who treat public opinion either as a datum to be taken into account or as a variable to be manipulated. The acceptability of such a constitutional system is tested only by its ability to survive without undue use of coercive force.

In the area of distributive values, one might anticipate a reinforced emphasis on rank and privilege, since the dominant allies—industry and military both—operate through hierarchical structures. Authority would be shored up with privilege in both civil and military walks of life. At the same time one might expect greater equality of condition *within* the ranks, and a continued emphasis on the principle of meritocracy. It is entirely compatible with such an outlook that racial equality would be more nearly enforced. Although the military could be expected to clamp down hard on race extremists, those inciting racial protests, and youthful black depredators in the cities, they might well move more vigorously to correct the social and economic conditions adverse to black progress and personal development. Such a policy, if it emerged, would not be based on any social-service concept, but purely on a belief that only through amelioration of such conditions could stability and order be returned to the American scene, creating the necessary base for projecting an influential world position.

In sum, if such shifts in social values did occur as we have imagined under Scenario Three, as a consequence of the military's rise to dominant status coordinate with the corporate managers, we would expect a focal value stressing national unity and public welfare, accompanied by a strong element of pseudo-speciation, but with no larger conception of a *summum bonum* than material-based might; a constitutional value emphasizing hierarchical order and conformity in contrast to individualism and self-development; and a distributive value stressing equality within more clearly defined status levels, with opportunity for all who showed merit to rise through the ranks.

Conclusion

I have chosen the term "scenario" to apply to these three possible paths of value development to underscore their speculative, hypothetical, and highly tentative nature. They constitute "scripts" which contain some plausibility, viewing the future from where we stand now, in which the leading actors and their lines can be readily visualized. Other possible scenarios could be added; these have simply seemed the most likely, given the nature of the changing objective conditions around us.

Clearly none of the three outcomes envisioned here is very appealing. It would be hard to choose which among them is either preferable or more probable. Some reader no doubt will consider my inability to foresee a rosy prospect for America, in which it surmounts all its present troubles and goes on to an even brighter future, as indicative of insufficient faith in or regard for a country which has manifestly brought so much good to the world. I lack neither faith nor regard, but the adequacy of these to ensure a bright future for the United States depends not so much on their strength as on the objective conditions which they confront. Nevertheless, I readily concede that the future may bring a happier outcome than any I have pictured here, not because one can safely fall back on a mystical patriotic belief that somehow America will "come through," but because the future always gives rise to intrusive events—events not now contemplated or even foreseeable, which have a way of confounding even the most purposefully objective of analyses.

Notes

1. Theodore J. Lowi has written of present pluralism in this vein in *The End of Liberalism* (New York: Norton, 1969). I would demur only that his timing is off, or potentially so. In my judgment he underestimates the continuing dominance of large-scale corporate enterprise; even though it may not be as dominant as it once was, it remains the strongest among competing groups, by a degree which makes a significant difference. Both Lowi and Robert Paul Wolff (*The Poverty of Liberalism*) have argued the philosophic emptiness of a system which consists only in the mediation of contentious interests, without common values to give legitimacy to a social leadership. This, as I see it, is one of the possible directions in which we are heading, but not yet a destination at which we have arrived.

2. I take it that this is roughly the scenario which Andrew Hacker expects to be played out, as set forth in his *End of the American Era* (New York: Atheneum Publishers, 1970). Anthony Sampson, writing of contemporary England (*The Anatomy of Britain*, [New York: Harper & Row, 1962]), paints a somewhat comparable picture for that society. The country is not controlled by dominant interests but operates through the mutual tolerance and compromises of a number of circles of influence which overlap each other only slightly, each largely preoccupied with its own affairs, held together by government on an ad hoc basis, without program and with waning traditional values. "This, surely, is the greater nightmare of a democracy—not that the government is full of sinister and all-powerful *eminences grises*, but that the will of the people dissolves in committees . . ." (p. 627)

3. Eli Goldston, "New Prospects for American Business," *Daedalus*, Winter 1969, pp. 78, 86.

4. Stephen S. Cohen, *Modern Capitalist Planning: The French Model* (Cambridge, Mass.: Harvard University Press, 1969), p. 163.

5. *Ibid.*, p. 52.

6. As Cohen suggests, *ibid.*, p. 202, and as I have tried to lay out more generally and at greater length in *Private and Public Planning* (New York: McGraw-Hill Book Co., 1965), especially Chapter 8.

7. Cheit, *The Business Establishment,* p. 181.

8. François Perroux, *Le IVème Plan Français* (Paris: Presses Universitaires de France, 1962), p. 22, as trans. Malcolm MacLennan in *French Planning: Some Lessons for Britain* (London: Political and Economic Planning, 1963), p. 346.

9. Some rough indication of the probable consequence in this regard is provided by *Business Week,* a responsible and independent interpreter of the American business scene. In 1969, looking to the future, it predicted that "a new breed of [business] men will call the shots," meeting public needs "without losing out in the market place." 6 December 1969, pp. 144, 152. This comes close to suggesting the inside thruster class we have just pictured. Two years later, the same journal foresaw a GNP doubling within the next decade and a half—presumably during the period when its "new breed" would be having its effect.

10. Cohen refers to the present French discussions on this point. The conservative forces, both private and public, see the present business-government collaboration as "in the interest of all Frenchmen. Implicit is a conservative notion that the problem of democracy is one of convincing people that existing configurations of economic power are legitimate and should be actively supported, i.e., if everyone believed in planned capitalism then planned capitalism would be democratic." He notes that "such a view of democracy does not go unchallenged," and key social groups have called for a radical redistribution of economic power. *Modern Capitalist Planning: The French Model,* pp. 231–232.

11. Even as I write this the *Columbia Daily Spectator* (December 8, 1971) carries a letter from a group identifying itself as composed of "concerned and intelligent Black people," in this case addressed to the university community but no different from what business has already experienced.

"For years the Harlem community has been charitable enough to allow Columbia to operate in Harlem. Such charity borders on naïveté when one considers the amount of exploiting that has been done in the community by outsiders. As demonstrated in the 1968 altercations between Columbia and the Harlem community, it does not take much to arouse the community to force Columbia and its environs to change or to fall in its rigidity. May we remind the Columbia community that it is but a small white island in a vast Black sea; huge waves of humanity surround this island at all times."

Will the major corporations choose to commit further resources to similar islands, surrounded by such an angry sea? The problem is quite comparable to whether American corporations will choose to invest additional capital in developing countries which display a hostility to foreign capital as a form of external control. At issue is not whether blacks have a "right" to be angry but whether that anger, if threatening to white property and white control, will not inhibit corporate involvement in urban redevelopment.

12. Herman Kahn, *The Emerging Japanese Superstate* (Englewood Cliffs, N.J.: Prentice-Hall, 1970).

13. Max Frankel, "The U. S. at an Era's End," *New York Times,* 22 December 1971, p. 16.

14. Late in 1971, after President Nixon had publicly lamented that too

many Americans were expressing defeatism and self-doubt, and had warned that "Once a nation ceases trying to be Number 1, that nation will not be a great nation," the *Wall Street Journal* commissioned a national sample public opinion poll to test the President's fears. The poll disclosed that more than 30 percent did not care whether the United States was Number 1 in *everything*, including such areas as sports. But 80 percent expressed the view that the United States should be first in general military preparedness and world political leadership. *Wall Street Journal*, November 16, 1971. The quoted response which follows comes from the same source.

15. Quoted by James Reston, Jr., in a review article, *Saturday Review*, 9 July 1971, p. 28.

16. As one example of this learning experience, Max Frankel reports: "In the Soviet Union an experienced student of his Government remarks on its fear that Communists will reach power in France or Italy. Soviet influence has been challenged quite enough, he says, by ruling Communists in China, Rumania, Yugoslavia and even Cuba, and the containing of the power of Western Europe will really be much easier if its major countries remain divided and in "bourgeois" hands. *New York Times*, 22 December 1971.

17. Tocqueville, *Democracy in America*, Vol. 1, pp. 299–300.

INDEX

INDEX

Y

Z